Social History of Africa

VILIMANI

**Recent Titles in
Social History of Africa Series**
Series Editors: Allen Isaacman and Jean Allman

Pride of Men: Ironworking in 19th Century West Central Africa
Colleen E. Kriger

Gender and the Making of a South African Bantustan:
A Social History of the Ciskei, 1945–1959
Anne Kelk Mager

The African Rank-and-File: Social Implications of Colonial Military Service in the King's African Rifles, 1902–1964
Timothy H. Parsons

Memoirs of the Maelstrom: A Senegalese Oral History of the First World War
Joe Lunn

"We Women Worked so Hard": Gender, Urbanization, and Social Reproduction in Colonial Harare, Zimbabwe, 1930–1956
Teresa A. Barnes

Bo-Tsotsi: The Youth Gangs of Soweto, 1935–1976
Clive Glaser

History and Memory in the Age of Enslavement: Becoming Merina in Highland Madagascar, 1770–1822
Pier M. Larson

"I Will Not Eat Stone": A Women's History of Colonial Asante
Jean Allman and Victoria B. Tashjian

Making the Town: Ga State and Society in Early Colonial Accra
John Parker

Chiefs Know Their Boundaries: Essays on Property, Power, and the Past in Asante, 1896–1996
Sara S. Berry

"Wicked" Women and the Reconfiguration of Gender in Africa
Dorothy L. Hodgson and Sheryl A. McCurdy, editors

Black Death, White Medicine: Bubonic Plague and the Politics of Public Health in Colonial Senegal, 1914–1945
Myron Echenberg

VILIMANI

LABOR MIGRATION AND RURAL CHANGE IN EARLY COLONIAL TANZANIA

Thaddeus Sunseri

HEINEMANN
Portsmouth, NH

JAMES CURREY
Oxford

DAVID PHILIP
Cape Town

Heinemann
A division of Reed Elsevier Inc.
361 Hanover Street
Portsmouth, NH 03801-3912
USA
www.heinemann.com

James Currey Ltd.
73 Botley Road
Oxford OX2 0BS
United Kingdom

David Philip Publishers (Pty) Ltd.
208 Werdmuller Centre
Claremont 7708
Cape Town, South Africa

Offices and agents throughout the world

© 2002 by Thaddeus Sunseri. All rights reserved. No part of this book may be reproduced in any form or by any electronic or mechanical means, including information storage and retrieval systems, without permission in writing from the publisher, except by a reviewer, who may quote brief passages in a review.

ISBN 0-325-00183-9 (Heinemann cloth)
ISBN 0-325-00182-0 (Heinemann paper)
ISBN 0-85255-698-5 (James Currey cloth)
ISBN 0-85255-648-9 (James Currey paper)

British Library Cataloguing in Publication Data

Sunseri, Thaddeus
  Vilimani : labor migration and rural change in early
  colonial Tanzania.—(Social history of Africa series)
  1. Migrant labor—Tanzania—History 2. Working class—
  Tanzania—History 3. Labor mobility—Tanzania—History
  4. Tanzania—Social conditions 5. Tanzania—Rural
  conditions
  I. Title
  331.5'44'09678'09041
  ISBN 0-85255-648-9 (James Currey paper)
  ISBN 0-85255-698-5 (James Currey cloth)

Library of Congress Cataloging-in-Publication Data

Sunseri, Thaddeus Raymond.
    Vilimani : labor migration and rural change in early colonial Tanzania / Thaddeus Sunseri.
      p. cm.—(Social history of Africa, ISSN 1099-8098)
    Includes bibliographical references and index.
    ISBN 0-325-00183-9 (alk. paper)—ISBN 0-325-00182-0 (pbk. : alk. paper)
    1. Migrant labor—Tanzania—History. 2. Working class—Tanzania—History. 3. Labor mobility—Tanzania—History. 4. Cities and Towns—Tanzania—History. 5. Tanzania—Social conditions—History. 6. Tanzania—Rural conditions—History. I. Title.
  II. Series.
  HD5856.T34 S86 2002
  331.5'44'09678—dc21   2001024563

Paperback cover photo: Porters resting their loads on their shoulders. (Courtesy of Bundesarchiv, Koblenz, 146/84/67/25. Reprinted with permission.)

Printed in the United States of America on acid-free paper.

05 04 03 02 01 SB 1 2 3 4 5 6 7 8 9

Every reasonable effort has been made to trace the owners of copyright materials in this book, but in some instances this has proven impossible. The author and publisher will be glad to receive information leading to more complete acknowledgments in subsequent printings of the book and in the meantime extend apologies for any omissions.

CONTENTS

Illustrations	vii
Abbreviations	ix
Note on Currency and Land Units	xi
Glossary	xiii
Acknowledgments	xvii
Introduction: Peasant and Worker Agency in Tanzanian History	xix
1 Industrialization and the Labor Question in German East Africa, 1885–1914	1
2 Slavery and the Genesis of Colonial Labor Relations	26
3 Labor Migration and the Erosion of the Plantation Imperative	51
4 Environmental Collapse, Household Disruption, and Rebellion in Rufiji District	76
5 An Antidote to the Plantation Labor Shortage? The Peasant Cotton Campaign in Southeastern Tanzania	113
6 Migrant Labor and the Shaping of Plantation Work Culture	136
7 "*Wamekwenda Vilimani!*": Transformations in Rural Society	165
Epilogue	193
Bibliography	199
Index	215

ILLUSTRATIONS

MAPS

I.1	German East Africa	xx
4.1	Rufiji Basin	81

PHOTOGRAPHS AND SKETCHES

1.1	Colonial Minister Dernburg observing a steam tractor near Sadani.	12
1.2	The *Kulturland* model.	16
2.1	A certificate of freedom (*Freibrief, hati ya huru*) that registered freed or ransomed slaves with district offices.	34
2.2	Women in a chain gang c. 1900.	42
3.1	Porters on a caravan.	57
3.2	Porters resting their loads on their shoulders.	58
3.3	A worker village in 1908.	61
4.1	A wild pig, one of the most destructive crop pests in German East Africa.	79
4.2	A watchtower and system of clappers to guard fields against crop predators in Kilwa district.	85
4.3	*Mitumbwi* dugout canoes on the Rufiji River.	87
4.4	Captured Maji Maji chiefs from Songea district.	100

5.1 Children harvesting cotton in southeast German
    East Africa c. 1910. 121
5.2 Women transporting cotton. 124
6.1 Workers and their overseers on a
    plantation in German East Africa. 143
6.2 A row of plantation workers doing field
    work in German East Africa, c. 1905. 152
6.3 One of the steam tractors of the Otto
    Cotton Plantation near Kilossa, mired in mud. 154
7.1 Workers and overseers on the
    construction of the Central Railway. 170
7.2 The market at Tabora. 177
7.3 Women prisoners at the Tabora *boma*. 180

ABBREVIATIONS

BAB	Federal Archives, Berlin
BAK	Federal Archives, Koblenz
BLF	*Berichte über Land- und Forstwirtschaft*
DOAG	German East Africa Corporation
DOAR	*Deutsch-Ostafrikanische Rundschau*
DOAZ	*Deutsch-Ostafrikanische Zeitung*
EAAJ	*East African Agricultural Journal*
GStA	Geheimes Staatsarchiv-Preussischer Kulturbesitz, Berlin
IJAHS	*International Journal of African Historical Studies*
JAH	*Journal of African History*
KR	*Koloniale Rundschau*
KWK	Colonial Economic Committee
MaddS	*Mitteilungen aus den deutschen Schutzgebieten*
MMRP	*Maji Maji Research Project*
RKA	Colonial Office
SCOA	Société Commerciale de l'Ouest Africain
SFIO	Section Française de l'Internationale Ouvrière
SICAP	Société Immobilière du Cap-Vert
TNA	Tanzania National Archives
TNR	*Tanganyika/Tanzania Notes and Records*
TDB	Tanganyika District Books
UP	*Usambara Post*
WHO	World Health Organization

Note on Currency and Land Units

The currency in German East Africa was the rupee, divided into 64 pesas. After 1904 pesas were substituted for a new currency of 100 hellers to the rupee. One rupee equalled 1.33 marks or 32 cents. Germans measured land in hectares, 1 hectare equalling 2.47 acres.

GLOSSARY

SWAHILI WORDS USED IN THE TEXT

akida (**pl.** *maakida*)   A German-appointed sub-district governor.
akidat   The area under jurisdiction of an akida.
askari   An African soldier or policeman.
bakshish   A bribe or gratuity.
boma   Military station or district office.
boriti   Mangrove poles.
daladala   A commuter bus.
dawa   Medicine.
dsisla (**or** *shisla*)   About 360 lbs.
frasila   About 35 lbs.
hati ya huru   A certificate of freedom.
huru   A freedperson.
jumbe (**pl.** *majumbe*)   A village headman.
kanzu   A calico gown worn by men.
kibaba   A dry measure, about one and a half pounds.
kibarua   A casual worker.
kilala   Fallow land (Kimatumbi).
kofia   A cap worn especially by Muslim men.
konde   A cultivated plot of land.
liwali (*wali*)   Town governors, originally under the Sultan of Zanzibar.

maji   Water.
matimbe   In Umatumbi, strips of land adjacent to rivulets.
mganga   A spirit medium.
mlau   Floodlands of the Rufiji River or the heavy rain season.
mshenzi   "Heathen," Muslim pejorative for non-Muslims.
mtemi   A chief in Unyamwezi.
mtoro   A runaway slave or deserted worker.
mtumbwi   A dugout canoe.
mtumwa   Generic Swahili word for slave.
mzalia   A slave born into captivity.
ndugu   Brother, countryman.
ngoma   A drum or dance.
pembeni   Living "in the corners" of the land.
pombe   Millet or other grain beer.
pori   Uncultivated land or wilderness.
posho   Food rations.
shamba   A peasant field.
suria   Concubine.
tembo   Palm liquor.
vilimani   At the coast; in the hills.
vitabu vya kazi   Work books or records.
waajiriwa   Wage laborers working on contract.
walimu (**sing.** *mwalimu*)   Teachers, especially of the Koran.

GERMAN WORDS USED IN THE TEXT

Allmende   Common lands.
Arbeiterfrage   The labor question.
Baumwollfrage   The cotton question.
Dienstbote   A servant, messenger.
Dienstbuch   A service record or book.
Dienstherrschaft   Master-servant relationship.
Freibrief   A certificate of freedom.
Freizügigkeit   Freedom of movement.
Gesinde/Gesindewesen   Contract laborer or the institution itself.

Glossary

Grenzwildnis A border region or "no man's land."
Grossbetrieb A large-scale plantation or other undertaking.
Instwirtschaft A squatter economy.
Kolonialrat The Colonial Council, oversaw colonial matters before 1907.
Kommune District-level governing councils, usually settler-dominated, abolished in 1909.
krisenfest Secure from crisis, referring to a household.
Kulturland Cultivated or "civilized" land.
Landflucht Fleeing from the countryside into cities.
Sachsengänger Migrant laborers to Germany from eastern Europe.
Urproduktion "Aboriginal" agriculture, the German view of bush fallowing.

ACKNOWLEDGMENTS

I owe a great many debts to people and institutions who aided me in researching this book since it began as a doctoral dissertation a decade ago. My research in Germany and Tanzania would not have been possible without generous funding from the following sources: the Department of History and the Graduate School of the University of Minnesota; the Social Science Research Council; the German Academic Exchange Service, which provided three separate grants. My thanks also to the Fulbright Program for a research and teaching grant to Zimbabwe that gave me time to begin writing. The staffs of the following archives and libraries were especially helpful in facilitating my research: the Bundesarchiv Koblenz and Bundesarchiv Berlin; the Tanzanian National Archives; the Moravian Mission in Herrnhut; the Archive of the Berlin Mission; the Abteilung für Afrika und Orient of the Stadt- und Universitätsbibliothek in Frankfurt; Wilson Library, University of Minnesota; Morgan Library, Colorado State University. I was provided with stimulating forums to discuss some of the ideas in this book in Ralph Austen's seminar at the University of Chicago and the faculty seminars in the Department of Economic History of the University of Zimbabwe. I would like to thank the Tanzania Commission for Science and Technology (COSTECH) for permission to conduct research in Tanzania, and for supporting my fieldwork in Morogoro, Kilosa, Bagamoyo, Kilwa, and Mafia Island. I hope this book is worthy of the unlimited hospitality and assistance I was given by people living in each of these communities.

Many individuals have provided me with moral and intellectual support in the course of writing this book. David Anthony inspired me to begin studying African history. Fred Kaijage was generous in providing contact support while I conducted research in Tanzania. My cohorts at the University of Minnesota created a great atmosphere of collegiality and intellect, and I would especially like to thank Heidi Gengenbach, Osumaka Likaka, Maanda Mulaudzi, Elvis Muringai, Helena Pohlandt-McCormick, Mohamed Saidou N'Daou, Salim Wanambisi, Dwayne Williams, and Nkasa Yelengi. Michael Tuck has been a great friend from the earliest days of writing. Besides providing a sounding board for ideas in this book, he went beyond the call of friendship in reading the entire manuscript twice. Linda Shimoda helped with all the illustrations. I owe a great deal to many instructors at the University of Minnesota, especially Ron Aminzade, Susan Geiger, and Ben Pike. Special thanks goes to M.J. Maynes, who has always taken the time to encourage my work. My greatest intellectual debt goes to Allen Isaacman, whose presence is embedded in this book in countless ways. Allen has been a great adviser and friend through many travails and successes, and was right when he said that the smartest thing I ever did was to go to the University of Minnesota.

Finally, I would like to thank members of my family for the love and encouragement that has kept me grounded over the years. My mother Elaine has been my greatest inspiration. My father Alvin Sunseri encouraged me to become a historian by never pressing me to follow him in this profession. My siblings Janice, Jennifer, Leandra, Gina, and Anthony are still the people I most like to spend time with. Ken Baughman has always been there to help. My grandmother, Gladys Zerwas, helped me with language study overseas. Most of all, my deepest appreciation goes to my wife, Elizabeth Bright Jones. As my best friend, companion, and critic, she has helped me over the years to develop the ideas in this book, which I dedicate to her.

INTRODUCTION: PEASANT AND WORKER AGENCY IN TANZANIAN HISTORY

Entering modern Dar es Salaam, one is struck by the movement of people by car, bus, *daladala*, bicycle, or on foot from suburbs and townships to city center and back again (See MAP I.1). Traveling Tanzania's major arteries, the steady flow of long-distance buses laden with personal possessions, household goods, and people on the move echoes other parts of the African continent. In towns and villages throughout the country, households composed of women, elders, and children spend long months awaiting visits by husbands, children, and fathers away at work. While the movement of people to new cities and jobs characterizes all modern societies, the persistent pattern of migration from village to work site and back again is a distinctive feature of the developing world.[1] The origin and effects of these movements in turn-of-the-century colonial Tanzania is the subject of this book, when short- and long-distance migration to work sites on plantations, in towns and cities, and on railways emerged as a familiar life experience for many rural dwellers.

Beginning in 1885, the rulers of the German East African Protectorate constructed a wage labor economy on established patterns of work that included porterage, slavery, and local production for inland and Indian Ocean commercial networks that had dramatic repercussions for rural societies in Tanzania. As an ongoing feature of life for thousands of men and women, wage labor was revolutionary for this region, the product of the grafting of German industrialization onto an East African agricultural and extractive economy. Twenty-five years into German rule a colonial judge traveling in Unyamwezi region of western Tanzania, far from the major production arenas of the colony, reported one result of the colonial wage-labor economy.[2] In the countryside he came across several villages

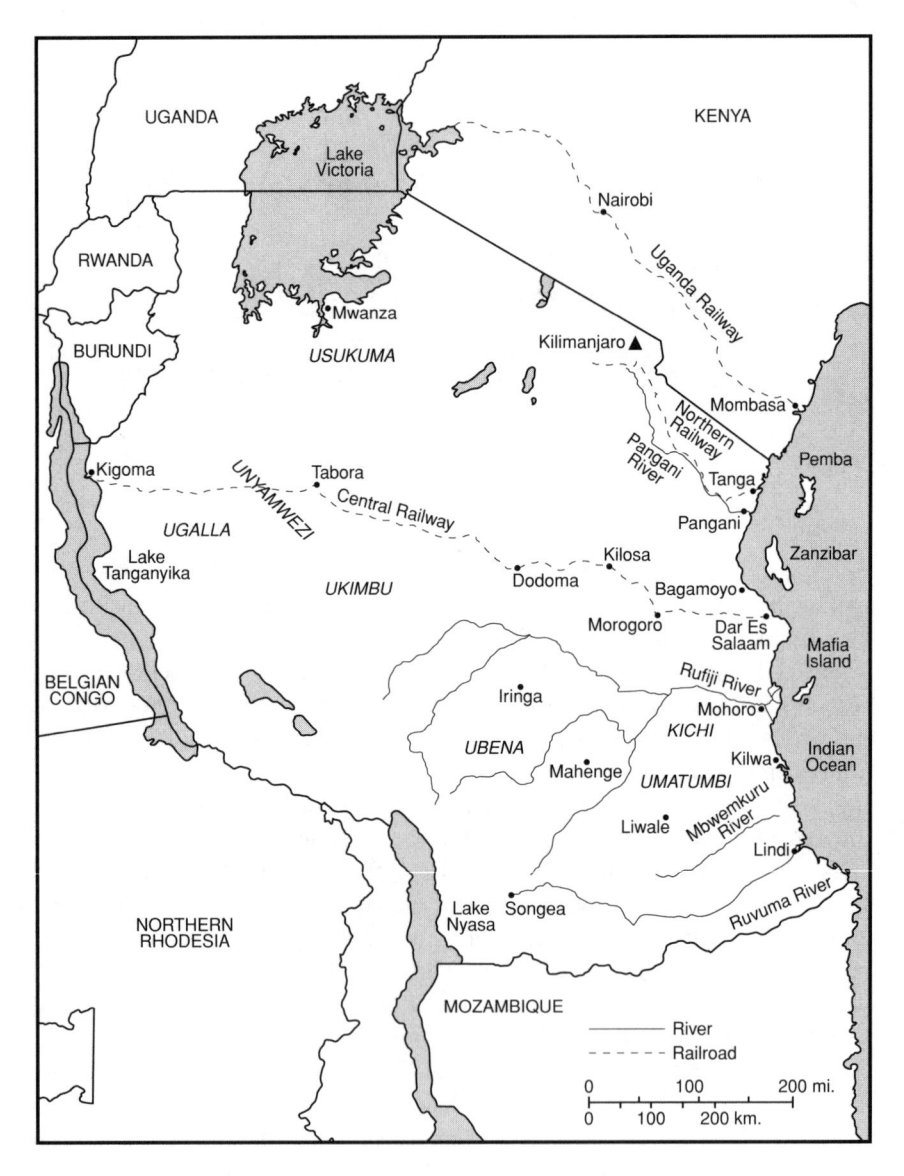

Map I.1 German East Africa
Source: Prepared by L.J.C. Shimoda

per day, many completely abandoned and decayed. Once-cultivated fields had been abandoned, palisades built to keep crop predators away had disintegrated, and the landscape itself seemed to have altered as dense

Introduction xxi

miombo bush encroached on formerly cleared lands. Some villages were inhabited by just a few elderly people, and few men were evident. When asked where all the people were, those remaining typically responded "*wamekwenda vilimani,*" "they have gone to the coast."[3] Such complaints were not confined to the region of Unyamwezi. In 1910 in Ukonogo, southwest of Unyamwezi, a district officer described many decayed and abandoned villages, others where seventy-five percent of the inhabitants were women.[4] Village elders and women complained bitterly that for years the men had been working on the coast. The word *vilimani,* therefore, suggests an ongoing *process* of migration that had severe repercussions for the countryside. As this book will demonstrate, women and elders coped with the prolonged absence of husbands and sons by abandoning and reconstituting their villages, by reshaping the agrarian landscape, and by establishing new social norms.

The wage labor economy, though predating colonial rule, emerged in force with the German conquest of the coast, mainland caravan routes, and inland societies in the fifteen years after 1885.[5] Not until colonial rule was in place could the state begin to establish the direct and indirect mechanisms of control that enabled them to channel rural people to colonial pursuits. With the founding of the first German plantations in 1885, colonialists strove to muster the labor of nearby villagers and hundreds of slaves owned by coastal Arab, Indian, and Swahili planters and traders. In time, Asian indentured laborers and African porters from the inland who could be hired temporarily between sojourns to and from the coast were added to the labor force. The introduction of a general 3 rupee hut tax in 1898 forced many people temporarily into wage work, and those who refused or were unable to pay were compelled to work on road construction or other corvée projects. Increasingly after 1896 colonial authorities diverted penal labor to private concerns or public construction. By 1910 thousands of men and some women migrated as laborers to German plantations throughout the colony, while many others worked on the Northern and Central railways. Tens of thousands still worked as porters on long-established caravan routes that led to the coast, to Lake Victoria, or into Central Africa. Despite these many labor circuits, there were never enough workers for colonial undertakings during this period, and many Africans were able to shape their work environments in response.

While a handful of past studies catalogue labor migration in Tanzania, they focus on the period of British Tanganyika, when *manamba* labor migrants had to deal with radically changed circumstances exacerbated by the world wars and the Great Depression. This often meant that wage workers might face labor gluts rather than labor shortages.[6] Under German rule, in contrast, labor migrants had leverage in an economy desperately short of workers and exploited labor opportunities in ways that historians have not generally recognized. Moreover, previous studies of East African labor migration have not explored how the absence of men and some women transformed migrants' villages of origin.[7] Yet, in colonial Tanzania the experiences of labor migrants were part of a complex picture of rural change that affected villages and households in dramatic ways.

This study departs from past analyses of Tanzanian history in four ways. First, my analysis of the nature of the German colonial state is more discrete than those of past studies. The work of John Iliffe, the most influential historian of Tanzania, emphasized the colonial state as a force for modernization.[8] While ultimately concluding that the colonial state was a tool of white settlers and planters in the colony, Iliffe also saw the state as the harbinger of education, a capitalist economy, cash crop production, and an infrastructure that African modernizers ultimately responded to and sought to emulate. Dependency theorists who followed on Iliffe's heels, most notably Walter Rodney, viewed the colonial state as a tool of a world capitalist system that sought to make Africa a producer of primary products and raw materials for a world market whose terms of exchange were in the hands of a capitalist core.[9] For dependency theorists, the colonial state in Tanzania was not much different from those in other parts of Africa or the world, and German rule before 1917 was barely distinguishable from British rule that followed. They were both tools of a vaguely defined core capitalist class. More recently, Juhani Koponen has viewed the German colonial state in Tanzania as a relatively autonomous entity that mediated between a variety of capitalist forces, with development as the ultimate goal.[10] Interested equally in promoting cash crop production by settlers, capitalist plantations, and African farmers, Koponen depicts the German state as otherwise having no driving interest of its own.

This book departs from these analyses by viewing the German state as representing specific economic interests that stemmed from the German metropole. As I argue in Chapter 1, almost from the beginning of German rule the interests of the textile industry held greater weight than those of other colonial players. In the absence of a significant mining sector in the colony, policy makers sought ways to make German East Africa of economic benefit to Germany by focusing on the agrarian sector. While tropical products such as copra, rubber, sisal, and coffee certainly had economic value for German merchants, only one crop, cotton, had a clear connection to a major sector of German industry. Moreover, by the end of the nineteenth century state officials perceived the textile industry to be in a perpetual state of crisis. The crisis was both economic and social, since ruptures in the textile industry had their counterparts in working-class militancy, the rise of socialism, and even struggles between male and female textile workers. Policy makers at the highest levels of government believed that procuring colonial sources of cotton was a national duty. By easing the supply crisis they hoped to mitigate the textile industry's volatility, the source of labor unrest. Before 1900 they assumed that both small-scale German settlers and large-scale capitalized plantations were suitable models for cotton production. However, settlers' and planters' inability to overcome the obstacles of East African cotton growing, including poor soils, cotton pests, adverse climate, and the shortage of labor, led most policy makers to conclude shortly after the turn of the century that African householders must be the colony's primary producers of cotton. Colonial officials became wedded to the plan of preserving African rural society as a domain of cash crop production, even if that meant inhibiting the flow of workers to plantations. While the state still tolerated new plantations, privately these efforts were discouraged. They would not be supported by the use of state coercion to get workers onto plantations, nor were tax levels raised to labor-creating levels, as they were in many other parts of Africa such as Kenya and South Africa, where settler economies predominated.

This book's second departure from past studies is its serious consideration of the agency of African labor migrants and other rural dwellers in shaping colonial policy. German East Africa was sparsely populated, no more than seven million people inhabiting a territory far larger than Imperial Germany itself. Since the densely populated regions of Ruanda-Urundi, where forty percent of the colony's population lived, were effectively closed to labor migration during German rule, all German economic schemes relied on mustering the remaining four million people while still maintaining rural food production and social stability. In a labor-scarce environment that worsened every year of German rule, workers negotiated virtually all the terms of employment, including wage levels, housing, food allocation, treatment, social life, and sometimes even work regime. Planters competed with one another for a limited labor supply, and a plantation's survival depended on its ability to obtain workers. The peasant cotton campaign, the centerpiece of German economic policy after 1907, was in large part a product of twenty years of worker resistance to plantation labor.

Thirdly, this study highlights the gendered nature of labor migration and rural society that has been neglected in past analyses.[11] Alongside officially contracted laborers who were overwhelmingly men were thousands of women who worked for wages as local non-contracted labor, as slaves and ransomed slaves, as penal laborers, and many others who lived on plantations or along railway lines as wives, cooks, marketers, and traders. Increasingly under German rule rural society was the domain of women, and here I explore how women reacted to the prolonged absence of men who had departed for wage labor. Women responded to colonial pressure to grow cash crops by concentrating on subsistence production in light of the erosion of precolonial patterns of production that had relied on male and female labor. In order to evade domains of colonial control, women evacuated villages and carved out new fields in inaccessible areas, often changing the landscape of production itself. Women furthermore sought to reshape personal and village-level relations to cope with changed economic circumstances.

Finally, this work has been influenced by recent scholarship on East African environmental history. One of the major gaps in an earlier literature on African peasant societies was the failure to situate rural production within specific ecologies and environments.[12] While past studies traced rural differentiation, gendered divisions of labor, the effects of capitalist penetration of the countryside, and the ability of peasants to cope with or resist colonial expectations, they did not examine how people interacted with their specific environments and the constraints that those environments imposed on production. Nor was gendered work equated with gendered environments. Beginning with the work of Helge Kjekshus in the mid 1970s, Tanzanian historiography has attended to the role of disease zones, demographics, climate, famine, colonial conservation and wildlife policy, peasant perceptions of land and water use, and how people control and interact with their environments.[13] In this book I look at how German colonial policies affected rural dwellers in the specific environments of the Rufiji River in the southeast and Unyamwezi region in the far west, both regions where the loss of male labor had cataclysmic repercussions in the last decade of German colonial rule. The departure of hundreds of thousands of people for indefinite periods necessitated changes in how people used the land and interacted with their environments. I also trace how German conservation policies, especially regulations that affected wildlife control, forest use, hunting, and the use of fire to open up new fields, constrained rural dwellers' control over their environments and in turn how that shaped peasant use of natural resources.

A study of colonial labor migration necessarily has implications for the entire territory of German East Africa. While early migrants and workers were coastal dwellers and caravan porters from inland societies,

Introduction xxv

by 1907 patterns of labor migration affected most of the colony, with perhaps the exception of the densely populated regions of Urundi, Ruanda, and Bukoba in the northwest. Nevertheless, a study of labor relations throughout the territory goes beyond the scope of this study. Instead I present regional case studies of how labor migrants and other workers shaped the colonial economy, and how rural societies were transformed as a result. Chapter 1 examines first the German industrial background to colonialism in East Africa and its bias for large-scale cash crop enterprises, or what I refer to as the "plantation imperative." In the first twenty years of German rule industrialists and policy makers believed in a model of cash crop production that resembled that of American cotton plantations or German grain-producing estates. The plantation imperative meant that, for the first twenty years, the state attempted to transform African men and available women into labor migrants and plantation workers. Even after the state turned away from this labor agenda, German industrialists, banks, and other investors continued to favor large-scale plantation production that relied on wage labor. This chapter details how cotton assumed a privileged position among cash crops in policy making decisions, a point essential to understanding the particular interests of the German state at this period in its history. Historians have long noted the contradictory policies that the German state pursued in colonial Tanzania that seemed to sometimes favor plantations and settlers and other times protect peasants. Those tensions are attributed to a variety of factors, including political disputes in the metropole and colony, the uneven articulation of a capitalist world economy within a preindustrial colonial environment, or "the advancing commodification of labor power without concomitant proletarianization."[14] I argue that German policy was fairly consistent in seeking colonial sources of cotton to stabilize the German economy and society. However, policies that favored cotton planters in the first fifteen years shifted to those aimed at peasant-scale cotton production after the turn of the century. The basic goal of emancipating German industry from American cotton sources always remained central to German policy making in German East Africa.

Chapter 2 examines how the plantation imperative led German colonialists to tap into the most available coastal labor force, slave men and women, who were among the first generation of colonial wage laborers, and who have long been ignored as part of colonial society. The interaction between slaves and free wage laborers working on plantations was central to labor relations. This was especially true in light of a German policy that allowed planters to pay for a slave's freedom, then require that slave to work off the ransom for several years on a waged basis. Slave resistance to plantation work regimes often percolated to other plantation workers, creating a common subaltern work culture. Conversely, the ability of labor migrants to leave plantation regimes almost at will imbued slave coworkers with similar aspirations for autonomy.

Focusing on the plantation districts of the northeast coast and its hinterland, Chapter 3 picks up the story of early colonial labor relations and the formation of work culture. Here I examine German attempts to create a pliable plantation labor force between about 1885 and 1907. I demonstrate that in this period when German settlers and state officials were most apt to use direct and indirect force to muster labor, peasants in proximity to plantations and towns were able to resist working for planters for long periods of time. Furthermore, labor migrants from the inland, especially porters, also maintained control over their labor power despite pressures to become a sedentary work force. Whereas past studies have emphasized this period as one in which the colonial state broke the backs of peasants through oppression, I demonstrate ways in which rural people maintained control over their working lives and, in so doing, convinced German policy makers that the plantation imperative and support for settlers must be abandoned. Efforts to draw on other potential plantation workers, especially Asian indentured servants, also failed to solve the incessant labor shortages. One result was that the colonial state turned to a labor force that it could control, men and women convicted of colonial-era crimes, who increasingly were sentenced to chain gangs to work on settler estates or corvée work projects. By the end of this period, the colonial state abandoned its role as a principal supplier of labor for German plantations.

Based on an analysis of Rufiji district, Chapter 4 looks at the effects of German labor policies leading up to the Maji Maji rebellion in 1905, long regarded as the most cataclysmic episode in Tanzanian colonial history. Here I examine how the cumulative impact of a decade of colonial labor demands coupled with a concerted German drive to get peasants to produce marketable products shaped the rebellion. I break with past analyses of the rebellion in several ways. First, I explore a wide array of colonial economic and conservation policies that altered the environment of production in Rufiji region in the years leading up to the rebellion. While past studies have viewed the grievances through the lens of a forced cotton campaign that began in 1902, the cumulative effect of forest-use policies coupled with wildlife regulations in Rufiji district were more important in gauging the actions of rural dwellers who mostly did not participate in the uprising. Secondly, I argue that the major carriers of the rebellion in the outbreak region were *majumbe* headmen attempting

Introduction

to reassert a local authority that colonial rule had eroded, tempering the nationalist interpretations that have dominated the literature on Maji Maji for over thirty years. Here I conclude that, rather than acting as willing participants in the war, most rural dwellers were refugees coping with the onset of famine that the war brought. Finally, I reassess past views that see Maji Maji as a decisive caesura between early and late German colonialism by examining how labor relations and agrarian policies unraveled before and after the rebellion.

Chapter 5 traces the state's intense efforts to channel rural dwellers toward cotton production in the Rufiji-Kilwa region through agricultural training, marketing networks, and by reviving the authority of *majumbe* elites. I argue that patterns of refugee movement particular to rural women during the war became generalized in the last decade of colonial rule, frustrating the state's cotton campaign. While past studies have described this as an era when peasants embraced cash crop production, I argue that the danger to food security that cotton posed led peasants to resist the crop. Many rural dwellers responded to the cotton campaign by fleeing centers of colonial control and opening up new fields in inaccessible regions of the forests to concentrate on food production. German authorities and African elites attempted to halt these movements by creating forest reserves throughout the Maji Maji–outbreak region that were off-limits to peasant use. In the last decade of German rule colonial authorities struggled to control peripheral regions such as forests and district borders that were becoming bastions of rural disorder and resistance.

The last two chapters return to the story of labor migration and its effects on rural societies in the last decade of German rule. This was a period characterized by a laissez-faire labor market that rested on the principle of freedom of movement throughout the colony. Chapter 6 breaks with past studies of labor recruitment in Tanzania by demonstrating that, in spite of abuses in labor recruitment, labor migrants held the upper hand in a labor-scarce environment, and learned to exploit both the recruitment process and work patterns on plantations. Focusing on case studies from Morogoro district, a region of intense plantation development along the Central Railway, I argue that while capitalist planters sought to create industrial-style labor relations in the colony, migrants and other plantation workers carved out realms of autonomy on plantations that resembled peasant work environments and social conditions, limiting the ability of plantations to survive. Colonial policy makers refused to prop up settlers and planters who, they believed, thwarted state efforts to develop the colony for the benefit of the German metropole. My conclusion contradicts studies that have argued that Tanzania was moving in the direction of a settler colony in the last years of German rule based on the state's command of forced labor.[15]

Chapter 7 brings the themes of this book together by examining how labor migration transformed rural society in Unyamwezi region of western Tanzania. Long the most important source of colonial labor migrants, therefore fundamental to this study, the colonial state also targeted this region to become eventually the colony's most important arena of peasant cotton growing. However, as the Central Railway neared Unyamwezi in 1911, the effects of two decades of labor migration were clear. Many villages lay in decay as women householders sought to escape the predations of local elites and demands of the colonial state. While some migrated to railway work or town life, others opened up new fields in the forests, away from elite and colonial control, acting in ways reminiscent of women elsewhere in the colony. In so doing they entered into what were previously men's domains. Actions such as these led colonial officials, African elites, as well as husbands, to view women as unruly and out of control. I argue that women did not become victims of a rural economy that lacked adequate labor now that husbands and sons were away at work. Rather, by reshaping rural norms, work, residence patterns, and the landscape itself, women were able to cope with changed circumstances and maintain subsistence security. In so doing, women subverted the cotton campaign and the colonial goal of developing the interior in the years leading up to World War I.

SOURCES AND METHODOLOGY

This book is based on a decade of research in Germany and Tanzania. The German period of Tanzanian colonial history is underresearched compared to the many studies of Tanganyika—the British period—that all but ignore the thirty years of German East Africa (1885–c.1914) that is the subject of this book. This gap in scholarship does not stem from a paucity of sources, as some historians contend.[16] An abundance of archival and published sources provide ample, though fragmentary, evidence for the reconstruction of this period.

Perhaps a dozen newspapers and periodicals in German and Swahili recorded early colonial history. Some, like the *Usambara Post*, its affiliated *Meru- und Kilimanjaro Zeitung*, and the *Deutsch-Ostafrikanische Zeitung* had a decidedly pro-settler bias.[17] That bias was primarily directed against Africans who refused to work for settlers and plantations under terms that favored employers. By 1905 these organs also vilified colonial policies that they deemed to favor Africans, including tax policy, the colonial cotton campaign, and almost all ordinances that dealt with labor matters. Many of the contributors to these newspapers were planters themselves, who freely expressed their disillusionment with colonial policies. The attitudes of settlers and government officials are also accessible in the many autobiographical works that were published during and after German colonial rule.[18] The short-lived *Deutsch-Ostafrikanische Rundschau* served the interests of the colonial government. Founded in 1908 to counter the anti-government bias of the *DOAZ*, the *DOAR* defended government policy and pointed to successes of African cash crop agriculture, rational means for planters to employ labor under free-market conditions, and also provided news of the day. Mission periodicals, such as the Berlin Mission's *Afrika*, the Benedictine *Missions-Blaetter von St. Ottilien*, and the Moravian *Missions-Blatt der Brüdergemeine* provided regional views of daily life near mission stations and more detailed reports on matters such as slave emancipation, the Maji Maji war, local experiments with new crops, and missionary conflicts with African chiefs and other elites. Missionary and humanitarian views were often expressed in *Koloniale Rundschau*, which provided a forum for discussion of issues such as labor, slavery, depopulation, and colonial economic policies. Newspapers based in Germany, including the pro-settler *Deutsche Kolonial-Zeitung* and the government's *Deutsches Kolonialblatt* and *Mittheilungen aus den deutschen Schutzgebieten*, often included travelogues and research reports culled from government-commissioned study visits to the colonies. To these must be added the Swahili periodical *Kiongozi*, the organ of the government school in Tanga. Written by and for Africans literate in Swahili, especially colonial functionaries, *Kiongozi*'s mission was to bolster government policy. Its articles often celebrated visits of German dignitaries, German national festivals, such as the birthday of the Kaiser, and extolled the colonial mission, including attempts to use modern technology to grow cash crops. The few articles on the Maji Maji war told of the foolishness of those heathen who dared to confront the German empire. Despite these biases, *Kiongozi* included reports on floods, famine, and agricultural successes and failures that enable the historian to get a sense of life in localities throughout German East Africa. Its classified ad section is important for its reports of worker desertions from plantations and government service, and planter attempts to hire overseers and recruit new workers. *Kiongozi* took over the role of *Fahndungsblatt*, "wanted bulletin," from the short lived *Askari*, which was dedicated to apprehending plantation and other work-site deserters. Ethnographic accounts of German East Africa that paint a more detailed, though invariably static, picture of local customs and life are also important sources for this period.[19] Read against the grain, these publications give us a sense of men and women wage workers under German rule, their age, ethnicity, and other aspects of their work lives.

This study has drawn on a score of state and missionary archives in Germany and Tanzania. The most important repository in Germany is the Federal Archive in Berlin (formerly in Potsdam) that houses the files of the foreign and colonial offices. The German Federal Archive in Koblenz and Federal Military Archive in Freiburg provide further documentation of economic development, plantation conditions, and colonial wars and other forms of resistance to German rule. State archives from regions where traders and industrialists had colonial interests, such as Dresden, Leipzig, Hamburg, Bremen, and Stuttgart include important files dealing with colonial economic undertakings. Component states of Imperial Germany, such as Saxony, had separate foreign ministries and foreign policies that did not always mesh with that of the imperial government. Local economic archives throughout Germany house files of specific plantation and trading corporations that operated in the colony. Repositories of colonial officials (Nachlässe) such as those of the Colonial Ministers Dernburg and Solf in Koblenz, include diaries and personal accounts of colonial matters. The Schnee Nachlass at the Geheimes Staatsarchiv in Berlin-Dahlem houses a dozen Swahili files from German East Africa that include Swahili epic poems in both Arab and Latin scripts, and an array of other Swahili writings, including testaments, newspaper fragments, district court cases and directives, lesson plans for *askari* troops, business transactions from coastal communities, and disputes over marriage, land, and inheritance.

For this work the most essential mission archives are those of the Berlin Mission that was active in the Dar es Salaam hinterland and southwest Tanzania, and the Moravian Mission that was active in Unyamwezi. In contrast to government records, missionary accounts give a much more localized account of African conditions and experiences during colonialism, often recording the lives of individual mission adherents and people living near their stations. The politics of local land disputes, labor recruiting, and missionary conflicts with the government and settlers appear in these accounts. Missionary accounts are by no means exhaustive, usually concerned with affairs in a discrete radius around their stations. However, they provide a local view that is important for a social history such as this. Unfortunately, there were no mission stations in the greater Rufiji-Kilwa region before World War I, where much of this book is focused, and where the Maji Maji war had its outbreak. This was furthermore the most important region of German efforts to foster cotton production and experiment with forest conservation policies. However,

Introduction   xxxi

missionary travel accounts published in the *Missions-Blaetter* helped to piece together the history of this region following the uprising.

The Tanzanian National Archives are indispensable for a thorough examination of this period. Housing most of the files of the administration of German East Africa that survived World War I, this often fragmentary collection nevertheless provides many local-level district reports, information on tax collection, land transactions, conservation policies, health and disease, crime statistics, and court cases dealing with matters of worker abuse, labor recruitment, and moral transgressions.

In this work I highlight the agency and intentions of workers, peasants, and slaves—men and women—who shaped the colonial economy. Toward this end I have drawn on the oral testimony of modern Tanzanians who recalled the German era or who heard about it from their parents. I conducted interviews in 1990 when it was still possible to find people who remembered German times, sometimes in surprising detail. Elders in Kilwa-Masoko and Kilosa, for example, were able to remember German settlers, planters, and district officials by name, and describe local relations with them and peoples' attitudes about working on plantations or growing cash crops. In coastal towns like Kilwa, Bagamoyo, and Kilindoni and Chole on Mafia Island, people could recall slavery and its importance for local society. Oral methodology brought with it several difficulties. One was that elders tended to conflate the British and German periods of rule in Tanzania. For example, when elders used the word *manamba* to refer to labor migrants, they were probably remembering British times when that Swahili word was introduced from English, and the conditions of labor migration had altered significantly from German times. Elders whom I interviewed often recalled paying taxes in shillings, not the rupees which were used during German times. I could find no one who recalled the massive Otto cotton plantation that was located just outside of Kilosa town, although several people readily talked about sisal plantations that emerged in the region under British colonialism. A further limitation of oral and archival evidence was in uncovering gendered changes in rural life that are an important theme of this book.[20] My oral research tended to elicit the richest evidence on occasions when I interviewed two or more elders together, whose memories reinforced and perhaps influenced each other.

I bring to bear the voices of African common people and their perspectives on labor migration and its effects on rural society furthermore by drawing on court cases and on district-level grievances brought by men and women. I have found in the course of writing this book that gendered dimensions of colonial history are most evident in records of district courts, where men and women sought to have their grievances redressed.[21] By their nature such sources are weighted in the direction of household conflict, such as when men and women sought divorce or control of children. Men sometimes appear in these records seeking the return of wives who deserted them. As these Swahili-language records show, women emerge in the historical record most frequently when their actions incurred the vilification and notice of colonial officials. This is particularly the case in the last decade of colonial rule, when women were condemned as unruly and not contributing to the colonial endeavor of growing cash crops or having sufficient numbers of children. Occasionally planters seeking women as workers complained of their actions when they refused to migrate locally for work. Despite their limitations, court records show that domestic conflict was one outcome of the kind of intense economic transformation that colonialism brought. Besides court records, women appear frequently in penal records and cases of slave emancipation. Mission accounts also describe different activities for men and women, in contrast to government records and newspapers that invariably speak of Africans in a collective sense, such as *die Bauer* (the peasants) or *die Leute* (the people), even when it is clear from the context that women are the main objects of discourse.

Voices of common people are available in some printed accounts of the oral record, most importantly the *Maji Maji Research Project (MMRP)*.[22] Undertaken in the late 1960s to record memories of the Maji Maji war, the *MMRP* is a largely untapped resource, offering peasant views of their history, relations with Germans and neighbors, attitudes about cash crops, taxation, and the war itself. However the *MMRP* also has its limitations. Because the *MMRP* was concerned with the origins of the Maji Maji rebellion, the University of Dar es Salaam students who interviewed their elders in the 1960s were guided by the nationalist-oriented agenda current at that time. Nevertheless, common people's testimonies about their experiences of famine, taxation, forced labor, and the deteriorating authority of *majumbe* headmen emerge poignantly in many of these accounts.

While oral evidence evokes the agency of ordinary people, and thus the limitations of the colonial state, this perspective is also reinforced by evidence from the metropolitan background of German colonialism. Here many of the problems that Germans confronted in East Africa mirrored those in Germany, which by the turn of the century had not yet evolved completely from an agrarian to an industrial state. Thus Germans in the metropole struggled to control problems associated with labor migration, the erosion of rural society, competition over labor between business and industry, agricultural contract-breaking, the employment of women and

Introduction

children, and even remnants of serfdom called *Gesindewesen*. In some instances labor migrants in German East Africa succeeded in wresting greater gains than their counterparts in Germany in matters that included freedom of movement, pass controls, length of officially-sanctioned work days, and plantation working conditions. In the first few chapters I suggest that Germans drew on their metropolitan experiences in responding to these issues, and used them as a lens through which to view problems of subaltern resistance in colonial Tanzania.

My approach to this subject is to use regional case studies to illustrate the complex interplay between different labor regimes throughout German East Africa.[23] This is in part because the sources are extremely checkered for this period. While Rufiji offers the best sources for the impact of the colonial cash crop economy and conservation policies on rural societies, labor migration affected Tabora region far more dramatically. Aside from source limitations, Tanzania during this period (as in the present) did not exhibit a cohesive, balanced economy, nor could it owing to stark demographic, environmental, and ecological contrasts throughout the colony. The geographical scope of this book furthermore mirrors the chronological unraveling of German colonialism in East Africa. Beginning with the industrial backdrop of the metropole, I turn to the emergence of free and slave wage labor along the northern and southern coasts before examining the genesis of rural production regimes in the southern coastal hinterland, and their contribution to the Maji Maji rebellion. The second half of the book begins with the southeast, analyzing the rural economy in the last years of German rule before moving inland, much as the wage labor economy itself did, to examine the process and effects of labor migration in Morogoro and Tabora districts. A focus on any one region would invariably exclude some of the issues I have sought to deal with in this book.

In putting the actions of peasants and workers at center stage, I try to demonstrate how colonial policy evolved in response to those actions. While cataclysmic events like the Maji Maji war clearly influenced colonial policy, the day-to-day strivings of householders and migrants for better lives at a difficult moment of Tanzanian history were far more important than has previously been appreciated in shaping colonial policy. This study is a contribution toward correcting that omission.

NOTES

1. The informal economy in modern Tanzania has been discussed in many works. Recent analyses include Aili Mari Tripp, *Changing the Rules: The Politics of Liber-*

alization and the Urban Informal Economy in Tanzania (Berkeley, 1997); T.L. Maliyamkono and M.S.D. Bagachwa, *The Second Economy in Tanzania* (London, 1990); E.P. Mihanjo and N.N. Luanda, "The South-East Economic Backwater and the Urban Floating Wamachinga," in *The Making of a Periphery: Economic Development and Cultural Encounters in Southern Tanzania,* ed. Pekka Seppälä and Bertha Koda (Uppsala, 1998), 222–32.

2. F.O. Karstedt, "Betrachtungen zur Sozialpolitik in Ostafrika," *Koloniale Rundschau* 13 (1914), 133.

3. The language of Unyamwezi is Kinyamwezi. The term *vilimani* was perhaps a corruption of the Swahili word *Mrima,* designating the coast. However it is just as likely that in local usage *vilimani* referred to the Usambara hills (the plural of *kilima,* Swahili for hill), where most German estates were located, and which was the destination for many colonial-era labor migrants. In this sense *vilimani* means "at the coast" or "in the hills."

4. TNA G12/165, Bezirksnebenstelle Bismarckburg to Imperial Government, 30 February 1910, 99.

5. On precolonial wages in cloth and other commodities see Stephen J. Rockel, "Wage Labor and the Culture of Porterage in Nineteenth Century Tanzania: the Central Caravan Routes," *Comparative Studies of South Asia, Africa and the Middle East* 15, 2 (1995), 14–24. Waged slave labor is discussed in Frederick Cooper, *Plantation Slavery on the East Coast of Africa* (New Haven, 1977) and Jonathon Glassman, *Feasts and Riot: Revelry, Rebellion, and Popular Consciousness on the Swahili Coast, 1856–1888* (Portsmouth, 1995).

6. C.M.F. Lwoga, "From Long-Term to Seasonal Labour Migration in Iringa Region, Tanzania: A Legacy of the Colonial Forced Labour System," in *Forced Labour and Migration: Patterns of Movement within Africa,* ed. Abebe Zegeye and Shubi Ishemo (London, 1989), 180–210; Issa Shivji, *Law, State and the Working Class in Tanzania* (London, 1986); Deborah Fahy Bryceson, *Food Insecurity and the Social Division of Labour in Tanzania, 1919–85* (New York, 1990); Walter Rodney, Kapepwa Tambila, and Laurent Sago, *Migrant Labour in Tanzania during the Colonial Period: Case Studies of Recruitment and Conditions of Labour in the Sisal Industry* (Hamburg, 1983). For Kenya see Sharon Stichter, *Migrant Labour in Kenya: Capitalism and the African Response 1895–1975* (London, 1982). *Manamba,* literally "numbers," is a Swahili word derived from English that refers to labor migrants during British and modern times. It was not used during German colonial rule.

7. Studies of South African labor migration have been better in this respect. Examples include Colin Murray, *Families Divided: The Impact of Migrant Labour in Lesotho* (Cambridge, 1981); Patrick Harries, *Work, Culture, and Identity: Migrant Laborers in Mozambique and South Africa, c. 1860–1910* (Portsmouth, 1994); Shula Marks and Richard Rathbone, eds., *Industrialization and Social Change in South Africa: African Class-formation, Culture and Consciousness, 1870–1930* (Hong Kong, 1985); Peter Delius, *A Lion amongst the Cattle: Reconstruction and Resistance in the Northern Transvaal* (Portsmouth, 1996).

8. John Iliffe, *Tanganyika under German Rule 1905–1912* (Cambridge, 1969) and *A Modern History of Tanganyika* (Cambridge, 1979).

9. Rodney collapses the German and British colonial periods in Tanzania in "The Political Economy of Colonial Tanganyika 1890–1930," in *Tanzania under Colonial Rule*, ed. M.H.Y. Kaniki (Singapore, 1980), 128–63.

10. Juhani Koponen, *Development for Exploitation: German Colonial Policies in Mainland Tanzania, 1884–1914* (Hamburg, 1995).

11. Henry Bernstein, "African Peasantries: A Theoretical Perspective," *Journal of Peasant Studies* 6, 4 (1979), 421–43; Rodney, "Political Economy"; Iliffe, *Modern History*.

12. An exception is Elias Mandala, "Peasant Cotton Agriculture, Gender, and Inter-Generational Relationships: The Lower Tchiri (Shire) Valley of Malawi, 1906–1940," *African Studies* 25, 2–3 (1982), 27–44.

13. Helge Kjekshus, *Ecology Control and Economic Development in East African History: The Case of Tanganyika, 1850–1950* (London, 1996); Gregory Maddox, James Giblin, and Isaria N. Kimambo, eds., *Custodians of the Land: Ecology and Culture in the History of Tanzania* (London, 1996); James Giblin, *The Politics of Environmental Control in Northeastern Tanzania, 1840–1940* (Philadelphia, 1992); Steven Feierman, *Peasant Intellectuals: Anthropology and History in Tanzania* (Madison, 1990).

14. Koponen, *Development for Exploitation*, 662.

15. Iliffe, *Modern History*; Werner Biermann, *Tanganyika Railways—Carriers of Colonialism: An Account of Economic Indicators and Social Fragments* (Münster, 1995), 11. Koponen is less adamant about the emergence of a settler colony, but views the structural trends as favoring planters. *Development for Exploitation*, 318–20.

16. Biermann, *Tanganyikan Railways*, 1. For a discussion of the sources in the Tanzania National Archives covering the German period, and the fate of some of the files during World War I, see National Archives of Tanzania, *Guide to the German Records* Vol. I (Dar-es-Salaam/Marburg, 1984).

17. Most colonial-era German newspapers can be found at the Stadt- und Universitätsbibliothek in Frankfurt am Main.

18. Examples include Richard Hindorf, *Der Sisalbau in Deutsch-Ostafrika* (Berlin, 1925); Carl Jungblut, *Vierzig Jahre Afrika 1900–1940* (Berlin, 1941); R. Kaundinya, *Erinnerungen aus meinen Pflanzerjahren in Deutsch-Ostafrika* (Leipzig, 1918); Wilhelm Methner, *Unter drei Gouverneuren: 16 Jahre Dienst in deutschen Tropen* (Breslau, 1938); Hermann Paasche, *Deutsch-Ostafrika: Wirtschaftliche Studien* (Hamburg, 1913); Otto Pentzel, *Heimat Ostafrika* (Leipzig, 1936); Albert Prüsse, *Zwanzig Jahre Ansiedler in Deutsch-Ostafrika* (Stuttgart, 1929).

19. Wilhelm Blohm, *Die Nyamwezi: Land und Wirtschaft* (Hamburg, 1931) and *Die Nyamwezi: Gesellschaft und Weltbild* (Hamburg, 1933); Karl Weule, *Negerleben in Ostafrika* (Leipzig, 1908), translated as *Native Life in East Africa* (Chicago, 1969).

20. Some gendered accounts of household change that include the German era in Tanzania include Marja-Liisa Swantz, *Women in Development: A Creative Role Denied?* (London, 1985); Marcia Wright, *Strategies of Slaves and Women: Life-Stories from East/Central Africa* (New York, 1993); Giblin, *The Politics of Environmental Control*.

21. These records are found in Geheimes Staatsarchiv-Preussischer Kulturbesitz, Berlin-Dahlem, Nachlass Schnee, Schriftstücke in Suaheli.

22. *Maji Maji Research Project: Collected Papers* (University College Dar es Salaam, Department of History, 1968).

23. Other historians of this period have offered fine regional studies that offer insights that will not always mesh with my findings. See Feierman, *Peasant Intellectuals;* Giblin, *Politics of Environmental Control;* Isaria N. Kimambo, *Penetration and Protest in Tanzania: The Impact of the World Economy on the Pare 1860–1960* (London, 1991); Thomas Spear, *Mountain Farmers* (Berkeley, 1997).

1

INDUSTRIALIZATION AND THE LABOR QUESTION IN GERMAN EAST AFRICA, 1885–1914

The twentieth century began with widespread perceptions among policy makers in Germany that the textile industry, one of the biggest employers of German labor, was in a state of crisis. Symptoms of that crisis included widespread strike activity and conflict between employers and employees; production curtailments and factory closings; the steady increase in the employment of women, whose labor power was cheaper than men's; and the electoral success of Social Democrats in capitalizing on general worker disgruntlement. Many government officials and industrialists alike believed that the procurement of German sources of cotton from its own colonies might be a panacea for these crises. Viewing the erratic but steady rise in raw cotton prices to be at the heart of the textile industry's problems, many hoped to emancipate German cotton spinners from an American cotton monopoly by founding cotton plantations in German East Africa. This conclusion implied that Africans in Germany's largest colony must be transformed into plantation wage laborers.

Germans entered into their colonial empire with a bias toward large-scale, mechanized production, especially for tropical products like rubber, tobacco, and coffee. While government officials, aware of successful peasant or smallholder production of cotton in regions such as West Africa, India, and the United States, were more flexible about scale of cotton growing, industrial backers insisted that they would only support plantation cotton projects. Until about 1905 most state officials accepted that view, creating a "plantation imperative" in the first twenty years of German rule in East Africa. The plantation imperative meant that the colonial state would use its resources to channel African peasants, slaves, and porters to plantation wage labor. This decision affected patterns of labor migration and rural society in German East Africa dramatically.

Cotton takes special place in the genesis and demise of the plantation imperative because of its connections to the German textile industry. No other tropical crop, including competing industrial raw materials like rubber and sisal, held such prominence because no other crop played a similar role in German economic and social stability. The industrial connection, in particular the crisis in the textile industry in the fifteen years before World War I, also explains the erosion of German state support of plantation-scale production. From about 1905 policy makers in German East Africa began to conclude that plantations could never become efficient cotton growers owing to problems of climate, crop disease, technological limitations, and especially labor procurement. While the Maji Maji rebellion of 1905–07 convinced some that German labor policies must be amended, the general resistance of Africans to permanent wage labor in the years preceding the rebellion was the key factor to end the plantation imperative. The state simply could not compel enough peasants to become wage laborers to sustain intensive plantation production. The plantation imperative ended when the colonial state began to channel its resources to peasant-scale cotton production, undermining any chance for a successful plantation economy in German East Africa.

While the colonial state moved away from support of plantations, textile industrialists and other investors in the colonies, including several hundred European settlers, remained committed to plantation production. Believing that policy makers were betraying the colonial mission, they mustered parliamentary and industrial supporters in Germany to pressure the state to maintain its commitment to wage labor creation. This point of conflict made the *Arbeiterfrage* and the *Baumwollfrage*—the labor question and the cotton question—the two most pressing issues in the political economy of German East Africa in the last decade of German colonial rule. Together they formed the context in which African labor migrants and peasants struggled to deal with colonial demands.

INDUSTRIALIZATION, SOCIAL INSTABILITY, AND THE COTTON QUESTION

Unlike other colonial cash crops such as rubber, sisal, coffee, and tobacco, there was a vigorous, ongoing demand for cotton from a powerful sector of German industry that employed about one-tenth of the industrial working class.[1] Other industrial crops that Germans grew in East Africa, notably sisal and rubber, either were destined for non-German markets or were gradually marginalized owing to better production zones in other parts of the world.[2] Cotton was at the heart of many policy debates because it was the most important industrial raw material to be imported into Germany, a fact many industrialists and figures in government noted when demanding support for promotion of the crop.[3] This meant that, from the beginning of colonial rule, German industrialists were intimately involved in colonial economic policy because they saw cotton procurement as a life-and-death matter for their industry.[4] Considered a German national interest, perhaps the only national economic interest associated with the colonies, most policy makers and textile industrialists felt that cotton production dare not be left to the vagaries of the world market. Because of its industrial importance, cotton had the power to shape labor policy in Tanzania and directly and consistently affect the lives of African men and women.

German cotton colonialism had its roots in the condition of the German textile industry after 1870.[5] Unlike Britain, the German textile industry did not have a long history of factory production. Well into the nineteenth century it was predominantly a cottage industry. Following German unification in 1871, the textile industry expanded rapidly as a mechanized and concentrated sector of the economy. The spinning sector increased from about 2.8 million spindles in 1870 to 5.5 million in 1890, and doubled again to 11 million spindles by 1912.[6] By 1909 Germany was the world's third biggest cotton yarn producer based on number of spindles, following Great Britain and the United States.[7] The weaving sector of the industry tripled between 1870 and 1910 from about 84,000 looms to about 260,000.[8] The expansion of the industry was driven by domestic consumption of cotton goods, which, by the end of the nineteenth century, replaced wool and linen as the preferred cloth in Germany.[9] However, the export of cotton textiles was also crucial to the health of the industry, doubling in the decade before 1907 to become Germany's single biggest export, making Germany second only to Britain as an exporter of cotton goods.[10] Although only a fraction of Germany's cotton goods were targeted for colonial lands, the colonial market was an expanding sector for the future growth of the industry, and cotton goods were the most desired imports into colonial territories, which no manufacturer could afford to disregard in the long run.[11] German industrialists sought to replace Asian, American, and British textile imports to East Africa with their own goods, going so far as to familiarize themselves with the cloth fashions that African consumers preferred.[12]

Germany, like other European textile producers, depended on overseas sources of raw cotton. The United States provided 70 to 80 percent of Germany's needs, with India and Egypt as secondary suppliers.[13] Raw cotton was Germany's single biggest import by the turn of the century, tripling between 1882 and 1907 from 155,000 tons to 476,000 tons.[14] Nationalist-minded industrialists lamented the dependency which the German industry had on American cotton growers, frequently invoking the "cotton famine" of the American Civil War years as a dangerous precedent that might return to haunt the industry.[15] With the 1860s disruption in mind, some German industrialists actively promoted cotton twenty years later in the new East African colony and other colonial regions, and attempted to garner industry-wide promotion of German-owned sources of cotton.[16]

Before 1900 German efforts to produce colonial cotton were sporadic and unsuccessful. Africans resisted growing the crop outright, and the destruction of the first European cotton estates in the Bushiri uprising of 1889 led some industrialists to back away from further investments.[17] One Alsatian industrialist recalled the failure of expensive cotton trials in Algeria and Senegambia during the American Civil War.[18] Many were skeptical that colonial cotton could match the quality of American lint, and most realized that in the short term sufficient supplies would not be forthcoming from the colonies to ease German dependence on American sources.[19] The first African cotton trials gave them little hope. Early cotton planters had no knowledge of African growing conditions, and were abusive handlers of African labor. The *Kolonialrat*, which coordinated German colonial policy before 1907, encouraged cotton growing by providing a premium for cotton exports from East Africa.[20] The German administration provided cotton seed, plows, and agricultural instructors to Muslim elites along the southern coast of Tanzania. Yet the 1890s saw few returns from these colonial projects. In part this lack of will stemmed from the downward trajectory of world cotton prices during the 1890s, which gave the illusion that cotton spinners faced no immediate crisis.[21] Furthermore, the early 1890s were a decade of bad blood between cotton promoters in government and German industrialists over labor and tariff issues, leading some industrialists to back away from government cotton projects.

Despite early setbacks, government and industry kept returning to the idea of colonial cotton as industrial instability loomed on the horizon. Textile organizations were uneasy about European and American cotton stocks, which declined by 40 percent between 1885 and 1889, pressuring world prices upward.[22] Another concern was the threat of American export tolls on cotton destined for Europe.[23] The protectionist-minded spinning sector was at the forefront of colonial cotton projects by the turn of the century.[24] Cotton industrialists in general agreed with a German official who concluded in 1891, "winning our own [cotton] production realm is desirable from the highest political standpoint."[25] Thus, Germany's desire for autonomy from American market domination was the basis of a colonial policy aimed at cotton production.

By 1898 several influential voices called for reinvigorated efforts to overcome the first cotton plantation failures in East Africa. Among them was a German agricultural expert in Washington, Freiherr von Hermann, who believed that Texas offered a viable model for Tanzanian cotton growing. Hermann felt the East African colony could provide all of Germany's industrial needs, and optimistically predicted that "we might be able to compete with the United States in their own market."[26] Hermann discussed these cotton plans with the German military attaché in Washington, Graf von Götzen, who, a few years later as governor of German East Africa, would implement an infamous cotton program using forced labor. In 1900 the Foreign Office removed then Governor Liebert from his post in Dar es Salaam owing in part to his lackluster efforts to foster cotton.[27]

The most important new stimulus to colonial cotton was the founding of the Colonial Economic Committee (KWK) in 1896 by a cotton industrialist, Karl Supf, who became the main proponent of colonial cotton production until World War I.[28] Spearheading cotton policy in all the German colonies as a "national duty," Supf and the KWK linked industry and government in formulating a colonial economic policy. Funded largely by textile spinners, the Cotton Börse in Bremen, the Interior Ministry, and the Foreign Office, the KWK raised four million marks for its colonial projects between 1896 and 1914.[29]

Fear of another cotton famine caused by "the rape of the cotton market by American speculators" awakened the textile industry to participate in colonial cotton projects by 1900.[30] Most threatening were sudden fluctuations and rises in cotton lint prices after 1897 that undermined industrial stability. In January 1899 the average cotton price at Bremen was 59 M per 100 kg.[31] By the end of the year prices reached 80 M/kg, and the average price for that year was 67 M/kg. Prices climbed steadily in 1900, averaging about 103 M/kg that year. Because German textile centers were located far from the port cities of Hamburg and Bremen, industrialists bought their cotton in advance, and often incurred losses because of dramatic price fluctuations. Even price declines put them at a competitive disadvantage with British spinners. Since spinners, as opposed to cotton weavers or finishers, suffered most from these fluctuations, they became the most consistent industrial supporters of colonial cotton. By 1900 the textile industry as a whole feared that the era of low cotton prices was over because, in spite of record cotton harvests, American industrialists were consuming more of their own cotton, and market speculation kept cotton prices high. An immediate result of the cotton crisis of 1900 was a jump in the number of textile industry bankruptcies from 118 in 1900 to 169 in 1901.[32]

The 1900 crisis was the spur for the Colonial Economic Committee to take up the cotton issue in full force, inaugurating fifteen years of frenzied cotton promotion in the colonies which did not end until World War I. In the next few years the Interior Ministry and the Foreign Office promoted colonial cotton as social disruptions in Germany took on greater significance. Perhaps the 1903–04 Crimmitschau textile workers' strike in Saxony did most to galvanize official and industrial opinion about the need to stabilize the industry so as to ease social disruptions and strike activity.[33] During the strike the Association of German Cotton Yarn Consumers in Dresden became an active campaigner for colonial sources of cotton, blaming industrial failures and worker layoffs on the "dearth of cotton at acceptable prices."[34] In the aftermath of the strike Chancellor von Bülow informed Kaiser Wilhelm of the efforts of the KWK to promote colonial cotton in light of the "industrial retrenchment and worker lay-offs" that by that time had become necessary because of massive price fluctuations in world cotton supplies.[35]

The crisis of 1900 was followed by another in 1907, and most industrialists concluded by then that instability would be a permanent feature of the textile sector as long as they were dependent on American cotton supplies.[36] The powerful Association of South German Cotton Industrialists, composed of over 100 firms, considered 1910 to be "the worst year for losses and problems since the American Civil War."[37] A Saxon cotton expert wrote that "the looming specter of 'cotton famine' that has been threatening the portals of industry for years has become a tangible fact."[38] Those who had refrained from participating in colonial cotton endeavors began to become involved in cotton colonialism by offering financial support to the KWK or founding their own plantations in German East Africa.

In March 1907 the Interior Ministry and the Colonial Department sponsored a conference which called upon regional states and chambers of commerce to take the lead in promoting colonial cotton in circles of business and industry.[39] Portraying the emancipation from American cotton as a life-and-death matter for German industry, the colonial budget for 1907 doubled the funds allocated for cotton promotion from 50,000 to 100,000 M. In 1907 the newly-appointed Colonial Minister, Bernard Dernburg, went on an inspection tour of German East Africa with a particular interest in gauging prospects for cotton growing. He was accompanied by representatives of textile industries, several of whom went on to found cotton plantations in German East Africa.[40] Further cotton conferences followed in 1909 and 1912, each motivated by the desire to see more of German industry participating in colonial cotton projects, even industries that did not benefit directly from cotton growing, such as the machine, iron, coal, and shipping sectors.[41] Referring to American price speculation as a permanent feature of the industry, one conference participant reminded others of their patriotic duty to support colonial cotton.

SOCIAL DIMENSIONS OF COTTON COLONIALISM IN GERMANY

An important component of the cotton question was its intersection with social instability and working class pressure to improve working and living conditions. The textile industry was unique because it was the major sector of women's industrial employment. In Germany as a whole the participation of women workers in the textile industry rose from 38 percent in 1882 to 45 percent in 1895 to 50 percent in 1907.[42] In the Kingdom of Saxony, the most industrialized German state, the number of women in the textile industry rose from 56,520 in 1883 to 86,647 in 1894, making up about 55 percent of the textile work force.[43] Many observers considered the textile industry to be a *Frauenindustrie* (women's industry), especially in the spinning branch, where women's presence increased faster than men's through the turn of the century.[44] Employers sought to expand their female work force, especially in times of economic crisis, because it was one means to cut production costs. Women's wages were 30–50 percent lower than men's, in part because they dominated in unskilled positions, creating "gendered hierarchies of skill."[45] As world cotton prices rose after the turn of the century, creating unstable buying patterns for the industry, women's levels of employment also rose.[46] The trend was for cheaper women workers to displace men in the industry because, as one male worker put it, "a factory crammed with women and girls is ideal for industrialists and their officials."[47] Women's "starvation wages" had a depressing effect on men's wages, and were a bellwether for workers' wage levels as a whole. In southern German textile factories average per capita wages declined between 1905 and 1910 as more women entered the industry.[48] The *Textilarbeiter-Zeitung* reported "many industries grasp toward cheaper female workers when the economy enters a downswing [because] the male and female labor markets work against each other."[49] For this reason trade unions were concerned about women's wage levels, and some industrial strikes after the turn of the century were fought mainly on the issue of women's wage levels.[50] In July 1912 unionized workers tried to force the Münch factory in Hof to dismiss a non-unionized female weaver, going on strike for five days before returning to work.[51] In 1912 twenty-nine women in a Göppingen (Württemberg) weaving factory went on strike over low wages, igniting a lockout that lasted four months and affected over one thousand workers and several factories.[52] Although the workers lost the strike, the affected firm lost some 67,831 worker days during the lockout. German industry as a whole viewed the increased employment of women as a practical necessity, and resisted attempts to de-feminize the work force.

While textile industrialists favored the unabated employment of women, government policy makers and social reformers viewed the employment of women, especially married women, as a social problem that threatened the physical and moral health of the nation and which therefore must be curtailed.[53] Though only about 20 percent of female textile workers were married, their employment became the subject of vigorous debate from the 1890s to World War I.[54] Some argued that, owing to married women's employment in factories, child mortality increased, family life suffered, children became wayward, and women did not have the opportunity to fulfill their "duties as housewife, mother and spouse."[55]

The "social problem" of women's industrial employment intersected with colonial cotton policy. In the early 1890s the Minister of Trade and Industry, Berlepsch, was among the cadre of officials most concerned about ameliorating the condition of women factory workers by decreasing the work week and improving the work environment.[56] Berlepsch also spearheaded the state's first efforts at bringing the textile industry and chambers of commerce on board in financing colonial cotton endeavors. After the turn of the century the Ministry of the Interior took the lead both in fostering colonial cotton production and decreasing the employment of married women in factories. For German policy makers, the social condition of factory women was directly related to the economic stability of the textile industry.

While many social reformers believed married women in factories to be the greatest danger to the "social body," others viewed *Landflucht*, the rural-to-urban migration of young people, especially women, as a more pressing problem.[57] The economic argument was that migration to textile centers created a shortage of girls and women on farms, leading to agricultural decline. Attracted by city life and factory wages, women refused to remain in the countryside. Such was the case with Franziska Narloch of Bautzen in Saxony, who in October 1906 was given two days in jail for leaving the service of a Pommritz estate owner before her service period had expired.[58] Although Franziska requested that her jail time be converted into a fine, local officials refused to ameliorate the sentence, so rife was the problem of desertion from rural estates. The estate worker Ida Bruder, who fled a Saxon estate late in 1906 for better work in a Leipzig factory, and was subsequently given eight days in jail for violating rural labor controls, exemplified the path of thousands of rural-to-urban migrants.[59] So severe was the problem of *Landflucht* in turn-of-the-century Germany that government officials sought to create legal prohibitions against the freedom of movement of young people from the countryside to the cities, a move intensely opposed by textile industrialists who relied on the labor of young women to cut production costs and compete with overseas producers.[60]

Beyond the economics of *Landflucht*, social reformers and conservative parties saw female migration as a moral danger to the nation. Viewing the countryside as the reservoir of German values and culture, they believed that the unabated loss of single women and men to the factories and cities was leading to the moral and physical corruption of the state. However, because industrialists had few options in cutting production costs so as to compete with foreign competitors, most policy makers saw rural-to-urban female migration as a necessary evil to create a cheaper work force. Because the textile industry was the single biggest employer of women, social reformers in government, and coordinators of colonial cotton policy like the KWK, argued that procuring German cotton from the colonies would enable industrialists to stabilize production costs and, implicitly, ease their dependence on cheaper female labor. Colonial cotton supplies would slow down the substitution of male for female labor, decrease the need for married women in factories, and help to stem *Landflucht* of young, unmarried women.[61]

Gendered aspects of the cotton question were buried in a discourse about Germany's need for colonial cotton in order to ensure social stability among the working classes. Recalling the cotton famine of the 1860s, Supf of the KWK emphasized that dependence on the American market threatened "one million worker families," or one-eighth of the industrial working class in Germany. Supf argued, "it is clear that if a crisis beset the cotton industry in its present state, it would bring with it an almost unimaginable social danger."[62] State officials believed that cotton production in the colonies would be good for industry, the working classes, and the nation.[63] Whereas industry and the working classes were divided on issues such as wage levels and length of work days, Supf and others believed that colonial cotton could be a unifying issue. Colonial cotton propagandists therefore took the issue directly to the working classes and their representatives in the Reichstag (parliament) and unions. The argument persuaded the Christian textile unions to support colonial cotton by affiliating with the KWK by 1903.[64] Thereafter the Christian textile unions were uncritical supporters of colonial cotton policy, which they used to distinguish themselves from the "unpatriotic" socialist unions.[65]

By portraying the cotton question as a national concern that directly affected textile workers, government and business leaders hoped to put pressure on socialist deputies in the Reichstag to vote for colonial budgets that included allocations for cotton growing. As one opponent of socialism stated, "The Social Democrats will have a confrontation with the spinnery workers when there is no more raw material."[66] Indeed, many socialists felt vulnerable on the cotton issue, and after the 1900 crisis often claimed that they supported colonial cotton production, but not the entire colonial endeavor or the repressive policies used to get Africans to grow cotton.[67] Socialist deputies argued that it was unrealistic to expect colonial cotton to influence the world market appreciably in the near future, especially as it was controlled by cotton speculators in America and Germany. Furthermore, they argued that efforts to promote cotton that relied on capitalist-oriented plantations had proven to be disastrous for the inhabitants of the colonies, as well as unprofitable. The socialist-allied textile trade unions followed this line, concluding in 1911 "the cotton question cannot be solved by growing cotton in the African colonies."[68] Nevertheless, by the outset of World War I, and perhaps wary of the possibility of a wartime "cotton famine," the socialist textile union conceded that colonial cotton cultivation might ease the "economic and social catastrophe" that would come with factory shutdowns.[69]

The cotton question after 1900 was inseparable from the social question for most policy makers. In general, cotton supplies from America and Egypt were adequate for Germany's needs throughout the colonial period, but price fluctuations made cotton buying insecure, even in years when raw cotton prices went down.[70] The trend toward lowering tariffs on cotton yarn imports after 1902 (going back to the 1890s) made German spinners vulnerable to overseas and Continental competitors.[71] Working class demands for improved living conditions, wage increases, and decreased work days exerted a continuous pressure on textile industrialists to find non-wage ways to cut costs, such as organizing regional associations, employing female labor, or procuring secure cotton supplies. Most understood that colonial cotton offered no quick hope of stabilizing the German industry and emancipating it from American-generated price fluctuations. Yet, the consensus was that German-controlled sources of cotton were not only highly desirable, but a national goal. Business and industry were steadfast, though financially reluctant, supporters of colonial cotton endeavors.

THE RISE AND FALL OF THE PLANTATION IMPERATIVE IN TANZANIA

The major issue dividing colonial cotton enthusiasts in the pre-war years was not whether cotton should be grown in the colonies, but whether cotton should be grown on highly capitalized *Grossbetriebe* (plantations), or on the *mashamba* (fields) of African peasants. This highly contentious issue had far-reaching consequences for Africans in the colonies, and ushered in struggles over the nature of colonialism itself.

From the beginning of colonial rule in 1885 German economic undertakings in Tanzania were based on the idea that production must be large-scale and capital intensive. Beginning in 1886 Germans grew cotton on a plantation basis along the Tanzanian coast. The scale of these estates was modest, in the range of 10–20 ha (hectares) in the first years, and rarely exceeding 250 ha actually cultivated in any given year of German rule, although thousands of hectares were often controlled by capitalist corporations. The plantation model assumed the need for a regular labor force in a colony where overall population levels were relatively low. While early planters sometimes resorted to expensive Asian indentured workers, African peasants were targeted as the major labor force for colonial projects in the long run. This meant that by favoring plantation production German colonialism disrupted African households and food production by demanding that men and women work for a wage for part of each year.

Unlike rubber and sisal, it was not a foregone conclusion that cotton would be produced on a plantation basis. Although the American model

Figure 1.1 Colonial Minister Dernburg observing a steam tractor pulling a plowshare on the Leipzig Cotton Plantation near Sadani, 1907. Steam tractors symbolized German attempts to create a capital-intensive agrarian economy. The plow was tethered to a cable attached to a tractor at each end of the field. (Courtesy of Bundesarchiv, Koblenz, 146/82/172/28. Reprinted with permission.)

of cotton production was predicated on plantations, other parts of the world, notably India and Egypt, offered examples of viable peasant cotton. Yet Germans began their tenure in East Africa with a preconceived notion that cash crop production, to be successful and profitable, had to be on a large scale, combined with scientific principles of farming: modern technology, irrigation, steam plows or draft animals, and agricultural research in soil, seeds, and crop pests (See FIGURE 1.1). Colonial planners considered large-scale agrarian production to be the only efficient method for an industrial state and a *Kulturland*, a civilized land. Based on this premise, the colonies in Africa emerged as an agrarian frontier of industrial Germany.

Aside from the predilections of economic thinkers, the plantation imperative stemmed largely from the efforts of the state to attract industrial financing. Textile industrialists insisted that colonial cotton must be on a plantation scale if they were to participate with funding, arguing that, in order to compete with American producers, colonial cotton had to be a uniform and high quality product to be used effectively in factories. The *Hamburgischer Kourier* expressed this view when it wrote, "For Europeans in the colonies large concerns are better suited, and are best begun by capitalist corporations which can absorb failed harvests better."[72] Likewise, in negotiating possible industrial support for colonial cotton ventures, the Hannover Chamber of Commerce emphasized:

> Whether or not German industry will participate in colonial cotton projects depends foremost on whether quality cotton can be obtained there. This will entail clearing of land and forests, irrigation, the establishment of transport routes, the creation of regular export connections; also in obtaining suitable cotton seed, cotton machinery, cotton teachers from the USA. . . . If these prerequisites are met, the Hannover industrialists agree that the necessary entrepreneurial spirit will not be lacking.[73]

Many proponents of the plantation model took it as a given that the state would oversee labor procurement, provide premiums for any cotton exported, and supply gins and presses for cotton processing. Although German officials who understood the situation in East Africa realized that these schemes were not realistic in the near future, they endorsed them nonetheless in order to attract industrial participation in colonialism.

The initial momentum for a plantation production zone in East Africa also came from the German East Africa Corporation (*DOAG*), a trading corporation that the German government chartered to administer the protectorate before 1891.[74] Those in Germany interested in investing in the colonies in the 1880s saw the *DOAG* as a panacea which, in one body, would promote trade in natural products, establish plantations, and create an infrastructure for administration. Some German textile industrialists invested in the *DOAG* and exerted their influence to get the company to begin cotton trials as soon as the colony was in German hands.[75] After several years of disappointing returns, the directors of the *DOAG*'s Kikogwe plantation near Pangani claimed to have planted about 276 acres in 1893, of which about 134 acres were in cotton.[76]

While officials in Germany encouraged the vision of a cotton plantation economy into the 1890s, those in the colony were more pessimistic. Governor Soden believed that the colonial infrastructure was too immature for a European-plantation economy, and, as an alternative, insisted that "native" cultivation—meaning the Muslim coastal elite—offered the best prospects for quick returns since they "are much cheaper producers," in part because they made extensive use of slave labor.[77] Soden took the lead in distributing cotton and sesame seed to Arabs, Swahili, and Indians along the coast to foster cash crop production. Other voices in government argued that cotton should be based on small-scale family undertakings like Indian or African-American farmers.[78] Small farms could withstand world price fluctuations more easily because much of their land was planted with food crops. Even this scale of production—about 10 ha—was much larger than typical East African peasant *mashamba*, and would require extra-family labor such as slaves, or the possibility of using the ox-plow, which was untenable in the tsetse zones of the colony that were infested with sleeping sickness.

THE LANDSCAPES OF TANZANIAN AGRICULTURE

German perspectives on the colony's agricultural potential were largely based on European realities that did not mesh with Tanzania's physical and social environment. A region of some 250 million acres during German rule, the population was roughly estimated at some seven million people, three million of whom lived in the region of Ruanda-Urundi that was never integrated economically with the rest of the colony.[79] With perhaps four million people in a land about twice the size of California, one would think that there was an abundance of land per capita. However, Tanzanian land varied widely in agricultural potential.[80] Poor soils, erratic rainfall, and insecure or impermanent sources of water characterize much of the country in recent centuries. Since most of Tanzania was not optimally arable, people concentrated in exceptional locations such as fertile volcanic highlands or along river systems. Population density was thus largely a factor of ecological niches. People gravitated to regions where crop productivity was highest on relatively limited areas of land, and it was there that intensive or semi-intensive agricultural systems developed, often leading to centralized political systems.[81] There were strong incentives to increase family or village size in such regions since more hands enabled better mastering of the landscape by building ridges and irrigation channels and fertilizing the land.

Most of the country, not suitable for intensive agriculture, was arable when peasants practiced bush fallowing. Bush fallowing required perhaps 80 percent of the land to lay fallow in any given year, creating limits on population densities and residence patterns.[82] Before the

German arrival, many societies established a precarious balance between land use and population level, so that surpluses could be produced in most years despite the limits of the land. Those that succeeded best, such as the Nyamwezi or Zaramo, were able to give up some male labor annually for porterage or hunting. Others, such as the Matumbi and Rufiji, refrained from porterage, concentrating men's and women's labor on agriculture to take advantage of regional grain exporting networks. The many different ecological zones of Tanzania, each with established crops and planting schedules, different rainfall patterns, soil types, and disease zones, meant that dwellers of the region often competed for available resources, but also established trade links that enabled them to weather times of crisis, such as famine caused by drought or locust plagues.

An important feature of Tanzanian rural economies was the use of *pori*, forests and other wilderness, as a commons. Forest and bush lands were reserves for fuel, timber, and trade products such as ivory, beeswax, honey, rubber, and copal. As hunting frontiers, the wilderness provided game to the diet, while on the negative side, forests and bush harbored crop predators, such as wild pigs, baboons, and antelopes, and disease-bearing insects, such as tsetse, which threatened rural economies and affected residence patterns.[83] If tsetse zones spread for any reason, people moved their villages and sometimes whole societies. The ability to control the environment was important for the success of crop systems. This meant that forest access was necessary to supplement agriculture or to keep the wilderness that threatened villages at bay. While women tended the agrarian economy, it was often the job of men to control the wilderness through collective hunting, clearing trees, and firing the bush. Alongside cultivated and fallow land, *pori* was part of Tanzanian agrarian systems.

The German vision of *Kulturland* contrasted sharply with their perception of African *Urproduktion*, "aboriginal" agriculture (See FIGURE 1.2).[84] The former model was one of intensive agriculture making use of draft animals, plows, machinery, seed selection, fertilizers, and family labor alongside hired laborers. Forests, too, should be regulated by this vision, allowing for a sustainable forest use that could easily mesh with the needs of agriculture and industry through management, tree selection, and regulated planting and cutting.[85] Thus, land, pasture, and forests were resources that should be protected from people. Some went so far as to see the German model of agriculture as a fundamental feature of civilization in a broad sense. The obverse was that African agrarian practices were the basis of backwardness, un-

Figure 1.2 The *Kulturland* model. Germans hoped to recreate rural Tanzania in this image. (From *Verhandlungen des Kolonial Wirtschaftlichen Komitees* 1 [1906], 5.)

derdevelopment, and "uncivilized" cultural practices such as polygamy and impermanent villages and households. German planners attacked African forest and land use, viewing fallow land as misused or unused land. In so doing they curtailed an important arena of men's agrarian activities. Forced to alter their relationship with the environment, many men entered into colonial labor circuits, ushering in changes in household divisions of labor.

The plantation imperative intruded into this environment in the 1890s. In the northeast Usambara region, *DOAG* trial plantations and a handful of independent settlers struggled to establish successful cash crop estates geared to the German market, mostly focusing on coffee, rubber, and eventually sisal. State efforts to foster plantations, on the other hand, were concentrated in the southeast coastal hinterland of Kilwa and the Rufiji delta, where the "wealthy, influential natives" of Samanga and Mohoro were brought on board for Germany's cash crop endeavors.[86] The colonial administration strove at this time to enlist Matumbi and Ngindo village headmen to get their people to grow cotton in the southern coastal hinterland.[87] Already in 1894 many of these efforts were stymied owing to locust plagues that destroyed rice, millet, and maize crops all along the coast, resulting in famine that ruled out the addition of non-food cash crops like cotton.[88]

Despite the first failures, Germans were intent on establishing a plantation economy in German East Africa, and by the end of the 1890s had implemented a reinvigorated production program. The plantation vision was kept alive throughout the 1890s by the few small plantations scattered up and down the coast and in the Usambara mountains. Increasingly these estates were strengthened by the immigration of a few hundred white settlers into East Africa, who most officials believed offered the best hope of making the colony economically profitable in the near future. Never a large group, and never able to open up large tracts of land to grow cash crops for a world economy, settlers nevertheless exerted an influence on the colonial administration beyond their numbers by the end of the 1890s. Settlers competed with the more ambitious undertakings of industrialists and other German capitalists for a limited African labor supply.

By the turn of the century the crisis in the textile industry created a great urgency for colonial cotton. With conquest all but complete, colonial officials were determined to put the colony on a sound economic footing. Some reports concluded that East Africa had a better potential for cotton growing than many American cotton districts.[89] The KWK laid out trial cotton plantations at Sadani and Mpanganya where it experimented with steam tractors, draft animals, and seed selection.[90] Urging settlers and missionaries throughout the colony to grow cotton, the German East African government laid out trial cotton estates at Kwai, Amani, and Gerengere near Kilwa to develop a scientific basis for the crop. Meanwhile, the Tanga district office settled several South Asians as model cotton farmers using ox-plows and irrigation on modest lands of about 15–18 ha.[91] These efforts were accompanied by a general policy of forcing Africans to work on German and Arab estates and village fields distant from their households.

The plantation imperative competed directly with the aspirations of labor migrants and local peasants to maintain household agricultural production. Plantations could not overcome the limitations of climate, rainfall, crop diseases, and especially labor to master the colonial environment. A labor shortage had become palpable throughout the colony well before 1905, and some colonial thinkers understood that Tanzania was too thinly populated to ever become a plantation or settler colony.[92] The Maji Maji rebellion that erupted in the fall of 1905 convinced most officials that the colonial state could not coerce sufficient African labor to work on plantations. After the uprising, the administration moved cautiously and quietly against plantations, discouraged the arrival of new settlers, and curtailed the use of force in mustering African workers.

While the government and the KWK moved away from plantation-scale production following the Maji Maji rebellion, the textile industry and its financial backers were more convinced than ever that industrial-scale textile production needed plantation-scale cotton, as one enthusiast made clear:

> Plantation agriculture is a necessity for German East Africa. Necessary for the quick use of many regions of our immense East African territory, necessary for training and stimulation of the natives to work, necessary as a defense of the European cotton industry against decline threatened by a feared cotton famine.[93]

The end of the Maji Maji rebellion coincided with the cotton crisis of 1907 in Germany that drove many industrialists out of business.[94] As the cotton question took on greater urgency in Germany, textile industrialists, backed by German banks, founded new cotton plantations in German East Africa in the hope of emancipating themselves from fluctuations in the world cotton market. The Leipzig Cotton Spinnery, for example, optimistically predicted that it could produce all of its cotton needs on its own plantation in the hinterland of Sadani.[95] In late 1908 the factory received the first bales grown on its plantation. The Stuttgart industrialist Heinrich Otto, backed by a consortium of southern German textile industrialists, founded plantations in 1907 along the Central Railway town of Kilosa and at Kikanda in the region of the Maji Maji outbreak, hoping to produce his own cotton supplies.[96] The boom in plantation rubber was reaching its apogee shortly thereafter, and sisal was beginning to achieve its first positive results on some fifty plantations and estates by 1911.

While the shift in state policy away from forced labor spelled the end of the plantation imperative, it did not mean the end of the plantation agenda for cotton industrialists and planters in the colony. Disgusted with the "extraordinary difficulties in labor procurement" created by the East African administration, industrial and planter organizations portrayed the new policy as a "brake on development" in the colony.[97] The debate over plantation or peasant production emerged as the most contentious issue in colonial circles after 1907, and set the stage for battles over labor policy in newspapers, the Reichstag, chambers of commerce, and German East Africa.[98] Ultimately these battles would be decided by how African peasants and workers responded to evolving colonial economic policies.

NOTES

1. Of some 8.6 million industrial workers in Germany in 1907, one million were textile workers, with cotton textiles predominating. Helga Nussbaum, *Unternehmer gegen Monopole: Über Struktur und Aktionen antimonopolitischer bürgerlichen Gruppen zu Beginn des 20. Jahrhunderts* (Berlin, 1966), 110. In contrast, only a few thousand workers were employed in the rubber industry before World War I, and only 54,000 as late as 1925. Rosa Kempf, *Die deutsche Frau nach der Volks-, Berufs-, und Betriebszählung von 1925* (Mannheim, 1931), 86.

2. Sisal, used for rope and agricultural cord, mostly went to non-German markets like Britain. The rubber boom in Tanzania came in the first decade of the twentieth century, then collapsed by 1911 owing to competition from Southeast Asian plantations. Juhani Koponen, *Development for Exploitation: German Colonial Policies in Mainland Tanzania, 1884–1914* (Hamburg, 1995), 544, fn. 1.

3. In 1900 cotton and its by-products led the list of "tropical" crops imported into Germany with a value of 461 million marks (of which 359 million marks included cotton lint). Cotton was followed by coffee (179 million), tobacco (150 million), maize (130 million), rubber (74 million), rice (48 million), palm oil (41 million), jute (30 million), and cocoa (30 million). BAB/R1001/7807, Denkschrift zur Frage der Ausdehnung landwirtschaftlicher Produktion in Deutsch-Ostafrika, 26 August 1901, 9–10. While sisal was destined to become the biggest export from German East Africa, in 1913 only 3,208 tons of 19,698 tons produced in the colony were imported into Germany. Rainer Tetzlaff, *Koloniale Entwicklung und Ausbeutung: Wirtschafts- und Sozialgeschichte Deutsch-Ostafrikas 1885–1914* (Berlin, 1970), 118–23.

4. Already in 1887 Theodor Hassler, chairman of the Association of South German Textile Industrialists, contributed 70,000 RM to fledgling cotton trials in German East Africa. BAB/R1001/8144, Hassler to Colonial Department, 4 February 1892, 35–36; Stadtarchiv Augsburg, Hassler Archive #19, Deutsche Kolonialgesellschaften.

5. On the German textile industry before World War I see W. Lochmüller, *Zur Entwicklung der Baumwollindustrie in Deutschland* (Jena, 1906); A. Oppel, *Die deutsche Textilindustrie* (Leipzig, 1912); Heinrich Sybel, "Die Baumwollindustrie," *Schriften des Vereins für Socialpolitik*, 105 (Leipzig, 1903), 127–55; Günter Kirchhain, "Das Wachstum der deutschen Baumwollindustrie im 19. Jahrhundert," (Ph.D. diss., University of Münster, 1973); Ernst Meyknecht, *Die Krisen in der deutschen Woll- und Baumwollindustrie von 1900 bis 1914* (Gütersloh, 1928).

6. Benas Levy, "Baumwolle," *KR* 9 (1910), 754. The 1912 figure comes from Benas Levy, "Die Baumwollfrage und die deutschen Kolonien," *KR* 12 (1913), 391–414. See also Meyknecht, *Die Krisen*, 24. An almost 100 percent jump from 1870 to 1880 included about one million spindles acquired when Germany annexed Alsace-Lorraine after the Franco-Prussian War.

7. Reichskolonialamt, *Die Baumwollfrage: Denkschrift über Produktion und Verbrauch von Baumwolle. Massnahmen gegen die Baumwollnot* (Jena, 1911), 165.

8. Levy, "Baumwolle," 754.

9. Per capita cotton consumption in Germany passed from .3 kg in 1840 to 5 kg in 1895 and 7 kg by 1909. Kolonial-Wirtschaftliches Komitee, *Unsere Kolonialwirtschaft in ihrer Bedeutung für Industrie und Arbeiterschaft* (Berlin, 1909), 49;

Ferdinand Fischer, *Die Industrie Deutschlands und seiner Kolonien* (Leipzig, 1908), 53–57.

10. Almost 90 percent of these manufactures went to Europe and North America, with Asia, Latin America, and Africa accounting for the remaining 10 percent. Oppel, *Deutsche Textilindustrie*, 93, 128; W.A. Graham Clark, *Cotton Fabrics in Middle Europe: Germany, Austria-Hungary, Switzerland* (Washington, 1908), 13–14.

11. As argued by Hermann Paasche, a pro-colonial member of the German parliament. *Stenographische Berichte über die Verhandlungen des Reichstages*, 288/129/4389, 8 March 1913.

12. "Die deutschen Kolonien als Absatzgebiet für Deutschlands Textilindustrie," *Leipziger Monatschrift für die Textilindustrie* 28, 2 (1913), 41–43; "Deutsch-Ostafrika als Einfuhrmarkt für Textilwaren," *Leipziger Monatschrift* 29 (1914), 20–22; "Deutsches Reich," MH/11/524 Bayerisches Hauptstaatsarchiv, 1–6; Laird Jones, "Target Wage Workers or Targeted Consumers?: Caravan Porters, Migrant Laborers and Imported Goods, 1880–1914," paper presented to the African Studies Association Annual Conference, Philadelphia, November 1999.

13. Levy, "Baumwollfrage," 393–99; Clark, *Cotton Fabrics*, 14. Saxon mills such as the Leipziger Baumwollspinnerei favored Egyptian cotton, which produced a staple better suited to their spindles. Staatsarchiv Leipzig, Leipziger Baumwollspinnerei AG, 146, Bericht 1906 and 1907.

14. Clark, *Cotton Fabrics*, 19; KWK, *Unsere Kolonialwirtschaft*, 50; *Kolonialpraxis. Handbuch für Kaufleute, Industrielle, Banken, Behörden und Kapitalisten* (Berlin, 1911), 194; Oppel, *Deutsche Textilindustrie*, 114.

15. For example BAB/R1001/8144, Ernst Vohsen, "Bericht über die Baumwollenkultur in den deutschen Schutzgebieten," 1891, 7; BAB/R1001/8178, Association of Silesian Textile Industrialist to Berlepsch, 27 January 1891, 68. The cotton famine has been discussed in W.O. Henderson, *The Rise of German Industrial Power 1834–1914* (London, 1975), 144–45. According to Henderson, many cotton mills in Saxony, Silesia, Berlin, and the Rhineland closed or worked part-time owing to the cotton famine, while Bavaria and Württemberg, with greater stores of raw cotton and less dependent on American sources, suffered less.

16. BAB/R1001/8178 Alsatian Industrial Syndicate to CVDI, 27 October 1890, 55–56; Association of Silesian Textile Industrialists to Berlepsch, 27 January 1891, 68–69; *Politische Nachrichten* (Berlin) 116, 23 May 1887.

17. BAB/R1001/8178 Jansen to Berlepsch, 5 November 1890, 35–38; Deutsch-Ostafrikanische Gesellschaft to Foreign Office, 30 May 1891, 106–08. The uprising is discussed in Jonathon Glassman, *Feasts and Riot: Revelry, Rebellion, and Popular Consciousness on the Swahili Coast, 1856–1888* (Portsmouth, 1995); J.A. Kieran, "Abushiri and the Germans," in *Hadith 2*, ed. Bethwell Ogot (Nairobi, 1970), 157–201.

18. The Alsatian industry in the 1860s was part of the French empire, and thus directed its cotton growing efforts at French colonies at that time. BAB/R1001/8178 Dollfus to CVDI, 27 October 1890, 54–55.

19. BAB/R1001/8178 Hannover Handelskammer to Berlepsch, 10 January 1891, 70–72; Osnabrück Handelskammer to Berlepsch, 16 November 1891, 73–75.

20. The *Kolonialrat*, created in 1890, was a semi-official body of German officials, businessmen, missionaries, and academics that advised the Foreign Office on

colonial policy. It was dissolved in 1907 when the Colonial Ministry was created. Paul Hacker, *Die Beiräte für besondere Gebiete der Staatstätigkeit* (Tübingen, 1903), 19–21; Koponen, *Development*, 279–80.

21. In the 1880s cotton prices hovered at around 11 cents per pound, and dropped to about 7 cents per pound by the 1890s. Karl Supf, "Zur Baumwollfrage," *Der Tropenpflanzer* 4, 6 (1900), 268.

22. BAB/R1001/8178, Hassler to CVDI, 5 November 1890, 41–46.

23. BAB/R1001/8178, 78; BAB/R1001/8144, Vohsen, "Bericht über die Baumwollenkultur," 2.

24. Helmut Böhme, *Deutschlands Weg zur Grossmacht: Studien zum Verhältnis von Wirtschaft und Staat während der Reichsgründungszeit 1848–1881* (Köln, 1966), 72; Nussbaum, *Unternehmer gegen Monopole*, 116.

25. BAB/R1001/8144, Ballicher to Marschall, 23 June 1891, 12.

26. BAB/R1001/8178, Hermann memorandum, 2 September 1898, 200.

27. BAB/R1001/8178, Liebert to Foreign Office, 4 April 1900, 209–10.

28. The KWK was a far more influential colonial policy-making body than its much larger affiliate, the German Colonial Society (DKG). Historians have generally erred in taking the DKG too seriously as a formulator of colonial policy. There is no general history of the Colonial Economic Committee, but see Karl Supf, "Die Arbeit des Kolonial-Wirtschaftlichen Komitees, 1896–1906," *Der Tropenpflanzer* 10, 12 (1906); Richard V. Pierard, "A Case Study in German Economic Imperialism: The Colonial Economic Committee, 1896–1914," *Scandinavian Economic History Review* 26, 2 (1968), 155–67. Pierard, a historian of the German Colonial Society, dismisses the significance of the KWK.

29. Wilhelm Supf, *Das Ende deutscher Kolonialwirtschaft?* (Berlin, 1921), 12, cited in Pierard, "Case Study," 165, fn. 40. For a list of contributors to the KWK see Archiv des Handelskammers Hamburg, Bumwollbau-Kommission des Kolonial-Wirtschaftlichen Komitees, Beitragsliste.

30. Supf's words in *Verhandlungen des Kolonial-Wirtschaftlichen Komitees*, 10 November 1904, 2.

31. Meyknecht, *Die Krisen*, 20. These are average prices for Middling Upland cotton.

32. Meyknecht, *Die Krisen*, 39.

33. Lochmüller, *Entwicklung der Baumwollindustrie*, 74–76; Hans-Peter Ullmann, "Unternehmerschaft, Arbeitgeberverbände und Streikbewegung 1890–1914," in *Streik: Zur Geschichte des Arbeitskampfes in Deutschland während der Industrialisierung*, ed. K. Tenfelde and H. Volkmann (Munich, 1981); Dieter Groh, "Intensification of Work and Industrial Conflict in Germany, 1896–1914," *Politics and Society* 8 (1978), 349–97.

34. BAB/R1001/8147, Verband Deutscher Baumwollgarn-Consumenten to Colonial Department, 5 November 1903, 102–103.

35. BAB/R1001/8147, Bülow to Wilhelm, 11 June 1904, 166.

36. Meyknecht, *Die Krisen*, 62–76.

37. "Aus dem Jahresbericht des Vereins Süddeutscher Baumwollindustrieller," *Textilarbeiter-Zeitung* 13, 30, 23 September 1911, 301.

38. Moritz Schanz, "Der koloniale Baumwollenbau," *Verhandlungen des Deutschen Kolonialkongresses* (Berlin, 1910), 817.

39. Sächsisches Hauptstaatsarchiv-Dresden, Aussenministerium Nr. 6696, 2 January 1908, 26; *Handel und Gewerbe* 14, 25, 30 March 1907, 396; BAB/R1001/ 8148, 124.

40. BAB/R1001/300, Schubert to Dernburg, 18 February 1907; Sächsisches Hauptstaatsarchiv-Dresden, Aussenministerium 6696, 2 December 1907, 12.

41. BAB/R1001/58, Kolonial-Wirtschaftliches Komitee, Baumwollkonferenz 1912.

42. Helene Simon, *Der Anteil der Frau an der deutschen Industrie* (Jena, 1910), 17–18, 81. In 1907 some 558,400 women worked in the textile industry compared to 428,000 in 1895. Rose Otto, *Über Fabrikarbeit verheirateter Frauen* (Stuttgart, 1910), 101–03.

43. Rudolf Martin, *Die Ausschliessung der Verheirateten Frauen aus der Fabrik: Eine Studie an der Textil-Industrie*, (Tübingen, 1896), 118.

44. Kathleen Canning, *Languages of Labor and Gender: Female Factory Work in Germany, 1850–1914* (Ithaca, 1996), 3; Reichsamt des Innern, *Die Beschäftigung verheiratheter Frauen in Fabriken* (Berlin, 1901), 25; Simon, *Der Anteil*, 18.

45. Canning, *Languages of Labor and Gender*, 292–93.

46. Derek Linton, "Between School and Marriage, Workshop and Household: Young Working Women as a Social Problem in Late Imperial Germany," *European History Quarterly* 18 (1988), 387–408; Angelika Willms, "Modernisierung durch Frauenarbeit? Zum Zusammenhang von wirtschaftlichem Strukturwandel und weiblicher Arbeitsmarktlage in Deutschland, 1882–1939," in *Historische Arbeitsmarktforschung: Entstehung, Entwicklung und Probleme der Vermarktung von Arbeitskraft*, ed. Toni Pierenkemper and Richard Tilly (Göttingen, 1982), 37–77; Canning, *Languages of Labor and Gender*.

47. "Die Lage der Textilindustrie und ihrer Arbeiter," *Die Neue Zeit* 2, 19 (1900–01), 273.

48. Wirtschaftsarchiv-Hohenheim, Verband Süddeutscher Textilarbeitgeber, *Jahresbericht für 1912*, 9–10.

49. "Aus unserer Industrie," *Textilarbeiter-Zeitung*, 19 July 1913, 230; 27 December 1913, 414.

50. "Das zweite Crimmitschau," *Der Gewerkverein* 32, 11 August 1905 in *Die Sozialpolitik in den letzten Friedensjahren des Kaiserreichs,* ed. Hans-Joachim Henning (Wiesbaden, 1982), 440–42.

51. Wirtschaftsarchiv-Hohenheim, Verband Süddeutscher Textilarbeitgeber, *Jahresbericht für 1912*, 8–9.

52. Wirtschaftsarchiv-Hohenheim, Verband Süddeutscher Textilarbeitgeber, *Jahresbericht für 1912*, 12–15.

53. Canning, *Languages of Labor and Gender*, 194.

54. For example Martin, "Die Ausschliessung"; RdI, *Die Beschäftigung verheiratheter Frauen*; Otto, *Über Fabrikarbeit*.

55. Martin, "Die Ausschliessung," 108, 407–09.

56. Hans-Jörg von Berlepsch,'*Neuer Kurs*' *im Kaiserreich? Die Arbeiterpolitik des Freiherrn von Berlepsch 1890 bis 1896* (Düsseldorf, 1987); Karl Erich Born, *Wirtschafts- und Sozialgeschichte des Deutschen Kaiserreichs (1867/71–1914)* (Stuttgart, 1985); Canning, *Languages of Labor and Gender*, Chapter 4.

57. Kuno Frankenstein, *Schriften des Vereins für Sozialpolitik*, 54 (Leipzig, 1892), 344; Peter Quante, *Die Flucht aus der Landwirtschaft* (Berlin, 1933), 326; Karl

Bielefeldt, *Das Eindringen des Kapitalismus in die Landwirtschaft* (Berlin, 1910); Elizabeth Bright Jones, "Gender and Agricultural Change in Saxony, 1900–1930," (Ph.D. diss., University of Minnesota, 2000).

58. Sächsisches Hauptstaatsarchiv Dresden (SHD), Ministerium des Innern 15876, Kreishauptmannschaft Bautzen to Königliches Ministerium des Innern, 18 February 1907.

59. SHD, MdI 15876, Amtshauptmannschaft Leipzig to Königliches Kreishauptmannschaft Leipzig, 30 May 1907.

60. BAB/R1501/115485, Arbeiternoth in der Landwirtschaft, Unterstützungswohnsitz 1899–1904; Geheimes Staatsarchiv-Preussischer Kulturbesitz, Ministerium für Handel und Gewerbe, I.120BB.VII3/Nr.2, Bd.3, Verband der Textilindustriellen von Chemnitz und Umgebung to Reichskanzleiamt, Berlin, 1 December 1899; Ken Barkin, *The Controversy over German Industrialization* (Chicago, 1970).

61. In 1907 the Undersecretary of the Ministry of the Interior, Wermuth, coordinated industrial and regional participation in colonial cotton projects and the *Landflucht* problem. Deutscher Landwirtschaftsrat, *Sesshaftigkeit und Abwanderung der weiblichen Jugend vom Lande* (Berlin, 1905), 185; Sächsisches Hauptstaatsarchiv-Dresden, Aussenministerium No. 6696, 2 January 1908, 26–27.

62. Supf, "Zur Baumwollfrage," 269; Nussbaum, *Unternehmer gegen Monopole*, 110.

63. RKA, *Die Baumwollfrage*.

64. "Aus unserer Industrie," *Textilarbeiter-Zeitung*, 21 December 1912, 406.

65. "Sozialdemokraten über deutsch-koloniale Baumwollzuchtsbestrebungen," *Textilarbeiter-Zeitung*, 12 August 1911, 252–53.

66. "Die Baumwollfrage vor dem Reichstage," *Der Textil-Arbeiter*, 21 March 1913, 89.

67. *Stenographische Berichte*, 259/27/937, 31 January 1910; 264–65/155/5793, 23 March 1911; 288/129/4386, 8 March 1913; "Ein Sozialdemokrat zur deutschkolonialen Baumwollfrage," *Deutsch-Ostafrikanische Zeitung*, 27 July 1910, 1.

68. "Die Baumwollfrage," *Der Textil-Arbeiter*, 21 July 1911, 226.

69. "Textilarbeiter und Koloniale Rohstoffversorgung," *Der Textil-Arbeiter*, 28 August 1914.

70. Bayerisches Hauptstaatsarchiv, Verein Süddeutscher Baumwoll-Industrieller, *Jahresbericht für 1907*, 3–4.

71. Georg Benl, *Die handelspolitischen Interessen der deutschen Spinnerei und Weberei von Baumwolle und Wolle seit 1862* (Berlin, 1930), 22–34.

72. BAB/R1001/8144, *Hamburgischer Kourier*, 22 July 1891, 18.

73. BAB/R1001/8178, Hannover Handelskammer to Berlepsch, 10 January 1891, 70–72.

74. Like other examples of concession company rule in the early decades of colonialism in Africa, the *DOAG* period was short-lived. Following the Bushiri uprising of 1888–90, the German Reich assumed formal control over the East African colony. Koponen, *Development*, 77–84.

75. BAB/R1001/8144, Hassler to Colonial Department, 4 February 1892, 35–36; BAB/R1001/8178, Hassler to CVDI, 5 November 1890, 41–46.

76. "Plantagenwirtschaft," *Deutsches-Kolonialblatt*, 4 (1893), 11.

77. BAB/R1001/8178, Soden to Caprivi, 14 March 1892, 128–29.

78. BAB/R1001/8144, Report to Foreign Office, 14 June 1891, 13–16.
79. Juhani Koponen, "Population: A Dependent Variable," in *Custodians of the Land: Ecology and Culture in the History of Tanzania*, ed. Gregory Maddox, James Giblin, and Isaria N. Kimambo (London, 1996), 22. Rwanda and Urundi were severed from the rest of the colony following World War I.
80. L.A. Lewis and L. Berry, *African Environments and Resources* (Boston, 1988), 223–43. On population density and land use patterns see Robert McC. Netting, *Smallholders, Householders: Farm Families and the Ecology of Intensive, Sustainable Agriculture* (Stanford, 1993). In modern times about 5.1 percent of Tanzania's 232 million acres is under cultivation. C. George Kahama, T.L. Maliyamkono, and Stuart Wells, *The Challenge for Tanzania's Economy* (London, 1986), 49.
81. Intensive land use was not widespread in colonial Tanzania, and was practiced in regions of exceptional fertility or extraordinary population density, such as in the Usambara mountains or the slopes of Mt. Kilimanjaro or Mt. Meru. For discussions of intensive agricultural in Tanzania see Thomas Spear, *Mountain Farmers* (Berkeley, 1997); Isaria N. Kimambo, *Penetration and Protest in Tanzania: The Impact of the World Economy on the Pare 1860–1960* (London, 1991), 19–24; Donna O. Kerner, "Land Scarcity and Rights of Control in the Development of Commercial Farming in Northeast Tanzania," in *Land and Society in Contemporary Africa*, ed. R.E. Downs and S.P. Reyna (Hanover, 1988), 162–63; Sally Falk Moore, *Social Facts and Fabrications: "Customary" Law on Kilimanjaro, 1880–1980* (Cambridge, 1986), 15, 80, 364.
82. Thomas J. Basset, "Introduction: The Land Question and Agricultural Transformation in Sub-Saharan Africa," in *Land in African Agrarian Systems*, ed. Thomas J. Basset and Donald E. Crummey (Madison, 1993), 3–6.
83. See especially Helge Kjekshus, *Ecology Control and Economic Development in East African History: The Case of Tanganyika 1850–1950* (London, 1996); James Giblin, *The Politics of Environmental Control in Northeastern Tanzania, 1840–1940* (Philadelphia, 1992).
84. "Die Urproduktion der Eingeborenen," *Berichte über Land- und Forstwirtschaft* 1 (1903), 4; "Auszüge aus den Berichten der Bezirksämter," *BLF*, 2 (1904–06).
85. The term used for regulated forest management was *Plänterwald*, "plantation forests." M. Büsgen, "Forstwirtschaft in den Kolonien," *Verhandlungen des Deutschen Kolonialkongresses* (Berlin, 1910), 801–817; T. Siebenlist, *Forstwirtschaft in Deutsch-Ostafrika* (Berlin, 1914).
86. These elites included "Arabs, Shihiri, Beluchen and 'Mrima-people' (coastal dwellers)." TNA G8/48, Kilwa, 5 November 1891, 13.
87. TNA G8/19, Abgabe Baumwollsaat an Araber und Eingeborene, Kilwa, 7 September 1893.
88. TNA G8/19, Schroeder to Government, 17 March 1894, 34–35.
89. *BLF* (1903), 203–04, 460–65.
90. KWK, "Unsere Kolonialwirtschaft," 54–55.
91. *BLF* (1903), 221–22.
92. In 1901 the KWK concluded that peasant cultivation offered greater prospects for profit in the African colonies than European plantation cultivation. BAB/R1001/8179, Stuhlmann report, 10 August 1901, 33–35 and Antrag des Kolonial-

Wirtschaftlichen Komitees, 149; Supf to Handelskammer Hamburg, 10 October 1903, Archiv des Handelskammers Hamburg, 85.A.2.4.

93. Sächsisches Hauptstaatsarchiv Dresden, AM6696, Baumwollplantagen und Eingeborenen-Kultur in Deutsch-Ostafrika, 28 February 1908.

94. Meyknecht, *Die Krisen*, 62–76; BAB/R1001/8150, Verband Deutscher Baumwollgarn-Verbraucher, *Geschäftsbericht Frühjahr 1907 bis Ende 1908*, 6–9.

95. Staatsarchiv Leipzig, Leipziger Baumwollspinnerei, AG 78, Rechenberg to Colonial Office, 25 June 1907.

96. Wirtschafts-Archiv Baden Württembergs, Schloss Hohenheim, Heinrich Otto & Söhne; TNA G8/894, Angelegenheiten der Otto Pflanzung; BAB/R1001/8189–8190, Landwirtschaft.

97. BAB/R1001/8150, Handelskammer Munich to Colonial Office, 12 February 1910, 165.

98. BAB/R1001/8148, Supf to Dernburg, 2 July 1907, 204–06.

2

SLAVERY AND THE GENESIS OF COLONIAL LABOR RELATIONS

When Germans arrived in East Africa in the mid-1880s and began to set up plantations under the aegis of the German East Africa Corporation they drew on the model of scores of Arab, Indian, and Swahili cash crop estates along the coast and on the islands of Zanzibar and Pemba. These estates relied on the labor of slaves, men and especially women from interior societies, who had been captured in violent raiding expeditions or in warfare before the German arrival. Germans readily employed slaves on their plantations, typically renting them from merchant labor brokers or from slave owners themselves. Slaves remained part of the colonial plantation economy until the end of German rule, often working alongside long-distance labor migrants and local wage laborers and receiving a share of plantation wages. As the first generation of colonial workers, slaves played an important role in the genesis of labor relations on plantations, on caravans, and in towns. Yet slaves have generally been invisible in past studies of the economy of German East Africa.

Although Germans readily accommodated themselves to slave labor relations in the colony, they also arrived with preconceived notions of how to regulate partially free labor based on their experiences in Germany. After serfdom was abolished in many German states at the beginning of the nineteenth century it was replaced with an institution of semi-free rural labor called *Gesindewesen*.[1] *Gesinde* were primarily single young men and women who worked on rural estates and farms as agricultural laborers or as household servants. *Gesindewesen* was a personal relationship between masters and servants that upheld the patriarchal authority of rural employers. As Germany industrialized at the end of the nineteenth century, laws regulating *Gesindewesen* were tightened to prevent young people from fleeing to better-paying jobs and fewer controls in cities. German colonial officials in East Africa combined *Gesinde* ordinances with Swahili customs of slave pawning, hiring, and ransoming to control slaves working on German plantations.

Under the pressure of a labor shortage that appeared early in German rule, colonialists rejected the outright abolition of slavery in East Africa, opting for a policy of gradualism. Only in 1912 did the *Reichstag* (German parliament) pass an amendment to end slavery conclusively by 1920.[2] Final abolition did not come until 1922 with the new British administration.[3] Fearing social and economic disruption as happened when the British abolished slavery in Zanzibar, Germans opted for a series of measures that allowed for a controlled manumission of slaves within the framework of the emergent European plantation economy.[4] This framework aimed at channeling slaves into the German cash crop economy, gradually weaning them into a wage labor environment. As far as colonial rulers were concerned, the slave population was too important to be excluded in the development of the colony. While probably not exceeding 10 percent of the total population of German East Africa, slave numbers were high in coastal districts where most early German plantations were located. Around Tanga town in 1900 slaves were estimated at about 15 percent of the population, while Pangani, Kilwa, and Lindi officials believed that slave numbers were much higher in their districts.[5] As late as 1914 colonial officials estimated that there were still over 180,000 slaves in the colony (excluding Ruanda and Urundi), surpassing the 172,000 contracted wage laborers in German East Africa at that time.[6]

As important as its contribution to German plantation development, Germany's gradualist emancipation policy upheld the indigenous slave-owning elite as an arm of colonial rule. *Majumbe* village headmen and *maakida* subdistrict rulers in German East Africa alone owned an estimated 185,000 slaves at the end of colonial rule.[7] "One can accept that not only most *akidas, jumbes, walis* and so forth own domestic slaves, but also most chiefs and their presumptive successors," read one memorandum on this issue.[8] Slaves were the "major component of wealth of the indigenous property-owning classes of the coast," and Germans were loathe to undermine this class economically or socially through outright abolition.[9] In retaining slavery, German policy makers weathered the recriminations of the humanitarian lobby in Germany, represented by the Catholic Center party, the Social Democrats, and missionaries in the colonies, who continuously pressed for abolition.[10]

The ambiguity of German plantation development was that it upheld semi-free labor relations while providing slaves with an opportunity to leave their masters among the coastal Muslim elite. This was particularly true after 1891 when German ordinances allowed slaves to work off the price of their freedom for planters or other employers. Many slaves availed themselves of this opportunity of *Freikauf* ransoming (Swahili *ukombozi*) to sever relations with their masters, reunite families, or assert greater control over their earning power and daily lives. However, until the ransom price was paid, slaves often worked alongside free laborers who received higher wages and had greater autonomy. The plantation economy thus became a crucible of interaction between slaves and other wage laborers, who together created a shared subaltern culture. German officials formulated labor policy in large part in order to control the actions of slaves and other laborers who resisted plantation work regimes. Disobedience, neglect of work, and desertion were common traits of free and slave workers on plantations. Ultimately, ongoing slave and worker resistance to proletarian status was an important factor in the erosion of the plantation imperative in German East Africa.

SLAVE TRANSFORMATIONS IN EARLY COLONIAL TANZANIA

Before the German conquest of East Africa after 1885, the rise of the Omani commercial state of Zanzibar opposite the Tanzanian mainland ushered in major economic and social transformations.[11] Plugging the mainland into Indian Ocean trade networks that Europeans increasingly dominated, the Zanzibar empire intensified the slave trade and its associated violence, leading to the defensive centralization of many mainland African societies. Zanzibar commerce spawned plantations on the coast and along caravan routes in the interior that produced commodities such as sugar and grain for local trade and export to Zanzibar and Pemba. These trade networks brought Africans from the inland to the coast both as slaves and as professional caravan porters, where they contributed to, and became part of, coastal Swahili culture.[12]

Slaves on the Swahili coast became part of a complex society in which they often lived in autonomous villages, among free villagers in towns, or in the households of their masters. The status of slaves differed according to gender, religion, occupation, recency of enslavement, relationship with their master, and whether they had succeeded in garnering property or skills.[13] Slaves of lowest status were newcomers from the interior, especially women, who were denied full participation in Muslim or Swahili culture. Such *watumwa wajinga* or "ignorant slaves" (also called *waja*, newcomers) most commonly worked as field slaves overseen by the master's retainers. Typically field slaves worked for four or five days on the *mashamba* of their masters, and for two to three days on their own *makonde* plots.[14] *Makonde* were important in several ways. They offered slaves a "peasant breach," a basic subsistence independence that allowed them to preserve traditions derived from the agrarian societies from which most stemmed.[15] The German geographer Baumann believed that *waja* slaves from inland societies, often recognizable by their cultural scarification, were most adept at preserving their languages and customs.[16] Even during German rule many *waja* were enslaved as a result of economic crises. In the 1890s a spate of locust plagues created famine on the southern coast, leading some people to pawn members of their extended families so as to withstand the crisis. Mohamedi, a slave on Mafia Island, claimed that his uncle sold him at Kilwa "in the year of the locusts."[17] Many Maasai and other pastoralists from the interior became slaves during the Rinderpest plague that devastated their economy in the 1890s.[18] Contemporary Tanzanians recall that during the famine that followed the Maji Maji uprising along the southern coast people were pawned as a survival tactic.[19] This seems to be why Samaradi and her father, Halfan, two slaves on Mafia Island, were sold in Kilwa in 1908.[20]

Women among the newly enslaved were most likely to retain non-Islamic cultural practices, such as life-cycle rituals, by preserving independent agrarian traditions.[21] *Makonde* plots provided the means for such newcomer slaves to resist German efforts to make them into proletarians as colonial rule coalesced. The peasant breach also made it unlikely that field slaves would become assimilated into dominant Swahili society. Thus, newcomers were most likely to resist their masters' demands, to desert, or to take advantage of ransoming laws, as colonial observers noted and the archival record demonstrates.[22] Although we cannot know when they were enslaved, some 350 slaves were convicted of desertion, refusing work, or disobedience in Kilwa district in the immediate aftermath of the Maji Maji rebellion, belying any notion that slaves were content with their condition, as German propagandists often asserted.[23]

Wazalia slaves, born in captivity, were more acculturated into their masters' society.[24] They were typically given domestic tasks, such as washing clothes, fetching water, cooking, and cleaning the master's house. Some *wazalia* were chosen as *masuria* concubines.[25] Though this might entail a privileged position in the master's household for a time, during the course of their lives *masuria* might be relegated to the status of domestic servants or even field hands. Male *wazalia* had a good deal of independence, often plying a trade, such as sewing, carpentry, or building. Other male slaves worked as stevedores, porters, sailors, and even dhow captains, earning a specified share of the trade goods they carried. Skilled slaves had access to independent earnings, one-third to one-half of which was remitted to their master. Many skilled slaves lived apart from their masters and simply remitted an annual *"taja"* payment that might range from about 10 to 24 Rp per year for men, and 6 to 12 Rp annually for women.[26] Such autonomy led some *wazalia* to seek independence through ransoming since they were able to pay the ransom price with their earnings. Planters employed skilled laborers such as these in positions of authority or as craftsmen.[27] Plantations furthermore created a demand for prostitutes, many of whom were likely to have been *wazalia* who show up as "Swahili" in the colonial discourse.[28]

Like other European powers involved in colonizing Africa at the end of the nineteenth century, Germany asserted that part of its mission in Africa was to end the slave trade.[29] As signatories to the Brussels anti-slavery conference in 1890 German rulers outlawed slave trading in East Africa. Occasionally slave traders were prosecuted in German-controlled towns, especially when force was used or slaves were exported from the colony in violation of international laws, and Germans posted a bounty for information leading to the capture of slave traders, especially those who exported slaves by sea.[30] Rescued slaves were immediately freed, as was the case with twenty-five slaves who were brought to Wanga on the mainland from Pemba Island in 1892.[31] Generally speaking, however, slaves could be sold or transferred to other masters in the colony with official approval if it did not raise too much attention and if the slaves did not object. In 1909, for example, the *akida* of Pongwa informed the Tanga district officer that the Manyema woman Mama Kibibi agreed to sell her slave, an Mrundi woman, to Mama Hasani for 40 Rp.[32] German officials registered and taxed these public transactions.

In lieu of slave selling, the practice of hiring or "renting" slaves to third parties was fairly common.[33] Because Indians were prohibited from owning slaves, they often hired them from their owners or acted as labor brokers for coastal planters and merchants. Typical was the agreement between Asmuni bin Ayubu and Muhamadi bin Ganji el-Hindi, whereby the former rented five slaves to the latter for a period of three years.[34] Each slave was to receive 4 Rp per month plus food, with the provision that they were not allowed to work for another

Slavery and the Genesis of Colonial Labor Relations

party during that time. Owners often mortgaged or pawned their slaves to creditors to settle a debt. Mwenyi Bakari bin Mfaume mortgaged his slave girl Chekanao to Mpate binti Omar for one-and-a-half years as surety for a bride price debt of 30 riale.[35] According to their contract, if the debt were not paid in that time, Chekanao would become binti Omar's property. Lumwe bin Kizungu, a Zigua man, pawned his female slave Bahati for ten months to the Indian Musaji Malji to pay off a debt.[36] During that time Bahati received the going wage of 4 Rp per month plus food and clothing. In such matters of mortgage or pawning it was often specified that the slave agreed to the transaction, as was true in Bahati's case.

German policy on slavery evolved in response to colonial economic needs. Drawing on Prussian law, officials initially claimed that they did not recognize the legality of slave relations in East Africa.[37] In 1891 the German governor pronounced that any slave who wanted to claim his or her freedom had that right.[38] That right dissolved as a labor shortage along the coast exposed the German reliance on slavery. In 1894 Governor Schele wrote that "the cultivation of the land, done best by slaves, would come to an almost complete halt if slaves were emancipated."[39] The "needs of commerce," according to a German exposition on slavery in the colonies, required that non-natives in the colonies make use of slaves.[40] Slaves who simply fled from their masters were punished and returned if caught, as hundred of cases from crime records attest.[41] This was because the colonial state taxed the exports of the Muslim elite, who had long used slaves on their coconut, sugar, and rice plantations. Already in 1891 Governor Soden coopted this planter class to produce tobacco, sesame, and cotton for export.[42] Some 500 slaves worked on the estate of the German ally Wedin Mputa near the Rufiji delta.[43] German officials relied on planters like Mputa as sub-district and town administrators, therefore they upheld their authority by punishing recalcitrant slaves and plantation deserters.

After the turn of the century slavery intersected with the cotton-growing schemes of the colonial administration. In the "communal cotton" years of 1902–05 (discussed in Chapter 4) officials expected slave owners along the coast to get their people to grow cotton and other cash crops on estates located near centers of colonial control.[44] In the last decade of colonial rule "peasant" cotton growing was largely under the aegis of indigenous elites who controlled slave labor, as was clear in Lindi district.[45] For the duration of German rule officials saw the slave-owning elite as an essential layer of colonial administration, social control, and cash crop production, and therefore refused to abolish slavery.

GESINDEWESEN, SLAVE RANSOMING, AND THE EVOLUTION OF WAGE LABOR

As planters trickled into German East Africa throughout the 1890s, creating what some hoped would be a colony of white settlement, slavery offered a ready source of labor. While it was illegal for Germans to own slaves, they obtained slave labor by establishing business relations with the Muslim elite of the coast. Slave-hiring was facilitated by a cash economy since a wage in coins was more easily divided between slave and master than pieces of cotton cloth that were often used as a wage. Several German cotton planters in the 1880s hired slaves in the Witu enclave along the Kenya coast, dividing a 6 Rp per month wage between the slaves and their masters.[46] The earliest German planters in coastal Tanzania tapped the slave labor of Zanzibar and Pangani sugar, clove, and coconut plantations.[47] In 1888, for example, Friedrich Schroeder of the Lewa tobacco plantation hired 500–600 slaves from the Zanzibari Indian merchant Sewa Hadji.[48] By the 1890s German planters and travelers were accustomed to hiring "whole cadres" of slaves as porters, sailors, domestic servants, and plantation workers.[49] There was always some risk in hiring slaves, as the planter Rowehl of Msasa learned in 1892. Rowehl hired the slave Ali on contract from his master at 20 Rp for two months (to be divided between master and slave).[50] However, the agreement stipulated that Rowehl would be reimbursed the entire sum if Ali ran away, as he did after only four days.

In part because hired slaves often deserted or resisted work, German planters turned to other mechanisms to bring slaves to their plantations as wage laborers. This was done by adapting the German institution of *Gesindewesen* to East Africa.[51] In Germany, *Gesinde* were primarily single young men and women who performed farm tasks like tending cattle, plowing, and milking, or domestic services.[52] *Gesindewesen* was a personal relationship between masters and servants (called *Dienstherrschaft*), and like East African slavery was both an economic and a social institution. As the German economy industrialized and a free wage labor market and cash economy emerged in the German countryside in the late nineteenth century, the patriarchal controls on *Gesinde* declined. Relations between *Gesinde* and their employers loosened, and contract breaking and hostility increased.[53]

In response, officials tightened laws regulating *Gesinde* and strengthened the contractual nature of the working relationship to stem the exodus of workers from the rural sector to industrial centers. *Gesindewesen* provided Germans with a model for adapting East African slavery to the colonial plantation economy because it provided a pre-existing corpus of legislation to regulate contracts, curtail freedom of movement, prosecute desertion, and uphold patriarchal authority, all problems that Tanzanian slave owners and German planters shared from the outset of colonial rule.

Like *Gesindewesen*, Germans agreed that slave emancipation "must not deteriorate into an unregulated freedom, rather [it] requires a firm legal orderliness as the basis for healthy development."[54] Toward this end, Germans in East Africa implemented a series of laws between 1891 and 1901 that legalized *Sklavenfreikauf*, "slave ransoming."[55] After 1891, with the master's consent, a slave or a third party could pay an agreed-upon sum to buy his or her freedom. By 1896 in Tanga district slaves didn't need their masters' approval to be ransomed and in 1901 this law was generalized for the colony as a whole.[56] In practice, however, colonial officials sought the master's consent. Few slaves could muster the 50–60 Rp needed for ransom, so the old custom of slave hiring was used to work off the ransom price. Typically a slave initiated the ransom by working as a plantation laborer or domestic servant to gradually pay off the debt. Half the monthly wages went directly to the slave owner as payment and half went to the slave. In this way a slave might be able to accumulate enough to pay for his or her freedom in about two years.

Once the ransoming process was begun, a slave received a *Freibrief* (or *hati ya huru*), a certificate of freedom that the local district officer recorded (See FIGURE 2.1). At that point the slave was no longer an *mtumwa* slave, but a *huru* "freedman." In German legal perceptions the *huru* also became a *Gesinde*, since he or she was bound by a service contract with an employer to pay off the ransom debt.[57] Employers usually withheld the *Freibrief* until the debt was paid off, creating an ambiguous status somewhere between slavery and freedom. In 1906, for example, the Pangani district office presented a *Freibrief* to the German planter Zwielich for the ransom of the slave Hamdalla.[58] Only when the 35 Rp ransom price had been worked off could Hamdalla receive the freedom certificate, giving Zwielich considerable leverage over the *huru*. Likewise, Mpendunga Kitomaro, sent to the Kilwa Cotton Plantation to work off his ransom price of 50 Rp in July 1913, still owed 30 Rp of his debt by May 1914.[59]

Figure 2.1 A certificate of freedom (*Freibrief, hati ya huru*) that registered freed or ransomed slaves with district offices. (From *Kolonie und Heimat* 2, 7 [1908–09], 8.)

By the turn of the century European planters, labor recruiters, or other employers ransomed many slaves with official encouragement.[60] Like German *Gesinde*, ransomed slaves received a *Dienstbuch* (service record) that recorded provisions of the ransoming contract, such as wage levels and type of work. The ransomed slaves thereby entered into a service relationship in which the employer became a contractual master. While working off one's debt, *huru* were bound to the worksite and to service for their employer, so much so that German officials worried that ransomed slaves would not be able to tell the difference between slavery and their new status as *huru*.[61]

Ransoming laws had a modest effect in the first few years after their enactment. In 1893 some eighty-five men and women were ransomed, accounting for about one-sixth of all persons receiving *Freibriefe* that year.[62] About the same number of slaves were manumitted by their masters, while twice that many were declared free by local authorities, suggesting cases of abuse, slave trading, or resistance to German rule by slave owners. Women made up about 60 percent of all freed slaves in 1893, a figure that probably accords with their overall percentage of the slave population. Ransoming was fairly evenly distributed in coastal districts, with Lindi, Tanga, and Sadani accounting for about 70 percent of cases, areas where German plantations were taking root in the first twenty years of colonialism. Plantation production thus emerged as an important stimulus to ransoming. However, relatives of slaves also used ransoming to free their spouses and children. This was possibly the case in Kilosa district in 1893, where the only two slaves receiving freedom certificates were two women who were ransomed.

In 1901 the customary right of coastal slaves to two or more free days per week was adapted to ransoming policy. Henceforth, for two days per week slaves could claim a wage compensation from their masters that they could use to begin paying for freedom.[63] Ransoming prices varied throughout the colony, a typical price for a woman being about 60 Rp compared to 50 Rp for a man.[64] These prices meant that slaves only able to work two days per week might remain in a state of semi-freedom for perhaps a decade. Colonial officials rejected demands from the humanitarian lobby to set ransom prices uniformly low throughout the colony so as to expedite freedom, even though some small-scale German settlers favored lower prices so as to obtain labor more cheaply.[65] High ransom prices shored up the authority of slave owners while preserving the contractual *Gesinde* status of ransomed slaves for as long as possible so that planters could make full use of their labor. Women *huru* in particular worked as contracted laborers longer than men because of their higher ransom prices and lower wages. As the majority of coastal slaves, women were more highly prized as unskilled plantation workers.[66]

An ordinance of December 24, 1904, stated simply that all children of slaves born after 31 December 1905 were free.[67] A response to humanitarian criticisms of the slow pace of abolition in Germany's biggest colony, the law had no immediate effect. Free children born after 1905 were still dependent on slave parents and their masters, and, until old enough to care for themselves, were bound to a slave culture. The archival record includes many instances of children born after 1905 still ransomed or retained as slaves, and colonial officials admitted that they could not police this provision effectively.[68] In cases where the age of the child was questionable, local officials were instructed to treat slave owners with "caution and indulgence" since "it seems completely inconsequential whether here and there a slave child born after December 31 1905 is still considered a slave."[69] After 1905 German officials enacted no other laws to ameliorate slavery in German East Africa.

SLAVE RANSOMING AND SLAVE ASPIRATIONS

Some 50,000 slaves received *Freibriefe* (certificates of freedom) through ransoming, manumission, official freeings, and other legally sanctioned mechanisms in the twenty-year period after 1892.[70] Official freeings were the most important medium for a slave to become free in the first ten years of German state rule, closely followed by voluntary manumissions. In the former cases officials punished masters' abuse of their slaves or active resistance to German rule by freeing their slaves. The slave Sadiki of Tanga was pronounced free after his master fled to British-controlled Pemba Island in 1892.[71] Under such circumstances the freed slaves might be sent to a German plantation to work off a redemption cost, as seems to have been the case with Mtunda, who was brought to the Kilwa Cotton Plantation to work off a 50 Rp debt in 1912.[72] The number of official freeings also dropped abruptly in the few years after 1905 from an average of about 700 per year to about 400 per year, reflecting the need to bolster the loyalist slave-owning class following the Maji Maji rebellion.

Manumissions increased steadily from about 600 per year in 1897 to about 1400 per year a decade later. Masters manumitted slaves for a variety of reasons, including loyal service, paternity of slave children, or in bequests. Many of the surviving bequests suggest that manumission usually resulted from a personal relationship between master and slave. Individual slaves were more likely to receive manumission than groups of slaves. One bequest specified that the manumitted slave could not henceforth be mortgaged or inherited.[73] Most surviving cases of manumission are of women freeing other women, sometimes specifying that the manumitted slave should receive a plot of land, a hut, fruit trees, or a few rupees along with her freedom.[74] However, slaves did not automatically obtain freedom upon their master's death, especially when an owner had large numbers of slaves. They were usually inherited and sometimes immediately sold as slaves to another party, as many surviving Kilwa cases from 1911–14 attest.[75] Several bequests survive that enumerate slaves along with other property to determine how they will be divided among heirs and other claimants.[76] Slave manumissions never exceeded 1 percent of all slaves in the colony in any year of German rule, and were usually far fewer.[77]

Slave ransoming is the most important mechanism of freeings for this discussion because it offers evidence of slave volition. Slaves could not be ransomed without their consent. Indeed, the evidence shows that slaves sought ransom as a means of ending bondage and starting a new life in which they could control wages, offspring, and property. Ransoming was the most direct way in which slaves entered the wage labor force as *Gesinde*. Ransoming offered slaves clear advantages over continued enslavement or hiring, giving them a possibility of uniting their families that was often denied them under slavery.[78] Slaves could increase their earning power once their ransom debt was repaid, since they no longer had to share a portion of wages with their masters like *taja* slaves or hired slaves.

The most thorough reports of ransoming come from Mafia Island off the southeast coast, which was part of a social and economic realm connected to the Rufiji delta and Kilwa town. Captured quickly by the British during World War I, colonial records from the island survived while many records from the mainland dealing with slavery perished or were destroyed.[79] Mafia was exceptional in that half its 1907 population of about 14,000 were slaves, and its economy was based almost exclusively on coconut plantations and food crops for local use.[80] Slaves tended the plantations for absentee landowners, many of whom lived on Chole, a small island off the southern coast and the island's historic center of administration. After 1907 Germans founded about half a dozen plantations on Mafia to produce copra for export, while some experimented with cotton.[81] German plantations were the destination of slaves who sought to establish autonomous family life through ransoming, as shown by the rich evidence from the island.

In the period after 1907 hundreds of Mafia slaves were convicted of fleeing their masters, some showing up on German plantations to seek ransom.[82] In January 1914, for example, four slaves, each with a different master, appeared at the Minaki plantation requesting to be ransomed.[83] Although their masters refused to negotiate ransom prices, the German director was willing to take them on. The refusal of slave owners to part with their slaves was not unusual, despite legislation that guaranteed slaves the right to seek ransom. The owner of Inserani, for example, charged her with escape when she showed up at the Mafia plantation to be ransomed.[84] The owners of the slaves Maktabu and Manharuri set a ransoming price of 300 Rp for them, almost three times the going rate.[85] Said Ali bin Ahmed flatly refused to negotiate a ransom price for his slaves Suria binti Serenge and Siwatu bin Mjaliwa.[86] Pungu Nyombora obstructed the ransom of his slave Hamadi by falsely claiming that it would cause him hardship, as Hamadi and his wife were his only slaves.[87] Many masters made claims on the property of their slaves (fruit trees, crops, and even huts) after they were ransomed as apparent retribution.[88]

While ransoming was a strategy for slaves to reunite their families, sometimes free commoners helped to pay the ransom for their slave wives, children, or relatives. In 1912 Mwanawetu binti Kitwanga appeared at the Chole *boma* requesting to be ransomed onto one of the estates of the Mafia Plantation Corporation.[89] Her free husband, Sultani, father of their three children, aided Mwanawetu in paying her ransom price. Other instances of free men attempting to obtain their families' freedom include that of the plantation worker Surubica, who insisted that his son (whose mother was a slave) should have freedom according to the 1904 statute.[90] The slaves Mohamedi and Alima, who were married, together sought ransom onto the Mafia plantation.[91] The slaves Salimini and his two wives and two children collectively sought ransom onto the Lessel plantation in Ngombeni in 1912.[92] Suria binti Serenge and Siwatu bin Majaliwa, who had a child together, sought to be ransomed onto the Minaki plantation.[93] On the mainland near Kilwa a slave man, woman, and child fled their master together in 1908, perhaps seeking ransoming on one of the German plantations in the region.[94] On Mafia the male slave Hajari and the female Mwanaradi binti Amdalla fled their master and were jailed in chains as punishment.[95] These examples of families seeking ransom or escape are an important dimension of slave emancipation often neglected in discussions of East African slavery that view slaves as mainly single men. While many slaves lived independent lives in semi-autonomous villages, families were sometimes separated through sale or lived apart because of work. Ransoming allowed slaves a strategy to recreate autonomous households that they were denied under bondage.

Although many slaves sought to be ransomed, the transition that slaves made to wage labor was by no means a smooth one. Slaves were often subjected to poor plantation conditions and a rigorous capitalist-style work regime that they were unaccustomed to. Some slaves preferred to build their own huts rather than live in the plantation barracks, a pattern that free wage laborers would also follow. An overseer on the Minaki plantation, Abu Omar, took the unusual step of writing to the district office to complain of deficient food rations on the plantation. "The people of Bwana Ingalls are very hungry," he wrote, "they don't have food, they don't have the energy to work."[96] Poor living conditions perhaps explain why some *huru* resisted plantation life shortly after being ransomed. Dauda, ransomed onto the Minaki plantation in 1913, worked for nine days and then ran off with the woman Asmini.[97] On the mainland, Brahimu, a *huru* from Kilwa, received his *Freibrief* in January 1906 to work off his debt on the Ngambo coffee and rubber plantation near Tanga.[98] Six months later he fled the plantation before his ransom debt had been paid and was charged with desertion. Almasi, a slave of the carpenter Faramba of Tanga, became *huru* no. 2312 for Tanga district in 1907 by agreeing to work on the Rheinische coffee and rubber plantation.[99] Almasi eventually deserted the plantation and was reported to district authorities as a contract breaker with a 5 Rp reward for his capture. By that time officials did not regard Almasi as an escaped slave, but as a runaway *Gesinde*, a contract breaker, like thousands of rural youth in Germany and increasing numbers of free plantation laborers in German East Africa.

As slaves were ransomed onto European plantations or worked on plantations as hired slaves for a partial wage, the boundaries between slavery and freedom were blurred. Arriving on German plantations, slaves entered the realm of *Gesindewesen,* expected to respect the authority, the *Dienstherrschaft*, that was implicit in the wage-labor relationship. Planters had the same expectations of slaves as they did of contracted wage laborers and personal servants, viewing all workers in a "*Gesinde*-like status."[100] Plantations in effect became sites for the creation of a subaltern culture that brought together hundreds of workers of varying degrees of freedom, including long-distance migrants, local workers, Asian indentured laborers, and penal laborers. This common subaltern work environment incubated a culture of resistance that was increasingly shared by workers regardless of gender or status.

CRIMINALITY AND SLAVE CONSCIOUSNESS

In his work on relations between slaves and their masters along the Swahili coast, Jonathon Glassman argued that slaves were imbued with a consciousness that led them to seek greater inclusion in the dominant Swahili society.[101] Positing Gramsci's notion of hegemony in the circumstances of coastal slave society, Glassman asserted that slaves sought closer incorporation into town culture, and in effect took on the trappings of that culture even as they sought to lessen ties of dependency. Glassman rightly identifies a complex coastal culture that belied simple categorization as master and slave. In trying to come to terms with slave aspirations, however, it is important to consider the status of any particular slave in coastal society since there was no single slave consciousness. There was little in common between an *mzalia* coastal-born man pursuing an independent trade and a *waja* newly enslaved woman working on a sugar or coconut plantation. Glassman's subjects are really those male slaves whose social inclusion was already profound. However, most slaves, whose bondage was still quite recent, and whose status would never move beyond that of agricultural laborer or dependent worker, reacted differently to the superordinate Muslim culture. Slave ransoming suggests a much more refractory consciousness for such slaves, who were often women preserving distinct, non-Swahili subcultures. Because women and other *shamba* slaves were also inarticulate in the historical record, their consciousness is the most difficult to assess. Colonial crime statistics provide an important picture of slave women and men confronting both Arab/Swahili and colonial authority and not acquiescing in their status as subalterns or seeking greater inclusion in Swahili society. This refractory slave consciousness is important because it seems to have influenced other early colonial workers. Slaves in coastal communities and caravan towns interacted with non-slave town and rural dwellers, worked alongside them, formed relationships, and created an increasingly shared subaltern culture.[102] For their part, planters and other German employers treated both groups as *Gesinde* contract laborers, disciplining them in similar ways, and thereby inadvertently contributing to worker solidarity.

Slave resistance was clear in the first few years of colonial rule. This ranged from individual slaves simply running away from their masters to collective resistance, whereby several slaves fled or even attacked their masters together. In 1891 the masters of the slaves Mabruki and Hamisi reported them as runaways to the Tanga district office, and cases like this of escape appear regularly in crime statistics.[103] More dramatic was the petition that twenty-nine Arabs of Pangani town wrote to the German administration in 1895 to complain about slave rebelliousness.[104] In 1894 locust plagues infested coastal regions, destroying sugar cane and food crops of the Pangani hinterland. The famine that followed led many slaves of the region to flee their masters, while others refused to work. "Our slaves don't listen to our orders and won't work for us as in times past, they just do what they want," read the petition. Pointing out that they couldn't afford to hire people to work, the Pangani Arabs warned of the destruction of the sugar cane industry if the situation did not change. Because of cases like this, German authorities worked to shore up the authority of slave-owning elites.

Slave recalcitrance in the first years of German rule led German officials to reassert control of subalterns through the use of criminal law (See FIGURE 2.2). In 1896 Germans established a framework of criminal legislation that sought to control the laboring classes, especially in the towns of the coast and interior. In that year the state required German district officials to record criminal activity and how crimes were punished.[105] Because the crime records often identified transgressors by name, gender, occupation, and age, they reveal subaltern identities in a much more specific way than most colonial records, which generally only refer to slaves as an amorphous mass. While it is difficult to gauge the percentage of slaves to overall population, the criminal records from coastal district offices from 1896–97 include a substantial proportion of slave men and women, especially in work-related crimes. In the southern coastal town of Mikindani in 1896–97, 28 percent of all criminals were recognizably slaves.[106] Yet, in that town slaves appear in 60 percent of cases involving disobedience, desertion, or avoiding work. In Kilwa, where 21 percent of criminals were recognizably slaves, about half of all cases of desertion or avoiding work included slaves in 1896–97.[107] Pangani provides a somewhat more complete record.[108] There about 20–25 percent of all Pangani criminals were slaves, 65 percent of whom were women, who were typically convicted of running away from their masters. Slaves often exhibited a great hostility to their masters. The women Saferan and Salia of Kilwa were each charged with striking their masters, while Mama Kaporo received one month in chains for opposing her master.[109] Buriani, a slave from Lindi, was brought before the district court for inciting fellow slaves against his master. Other slave men and women were charged with fighting, public drunkenness, bodily injury, unruliness to and theft from their masters, slander, and repeated disobedience. Six slaves of Wedin Mputa deserted work with a slave of Binti Sueni.[110]

Figure 2.2 Women in a chain gang c. 1900. Slaves and free convicted of colonial crimes were usually sentenced to labor on public works or on private plantations. (© Bildarchiv Preussischer Kulturbesitz Berlin, 1401 f. Reprinted with permission.)

Slaves carried their refractory relationship with their masters into the public arena, and often directed their recalcitrance against German officials or their functionaries, many of whom were slave owners. Sanja, a female slave in Kilwa, was given fourteen days in chains for insulting a policeman.[111] Taja and Adman were both convicted of repeated disobedience to their master, the *liwali* of Mikindani.[112] Public confrontations with officialdom, including disobeying the orders of Germans and their deputies, refusing to appear at the *boma* when summoned, insulting officials, insolence, and "recalcitrance" were typical crimes of slaves against the colonial order.

The evidence suggests that slaves worked and interacted continuously with free commoners. This was the case with Bascha bin Bakil of Mikindani, a free commoner who was given fifteen canings for inciting a slave against his master.[113] Binti Katema was jailed for three months in Kilwa for "seducing slaves to flee their master," and in Pangani Madjiani was sentenced to three months and twenty-five whippings for "continuously inciting a slave to flee from his master."[114] Crime reports and anecdotal evidence demonstrate that free and slave men and women sometimes attempted to assert a free life together. In Kilwa, for example, the slave woman Frida was sentenced to one month in chains for running away from her master, assisted by Korshen Hadimu Ahmed Bakari, a free man who received fourteen days for complicity.[115] Kamkunje of Mikindani was given one month in chains for enticing a slave of Binti Haneroi to escape.[116] In 1909 the slave woman Ena was charged with running away with four free men who were charged as contract breakers.[117]

Slave rebelliousness was still profound over twenty years after the beginning of German rule. The evidence is richest for Kilwa district, where the crime records for the three years that followed the Maji Maji rebellion survive.[118] In April 1908, for example, four slaves ran away together and were subsequently given one month each in chains. In the three years after 1907 some eighty slaves around Kilwa town were charged with crimes that included recalcitrance (*Widersetzlichkeit*), disobedience, assaulting their masters, and negligence at work. On one day in 1909 ten slaves in Kilwa district, men and women, were collectively charged with unruliness.[119] On Mafia Island twelve slaves were charged in 1909 for "refusing work and conspiring with other slaves."[120] Slave resistance was clearly a reaction to the brutality of life under bondage. Slave owners appear in the crime reports repeatedly for transgressions against their slaves, including mistreatment, neglect (such as in caring for their elderly slaves), and child abuse.[121]

The high incidence of slaves fleeing their masters at this time period also reflects the intensity of the colonial cash crop regime that followed the Maji Maji war. As Germans targeted southeast Tanzania for cotton regimes, they coopted the slave-owning elite of the region. It is tempting to see slave desertion at this time as a response to greater intensity of exploitation, as was the case in other parts of Africa that experienced colonial cash crop regimes.[122] However, it is also possible that the struggle for labor among German planters led many of the region's slaves to seek ransoming or employment as free wage laborers for high wages in order to better their condition.

Their refusal to participate in hegemonic society on terms that they could not control led many slaves, including the relatively privileged, to assert autonomy from their masters. Slave porters and sailors, who by virtue of their work had more independence than plantation slaves, nevertheless sometimes deserted their caravans and dhows.[123] The picture of an orderly functionalism existing between slaves and masters that we get from colonial-era accounts, such as those of Mtoro bin Bakari and others, is belied by reports of slaves absent without consent from their masters for three years on end, and of others convicted of theft, drunkenness, fighting, attacking their masters, disrupting *ngoma* festivals, and deserting work, often in large groups. A concerted action between slaves and free also emerges from the crime records. The rebellious consciousness of subalterns that became a regular feature of the mature colonial wage labor economy had many precedents in the slave economy of the 1890s. Just as employers came to view all contracted workers as *Gesinde* regardless of their origins, they came to regard all deserters as *watoro* runaways.

The evidence in this chapter suggests that the interaction between slave and free on plantations had a transformative effect on all subalterns. Sometimes free workers formed relationships with slaves and helped to ransom their slave spouses and children. Hired and ransomed slaves were influenced by the greater autonomy, freedom of movement, and control over wages that local and long-distance labor migrants enjoyed, and many deserted German plantations shortly after being ransomed. Likewise, slaves appear to have infected free workers with their own rebelliousness. Such was the case with the *huru* Niamia binti Hamis of the Minaki plantation, who was charged with breaking contract, disobedience, and refusal to work. Niamia was frequently absent from the Minaki plantation, and, according to the complaint of the director Ingalls, "she has led two other women, who had been obedient workers, to follow her example."[124] While planters overwhelmingly supported ransoming policy as a means of obtaining cheap labor for long durations, some recognized that slaves working alongside free created problems of labor management.[125] Slaves, otherwise invisible in the archival record, appear prominently in crime statistics as a rebellious underclass accustomed to confronting their masters and other representatives of colonial authority. As part of the plantation underclass, slaves contributed to the problems of desertion and resistance that emerged as the biggest issue affecting plantation viability in the last decade of German rule.

NOTES

1. Wilhelm Kähler, *Gesindewesen und Gesinderecht in Deutschland* (Jena, 1896); Verein für Sozialpolitik, *Bäuerliche Verhältnisse im Königreich Sachsen* (Leipzig, 1892), 328–42.

2. Otto Stollowsky, "Die Aufhebung der Sklaverei in Deutsch-Ostafrika," *Koloniale Zeitschrift*, 31 April 1912, 348–49.

3. Thaddeus Sunseri, "Slave Ransoming in German East Africa, 1885–1922," *IJAHS* 26, 3 (1993), 481–511.
4. F.O. Karstedt, "Zur Sklavenfrage in Deutsch-Ostafrika," *KR* 12 (1913), 616–17; "A Word on the Slave Question," *DOAZ*, 11 April 1903; Frederick Cooper, *From Slaves to Squatters: Plantation Labour and Agriculture in Zanzibar and Coastal Kenya 1890–1925* (New Haven, 1980).
5. Slave estimates for Pangani, Kilwa, and Lindi districts in 1900 were 17,500; 40–50,000; and 50,000–100,000 respectively. Tabora officials estimated over 200,000 slaves in their district, or two-thirds of the population. BAB/R1001/1006, Berichte der einzelnen Verwaltungsstellen in Deutsch-Ostafrika über Sklaverei.
6. BAB/R1001/1007 "Denkschrift über die Haussklaverei in Deutsch Ostafrika," 11; Adalbert Bauer, *Der Arbeitszwang in Deutsch-Ostafrika* (Würzburg, 1919), 32; Rainer Tetzlaff, *Koloniale Entwicklung und Ausbeutung: Wirtschafts- und Sozialgeschichte Deutsch Ostafrikas 1885–1914* (Berlin, 1970), 194.
7. BAB/R1001/1007, "Runderlass an alle Bezirksämter, Militärstationen und Residenturen," 28 October 1913, 54b; "Auszug aus A I 286/16," 64; BAB/R1001/1006, Götzen to Auswärtiges Amt, 9 September 1905, 58.
8. BAB/R1001/1006, "Denkschrift über Haussklaverei und deren Abschaffung," 28 October 1913, 197.
9. BAB/R1001/1006, Götzen Memorandum, 9 September 1905.
10. *Stenographische Berichte*, 294/232/7970 and 7986, 10 March 1914; *DOAR*, 22 June 1912, 2 and 26 June 1912.
11. Frederick Cooper, *Plantation Slavery on the East Coast of Africa* (New Haven, 1977); Jonathon Glassman, *Feasts and Riot: Revelry, Rebellion, and Popular Consciousness on the Swahili Coast, 1856–1888* (Portsmouth, 1995); Abdul Sheriff, *Slaves, Spices and Ivory in Zanzibar* (London, 1987).
12. On slave employment in caravans see Glassman, *Feasts and Riot*, 74–78; BAB/R1001/1006, Berichte der einzelnen Verwaltungsstellen in Deutsch-Ostafrika über Sklaverei, 43.
13. Information on slave differences is derived from Mtoro bin Mwinyi Bakari, *The Customs of the Swahili People* (Berkeley, 1981), 169–77; Fritz Weidner, *Die Haussklaverei in Ostafrika* (Jena, 1915), 31–35; A. Leue, "Die Sklaverei in Deutsch-Ostafrika," *Beiträge zur Kolonialpolitik* 2 (1900–01), 606–08; F. v. Eberstein, "Über die Rechtsanschauungen der Küstenbewohner des Bezirkes Kilwa," *MaddS* 9 (1896), 178–80.
14. Carl Velten, *Swahili Prose Texts*, ed. and trans. L. Harries (London, 1965), 207–08.
15. On the concept of peasant breach see Sidney Mintz, *Caribbean Transformations* (New York, 1989), 146 and "Slavery and the Rise of Peasantries," *Historical Reflections* 6, 1 (1979), 213–42; Allen Isaacman, "Peasants and Rural Social Protest in Africa," in *Confronting Historical Paradigms: Peasants, Labor, and the Capitalist World System in Africa and Latin America*, ed. Frederick Cooper, Florencia E. Mallon, Steve J. Stern, Allen Isaacman, William Roseberry (Madison, 1993), 232–33.
16. Oskar Baumann, *Usambara und seine Nachbargebiete* (Berlin, 1891), 61–63.

17. TNA G55/2, Mafia Plantation to District Branch Chole, 2 December 1912.

18. BAB/R1001/1006, Berichte der einzelnen Verwaltungsstellen, Besirksamt Tanga, 42. On Maasai pawning following Rinderpest in Kenya see Richard Waller, "Emutai: Crisis and Response in Maasailand, 1883–1902," in *The Ecology of Survival: Case Studies from Northeast African History,* ed. Douglas Johnson and David Anderson (Boulder, 1988), 73–112.

19. Interview with Kasam Makao and Hamadi Duma, Kilindoni (Mafia Island), 26 May 1990.

20. TNA G55/39, Angelegenheiten Pflanzungen, Minaki Plantation to District Branch Kilindoni, 20 March 1914.

21. Differences between the culture of male and female slaves on the Kenyan coast have been discussed in Carol M. Eastman, "Women, Slaves, and Foreigners: African Cultural Influence and Group Processes in the Formation of Northern Swahili Coastal Society," *IJAHS* 21, 1 (1988), 1–20; Pat Caplan, "Gender, Ideology and Modes of Production on the Coast of East Africa," *Paideuma* 28 (1982), 29–43.

22. Baumann, *Usambara,* 153.

23. TNA G11/1, Kilwa Strafbuch 1908–1910. The bulk of these cases (some 270) come from Mafia Island. Another 80 come from the mainland around Kilwa.

24. Bakari, *Customs,* 170.

25. Bakari, *Customs,* 175.

26. Weidner, *Haussklaverei,* 21–22; BAK, FA 1/4–7, 44.

27. R. Kaundinya, *Erinnerungen aus meinen Pflanzerjahren in Deutsch-Ostafrika* (Leipzig, 1918), 89.

28. M. Klamroth, *Der Islam in Deutschostafrika* (Berlin, 1912), 12–13.

29. Klaus Bade, "Antisklavereibewegung in Deutschland und Kolonialkrieg in Deutsch-Ostafrika, 1888–1890: Bismarck und Friedrich Fabri," *Geschichte und Gesellschaft* 3, 1 (1977), 31–58.

30. In 1896 in the southern coastal town of Mikindani, for example, Ali bin Abed was sentenced to 1 1/2 years in prison and chains for exporting slaves. Later that year nine other men in Mikindani were prosecuted for profiting from the slave trade. Examples abound of slave traders, men and women, being prosecuted in other cities as well. BAB/R1001/5075, Strafverzeichnisse, Mikindani, 35a, 93b; GStA, Nachlass Schnee, File #64, "amri ya serkali."

31. GStA, Nachlass Schnee, File #61, "bismillah errahman errahim."

32. GStA, Nachlass Schnee, File #73, Athmani bin Pongwa to Tanga District Office, 9 August 1909; BAB/R1001/1006, 3 February 1913, 192–93. A register of almost a thousand slave sales in Kilwa district from 1912–14 is found in TNA G38/7, Verzeichnis über Sklavenkäufer und -Verkäufer 1911–1914.

33. "Hörigkeit in Deutsch-Ostafrika," *DOAR,* 15 June 1912, 1–2; F.O. Karstedt, "Zur Sklavenfrage in DOA," *KR* 12 (1913), 619–20; Weidner, *Haussklaverei,* 155–57.

34. GStA, Nachlass Schnee, File #71, "Mimi Asumuni bin Ayuba," 1315 a.H. (1897).

35. GStA, Nachlass Schnee, File #71, "khatti yangu Mwenyi Bakari."

36. GStA, Nachlass Schnee, File #67, "Hati ya mapatano."

37. By Prussian law of 1857 "from the moment slaves step on Prussian territory they are free, and the proprietary right of the master from that time on is dissolved."

Slavery and the Genesis of Colonial Labor Relations 47

This meant that, as residents of "Prussian" territory (as part of the German Empire), slaves in the colonies were free. Governor Soden wrote in 1891 " . . . anyone who no longer wants to be a slave can revoke his slavery without being hindered by officials." BAK, FA1/47/4–8, "Civilrechtliche Behandlung"; FA1/47/5–8, "Bericht des kaiserlichen Gouverneurs von Deutsch-Ostafrika," 30 August 1891.

38. BAK, FA 1/47, 3.
39. *Deutsche Kolonialzeitung* 7 (1894), 12.
40. BAK, FA 1/47 4–8.
41. TNA G11/1, Kilwa Strafbuch 1908–10.
42. BAB/R1001/8178, Soden to Caprivi, 24 March 1892, 128–29; TNA G8/48, Eberstein to Soden, 5 November 1891; TNA G8/19, Eberstein to Kaiserliches Gouvernement, 7 September 1893, 38–39; Schroeder to Kaiserliches Gouvernement, 21 September 1893, 49b.
43. TNA G8/19, Schroeder to Government, 21 September 1893.
44. TNA G4/40, Angelegenheiten Bagamoyo, 1898–1906.
45. KWK, Verhandlungen der Baumwollbau-Kommission des Kolonial-Wirtschaftlichen Komitees, 27 November 1911, 36.
46. W.W.A. FitzGerald, *Travels in British East Africa, Zanzibar and Pemba* (London, 1898), 361–65. F. Elton describes slave-hiring as a means to circumvent the slave trade in "On the Coast Country of East Africa, South of Zanzibar," *Journal of the Royal Geographical Society* 44 (1874), 235–36.
47. On Pangani sugar estates and slave labor see BAB/R1001/1006, Berichte der einzelnen Verwaltungsstellen, Besirksamt Pangani, 48–56; Glassman, *Feasts and Riot*, 96–106.
48. Friedrich Schroeder, "Einiges über Arbeiterverhältnisse in Usambara," *DKZ* 5, 28 (1888), 220–22; Fritz Ferdinand Müller, *Deutschland-Ostafrika-Zanzibar: Geschichte einer deutschen Kolonialeroberung 1884–1890* (Berlin, 1959), 243.
49. BAK, FA 1/4–7, 44.
50. GStA, Nachlass Schnee, File #66, "Bimenehi taala."
51. The *Gesindeordnungen*, laws regulating *Gesinde* in Prussia (and hence applicable to the German colonies), were promulgated 8 November 1810 and periodically amended in the nineteenth century. These laws were the basis for slave ransoming in German East Africa. BAK, FA 1/47, 4–8.
52. Kähler, *Gesindewesen und Gesinderecht*; Karl Bielefeldt, *Das Eindringen des Kapitalismus in die Landwirtschaft* (Berlin, 1910), 120–45; Verein für Sozialpolitik, *Bäuerliche Verhältnisse im Königreich Sachsen* (Leipzig, 1892), 328–42.
53. Bielefeldt, *Eindringen des Kapitalismus*, 342.
54. Kähler, *Gesindewesen*, VII–VIII.
55. This legislation has been discussed previously in Weidner, *Hausssklaverei*; Sunseri, "Slave Ransoming"; Georg Deutsch, "The 'Freeing' of Slaves in German East Africa: The Statistical Record, 1890–1914," *Slavery and Abolition* 2 (1998), 109–32. German ordinances on slave emancipation are found in *Landesgesetzgebung*, Verordnung betreffend den Freikauf von Sklaven, 4 September 1891, 329; Verordnung des Reichskanzlers, betreffend die Haussklaverei in Deutsch-Ostafrika, 29 November 1901, 331–32.
56. GStA, Nachlass Schnee, File #64, "i'lan," 21 July 1896; *Landesgesetzgebung*, 331.

57. The term was *Dienstmietvertrag*, which gave the slave working off the debt the same status as a contracted *Gesinde*. BAK/FA 1/47 4–8, Abschaffung der Haussklaverei.

58. Fr. Kuntze, "Der Sklaven-Freikauf in Deutsch-Ostafrika," *Kolonie und Heimat* 2, 7 (1908–09), 8.

59. The time needed to work off the ransom price varied considerably. With a wage of about 10–12 Rp per month, a *huru* should have been free after about ten months (since half of the wage was used to pay off one's debt). In practice, no worker worked for thirty days in a month. Twenty days was typical, but sickness, injury, and the incursion of added debt all combined to lengthen the ransom period. TNA G55/7, Kilwa Cotton Plantation to District Branch Kibata, 6 May 1914.

60. The Pangani District Officer in 1905/06, Theodor Gunzert, negotiated ransoming between slaves and planters of the region. T. Gunzert, "Service in German East Africa," 24.

61. BAK, FA1/47, 4–8, Civilrechtliche Behandlung, 3.

62. The following discussion is based on BAK, FA1/47 3–8, Verzeichnis der im Jahre 1893 in Deutsch-Ostafrika ertheilten Freibriefe; Weidner, *Haussklaverei*, 138–39. Deutsch gives the figure of seventy-four ransomed slaves in 1893 based on Colonial Office records in "The 'Freeing' of Slaves," 114.

63. *Landesgesetzgebung*, Verordnung des Reichskanzlers, betreffend die Haussklaverei in Deutsch-Ostafrika, 29 November 1901, 331–32.

64. Ransom prices varied according to factors such as original cost of the slave, age, and gender. Because female slaves generally cost more than males, their owner demanded higher ransom prices. Ransom prices are derived from Benediktiner Archiv, St. Ottilien, Spreiter to Schnee, 31 July 1912; Karstedt, "Zur Sklavenfrage," 619; Verhandlungen des Gouvernementsrats des deutschostafrikanischen Schutzgebietes, 19 June 1914, 45; TNA G55/1, Minaki Plantation; TNA G55/2, Mafia Plantation; TNA G55/7, Kilwa Plantation; TNA G55/39, Plantation Matters.

65. BAB/R1001/1006, Reichstagsverhandlungen 1913, 189–90; Schnee to Reichskolonialamt, 28 October 1913, 197–98. Governor Schnee wrote "An abolition of slavery without pecuniary compensation to the owners is absolutely not negotiable."

66. Although precise gender demographics are unavailable, some German districts reported far greater numbers of female than male slaves. BAB/R1001/1006, Berichte der einzelnen Verwaltungsstellen, Bezirksamt Dar-es-Salaam, 60; Bezirksamt Rufiji, 63; Bezirksamt Kilwa, 65.

67. Verordnung des Reichskanzlers, betreffend die Haussklaverei in Deutsch-Ostafrika, *Landesgesetzgebung*, 332.

68. TNA G55/39, Minaki Plantation to District Branch Kilindoni, 23 January 1914; Minaki Plantation to District Branch Kilindoni, 14 March 1914; TNA G55/2, Mafia Plantation to District Branch Chole, 31 July 1912; Mafia Plantation to District Branch Chole, 30 September 1912; District Branch Chole to Lessel Plantation, Ngombeni, 4 December 1912.

69. BAB/R1001/1006, Runderlass betreffend die Haussklaverei, 31 May 1905, 134b.

70. Weidner, *Haussklaverei*, 138–39; BAB/R1001/1007, Denkschrift über die Haussklaverei, 12.

71. GStA, Nachlass Schnee, File #71, 29 January 1892.

Slavery and the Genesis of Colonial Labor Relations 49

72. TNA G55/7, Kilwa Cotton Plantation to District Branch Kibata, 2 August 1912.
73. GStA, Nachlass Schnee, File #71, "Bismillah errahman errahim," a.H. 1306 (1888).
74. Seven out of nine of the surviving cases, mostly from 1900, show women freeing other women. GStA, Nachlass Schnee, File #71.
75. TNA G38/7, Verzeichnis über Sklavenkäufer und -Verkäufer 1911–1914.
76. GStA, Nachlass Schnee, File #61, 1309 a.H. (1891) and 1315 a.H. (1897).
77. In 1911, 1534 slaves were manumitted when there were probably well over 200,000 slaves still in the colony. Weidner, *Hausklaverei*, 138.
78. It was illegal to separate family members who were slaves, but nevertheless this occurred. Eberstein, "Über die Rechtsanschauungen," 180.
79. On the fate of the German records during and after World War I see *Guide to the German Records*, ed. Eckhart Franz and Peter Geissler, 2 Vols. (Dar es Salaam/Marburg, 1984), 48–67.
80. BAB/R1001/537, von Rode to Dernburg, 25 March 1907.
81. Pflanzungs-Gesellschaften, *Kolonial-Handels-Adressbuch* (1911), 63–77.
82. TNA G11/1, Strafbuch Kilwa, 2–5, 7–10, 120–36, 158–63, 173–76, 219–30.
83. TNA G55/39, Ingalls to District Branch Kilindoni, 31 January 1914.
84. TNA G55/2, Bresch to District Branch Chole, 1 April 1912.
85. TNA G55/39, Ingalls to District Branch Kilindoni, 29 October 1913.
86. TNA G55/39, Minaki Plantation to District Branch Kilindoni, 20 January 1914.
87. TNA G55/39, Ingalls to District Branch Kilindoni, 23 February 1914.
88. TNA G55/1, Minaki Plantation to District Branch Chole, 28 October 1911.
89. TNA G55/2, Bresch to District Branch Chole, 30 September 1912; KWK, *Kolonial-Handels-Adressbuch* (1911), 67.
90. TNA G55/2, Bresch to District Branch Chole, 31 July 1912.
91. TNA G55/2, Bresch to District Branch Chole, 2 December 1912.
92. TNA G55/2, Mannesschmidt to Lessel Plantation, 4 December 1912.
93. TNA G55/39, Ingalls to District Branch Kilindoni and District Branch Kilindoni to Ingalls, 20 January 1914; Ingalls to District Branch Kilindoni, 23 January 1914; District Branch Kilindoni to Ingalls, 24 January 1914.
94. TNA G11/1, Strafbuch Kilwa, 37.
95. TNA G11/1, Strafbuch Kilwa, 9.
96. TNA G55/39, Abu Omar to District Branch Kilindoni, 31 December 1913.
97. TNA G55/39, Minaki Plantation to District Branch Chole, 13 April 1913.
98. GStA, Nachlass Schnee, File #69, *Askari*, 8 September 1907; Deutsch-Ostafrika Pflanzungsgesellschaften, *Kolonial-Handels-Adressbuch* (1911), 68.
99. GStA, Nachlass Schnee, File #69, *Askari*, October 1907; Deutsch-Ostafrika Pflanzungsgesellschaften, *Kolonial-Handels-Adressbuch* (1911), 68.
100. "gesindeartige Stellung." "Arbeiterverhältnisse," in *Deutsches Kolonial-Lexicon*, ed. Heinrich Schnee, Vol. I (Leipzig, 1920), 77.
101. Glassman, *Feasts and Riot*, 17–20, 85–96 and "The Bondsman's New Clothes," 288.
102. Frederick Cooper explores similar relations between slaves and casual laborers on the Mombasa docks in *On the African Waterfront: Urban Disorder and the Transformation of Work in Colonial Mombasa* (New Haven, 1987), 13–26.

103. GStA, Nachlass Schnee, File #64, "Muhebhana shausch Fresh bin Hedebu"; File #73, "muhibhena Mfuri."

104. GStA, Nachlass Schnee, File #66, "sisi waarabu," 30 May 1895.

105. BAB/R1001/5075, Strafverzeichnisse der Eingeborenen, 1896–1900. The criminal records are fragmentary beyond 1896–97, but see TNA G11/1, Kilwa Strafbuch 1908–10; TNA G50/10, Tabora Strafbuch.

106. BAB/R1001/5075, Strafverzeichnisse Mikindani, 35, 92–93, 144–45.

107. BAB/R1001/5075, Strafverzeichnisse Kilwa, 31–34, 84–89, 134–39.

108. BAB/R1001/5075, Strafverzeichnisse Pangani, 10–13, 113–16.

109. BAB/R1001/5075, Strafverzeichnisse Kilwa, 137; Lindi, 140.

110. BAB/R1001/5075, Strafverzeichnisse Kilwa, 137.

111. BAB/R1001/5075, Strafverzeichnisse, 3 July 1896, 32b.

112. BAB/R1001/5075, Strafverzeichnisse, 12 December 1896, 92b, 93a.

113. BAB/R1001/5075, Strafverzeichnisse, 3 October 1896, 92a.

114. BAB/R1001/5075, Strafverzeichnisse, 25 January 1897, 136a; 12 January 1897, 114a.

115. BAB/R1001/5075, Strafverzeichnisse, 14 September 1896, 33a.

116. BAB/R1001/5075, Strafverzeichnisse, 4 November 1896, 93a.

117. TNA G11/1, Strafbuch Kilwa, 142.

118. TNA G11/1, Strafbuch Kilwa, 1908–1910.

119. TNA G11/1, Kilwa Strafbuch, 18 March 1909, 152.

120. TNA G11/1, Kilwa Strafbuch, 229–30.

121. BAB/R1001/5075, Strafverzeichnis Lindi, 38–39; Strafverzeichis Mikindani, 144; TNA G11/1, Strafbuch Kilwa, 61, 166.

122. Richard Roberts and Suzanne Miers, eds., *The End of Slavery in Africa* (Madison, 1989); Richard Roberts, "Representation, Structure and Agency: Divorce in the French Soudan during the Early Twentieth Century," *JAH* 40, 3 (1999).

123. BAB/R1001/5075, Strafverzeichnisse, 31 August 1896, 34a; 8 March 1897, 137a.

124. TNA G55/39, Minaki Plantation to District Branch Chole, 18 June 1913.

125. "Ein Wort zur Sklavenfrage," *DOAZ*, 11 April 1903, 1. "Wollen wir Sklaven oder freie Arbeiter?" *UP*, 15 June 1907, 1; "Zum Freikauf von Sklaven im Bezirk Pangani," *UP*, 27 July 1907, 6; BAB/R1001/812, Verhandlungen des Gouvernementsrats, May 1905, 50b.

3

LABOR MIGRATION AND THE EROSION OF THE PLANTATION IMPERATIVE

Historians of Tanzania have viewed the early colonial period through the lens of the Maji Maji rebellion (1905–07) that ended the first twenty years of German colonialism. This prevailing view holds that the accumulation of grievances that came with German rule, including forced labor, burdensome taxation, misrule by German-appointed local elites, and wide-scale European settlement gave African peasants little alternative but to rise up against German rule.[1] Although Africans lost the ensuing war, the disruptions it caused were so severe as to lead to changes in German policy. After the war Germans ameliorated their policies by concentrating on peasant cash crop production while still maintaining an agenda of developing a colonial economy based on European plantations and white settlement. The age of brutality that preceded Maji Maji was followed by an age of improvement after the war.

The problem with this paradigm is that it masks the leverage and continued control over their lives that most peasants and wage workers still maintained two decades into colonial rule, on the eve of the rebellion. With the knowledge that German policies would lead to war in 1905, historians have written early colonial history as a teleological explanation for the rebellion. The result has been that historians have exaggerated the power of the colonial state and underestimated the ability of peasants and workers to shape the colonial environment. In fact, labor migrants and peasants living in plantation zones had helped erode the colonial state's plantation agenda several years before the rebellion. Both local peasants and long-distance migrants resisted working on plantations under poor conditions and low wages, thereby forcing planters to expend great sums to obtain a work force. No planter could obtain sufficient workers to cultivate more than a fraction of his land. Furthermore, no workers willingly resided on plantations unless food rations were regular. Planters therefore developed an early dependence on local villages for food production in order to feed their workers.

The result of the labor squeeze was that plantations quickly reached limits of production that mitigated against adopting a burdensome annual crop like cotton. Many planters, especially small-scale settlers, came to believe that it would never be profitable for them to grow cotton in spite of German industry's interest in the crop.[2] Although the government encouraged plantation cotton growing by providing cotton gins, presses, guaranteed minimum prices, and transport subsidies, as late as 1905 virtually no private planter grew cotton in the northeastern plantation districts.[3] The few Germans who did take up the crop before 1905 were located along the southern coastal hinterland near Kilwa and Lindi. Even in those vast regions planters could not obtain sufficient local labor without state intervention. One planter argued that cotton would only be profitable if the government ensured that twice as many Africans were available in plantation districts as planters actually needed for most of the year.[4] The result of this labor dearth was that shortly after the turn of the century the colonial government and the Colonial Economic Committee turned away from a plantation cotton program and began to shift their resources to African cotton growing.[5] While this signified the end of the plantation imperative and the colonial vision of a colony of white settlement, it also marked the beginning of intensive struggles over labor and rural production in Tanzania.

This chapter examines the struggle over labor in the first twenty years of colonial rule and how it contributed to the erosion of the plantation imperative. In the mid 1890s, when the plantation vision still shaped German perceptions of colonial development, the German state began its first efforts at labor management in a series of laws modeled after the *Gesindeordnungen* discussed in Chapter 2. These masters-and-servants ordinances sought to control the work force by introducing labor contracts and a corpus of legislation that criminalized contract breaking and desertion. The state furthermore attempted to divert porters and other long-distance migrants to German plantations and towns as contractual wage laborers. Finally, the state introduced taxation and corvée labor obligations by the turn of the century even before conquest of the inland had been completed. In spite of these measures, planters could not escape the limits of labor coercion. Every year colonialists founded new estates and plantations, began new construction projects, including roads, railways, and harbors, and pushed the colonial frontier from coastal districts and caravan routes to inland societies. These moves created an escalating demand for labor that could not be met with available workers. The result was that those people willing to work for a wage for part of the year had great leverage in determining their conditions of work. Such leverage led state officials to seek additional sources of labor among indentured Asians outside the colony. Furthermore, colonial officials channeled African convicts onto plantations as penal laborers. Finally, slave emancipation policy sought to channel slaves onto German plantations (as discussed in Chapter 2). The most prescient colonial officials realized that the state's inability to control free local labor meant the end of the plantation imperative.

Despite these moves to bail out the plantation sector with indentured and convict labor, the escalating demand for cotton in Germany by the turn of the century combined with poor returns from plantations led state officials to seek "peasant" methods of cotton growing. One strategy was to settle porters and other long-distance migrants in coastal districts as cotton farmers. Another was to enlist African elites in an intensive cash crop campaign after 1902. While the first campaign was based on incentives, the second made widespread use of force, drastically affecting the rural economy, and was a factor in the outbreak of the Maji Maji rebellion in 1905. Although both strategies failed to solve the problem of cotton growing, they marked the beginning of a revised colonial program that would use state resources to draw peasants into cash crop production. This program meant that the German colonial state would not use every means at its disposal to make East African peasants into wage laborers, as it did in German Southwest Africa. The period before Maji Maji ends, then, not with a colonial state and planter class that had succeeded in mastering labor, but with a state desperately seeking to draw rural dwellers into a cash crop economy as peasants rather than workers.

LABOR SCARCITY AND EARLY COLONIAL PLANTATIONS

About fifty-three German coffee, tobacco, and coconut estates cropped up in the hinterlands of the coastal towns of Tanga, Pangani, Bagamoyo, and Dar es Salaam before 1898.[6] That number grew to about 120 in 1905, some beginning to snake their way up the Pangani river valley into the Usambara mountains.[7] About one-third of all estates were controlled by several trading corporations, most notably the German East Africa Corporation (*DOAG*) that had administered the coast before 1891. By 1903 German plantations and settlers of the northeast employed perhaps 10,000 workers. In addition, many thousands worked at railway construction, town and port development, and porterage.

From the start planters located their estates among African villages so that they could draw on local "day" laborers for much of their workforce. However, villagers did not come to work on these estates willingly. Friedrich Schroeder, a particularly brutal manager of the *DOAG*'s Lewa plantation near Pangani, described in 1888 how he obtained workers by threatening local villagers with a gun, demanding that "all but the children and the sick" show up for work.[8] In this way Schroeder obtained about eighty workers who joined a greater number of hired slaves. Shortly thereafter local villagers resisted Schroeder's labor demands either by force of arms or by moving far away from the Lewa plantation. Henceforth Schroeder only obtained sufficient workers when he doubled daily wages from 10 pesas to 20. The trend over the next decade for other planters was that day laborers were sometimes available if wages were sufficient, if coffee or tobacco planting did not conflict with seasonal household food production, and if plantations were located in close enough proximity to villages that day workers could return home every evening.

The greatest limitation to widespread availability of local day labor was plantation dependence on food supplies to feed their workers. As more plantations were founded each year, their food dependence escalated, giving local villagers a means of growing food for both subsistence and local markets. Peasant food production was furthermore essential to provision caravan porters, railway workers, and inhabitants of emerging colonial towns. With a steady demand for food there was no need for most rural dwellers to work for a wage, even after taxation was introduced in 1898.[9] Intended as labor reservoirs, villages instead became food stores for plantations and towns, a pattern that continued throughout German rule. Europeans therefore had to look beyond local villages for plantation labor.

Already in 1891 German planters sought labor from outside the colony "so that the plantations could be independent of the capriciousness of the native population."[10] In that year the policy-making *Kolonialrat* in Germany endorsed the use of indentured labor, demonstrating the government's eagerness to sustain early plantations and counter costly African wage demands by resorting to even costlier imported labor.[11] In 1892 the *DOAG* contracted some 462 Chinese and Javanese indentured laborers from Singapore to work on its coffee and tobacco plantations in Usambara.[12] The *DOAG* hoped that indentured workers would set an example of regular work for local Africans and suppress the upward pressure on wages that local villagers had succeeded in creating. The Asians worked ten-hour days with two days per month as rest days and were paid about twice the wages of African workers.[13] The Chinese and Javanese had identification passes that included their photographs, and found it difficult to desert plantations.[14] Nevertheless, indentured workers occasionally appeared in the crime statistics charged with disobedience, suggesting that they were not the compliant workforce that planters and the state hoped they would be.[15] Employment of several hundred indentured laborers continued throughout the 1890s, some on the government's experimental tobacco plantation in Mohoro region.[16]

The use of Asian indentured labor was a transient practice in German East Africa. Asian labor was expensive by East African standards, and the settler press castigated the "Asian alternative" as giving up on the colonial endeavor of controlling African labor.[17] By the late 1890s reports of abuse and discrimination directed at indentured workers in Africa made recruitment difficult.[18] Furthermore, recruitment was cumbersome, necessitating negotiations with rival colonial governments that were increasingly protective of exported workers in light of reports of poor working conditions in Africa.[19] The nascent Indian nationalist movement exerted pressure on the British government to curtail labor exports to South Africa, and as German plantations earned a reputation for harshness, officials in China and Singapore followed suit.[20] In 1902 an amendment to the Indian Emigration Act of 1883 allowed only skilled laborers to take up new contracts.[21] While few Asians worked in German East Africa after 1902, settlers and other employers periodically revived the call for Asian labor in response to continuous labor shortages in the colony.[22]

One alternative to local and indentured labor was to use penal workers for colonial development. By the late 1890s penal policy became a means for the state to channel hundreds of African men and women onto plantations and public works for periods ranging from about a week to several months.[23] Any criminal act—theft, disturbing the peace, fighting, gambling—could be punished with penal labor. From the start more convicts served time in chain gangs than in jails. For example, over a nine-month period in 1896–97 170 men and women worked as penal laborers in Tanga district while only 6 people did time in jails.[24] In Dar es Salaam during the same period 25 people were jailed while

293 worked as penal laborers.[25] Most of the communal district councils budgeted funds for the upkeep of prisoners in the first few years after 1900, using convicts to work on district and private plantations or road works.[26] Perhaps 10–20 percent of all workers at the turn of the century were penal laborers. Like slave ransoming and indenture, penal labor would never become the mainstay of plantation workforces in German East Africa. Nevertheless, it was typical for convict laborers to work alongside free wage laborers on plantations and other colonial pursuits by the turn of the century.

PORTERAGE AND THE ORIGINS OF LONG-DISTANCE LABOR MIGRATION

With local labor available only seasonally and indentured labor expensive and complicated to obtain, planters and other employers turned to long-distance labor migrants as the most promising steady source of labor. In particular, Nyamwezi and Sukuma porters from western Tanzania south of Lake Victoria began occasional wage work on European estates while awaiting the departure of caravans. With long-standing traditions of annual migration for caravan work, porters seemed the logical group to take up plantation work (See FIGURE 3.1).[27] Some 40,000 porters appeared on the northern coast annually in the mid 1890s and about one-tenth worked on nearby plantations for varying durations that rarely exceeded six months.[28] In light of the seasonality of porterage, northeast planters in 1901 called upon the Bagamoyo district office to sponsor a labor brokerage to enlist porters awaiting the mobilization of caravans for the journey inland.[29] The plan had modest initial success. In April 1902 the brokerage managed to supply 1,269 workers of some 1,499 whom planters requested.[30] However, porters were always a temporary source of plantation labor. As soon as caravans were outfitted, porters departed for the interior. In 1904 10,658 men were recruited for porterage at Bagamoyo at the start of the caravan season. By the time the caravans left, some 12,713 porters had been engaged, including many coastal men, leaving the labor brokerage several thousand men short of planters' needs. Such labor shortages forced all northern planters to sharply circumscribe the amount of acreage they were able to cultivate. The Tanga Planters' Association projected a deficit of 10,000 workers out of some 23,000 needed for the 1905 season.[31]

As colonial rule coalesced by the late 1890s, it created a greater demand for porters than in times past, since virtually any commodity that moved was transported by porterage. Attempts at other forms of

Labor Migration and Erosion of Plantation Imperative 57

Figure 3.1 Porters on a caravan. Porters were targeted by colonial officials and planters alike as a potential wage labor force. (From Otto Pentzel, *Heimat Ostafrika* [Leipzig, 1936], opposite 17.)

transport—donkeys, camels, ox-wagons—all failed, largely owing to the lack of sufficient water to provision draft animals and because of the death of large draft animals due to sleeping sickness.[32] By 1907 an estimated 100,000 porters left the coast annually for the interior,

Figure 3.2 Porters resting their loads on their shoulders. (Courtesy of Bundesarchiv, Koblenz, 146/84/67/25. Reprinted with permission.)

making porters by far the most numerous of all wage workers at that time.[33] Men who had previously not participated in caravan networks, such as many people of the south, began to take up loads to pay taxes, buy commodities, and avoid plantations.[34]

Labor Migration and Erosion of Plantation Imperative

Although some slaves worked at porterage, most porters took up loads voluntarily under terms that they negotiated. Among the Nyamwezi, for example, porterage was a rite of passage, and until a young man had made the journey to the coast he was a *mutini* "unripe fig" who did not know the ways of the world.[35] Porters guarded their autonomy and resisted attempts to regulate their movement. In southern Tanzania porters dug up the kilometer marker stones that Germans had set up along the Kilwa-Liwale road.[36] (See FIGURE 3.2.) This was done because colonial officials demanded that they reach six stones per hour instead of the four per hour that they were accustomed to. Long-distance porters were especially adept at dictating terms of their hire, choosing their own leaders, determining when they would take on work, and when they would return to their homes. When caravan conditions were not to their liking, porters deserted with impunity. The German engineer Gansser, commissioned to build signal towers in the Usambara mountains in 1898, frequently awoke to find that many of his porters had left:

Yesterday I told my porters that they must carry the loads for me up the mountain, and then they would be paid. They all slipped away in the early morning. This is the second or third time that the government has saved itself 30–40 Rps. in this way. . . . It is also characteristic of this rabble that, with the exception of two, all the other Zaramo have absconded. Of some 60 people hired in Dar es Salaam, and others who came from Tanga and elsewhere to make a total work force of 77 men, only about 38 are still around.[37]

Gansser characterized the desertion of porters as so common that it was hardly worth commenting on. "[Desertions] occur in this land in every safari and every caravan; sometimes more than half the people disappear in the night."[38] Porters were furthermore little regulated by colonial labor legislation because they refused to sign labor contracts, instead enlisting onto caravans collectively under a chosen leader.

By the turn of the century planters and government officials alike saw porterage as stymieing colonial development by depriving plantations of workers. They were especially concerned about the loss of Nyamwezi porters after the completion of the Uganda Railway in Kenya in 1902 increased the demand for inland porters to transport and market goods to Lake Victoria ports.[39] The settler press portrayed porters as a "cancer on the colony," disparaging them as *Sachsengänger*, drifters.[40] While Governor Götzen agreed with the planter indictment, he also recognized that there was no practical way to discipline and stabilize porters, so important were they to colonial development.[41] One means tried was to set up *caravanserais*, depots where porters encamped as a labor pool until needed. Both the government and private firms such as the *DOAG* established *caravanserais* in coastal and caravan towns like Dar es Salaam, Bagamoyo, Lindi, and Tabora.[42] Colonial officials punished desertion from government caravans severely. The slave Hassani, for example, received three months' labor in chains for deserting from a government caravan in 1897.[43] Ignas Kapile remembered, "If you tried to flee [government porterage] you were pursued and beaten many times with a cane."[44] Although punishment for desertion was severe, the state generally failed to bring professional porters under control. In a nine-month span from 1896–97 in the major caravan town of Bagamoyo only five men were prosecuted for deserting caravans, and only ten porters were convicted of desertion in all the other coastal towns combined.[45]

In the late 1890s, when Tanga district's population was halved by death and emigration, Tanga officials attempted to entice Nyamwezi porters to settle in the northeast as labor reserves for plantations.[46] By that time colonial officials noticed that many Nyamwezi men and women had founded market towns near Kilosa and Mpwapwa to supply caravans with grain, tobacco, hemp, and other wares.[47] Other Nyamwezi lived for extended periods in caravan villages and temporary camps while constructing the Usambara railway in the 1890s (See FIGURE 3.3). Drawing on this tradition, Tanga officials offered Nyamwezi migrants tax amelioration, land, seed, hoes, machetes, axes, and even cattle if they would settle around Tanga town and in plantation regions.[48] Four to five thousand Nyamwezi agreed to settle, some relocating with their wives.[49] The Nyamwezi settlements provided day laborers for coastal farmers and seasonal workers for the Usambara railway.[50] At this stage of colonial development, with the economic focus almost exclusively along the coastal hinterland, German policy makers were prepared to shift whole inland populations to the coast as labor reservoirs for plantations and other coastal development schemes.

The Nyamwezi settlements did not solve the labor shortage of the northeast. Rather than provide a steady pool of labor, the Nyamwezi instead used their land to grow and market crops to plantation workers or to coastal towns, much as local villagers had done for years. Nyamwezi market farming was lucrative. A planter reported that some Nyamwezi settlers purchased wares from his *duka* (shop) in the amount of 5–7 Rp per week, money that came from marketing of crops rather than working on plantations.[51] This was twice the annual hut tax re-

Figure 3.3 A worker village in 1908. Such villages were built near plantations, railways, or caravan routes to provide temporary shelter for workers and their families. German officials used this model to try to settle inland peoples near the coast before 1905. (© Bildarchiv Preussischer Kulturbesitz Berlin, 1401 f. Reprinted with permission.)

quired of African men after 1898. As Nyamwezi marketed crops, they refrained from working for a wage, incurring the anger of German planters and stalling railway construction for lack of workers.[52] Some characterized the Nyamwezi as "sports" who earned so much money that they could afford to buy trinkets. Planters came to resent the Nyamwezi colonies because, by making it too easy to farm, they attracted "a great number of old and reliable plantation workers" as farmers rather than workers.[53] One planter complained "if we don't decide soon to break up these 'labor reserves' we will lose our last worker to them."[54] A further grievance was that, located on the fringe of plantations, Nyamwezi colonies offered refuge to plantation deserters and were considered refuges for other suspect people, such as penal laborers who deserted their work sites.

Early in 1904 a report on the state of plantations in German Africa concluded that "all the plantations here have suffered because of the great deficiency in labor supplies, a situation that shows no end in sight."[55] The report attributed the drop in labor to increased competition from railway construction and newly founded sisal plantations, both of which drew workers away from smaller settler estates. The report also noted that Nyamwezi and Sukuma labor migrants had far greater opportunities for trade and work at good wages after the opening of the Uganda railway in Kenya, which by 1907 employed as many as 15,000 Nyamwezi regularly.[56] The backbone of the colonial wage labor force was filtering away from the coast back into the interior, and even out of the colony to British-controlled regions.

CONTRACT LABOR AND WORKER AUTONOMY

By the mid 1890s German officials responded to the success of coastal villagers and porters at avoiding plantation work by introducing *Gesinde* regulations into the colony. As described in Chapter 2, these laws sought to discipline rural workers by enforcing labor contracts, upholding *Dienstherrschaft*—the authority of employers over their workers—and punishing desertion. They were in effect masters-and-servants regulations like those introduced in other European colonies such as neighboring Kenya.[57] Along with *Gesinde* regulations, by the late 1890s the colonial state added taxation and corvée labor to the burdens faced by rural dwellers, all symptoms of the drive to get Africans to work for a wage.

Apart from laws that regulated slave labor, labor policy in German East Africa began in 1894 with the introduction of *Dienstbücher* work books (Sw. *vitabu vya kazi*) that recorded personal details of workers, including name, gender, age, homeland, physical characteristics, religion, and employment history. The law required employers to maintain a work book for all *Dienstboten*, "personal and household servants, sailors and all workers hired on a monthly basis."[58] Employers retained the *vitabu* until the period of employment was up, enabling them to maintain leverage over workers. Workers without books could be punished with up to three months labor in chains, which explains why many of those who broke contract first tried to obtain their *vitabu* before fleeing. The authority of employers was further bolstered by an 1896 law that regulated those "who enter into a contractual service or work relationship."[59] These laws were a direct outcome of the plantation imperative in that they sought to discipline a workforce at a time when German colonialism was wedded to a vision of developing the colony for plantation production. By 1896 colonial officials had the authority to punish work avoidance, dereliction of duty, recalcitrance, and desertion by using corporal punishment or penal labor in chains.[60]

Beginning in 1896 district officials were required to record episodes of crime and punishment, and therefore a picture of the laboring environment at this early stage of colonialism was created. Read against the grain, crime records provide a picture of worker resistance. In Tanga district in 1896–97 workers were punished for crimes that included desertion, negligence in service, breaking contract, and disobedience.[61] Workers often deserted in groups, sometimes repeatedly. Ten people were punished in Dar es Salaam in one three-month period in 1897 for refusing or avoiding work, typically receiving twenty-five lashes of the whip.[62] Crimes such as insolence and insubordination to employers, mistreatment of employers, and attacking overseers demonstrate both worker recalcitrance and the state's goal of disciplining the workforce. Each year hundreds of men and women were convicted of work-related crimes and returned to plantations as penal laborers.

Planters and district officials punished domestic servants and overseers who broke discipline much more fervently than other workers, perhaps to uphold the hierarchy of authority. The overseer Mabruki of the *DOAG*'s Lewa plantation, for example, was sentenced to one month in chains and fifteen lashes for "inciting workers."[63] Even more illustrative is a case of violence between a sisal planter named Meyer and his Comoran overseer.[64] Because Meyer lost an arm in a hunting accident he obtained a tandem bicycle that he used to tour the sisal estate, typically sitting in the front seat while his overseer peddled in the back. One day, bicycling back to the plantation house, Meyer, in a heavy sweat, turned around to see his overseer not peddling but ridiculing him, to the entertainment of surrounding workers. In his anger Meyer crashed the bicycle and threatened the overseer with a beating. The overseer ran off, first grabbing a shotgun from the plantation house. Meyer called for *askari* from the local district post to help him track down his servant. Cornered in an outbuilding, and realizing that he would be given up to the *askari*, whose reputation for brutality was well-known, the overseer emerged firing, mortally wounding Meyer before killing himself with the remaining shell. The extreme consequences of so minor an incident leading to the death of two men can only be explained as the result of a breach in authority that German rulers believed weakened them in the eyes of African workers. The tension of maintaining such authority explains why people in positions of relative prestige and autonomy—overseers, household servants, even *askari*—often fled their employers, to be pursued by officials with especial zeal, typically with rewards for their capture. Entrusted with money, property, sometimes guns, and given positions of responsibility, such as recruiting workers or overseeing laborers, "domestics" were more strictly controlled through the work book system than general plantation laborers.

Although work books implied a voluntary contractual relationship, they were widely abused by the African elite who were pressured by colonial officials to supply labor to plantations. In Msongozi village near Morogoro, for example, John Yogelo remembered "job cards" as simply being a means of conscripting workers:

> A Jumbe would be provided with job-cards which in turn he had to drop at the doors (of the people). Then if a person saw a job-card and if he did not report for work, he would receive twenty-five strokes. A German had no respect; he would flog even the jumbes and the foremen if they did not follow instructions.[65]

Yogelo's words show that many contract workers were really forced laborers, which explains why some people were criminalized for being "work shy" or for "resisting work."[66] The trend by the turn of the century was that many rural men fled plantation zones in order to avoid unwanted labor cards or other forced labor. Perhaps because labor migrants resented the loss of autonomy that work books entailed, many planters ceased using them for "unskilled day and monthly laborers" and relied on high wages to attract a work force.[67] Colonial officials often admitted that they could never police plantation desertion adequately. The result was that the contract system, intended to foster a disciplined work force, did not solve the labor shortage, and thus never evolved into a pass system for general plantation workers.

TAXATION AND THE LIMITS OF LABOR COMPULSION

Historians have often asserted that peasants were forced into wage labor by burdensome colonial taxation.[68] While taxation was onerous for rural dwellers, it did not transform peasants into permanent wage laborers in German East Africa. A general 3 Rp tax was placed on "all house and hut owners" in 1898 in order to draw workers into the colonial economy and to get peasants to produce marketable crops regularly.[69] Villagers could initially pay taxes in kind, which included oil crops such as peanuts, sesame, and copra; natural products like rubber, ivory, and wax; cash crops like cotton; and labor.[70] In inland districts livestock and grain taxes were used to supply military garrisons, feed prisoners, and provision caravans.

Taxation entailed counting huts, estimating population densities, and establishing the authority of *majumbe* and chiefs as tax collectors by rewarding them with 10 percent of collected revenues. Before each tax year local authorities made lists of taxable huts, a policy that was open to abuse since, once the lists were established, tax obligations existed that might not reflect the reality of population levels. As the colonial population declined through migration, mortality, warfare, and low birth rates, villagers left behind bore unrealistic burdens. Unlike the precolonial moral economy that weighed annual circumstances in gauging tribute, in coastal districts the first year of taxes coincided with drought and famine on top of ongoing problems with cattle disease, locust plagues, and other signs of breakdown in the political ecology.[71] Yet the state still expected its subordinates to collect taxes, eroding the authority that they once had.

In light of tax demands, men increasingly fled regions of effective administration, leaving women behind to assume the tax burden or incur conflict with *majumbe* headmen.[72] If no food, livestock, or other products were available for sale, women had to work as tax laborers at a wage rate half that of men's. It was inevitable under such circumstances that taxes engendered deep tensions in rural households.

In the first few years most peasants paid taxes by selling grain, cattle, goats, or other commodities. A 1901 report from the Bismarckburg military station on Lake Nyasa shows the diverse ways in which some 9,000 inland people paid the head-tax.[73] Some people of the area paid the tax in cash, while others signed on as porters or workers and had the tax immediately deducted from their wages. Still others sold a goat, some millet or maize, or paid the tax directly in kind, which the military station used to feed prisoners in its jails. Those who could not muster cash or provisions were put to work as tax laborers clearing roads, and some were sent to mission stations in the area to drain swamps, construct irrigation canals, or to build bridges.

By 1905, when the state required taxes to be paid in cash, the burden became more onerous. Mzee Ibrahim Uzengo of Msongozi recalled:

> Both taxes in millet and then in goats were easily obtained. Great difficulty was faced when they said, 'Now what is required is tax in Ru-

pees.' People suffered in finding them. A person could not get money unless he went out of this place to work in plantations near Kilosa or Morogoro. That was the problem of tax.[74]

If people could not pay, they were sent to work for a wage on plantations to settle the debt. Ignas Kapile recalled:

> People who were burdened with taxes and unable to pay were taken by the government and 'sold' to a plantation owner. There the government received its money and the planter had people to plant his fields. After working the people received tax receipts (*vyeti vya kodi*).[75]

Maakida subdistrict officials often pressured their subordinate *majumbe* to periodically supply workers for the state and planters. The *jumbe* Rajabu Lutewa in 1906 wrote to district officials in Bagamoyo complaining that an *akida* forcibly conscripted his villagers by using the pretext that they had not paid their taxes.[76] Rajabu noted that he had already collected taxes from "18 houses, 15 with tax receipts (*vyeti*) and three from strangers (*wageni*)," but the people were taken anyway. Because of incidents such as this, *majumbe* lost influence over their people as they failed to protect them from abuses of the state and settlers. Settlers exerted pressure on colonial officials to use tax policy to muster workers for their needs. Thus, the 1905 tax revisions ameliorated taxes for plantation workers by half and completely exempted those who worked for longer than six months.

In addition to taxes, villagers were required to construct and maintain roads and undertake other corvée obligations for the state. Until 1905 women and children were required to do corvée labor alongside men.[77] Corvée was unpaid, and workers were even required to provide their own food if work was undertaken close to their homes. Abdala Undi remembered taxes and corvée as operating hand in hand: "It was the practice of the government to have the roads cleared when the tax season began."[78] District officials often targeted peasants who refused to work for a wage for corvée labor even if they had paid their taxes. Cases of desertion from public works occasionally appeared in the crime statistics.[79]

Although burdensome for many peasants, taxes failed to solve the labor shortage or create a permanent working class. While it is clear that more people worked for a wage because of the tax obligation, especially in years of drought or other crises, it is also clear that the hut tax did not drive workers onto the plantations. At the turn of the century most Usambara plantations reported shortfalls of workers that made them curtail production.[80] Planters frequently complained that people in proximity to the plantations were the least likely to work for a wage. This was because "for the most part the people earn money to pay taxes by selling cattle."[81] In Tanga in 1902 the hut tax could be paid by selling a goat or three or four chickens. Selling one cow might pay the taxes of thirteen to twenty-seven households.[82] A "load" of potatoes earned 5 Rp while a sack of rice could pay taxes for three huts. Many peasants preferred to gather natural products to pay their taxes rather than work for a wage or sell crops. A *frasila* (about 35 lbs.) of wax could be sold for 22 Rp, a *frasila* of copal sold for 8–16 Rp, and the same amount of wild rubber could pay the taxes of twelve households. Hunters could pay taxes for two households by supplying one animal pelt, while a wild pig's head brought in a 3 Rp bounty.

Compared to tax levels in other African colonies, the 3 Rp hut or head tax was relatively low. In South Africa, for example, Zulu men were forced into the gold mines with a tax five times higher than that of German East Africa, and in the Belgian Congo taxes were two to four times higher.[83] Low taxes were not a colonial omission. They signified the state's recognition of its ongoing dependence on peasants to produce food and commodities of the forest, which brought in more revenue than settler cash crops.

CONTRACT BREAKING, DESERTION, AND WORKER AUTONOMY

By 1905 the planter demand for workers had reached a state of crisis along the northern coastal strip as about 100 plantations competed for labor with two railway lines and ongoing porterage.[84] Yet fewer workers were available since thousands of Nyamwezi who had once worked occasionally on plantations were now subsidized by the government as cotton farmers, building on their prior success at food production for local markets. Beginning in about 1904 the pro-settler newspapers *Deutsch-Ostafrikanische Zeitung* and *Usambara Post,* decrying the labor shortage as spelling economic ruin for northern plantations, called for state-sponsored labor compulsion as a means of solving the problem.[85] While Governor Götzen remained committed to plantation development and white settlement, those policy makers committed to cotton production, especially the Colonial Economic Committee and its backers in Germany, had begun to abandon the preference for plantations. This was in part because only a handful of German settler estates were willing to grow cotton in 1905. All planters struggled with production limits in light of the labor shortage, few able to bring much more than 10 percent of their lands under continuous cultivation. Under these circumstances, the ability of plantation workers to desert with relative impunity had important consequences for policy making in the colony.

In 1906 the Tanga district office, more sensitive to planter interests than were policy makers in Germany, responded to complaints of desertion and labor shortage by publishing a "wanted bulletin" that was dedicated to tracking down plantation deserters and other contract breakers.[86] The bulletin provides a picture of contract laborers and their ability to manipulate the labor environment twenty years after the founding of the colony. They also supply a profile of wage workers by the turn of the century, suggesting a comparison with South African labor migrants in the early stages of mineral development when the labor environment was clearly in their hands.[87] Based on a survey of fifty-seven workers sought for desertion in 1906–07, contracted workers were overwhelmingly young men with an average age of about twenty-four, representing many different Tanzanian ethnicities.[88] While about 50 percent of deserters were field laborers, others worked on plantations as sailors (along rivers and the coast), hunters, cattle herders, and labor overseers. About 30 percent worked as domestic servants, cooks, washers, or personal aides. Three workers from the sample were clearly identified as *huru* ransomed slaves. Mature and older men apparently avoided wage labor twenty years after the advent of German rule. Women also do not appear in the statistics as contract breakers and deserters, perhaps because most female workers were non-contractual day laborers who migrated from nearby localities.

Workers deserted plantations regardless of status. This was the case with Bakari Bwana, a Segeju man of about twenty-five years, reported as a deserter in February 1907.[89] Contracted as worker #158 in Tanga district, Bakari had formerly worked as an *askari* for the Tanga *boma* until hired by the West German Trade and Plantation Corporation to shoot the *kima* monkeys that plagued its Kiomoni coconut and sisal plantation. An overseer of the Ambangula coffee plantation named Hassani also deserted his employment and was pursued as a contract breaker.[90] More typical were the eight workers from the southern coast who in 1907 signed contracts to work on one of the *DOAG*'s sisal plantations near Tanga.[91] Each worker received a 5 Rp wage advance as an enticement to migrate to the northern plantation zones, and together they promptly fled with their advances.

By 1907 the settler economy took a back seat in colonial policy, and state officials under newly appointed Governor Rechenberg were less sympathetic about desertion than before. To bolster their claims to police aid, planters often accused deserters of more serious crimes. The settler von Dalwigk, for example, called on the police to apprehend his servant Stephanus for desertion and suspicion of stealing 200 Rp.[92] The planter Selke, accusing his worker Sefu of desertion and stealing a fellow worker's coat and clock, described him as dressing well in white clothes and khaki "that he probably stole."[93] Garimoshi, a Nyamwezi, was accused of running off with 15 Rp that he was given to recruit workers for the Kihuihui plantation.[94] Accusations of theft typically accompanied claims of desertion, suggesting that just as workers learned to manipulate the plantation system through desertion, planters used charges of theft and other crimes to enlist the colonial state to apprehend deserters.

The greatest inducement to desertion were planters themselves, competing for a scarce labor supply. Planters actively enticed their neighbors' workers onto their own estates, directing their overseers or workers to get others to come to work by providing a gratuity for every worker obtained.[95] Marketplaces and plantations were, in fact, the best recruiting grounds for the "Schlepper," whose job it was to obtain workers quickly for seasonal plantation needs, such as coffee harvesting. Under such competitive conditions plantations with reputations for abuse or low wages, or an overseer or planter nicknamed "*mkali*" (vicious), would soon lose their workers. Worker subcultures were important in the desertion process. *Ndugu* countrymen working for different estates often met in marketplaces or shared meals together, compared notes about plantation conditions, wages, food, and hours of work, and persuaded each other to desert.[96] As long as employers competed with each other, they were reluctant to create a rigid system of labor control for fear of not being able to obtain workers on short notice. The result was pressure on planters to improve working conditions, dismiss abusive overseers, increase wages or food rations, and thereby create conditions that could attract or at least retain a workforce for seasonal needs.

The ability of long-distance migrants to maintain control over their working lives was dramatically apparent in 1906 when migrants began withdrawing from coastal and plantation districts and returning to the interior. Late that year a group of northern planters sent an urgent telegram to the government in Dar es Salaam informing it of a shortage of silver coins that prevented them from paying their workers in cash. The letter warned that "the consequences of missing one or two wage payments are immense."[97] These consequences undoubtedly referred to the fear that unpaid plantation workers would ignite rebellion in the north, as their compatriots were doing at that moment with the Maji Maji rebellion in the south. Planters further feared that workers would not return to plantations that defaulted on their wage payments. Although the government sent some 40,000 Rp in paper money to make up for the silver shortage, it was not acceptable for many of the 8,000 workers of the north at that time, mostly Nyamwezi from the interior. Instead, workers began to leave plantation districts and withdraw from the coast. The opening of the Uganda railway gave them ample opportunity to participate in inland trading and porterage near their homelands. Twenty years after the advent of colonial rule planters had lost their moment. Labor migrants would only work for a wage under circumstances that suited them, and colonial officials would not muster state resources to create a proletarian economy.

Historians of Tanzania have long regarded the twenty years before 1905, when the Maji Maji rebellion broke out, as an era of unbridled labor coercion. However, the colonial state was not so omnipotent that it could reshape rural societies at will. While creating a legal framework to draw men and women into wage labor and market participation by 1900, villagers exploited the many breaches in the colonial economy, not the least of which was the ongoing shortage of labor that gave rural societies leverage over the labor process. The strains on colonial labor policy were clear by 1905. Each year more plantations were founded, leading planters to compete for an already limited labor force. By 1905 the two railway lines demanded some 12,000 workers annually.[98] Another 3,000 workers were swept up annually into the Dar es Salaam economy in tasks such as construction and harbor work. Every new economic pursuit created a demand for more porters and workers. Under these strains, the state used slave ransoming, indentured labor, and penal policy as stopgaps to enhance the labor force. It further exerted pressure on *majumbe* and *maakida* to find workers, especially in regions that had hitherto escaped colonial demands, such as the southeast and southwest. Some of these elites, however, began to resist colonial demands, and would participate most fully in the rebellion that hit southern districts late in 1905.

The autonomy of wage workers on the eve of Maji Maji had important consequences for the future of the colony. As Nyamwezi laborers withdrew from the northeast in 1906, demonstrating that they would resist becoming a sedentary coastal labor reserve, the settler-dominated northeast highlands moved to the periphery of German policy making. The most farsighted officials came to believe that the "opening up" of the colony could not be confined to the settler northeast, but had to rely on peasant production of cash crops in the south and inland. The refusal of villagers and porters to become a compliant labor force was an important factor in the erosion of the plantation imperative that had captivated policy makers in the first twenty years of colonial rule.

NOTES

1. The Maji Maji rebellion is discussed at length in Chapter 4, but see John Iliffe, "The Organization of the Maji Maji Rebellion," *JAH* 8, 3 (1967), 495–512 and "The Effects of the Maji Maji Rebellion of 1905–1906 on German Occupation Policy in East Africa," in *Britain and Germany in Africa*, ed. Prosser Gifford and William Roger Louis (New Haven, 1967), 557–75. For examples of how this narrative has made its way into Tanzanian textbooks see Taasisi ya Elimu, *Historia Shule za Msingi* (Dar es Salaam, 1985) and Tanzanian Institute of Curriculum Development, *East Africa from 1850 to the Present* (Dar es Salaam, 1988).

2. A. Pfüller, "Über Baumwollkultur," *Der Pflanzer* (1905), 97–100.

3. KWK, "Baumwoll-Unternehmen in Deutsch-Ostafrika," *Verhandlungen des KWKs*, 22 January 1903, 21–25; *Verhandlungen des KWKs*, Spring 1905, 6–12.

4. Gustav Eismann, "Über Baumwolle in Deutsch-Ostafrika," *Der Pflanzer* (1905), 56–57.

5. KWK, *Verhandlungen des KWKs*, 2 June 1902, 14–15.

6. "Verzeichnis der im Schutzgebiete Deutsch-Ostafrika thätigen Firmen und Erwerbsgesellschaften," *DKB* 9 (1898), 350–53.

7. "Nachweisung über die in Deutsch-Ostafrika vorhandenen Plantagen und deren ungefähren Stand," *BLF* 2 (1904–06), 110–16.

8. "Einiges über Arbeiterverhältnisse in Usambara," *DKZ* 5 (1888), 220–22.

9. John Iliffe, *A Modern History of Tanganyika* (Cambridge, 1979), 152.

10. TNA G8/67, DOAG, Lucas Bericht, October 1892, 112; Juhani Koponen, *Development for Exploitation* (Hamburg, 1995), 336–39.

11. BAB/R1001/8144, Kolonialrath I. Sitzungsperiode 1891/92, Bericht über die Baumwollenkultur in den deutschen Schutzgebieten, 8.

12. TNA G8/67, Deutsch-Ostafrikanische Gesellschaft, Report by Lucas, October 1892, 113b–114a, October 1892; *DKB* 5 (1894), 67.

13. "Zur Arbeiterfrage in Ostafrika," *DKZ* 5 (1892), 57.

14. "Kontraktbruch," *UP*, 10 August 1907, 1–4.

15. In 1896 five Chinese workers were charged in Tanga with disobedience and given ten lashes each as punishment. BAB/R1001/5075, Strafbuch Tanga, 5.

16. BAB/R1001/8647, Versuchspflanzung Mohoro, Liebert to Hohenlohe-Schillingsfurst, 4 October 1897, 32, 50.

17. "Chinesische Arbeiter," *DOAZ*, 19 May 1906, 1; "Chinesische Kulis für Deutsch-Ostafrika," *UP*, 11 January 1913, 2.

18. BAB/R1001/812, Verhandlungen des Gouvernementsrats, 125–26.

19. *DKB* 6 (1895), 353; "Kuli," in *Deutsches Kolonial-Lexicon,* ed. Heinrich Schnee (Leipzig, 1920), 386–89. For similar circumstances in Natal, see Bill Freund, *Insid-*

ers and Outsiders: The Indian Working Class in Natal (Portsmouth, 1994); Joy Brain, "Natal's Indians, 1860–1910," in *Natal and Zululand,* ed. Duminy and Guest (Pietermaritzburg, 1989), 249–74; Robert G. Gregory, *India and East Africa* (London, 1971), 103–05.

20. Brain, "Natal's Indians," 268–70; Koponen, *Development,* 336–39.

21. "Zwei Antworten," *UP,* 1 September 1906, 1.

22. For example "Einfuhr fremder Arbeiter," *UP,* 24 March 1906, 1–2. In 1906 the Holzmann firm attempted to contract 500–1,000 Chinese to help construct the Central Railway. "Zur Chinesenfrage," *UP,* 2 June 1906; "Es muss etwas geschehen," *DOAZ,* 20 January 1906, 1.

23. In 1898 imprisonment was specified as "any curtailment of liberty, especially labor in chains." *Landesgesetzgebung,* 200, fn. 1.

24. BAB/R1001/5075, Strafverzeichnisse Tanga, 6–7, 56–58, 111–12.

25. BAB/R1001/5075, Strafverzeichnisse Dar es Salaam, 25–29, 78–81, 128–30.

26. *Amtlicher Anzeiger für Deutsch-Ostafrika,* 3, 6–12 (1902).

27. Stephen J. Rockel, "Caravan Porters of the *Nyika*: Labour, Culture, and Society in Nineteenth Century Tanzania," (Ph.D. diss., University of Toronto, 1997) and "Wage Labor and the Culture of Porterage in Nineteenth Century Tanzania: the Central Caravan Routes," *Comparative Studies of South Asia, Africa and the Middle East* 15, 2 (1995), 14–24; Jonathon Glassman, *Feasts and Riot: Revelry, Rebellion, and Popular Consciousness on the Swahili Coast, 1856–1888* (Portsmouth, 1995), 55–78; S.C. Lamden, "Some Aspects of Porterage in East Africa," *TNR* 61 (1963), 155–64.

28. BAB/R1001/6475, Arbeiter-Verhältnisse, 204, reprinted in Achim Gottberg, ed., *Unyamwesi: Quellensammlung und Geschichte* (Berlin, 1971), 388–89. These correspond roughly with Rockel's figures in "Caravan Porters," 342.

29. TNA G4/46, Arbeitervermittlungsstelle Bagamoyo, 1901–1904.

30. TNA G4/46, Kommunalverband Bagamoyo, 10 August 1904; "Zur Arbeiternot," *UP,* 17 December 1904, 3.

31. *UP,* 17 December 1904, 2.

32. BAB/R1001/819, Transportverhältnisse in Ostafrika, Götzen to Bezirksämter, 26 August 1901.

33. "Die Karawanen-Verkehr: eine Gefahr für unsere Kolonie," *DOAZ,* 27 July 1901, 1; "Zur Arbeiternot," *UP,* 17 December 1904, 3.

34. "Zur Arbeiternot," *UP,* 17 December 1904, 3.

35. Edmund Dahl, *Nyamwezi-Wörterbuch* (Hamburg, 1915), 210; Rockel, "Caravan Porters," Chapter 5.

36. "Die Reise des hochwürdigen Herrn Bischof Thomas Spreiter nach Matumbi und Kwiro," *Missions-Blaetter* 13 (1908–09), 67, 82.

37. Heinrich Dauber, *"Nicht als Abentheurer bin ich hierhergekommen . . . ": 100 Jahre Entwicklungs- "Hilfe". Tagebücher und Briefe aus Deutsch-Ostafrika, 1896–1902* (Frankfurt am Main, 1991), 107.

38. Dauber, *"Nicht als Abentheurer,"* 90.

39. "Die Wanyamwezis sollen Träger bleiben!" *DOAZ,* 18 March 1905, 1; "Arbeiterfrage," *UP,* 16 September 1911, 1–2.

40. *Sachsengänger* referred to eastern European labor migrants in Germany who refused to become sedentary workers. "Die Karawanen-Verkehr," *DOAZ,* 27 July 1901,

1; W. Schwarze, *Deutsch-Ost-Afrika* (Berlin, 1907), 33; "Zur Arbeiter- und Trägerfrage," *DOAZ*, 3 March 1900, 1.

41. BAB/R1001/819, Götzen to Bezirksämter, 26 August 1901, 5.

42. For example in 1906 Lindi District budgeted 5,000 Rp for upkeep of its caravanserai. TNA G4/74, Wirtschaftsberichte Mikindani, 73. One observer claimed that the Bagamoyo caravanserai was capable of providing shelter for 10,000 porters. Schwarze, *Deutsch-Ost-Afrika*, 31; Karl Weule, *Native Life in East Africa* (Chicago, 1969), 83.

43. BAB/R1001/5075, Strafverzeichnisse, 137a.

44. *MMRP*, Mzee Ignas Kapile, Mtama, 7/68/2/3/6.

45. BAB/R1001/5075, Strafverzeichnisse Bagamoyo, 14–19, 66–70, 117–24; Strafverzeichnisse Tanga, Pangani, Sadani, Dar es Salaam Kilwa, and Mikindani.

46. "Bericht des Bezirksamts Tanga," *BLF* (1903), 217.

47. "Jahresberichte allgemeinen Inhalts aus Ostafrika 1894–96," in Gottberg, *Unyamwesi*, 388. In 1903 Captain Schleinitz noted Nyamwezi settlements in Kilosa district encompassing about 1,000 people. BAB/R1001/224, "Bericht über Wegeverhältnisse," 10 June 1903, 28; Lambrecht report, 1 March 1902, 15; BAB/R1001/1034, Glauning report, 11 June 1896.

48. "Zur Arbeiterfrage," *UP*, 6 May 1905, 2.

49. Paul Fuchs, *Die Wirtschaftliche Erkundung einer ostafrikanischen Südbahn* (Berlin, 1905), 230–31.

50. BAB/R1001/6479, Januar 1905 bis September 1905, in Gottberg, *Unyamwesi*, 205; C. Gillman, "A Short History of the Tanganyika Railways," *TNR* 13 (1942), 17–21.

51. "Noch ein Beitrag zur Arbeiterfrage," *UP*, 31 March 1906, 1.

52. Gillman, "Short History," 18.

53. BAB/R1001/812, Verhandlungen des Gouvernementsrats, May 1905, 26; "Njaa," *UP*, 14 January 1905, 2–3.

54. "Njaa," *UP*, 14 January 1905, 3.

55. F. Stuhlmann, "Vierter Jahresbericht des Kaiserlichen Biologisch-Landwirtschaftlichen Instituts Amani," *BLF*, 1904–06, 466.

56. *UP*, 16 November 1907, 1.

57. David M. Anderson, "Master and Servant in Colonial Kenya, 1895–1939," *JAH*, 41 (2000), 459–85; Bruce Berman and John Lonsdale, *Unhappy Valley: Conflict in Kenya and Africa* (London, 1992), 112–14, 147–48.

58. *Landesgesetzgebung*, Gouvernementsverordnung, betreffend die Führung von Dienstbüchern, 23 April 1894, 309–10. It was illegal for whites to employ "servants" without a service book.

59. *Landesgesetzgebung*, Disziplinarbefügnis der Bezirksamtmänner und der Stationschefs im Innern, 202. A contract decree of 1896 was dropped after several years as being ineffective. Koponen, *Development*, 374–75.

60. *Landesgesetzgebung*, Verfügung des Reichskanzlers wegen Ausübung der Strafgerichtsbarkeit und der Disziplinargewalt gegenüber den Eingeborenen, 22 April 1896, 200.

61. BAB/R1001/5075, Strafverzeichnisse Tanga, 5–7, 55–58, 111–12.

62. BAB/R1001/5075, Strafverzeichnisse, 125–30.

63. BAB/R1001/5075, Strafbuch Pangani, 12.

64. Wilhelm Methner, *Unter drei Gouverneuren: 16 Jahre Dienst in deutschen Tropen* (Breslau, 1938), 36–39.

65. *MMRP* 1/68/2/4/2, Mzee John Yogelo, Msongozi, 29 March 1968. See also the following informants from Lindi district: 7/68/2/3/1, Mzee Abdala Undi; 7/68/2/3/2, Mzee Yonas Mtepa; 7/68/2/3/3, Mzee Ludger Amani.

66. BAB/R1001/5075, Strafbuch Dar es Salaam, 74–81; Strafbuch Tanga, 56.

67. "Ein Fahndungsblatt für Farbige," *UP*, 1 December 1906, 3.

68. Walter Rodney, "The Political Economy of Colonial Tanganyika 1890–1930," in *Tanzania under Colonial Rule*, ed. M.H.Y. Kaniki (Singapore, 1980), 133–34; Issa Shivji, *Law, State and the Working Class in Tanzania* (London, 1986), 7–8; Helmuth Stoecker, ed., *German Imperialism in Africa* (London, 1986), 110–11; Koponen, *Development*, 339–415; Iliffe, *Modern History*, 151–53.

69. Alexander Bursian, *Die Häuser- und Hüttensteuer in Deutsch-Ostafrika* (Jena, 1910), 10–11, 63.

70. *Landesgesetzgebung*, Verordnung, betreffend die Erhebung einer Häuser- und Hüttensteuer, 22 March 1905, 367; Bursian, *Häuser- und Hüttensteuer*, 19.

71. Giblin, *Politics of Environmental Control*, 124–27.

72. Bursian, *Häuser- und Hüttensteuer*, 64.

73. BAB/R1001/1053, Danker to Imperial Government, 24 January 1901 in Gottberg, *Unyamwesi*, 386.

74. *MMRP* 1/68/2/4/6, Ibrahim Uzengo, Msongozi.

75. *MMRP* 7/68/2/3/6, Mzee Ignas Kapile, Mtama, 5 May 1968.

76. GStA, Nachlass Schnee, File #63, 11 July 1906.

77. Bursian, *Häuser- und Hüttensteuer*, 19; TNA G8/177, District Office Mohoro to Imperial Government, Dar es Salaam, 1 October 1911; *Landesgesetzgebung*, Verordnung, betreffend die Heranziehung der Eingeborenen zu öffentlichen Arbeiten, 22 March 1905, 308.

78. *MMRP* 7/68/2/3/1, Mzee Abdala Undi, Mtama, 24 May 1968.

79. BAB/R1001/5075, Strafbuch Tanga, 111.

80. "Aus Tanga," *DOAZ*, 9 February 1899, 2.

81. "Der Erfolg der Hüttensteuer in Usambara," *DOAZ*, 7 May 1899.

82. *Anzeigen für Tanga* 8, 2, 22 November 1902, 2.

83. Schwarze, *Deutsch-Ost-Afrika*, 22; John Lambert, "From Independence to Rebellion: African Society in Crisis, c. 1880–1910," in *Natal and Zululand from Earliest Times to 1910*, ed. Andrew Duminy and Bill Guest (Pietermaritzburg, 1989), 389.

84. Plantation numbers are difficult to gauge for this time. The *Usambara Post* put the number in Tanga, Pangani, and Wilhelmstal districts at eighty-eight by 1906. "Führer durch Tanganital," *UP*, August 1906, 7–9. To these should be added a handful of estates around Dar es Salaam, Morogoro, and Kilwa. See also Koponen, *Development*, 366–67.

85. "Die Aussichten der Arbeiterbeschaffung für das Plantagengebiet," *UP*, 17 December 1904, 5–6; "Arbeitserziehung und Arbeitszwang," *DOAZ*, 2 June 1906, 1.

86. Selected issues of *Askari* are found in GStA, Nachlass Schnee, File #69.

87. This evidence on Tanzanian workers is derived from GStA, Nachlass Schnee, File #69, *Askari*, December 1906–October 1907. On early South African labor migrants see William Worger, *South Africa's City of Diamonds* (New Haven, 1987), Chapter 2; Patrick Harries, *Work, Culture, and Identity: Migrant Laborers in Mozambique and South Africa, c. 1860–1910* (Portsmouth, 1994), Chapter 6.

88. These included Swahili, Nyamwezi, Zaramo, Nyasa, Zigua, Gogo, Maasai, Nyagatwa, Shambaa, Segeju, Bondei, Digo, and Ngindo.
89. *Askari*, 1 (February 1907).
90. *Kiongozi*, "Watu wanaotafutwa," (December 1906).
91. *Askari*, 1, 5 (May 1907).
92. *Askari*, 1, 6 (June 1907).
93. *Askari*, 1 (September 1907).
94. *Askari*, 1 (September 1907).
95. "Kontraktbruch," *UP*, 10 August 1907, 1–4.
96. Such camaraderie resembled that of Zulu laborers in Natal and nineteenth century caravan porters. Keletso Atkins, *The Moon Is Dead! Give Us Our Money! The Cultural Origins of a Zulu Work Ethic* (Portsmouth, 1993), 122–29; Rockel, "Caravan Porters," 268–70.
97. "Wer trägt den Verlust?" *UP*, 1 September 1906, 1–2.
98. "Zur Arbeiterfrage und Karavanserai," *DOAZ*, 21 January 1905, 2.

4

ENVIRONMENTAL COLLAPSE, HOUSEHOLD DISRUPTION, AND REBELLION IN RUFIJI DISTRICT

At the turn of the century many Tanzanian villagers still managed to avoid full participation in the colonial economy as local and long-distance wage laborers. This was particularly true in regions off the main caravan routes or distant from administrative posts, such as the southern coastal hinterland between Dar es Salaam and Kilwa. However, in the few years before 1905, the colonial administration began a concerted effort to draw men and women outside of plantation regions into market production. In part because of the extensive control over the labor market that long distance migrants and local people of the northeast preserved, colonial officials looked to the south and inland districts for marketable cash crops and forest products. There they demanded that *majumbe* grow cotton or other cash crops in their villages virtually as an obligation to the state, with minimal compensation. As a handful of German settlers trickled into the south and increasingly took up cotton, colonial authorities sought to supply them with labor. Furthermore, by the turn of the century officials sought to exploit the forests for revenue and colonial needs. Toward this end they introduced laws to protect the forests from peasant use by regulating wood procurement, hunting, and field burning. Taken together, the accumulation of burdens greatly encumbered rural society and ushered in deep social and household conflicts.

This chapter examines how labor migration, mandatory cash crop production, and state attempts to reshape peasant farming through conservation affected households and villages after the turn of the century. These policies spawned conflicts between villagers and *majumbe* and between men and women, and shaped peasant responses to the Maji Maji rebellion that broke out late in 1905. Many men increasingly spent months participating in the colonial economy as porters, wage laborers, forced laborers, or refugees, and some left their villages indefinitely. Absent from the rural economy for prolonged periods, men neglected tasks that previously had been their domain, especially hunting and field clearing, leaving these tasks to women, children, and elders. *Majumbe* received orders to grow cash crops, and if labor was not forthcoming for village-level projects, grain stores were simply confiscated as tribute to the state, making rural society vulnerable to famine. Formerly able to respond to the needs of villagers by organizing hunting parties or distributing grain reserves, *majumbe* now were first and foremost expected to collect taxes or muster workers for colonial undertakings. Grain that was once stored now left villages in the form of tax. Labor that once went to secure fields from crop predators now might be employed on railway construction, plantations, or caravans. In 1904 a writer warned that if too much pressure were placed on *majumbe* to collect taxes, rebellion would erupt.[1] This is what happened late in 1905, when many *majumbe* responded to rumors of rebellion south of the Rufiji river.

The geographical focus of this chapter is Rufiji district in the southeastern coastal hinterland, the outbreak site of the Maji Maji rebellion. Rufiji district offers a unique case study for several reasons. It was one of the most important waterways in eastern Africa, with flood regimes that created a privileged, though precarious, farming environment. River flooding made Rufiji region largely inaccessible to concerted colonial control until the turn of the century. While colonial officials targeted the Rufiji delta in the early 1890s as a region of cash crops that included sugar, cotton, tobacco, and sesame, by 1900 they were determined to exploit the river's forest stands for colonial development. Because of the Rufiji's multifaceted production potential, colonialists brought conservationist policies to bear in this region at an early date, creating severe disruptions in household cropping regimes that shaped how villagers responded to the 1905 rebellion. While Rufiji is not representative of other regions of Tanzania, it was

COLONIAL CONSTRAINTS AND ECOLOGICAL CRISIS

For many rural Tanzanians 1905 was a crisis year largely due to wild pig infestations that destroyed food crops. A common pest in East Africa, peasants once dealt with wild pigs by guarding fields at night during the "pig season," and by organizing hunting to clear the bush of pig colonies before crops matured (See FIGURE 4.1). Twenty years after the beginning of colonial rule it appeared that pig infestations were increasing and the ability to control them had ended. Ndundule Mangaya, who lived in the Matumbi hills south of the Rufiji, recalled how difficult it was to deal effectively with wild pigs, especially in the major planting months locally known as *Ntandatu* and *Nchimbi*.[2] It was necessary to call upon women "with very strong hearts" to help men, Manganya remembered. The situation was similar in Uzaramo north of the Rufiji. There, late in 1905, a German missionary reported that many villagers "have given up planting the essential cassava crop because in light of the wild pig plagues the region has become depopulated."[3] Another report from the region concluded, "The wild pig problem in the district is so bad that the district office should intercede energetically."[4] *Akida* Kirumbi wrote to the Pugu forest administrator in May 1905 declining to send people for government forest work because "right now all the people are guarding against pigs."[5] So dire was the situation that district authorities approved a bounty of three rupees for every pig head brought in, the equivalent of one year's hut tax. On the eve of the Maji Maji rebellion, Rufiji district officials allowed a "lively sale of gunpowder" to Africans to combat the region's acute wild pig problem, and waived bans on collective hunting of pigs with nets.[6] One observer went so far as to relate the Maji Maji rebellion directly to the pig plagues, writing "an important factor in the genesis of the uprising that needs special emphasis is the damage caused by wild pigs."[7] A report from 1906 concurred that the ongoing need to fend off wild pigs was a major peasant grievance leading to the rebellion.[8] These reports belie assertions that the 1905 rebellion broke out in a region of Tanzania that was "clearly prospering."[9]

Pigs, of course, were not the only problem for rural Tanzanians on the eve of the rebellion. An array of burdens faced householders, including periodic locust plagues, drought, and famine, all which were exacerbated by colonial demands that included taxes, corvée labor, and

Figure 4.1 A wild pig, one of the most destructive crop pests in German East Africa. Wild pig devastations increased as a result of German conservation and labor policies. (From E. Werth, *Das Deutsch-Ostafrikanische Küstenland* Vol. I [Berlin, 1915], 202.)

the obligation to work on communal fields set up to grow cash crops. Wild pig plagues were a symptom of the breakdown of methods that peasants had once used to control their environment. Jim Giblin has offered a persuasive model of how peasants addressed their myriad environmental problems before colonial rule.[10] In the last half of the nineteenth century, in many regions of Tanzania, rural dwellers established relationships with patrons who held local authority. Some of these relationships were based on long-established kinship and village obligations, and some were more recent. Owing to threats from slave raiders or periodic plundering from militarized societies of the interior, many people became clients of local power holders who offered them protection in exchange for periodic labor obligations and tribute in the form of cattle or grain. Patrons in turn aggrandized power by trading grain and cattle along caravan routes, thereby amassing wealth that they used to acquire more dependents, wives or slaves, whose labor they used in the rural economy.[11] Patrons facilitated "environmental control" by organizing clients to clear and burn bush surrounding villages and fields, which otherwise harbored insects, snakes, and field predators, like antelopes, baboons, and wild pigs. Patrons also organized communal hunting, which made use of nets and traps to kill crop predators before they could devastate fields. Patrons prepared for famine and drought by storing tribute grain to redistribute to clients in times of crisis. Finally, chiefs and other patrons were responsible for "healing the land" by bringing rain and organizing rituals.[12]

Even in societies with no strong ties of patronage, villagers prepared for drought, locusts, crop diseases, and predators through complex systems of crop and field management.[13] Such preparations included using different fields in varied ecological niches, growing many varieties of crops every year, and staggering production throughout the year so that there was always a crop in the field waiting to ripen while harvest was taking place elsewhere. If locusts hit, a temporary famine could be weathered for a few months with grain stores, hunting, or foraging until new crops were harvested.[14] Locusts might hit one field while sparing another. These preparations often rested on the role of village authorities in making the system work by requiring grain and labor tribute for environmental management.

Colonial rule eroded local patronage by undermining the authority of chiefs, headmen, and elders as it drew them into the colonial power structure and made them responsible for placing unrealistic tax, labor, and corvée demands on villagers. Perhaps more importantly, colonialism took men and some women out of the household economy for varying lengths of time, leaving insufficient labor for environmental control. It is not surprising, then, that rural dwellers associated colonial rule with intensified natural disasters, including wild pig plagues.

RUFIJI AGRICULTURAL AND ECOLOGICAL ZONES

Peoples of the Rufiji had diverse origins among Bantu-speaking migrants from the Tanzanian interior. Most immigrant clans followed the many tributaries of the river down to the coast, some claiming traditions of origin as far as the Katanga region of the Congo.[15] Others gravitated from the south and north of the river, forming a complex mix of people.[16] Closely related neighboring peoples included the Zaramo and Ndengereko to the north, the Pogoro on the upper Rufiji, and the Matumbi and Ngindo in the Kilwa hinterland.[17] Lacking a singular linguistic identity and centralized political system, Rufiji people often identified themselves according to location, such as Mohoro town, the Kichi hills, or the Rufiji river itself. The diversity of the Rufiji people reflected the complex ecological matrix of the region.

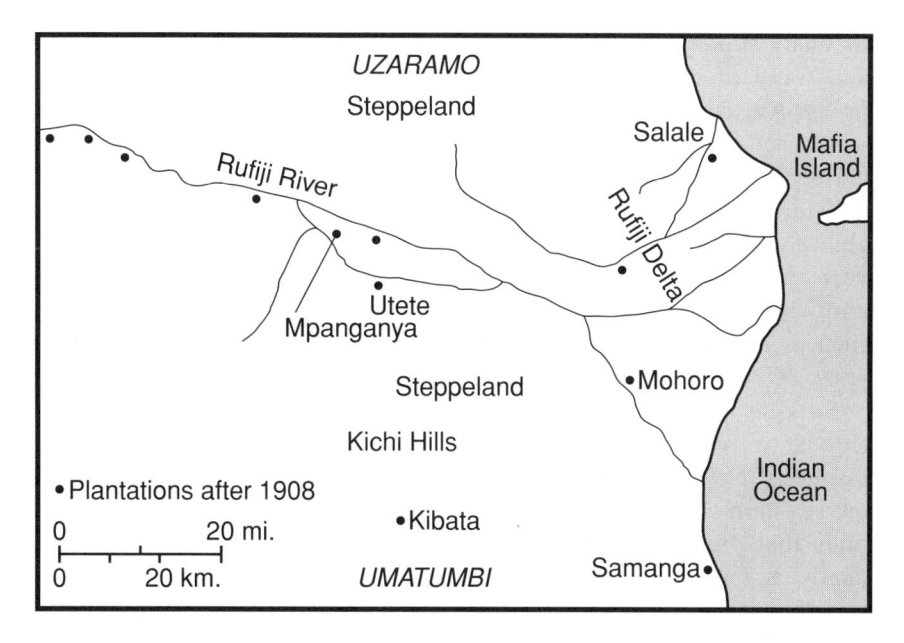

Map 4.1 Rufiji Basin. *Source:* Prepared by L.J.C. Shimoda.

Unlike northeastern plantation districts, Rufiji region was not a place of significant European settlement, with only about six planters scattered between the Rufiji and Kilwa town before 1905 (See MAP 4.1).[18] Although Kilwa district officials founded a trial cotton plantation at Geregere outside of Kilwa in the early 1890s, they concentrated their efforts at cash crop promotion in the Rufiji delta, where Arab, Indian, and Swahili estate owners grew tobacco, sesame, sugarcane, cotton, and rice.[19] Officials furthermore hoped to exploit the dense mangrove forests of the river delta, which had long supplied Indian Ocean traders with timber, poles, and fuel wood. The navigability of the Rufiji river for some 150 km inland gave it a transport advantage over other parts of the colony. The agricultural potential of the wider Rufiji basin also seemed clear. Nineteenth-century travelers described the region as a "land of plenty" that had long been a granary for the Zanzibar commercial economy.[20]

Fed by the rain forests of the Southern Highlands, the Rufiji was a perennial waterway for its entire length, draining an area of some 68,500 square miles.[21] About 200 km from the coast the river formed a fertile alluvial plain about 20 km wide that made Rufiji into a regional breadbasket. The productivity of the region was in large part due to its many ecological zones, including open savanna, wooded hills north and south of the river, and floodlands along the Rufiji and its tributaries. Agriculture in the Kichi and Matumbi hills south of the river was based on bush fallowing, using complex cropping patterns and a variety of landscapes.[22] Hill land was dependent on rainfall for soil moisture for the major staple crops of rice, maize, millet, and sorghum, grown on the *shamba* land that village *majumbe* allocated each year to households in their locales. The southern hills were interspersed with river valleys, where *ngwenda* land allowed for dry season crops such as maize, beans, and sweet potatoes that were important famine reserves.[23]

So central was the river to everyday life that Rufiji people used floods to record significant events, like war, famine, and locust plagues.[24] The river floodlands allowed for exceptional agriculture based on a system called *mlau* cultivation, named after the long March–April rains that preceded flooding.[25] Village elders allocated river land annually according to each household's labor availability, a right that was lost if men were absent too long as porters or labor migrants.[26] Peak flood levels usually occurred in mid-April, after which waters receded over the next few months, leaving behind a layer of loam one to six inches deep that fissured when it dried. Planting began once the ground was dry by lifting the surface crust, poking a hole in the subsoil, depositing seeds, and replacing the crust. *Mlau* planting offered several labor-saving advantages over bush fallowing. All riverside land could be used every year, obviating the need for fallow and annual clearing. Loam deposits provided exceptional fertility while inhibiting weeds. Flood waters enabled a high level of soil moisture independent of rainfall. Villagers balanced *mlau* planting with the *mvuli* short-term rains from about November to January, which provided a second crop season to supplement the major harvests.

The Rufiji delta, formed as the river broke into eight major arms before emptying into the Indian Ocean, made up a third ecological zone. Despite greater soil salinity from ocean tides, delta agriculture was exceptional. Floods were easily absorbed by myriad small rivulets, which lessened their destructive potential while retaining the benefits of silting.[27] The delta flood regime allowed for intensive wet rice, sugarcane, and permanent crops like coconut palms and bananas. In the late nineteenth century a wealthy Muslim elite came to monopolize the best delta lands under the aegis of the Sultan of Zanzibar, relying on the labor of slaves from the Tanzanian interior.[28] Colonial officials quickly coopted this plantation class for cotton and tobacco projects in the 1890s, and appointed some delta planters as *maakida* of the district. With this social base, colonial rulers targeted the delta as the hub of Rufiji agriculture.

Crop mixes were an important part of the Rufiji agrarian economy. Rufiji people favored rice for local consumption and for export, growing some thirty-four varieties in both the *mvuli* and *mlau* seasons to lessen the risk of crop diseases. Some rice varieties favored the inundated land near the river, and others the rain-fed steppe and hill lands.[29] In the 1890s Ziegenhorn reported three rice crops annually when flood regimes were favorable.[30] Rufiji peasants also grew maize, cassava, millet, beans, and sesame that they traded with Indian merchants at Samanga, Kilwa, and Mohoro in exchange for cotton cloth and other imports.[31] The Rufiji people sold surplus grain to caravans that traversed the coast in the late nineteenth century, including slavers forced overland by British efforts to curtail the slave trade on the seas. Although grain was sometimes bartered for cloth, a money economy penetrated the region by at least the late nineteenth century. In 1881, during a period of famine, Rufiji villagers approached the explorer Beardall's party to purchase grain with Maria Teresa dollars.[32] Others purchased food with cloth or money at various market towns along the river.

The varied Rufiji ecological zones and crop mixes offered an important hedge against famine. It was unlikely that in any given year all the available lands would suffer drought or locust plagues. Different crops grown throughout the year meant that disease or pests that damaged one crop might spare another. Established trade networks along the river provided a recourse in case famine occurred in one region. The complexity of the agrarian system and Rufiji peasants' willingness to innovate with crops (such as the historical adoption of cassava, maize, and some Asian rice varieties) helped ensure food security. However, the whole system was based on the availability of sufficient labor throughout the year.

Although flood regimes on balance facilitated Rufiji agriculture, they were frequently destructive.[33] Destructive floods occurred in local memory every twelve to fifteen years, often changing the course of river tributaries and completely inundating once-planted land.[34] Destructive floods ruined *mvuli* crops and delayed *mlau* planting until waters receded. Thereafter it was essential to get a new crop in the ground quickly to make up for lost rice.[35] Writing in the 1930s Barker observed, "After these floods the Rufiji inhabitants do not lament their lost rice but grow bumper crops of maize and cotton in the silt deposit left by the receding waters."[36] Yet this probably underestimates the devastation of floods that continues to this day. The same observer noted, "A few miles up-river there was once an extensive area of cultivation since carried away by floods causing a whole settlement to migrate in search of more alluvial flats for growing their crops."[37] Flooding prevented a permanent, intensive agrarian economy from developing in this region. River tributaries frequently shifted their courses, once-cultivated lands came under water, villages moved, and permanent field use was ruled out.

GENDERED DIMENSIONS OF RESOURCE USE

In an ecologically and ethnically complex region like Rufiji, the lack of detailed sources make it difficult to generalize about how labor was divided between men and women and how gendered labor patterns changed over time. Yet establishing the gender division of labor in the late precolonial period is important in order to understand how changes that accompanied colonialism affected people at the household level, and, in turn, how household changes shaped how people reacted to the Maji Maji rebellion in 1905. Nineteenth-century visitors observed Rufiji men and women working together in the fields, though men were clearly active at other pursuits, including copal digging, occasional porterage, and hunting.[38] These visitors noted that Rufiji men were active farmers, refraining from long ventures as porters so that they could be on hand for the planting season.[39] Men also cleared brush and trees to open up new fields in the hill and steppe lands. Apart from clearing land for new fields, the most important agrarian task for men was arguably the organized hunting of the many predators that posed a threat to crops in the fields. With dense mangrove forests along the river delta and forest parcels in hill and steppe lands that offered refuge to wild pigs and antelopes, it was necessary for men to set traps and construct nets to keep predators from the fields, especially in the seasons when crops were most vulnerable.[40] Hunting also provided a meat supplement to the diet called *kitoweo* that was especially important in a region with little livestock.[41]

Another predominantly male task, bush burning, was important as a means of fertilizing land with ash and preparing non-riverine land for planting while saving labor time clearing new fields. Bush burning furthermore destroyed the habitat of crop predators and insects, such as locusts that frequently caused famine. Locusts laid their eggs in the bush preceding the *mvuli* season, which was the optimum time to burn grass to destroy the larvae.[42]

While Rufiji men cleared fields and protected crops by hunting, women were the principle tillers of the soil and producers of food.[43] Women planted seeds, weeded riverine and hill lands, harvested rice, maize, and millet,

Environmental Collapse, Household Disruption, Rebellion 85

Figure 4.2 A watchtower and system of clappers to guard fields against crop predators in Kilwa district. It was often the job of women to procure construction materials from nearby fields and forests. German forest regulations curtailed such activity. (From Otto Peiper, "Ethnographische Beobachtungen aus dem Bezirke Kilwa," *Baessler-Archiv* 10 [1926], 27.)

and stored and pounded grain. Apart from staple crop lands, women typically had household gardens for beans, onions, and greens. Along the Rufiji river it was necessary for people to expend some time constructing stilted platforms above their huts in anticipation of annual flooding, harvesting mangrove poles from the forests for this task.[44] Women also constructed wooden watch towers and huts to guard the fields from "the frequent invasions of wild pigs and apes" (See FIGURE 4.2).[45] Children often used sling shots and systems of wooden clappers to scare away pests.

While the complex mix of crops and land use increased the labor burden, it helped guarantee food security. Root crops such as cassava and sweet potatoes offered protection from locusts and birds that millet, maize, and rice did not allow. Many of the societies around the Rufiji became more dependent on cassava as a staple during the nineteenth century, reflecting a famine consciousness.[46] Elevated granaries, baskets, and underground grain caches also protected harvested crops in case locusts or pigs destroyed crops in the fields.

Rufiji region was not so abundant in food that it was spared famine. Food shortages were likely whenever rains were deficient, especially at the outset of the planting season before the two major rainy-season crops were ready for harvest. Beardall, traveling in December and January, noted great reluctance on the part of upriver villagers to part with grain during a year of famine.[47] Traders from the coast used annual food shortages to their advantage by purchasing grain cheaply after harvests, then waiting for the days of hunger at the end of the year to sell their stores of grain at five to six times the original price.[48]

Rufiji people had been active for generations in regional trading networks, producing rice and extracting forest products like copal, wax, mangroves, and rubber for export. Managing the forests was important for protecting fields, and as a supplement to the agrarian economy. Many Rufiji people were continuously employed in the forests. Throughout the delta, villages of several hundred people each dotted the river branches.[49] During the rainy seasons, men and women gathered gum copal, the resin from the *msandarusi* tree, for trade to Indian merchants in exchange for cotton textiles, muskets, and gunpowder, before it was ultimately shipped to Europe and North America for varnishes and lacquers.[50] Copal was second only to grain as an exported commodity in the late nineteenth century.[51] Rich in mangrove forests, the delta was also a major supplier of mangrove poles to Zanzibar and Mafia islands to be used as masts and planking for the dhows that carried the Indian Ocean trade, and for construction of Swahili houses and other structures. In the mid 1890s mangroves with a value of about 46,000 Rp were exported to Zanzibar annually, and a further 40,000 Rp worth of wood was used on the coast for construction.[52] In 1899, the first year when Germany kept statistics on Rufiji wood use, almost 7,000 cubic meters of wood intended for *boriti* roofing beams were exported from the delta.[53] Different lengths and girths of mangroves were used for the roof poles of more modest houses, for walls, oars, dhow planking, flooring, and masts. In the same year, 2,516 cubic meters of firewood were exported from the delta. Altogether, 12,000 cubic meters of wood were exported in 1899. This figure is probably low compared with the period of Zanzibar hegemony over Rufiji forests when there were few restrictions on forest access like colonial export tolls. In the 1890s Rufiji delta dwellers could still earn one half to one rupee daily cutting wood—enough to pay a year's hut tax in one week.[54] In this difficult environment men used dugout canoes called *mitumbwi* to navigate myriad rivers to obtain wood and other natural products such as rubber, for which there was a high demand from delta merchants (See FIGURE 4.3).[55] Villagers used money earned from marketing forest products to purchase grain from Rufiji markets

Figure 4.3 *Mitumbwi* dugout canoes on the Rufiji River. Canoes were the chief means of transporting grain, mangroves, and other forest products from upriver to delta markets on the Indian Ocean. (From Rufiji-Baumwoll Syndikat, *Deutsche Rufiji-Baumwollgesellschaft* [1909], 15.)

in times of famine, and to import textiles and other wares when times were good.[56]

Aside from exported wood, Rufiji peasants used forest wood for houses, field watchtowers, and elevated granaries. The region's iron smiths used forest hardwoods for charcoal. Mortars and pestles for grinding grain, household tools, and dugout canoes all came from forest woods. Women went to the forests daily for firewood. Finally, men burned forest stands contiguous to fields seasonally in order to clear away the habitat of wild pigs and other predators. The agrarian economy of Rufiji region was based in large part on the use of the forests as a commons.

COLONIAL ECONOMY, COLONIAL CONSTRAINTS

From the early 1890s, German officials were keen on making Rufiji region part of the colonial economy by urging Arab and Swahili planters of the coast to plant marketable cash crops on their plantations.[57] Since 1891 Germans also sought to exploit the Rufiji forest reserves.[58] Early in the decade the colonial government established a toll station to tax exported woods, and granted a concession to the Rufiji Industrial Corporation to provide lumber to coastal ports. Railway construction in the northeast and as far afield as South Africa, where wood was scarce, created a heavy demand for Rufiji mangroves.[59] The colonial government in 1902 made Rufiji into a separate district (carved out of parts of Dar es Salaam and Kilwa districts) in order to exploit forest stands adjacent to the river more effectively. The new district office segregated forests from agricultural zones, splitting the peasant economy of the region in a way highly detrimental to local production. Along with this split came a series of regulations that encumbered forest and land use, creating deep divisions within households and villages.

German officials treated Rufiji forests as zones to be protected from peasants, not believing that African forest use was a legitimate form of *Allmende*, commons, as existed in German villages.[60] In so doing, they dramatically reshaped African land use. This was seen in the competing ways Africans and Europeans combated locusts. Knowing very little about locusts in Africa, German entomologists believed that they could be fought by planting more trees to increase the habitat of locust eaters, and by extending European-style cultivation (*Kulturland*) "since locusts avoid laying their eggs in well-cultivated, loose soil."[61] In contrast, Africans of Rufiji region used bush firing as a means of destroying locust larvae in the months preceding the *mlau* rains. Colonial rulers viewed bush firing as a primitive and destructive practice and particularly threatening to valuable forest stands that they wished to market. Beginning in 1894 in Rufiji region *maakida* were directed to curtail the "foolish native bush burning" and the "reckless devastation of the forests."[62] District officials ordered *majumbe* to make sure that their people not burn "grasses of fields, the bush, or riverbanks" under threat of a 100 Rp fine, or, for those who could not pay, penal labor at the *boma* "for many months." The wives of anyone who burned a field and ran away had to pay the fine or were subjected to penal labor. The only acceptable burning was to rake grasses and bush into heaps in the center of fields, a method that required much more labor than general field burning. The ban on field burning might have exacerbated the locust plagues that affected the southern parts of the colony in 1894.[63] In that year locusts "radically devoured" the rice crop in Mohoro in February, creating a regional famine. After the turn of the century the colonial forest administration increased their surveillance of field burning, viewing it as an essential feature of forest protection.[64] In 1900 the governor banned general field burning with the justification that "the native method of cultivation by which no fertilizer is used and the fields are changed frequently and carelessly burned . . . is leading to the economic ruin of the colony."[65]

Colonial officials sharply curtailed peasant wood use as the forests emerged in colonial thinking as a major asset for the colony. Already in 1894 a local ordinance required a fee of 5 Rp per year (almost twice the 1898 hut tax) to obtain wood for hut construction, but only if one were endorsed by the village *jumbe* as an "*mtu mzuri*" (reputable person).[66] Disreputable people, on the other hand, perhaps those seeking to sell wood for profit, were denied permits, and their *majumbe* were reproached, fined up to 100 Rp, or sentenced to penal labor if they did not bring forest use under control.[67] Those who reported infractions were rewarded with "*bakshish*." Some districts also employed African wardens to guard forest reserves from illegal use.[68] Dressed in a khaki uniform and red fez with the insignia of the German eagle, wardens (sometimes called "*askari wa bwana miti*") resembled *askari* police and developed a reputation for brutality.[69] Their job was to ensure that "no native clear forest stands for agricultural use or cut wood for personal use without a permit."[70] Though we cannot know how effectively forest laws were enforced, several people appear in the 1897 crime statistics in Bagamoyo for "unauthorized wood cutting," some incurring 10 Rp fines while others received two weeks labor in chains.[71] Forest regulations upset environmental control fundamentally by changing the role of a *jumbe* from that of environmental protector to that of forest warden, by preventing people from bush fallowing, and by taxing people for basic forest use. While free permits were issued to "all Swahili and *washenzi* [heathens]" to collect wood for household cooking, regulations even curtailed this use by demanding that peasants use prescribed cutting sites, often far from their dwellings.[72] *Maakida* demanded bribes for forest permits, sharply curtailing use for those peasants who could not pay. In the last eight months of 1905 in Dar es Salaam district, a region of perhaps 25,000 households, no more than ninety free permits were issued for household forest use.

Colonial regulations sharply curtailed the sale of wood, impairing the ability of Rufiji peasants to cope with food shortages by marketing forest products for cash. Peasants had to pay 1 Rp for every thirty mangrove poles they sold, taking away about one-third of the profit, leading many to give up the practice.[73] Forest wardens stopped people bringing charcoal or wood to Dar es Salaam for sale and confiscated the wood if they did not have a permit. Perhaps because wood access was so intensely regulated, dhow construction on the southern coast sharply declined by 1905, and African housing construction in Dar es Salaam, dependent on Rufiji mangroves, came almost to a standstill. Meanwhile the Schultz beer brewery in Dar es Salaam consumed about 5,000 Rp of Rufiji fuel wood annually.[74]

The most severe result of forest conservation was that it created protected zones for crop predators at a time when hunting was sharply inhibited by colonial laws. This explains the ubiquitous reports of wild pig outbreaks on the eve of Maji Maji. The bounties of 2 to 5 Rp per pig did not outweigh hunting bans.[75] Beginning in 1896 hunting required a license of 5 Rp, and in 1898 colonial authorities expressly prohibited net hunting in an effort to restore game that had been decimated by the Rinderpest epidemics of the 1890s.[76] Villagers could not simply take to the forests or bush to root out predators before they caused damage.[77] The effect was to inhibit protective hunting. In Rufiji district in 1902–03 officials reported:

> the sows have become noticeable in unfortunate ways. Their increase in the last years is enormous, and the damage they cause everywhere in the fields is considerable. Natives report that almost half of their harvests have been destroyed by these beasts.[78]

Wild pigs appear to have proliferated twenty years after German rule began.[79] Pigs recovered faster than other wildlife from the Rinderpest epidemic of the 1890s, and thus were able to take advantage of habitats free of competitors for food resources.[80] Furthermore, European settlers and sportsmen with modern rifles hunted lions and leopards, killing so many of the natural predators of wild pigs that villagers asked that lions not be shot.[81] Hunting laws prevented peasants from using guns to master the wild pig problem. Some Rufiji delta villagers had almost managed to eradicate wild pigs with guns from some areas by the 1890s, when hunting bans and license requirements had not yet taken force.[82]

Although many factors contributed to pig increases, it seems clear, based on peasant complaints, that the reason peasants could not control them was because colonial laws curtailed collective African hunting in the decade preceding the Maji Maji rebellion. *Majumbe* were expected to uphold hunting laws. Jumbe Amiri of Kilwa district for example, received 12 Rp monthly as a game warden.[83] While some *majumbe* organized net hunting north of the Rufiji to deal with wild pigs in spite of the regulations, the "smaller jumbes" hesitated because, as one Zaramo peasant stated, "these days everything is done by order."[84] Jumbe Matamba Safi of Msonga, just north of the Rufiji delta, explained that there had always been pigs in the area, "but in those days we hunted them more than now, when we are afraid to."[85] The government councillor Winterfeld viewed the prohibition on net hunting to be a major grievance of peasants at the time of Maji Maji, writing "after net hunting was abolished the pigs multiplied to critical levels, impairing native production."[86] The state enacted so many prohibitions on hunting that the overall effect was to hamstring an activity that was an integral part of the agrarian economy. Some villages of Rufiji region apparently gave up rice or millet as staple crops in favor of cassava, a root crop, because it afforded marginal protection from pigs and locusts.[87]

COMMUNAL FIELDS AND THE ASSAULT ON PEASANT AGRICULTURE

The assault on bush fallowing, forest use, and hunting was overtaken by colonial demands to produce cash crops and other marketable export products after the turn of the century. By 1902 German policy makers in the Foreign Office and Interior Ministry committed themselves to promoting cash crops in East Africa, with cotton given special priority due to the emerging crisis in the German textile industry.[88] Governor Götzen and his deputy Winterfeld were instrumental in organizing the new campaign, which urged settlers, missionaries, *maakida,* and other Muslim plantation owners near the coast to grow cotton and other cash crops of value to the German market.[89] In some districts, such as Kilwa, Lindi, and Morogoro, German settlers and missionaries took up cotton, aided by the willingness of local authorities to pressure Africans to work on their estates at marginal wages.[90] District *Kommunen* and subdistrict *maakida* oversaw many of the projects and founded their own trial fields, requiring *majumbe* to send their villagers to work.

South of Dar es Salaam officials demanded that all *majumbe* lay out a communal field on which adult men owed some labor during the year.[91] Winterfeld claimed it to be no more than 24 days in the year, or about 2 days of the week during peak agricultural seasons. The reality was that the communal system was an open-ended demand on household labor. The proceeds of the communal fields were divided equally among the Kommune, the *akida* or *jumbe,* and the workers. This meant that a man might receive the equivalent of one day's wage for a month's work, though usually no wage was paid.[92] Because conscripted workers had to journey to communal plots, their own household crops suffered in their absence. For this reason, villagers resisted the communal campaign, some by migrating from the region. A downward spiral of environmental involution was thereby set in motion.

Just north of the Rufiji the cotton campaign dealt a harsh blow to peasants. The 174 villagers under Said Magimbaro managed to produce 25 "loads" of cotton in the first year, but by 1904–05 the cotton was left unpicked in the field for lack of labor, and people supplied rice in its place.[93] Conditions were similar in Msanga village, where *jumbe* Pasi Kitoweo laid out a village field with minimal results. In the first year an 85 Rp profit was divided between Kitoweo and his people, which was at most a few pesas for each household. Thereafter the villagers neglected the cotton, not even bothering to transport twelve harvested loads to the *akida*. Kitoweo stated that his people did not mind paying taxes or building roads, but the communal fields were an unacceptable burden.

The village field system directly attacked bush fallowing. In some regions officials designated land for communal crops that householders used as *kilala* fallow. In Dar es Salaam district "mostly *pori* [bush] was selected."[94] Each year the fields were increased in size as more cotton was added, from 4.5 ha in 1902–03 to 7 ha the following year. Perhaps 25,000 workers per year were engaged on the communal fields in Dar es Salaam district alone. The initial demand of 2 days per week increased to 3–4 days, and "sometimes labor was needed continuously."[95] In addition to communal field work, people still had tax and corvée obligations. The head of the KWK described the village *shamba* system as "an unfortunate state intrusion into the productive life of the natives."[96]

Although officials had long targeted Rufiji as a cotton zone, before 1905 it was overshadowed by rice and mangrove production.[97] Rufiji region had long produced rice surpluses, often supplying much of the colony's needs so that imports from Zanzibar merchants were unnecessary.[98] After 1898 villagers often paid their taxes in rice, severely endangering the region's food supplies. In 1904, for example, some 22,000 Rufiji households paid a total of 66,000 Rp, the equivalent of 4,000 tons of rice or 8,000 tons of maize.[99] During the communal campaign officials requisitioned rice and other food crops from Rufiji peasants whose lands were not suited to cotton growing.

In Rufiji district, officials integrated forest work into the communal crop campaign. In 1902 peasants were prohibited from using the forest as a hedge against famine by marketing forest products—rubber, charcoal, and mangroves—to buy grain. Forest officials furthermore designated some fallow lands and *mlau* flood lands for forest regeneration, taking them out of peasant cropping systems. German officials simply saw much more profit to be made in the commercial exploitation of forests for fuel and construction than as an appendage to the peasant economy.[100] In exploiting the forests, the district office in Mohoro conscripted men to do forest work as a communal obligation. Seldom were "sufficient voluntary workers" available, therefore local *majumbe* had standing orders to force men to do forest work, often at moments when they were needed to hunt wild pigs or clear fields for planting. Tax defaulters and penal laborers were regularly rounded up for forest work for up to three months at a time.[101]

Men's reaction to communal obligations mirrors that of other regions of Tanzania at this time. Rather than work for virtually no pay, and with many of their agrarian tasks made redundant by colonial laws, many men signed on for colonial work on railways, plantations, or as porters, where they would be assured a competitive wage and food rations. Rufiji district officials had ongoing problems mustering labor for any type of work since men disappeared.[102] Women and children were often conscripted in their place. In the Rufiji delta women were put to work winnowing rice for 1 pesa per day plus *posho*—about one-tenth of the going daily wage for a man. The Mohoro district office conscripted tax-defaulters to harvest its maize and sesame fields, paying them 8 pesas per day, wages typical for a hired slave. *Majumbe* sometimes took women hostage until family members paid a ransom to free them.[103]

Before German colonialism it had been fairly typical for local patrons to muster the labor of clients, slaves, and wives for village field production.[104] Although the communal *shamba* system resembled this practice, there were important differences. Precolonial patrons had obligations to their people, which included distributing stored grain for famine relief, and protecting the environment by organizing communal bush burning and hunting. By 1902 the role of rural elites was turned upside down. They could muster labor to grow crops for the state, but colonial laws inhibited them from maintaining environmental control or ensuring food security. If a village failed to produce communal crops, it gave up its famine surplus as its share. This was the case in the village of Said Magimbaro of Undengereko, where about 2,000 pounds of rice were given up in 1904 after the cotton crop failed.[105] Pitted against their people by colonial laws, or otherwise jailed for recalcitrance, many *majumbe* came to resent the colonial system deeply. For this reason many joined the Maji Maji uprising shortly after fighting broke out late in 1905.

By 1904 environmental control had broken down completely. Rice grown on *mlau* land declined in the absence of men's labor, and officials pressured women to grow maize during the *mvuli* season because it germinated more quickly.[106] Rufiji peasants considered maize to be a "wage of famine" because twice as much was needed as rice to pay hut taxes. Furthermore, it was more dependent on bush fallowing that colonial laws circumscribed, and was far less productive than other grains in years of drought. At the same time, production was constrained by pig plagues, locusts, the prevention of grass burning, and the discouragement of fallowing. Due to such depredations, people living near centers of control abandoned their *mashamba* and fled into the bush, where they could hopefully evade colonial obligations. This would be a pattern for years to come.

By 1904 the reputation of many *majumbe* had deteriorated, and they could no longer be counted on to provide people with relief. The colonial state further encumbered people with meaningless regulations that affected their ability to deal with crises, such as a tax on *pombe ya kazi*, work beer, that women brewed to muster people for collective hunting and field work.[107] Officials required permits for *ngoma* dances, inhibiting an activity often used by rural dwellers as a spiritual recourse to famine, drought, or other rural problems. In some localities, including Uzaramo and the Kichi hills, colonial officials attempted to move rural dwellers to caravan roads for better oversight, labor conscription, and tax collecting at a time when people were doing just the opposite, moving away from centers of control so as to evade colonial burdens.[108] *Majumbe* who could not maintain communal fields or supply labor were fined, removed from office, or jailed in chains.

THE 1905 REBELLION IN RUFIJI DISTRICT

In 1905 two movements began in the greater Rufiji region in response to grievances brought about by German colonial policies.[109] One was a resistance movement of *majumbe* and their immediate followers, who sought to reassert the authority that they once had as patrons by attacking sources of grievance, including German settlers, Indian traders, missionaries, government *bomas*, and *maakida*, who were the main instruments of German authority. Throughout southern Tanzania many *majumbe* committed themselves to rebellion by accepting a *maji* water medicine. Soldiers of the uprising also wore blue cloth, millet stalks, or other shrubbery on their foreheads to distinguish themselves from villagers who did not participate in the uprising. Like hunting and war talismans used throughout Tanzania for generations, some participants believed the *maji* water would provide immunity from bullets, spears, and arrows if certain taboos were upheld, such as abstinence from sex.[110] Germans in particular were obsessed with the rebels' ritual use of water, and, perhaps with the recent Chinese Boxer rebellion in mind, christened the conflict the Maji Maji uprising.[111]

The second movement was an attempt by Rufiji peasants, mainly women, to reverse the breakdown of the rural environment by seeking *madawa* medicines to protect their fields. Women throughout the region had long used medicines, rituals, and talismans to protect their fields from drought and crop predators, especially in years of crisis. Typically this *dawa* took the form of water mixed with ash or grain, which was then sprinkled on fields.[112] Women and other villagers searching for *dawa* were not interested in warfare, which would lead to famine and further devastation. Although some German observers understood the distinction between the *majumbe* uprising and women's quest for field protection, most German accounts tended to conflate the two, highlighting the use of water and playing down colonial economic and environmental policies that created involution.

Most telling that a crisis was besetting rural society by 1905 were the journeys of Rufiji villagers seeking *madawa*. One destination was the Rufiji town of Mtondo, where "men and women, young and old, from Samanga, Kikale, Ndundu and many other places in the delta and on the coast" sought out an ash-and-water medicine to protect their crops from wild pigs and birds.[113] The treks were very public, with people even passing through the district headquarters at Mohoro, belying the later claim that these journeys were a covert preparation for war.[114] The Mtondo *dawa* was distributed by an old Matumbi woman for a fee of 2 pesas.[115] The *jumbe* at Mtondo, a German appointee, presided over the distribution of *dawa* and *pombe* beer, fulfilling his role as a local patron. When the event was reported to the Mohoro district officer, he believed it to be an unremarkable, mundane occurrence. Other Rufiji peasants trekked inland to the town of Mpanga on the upper Rufiji, where they received *dawa* from a Pogoro spirit medium, who claimed it would ensure a good harvest and offer protection from wild animals, including the leopards and lions that had become such a problem owing to male migration and hunting proscriptions.[116]

North of the Rufiji, as famine struck Uzaramo region in 1904, Zaramo women turned to the regional Koleo religious cult, which, they believed, protected fields from locusts, wild pigs, and other predators.[117] The appeals to Koleo were the strongest indicator of an agricultural crisis, since, as one informant stated, "When the crops thrive, the Zaramo don't think about Koleo."[118] Colonial officials and modern historians, misreading the evidence, tried to establish a causal link between the Koleo cult and the uprising.[119]

On the eve of the rebellion a gulf existed between *majumbe* and rural householders who considered village elites to be responsible for enforcement of colonial policies. Jumbe Said Magimbara explained, "the people told us that [we] jumbes were oppressing them with the work on village *mashamba*. We replied, 'that's the order of the district office,' and they said 'but you are the jumbes'."[120] *Majumbe* were clearly losing their local authority as they enforced colonial laws. This was perhaps best stated by a Hehe *jumbe* at the time of the rebellion, who, years later, recalled:

> Some jumbes were not on friendly terms with their people because they were cruel. I myself was not very much liked, probably because I was very young. For mere drunkenness people suffered corporal punishment. These jumbes were very subservient to the German administrators. We were not very popular with our people.[121]

Writing in 1937, Ali bin Abdallah Muhape remembered the time before the rebellion as one of famine, when chiefs extorted grain, cooking oil, and salt from rural dwellers by taking men hostage until women ransomed them with food, money, or even slaves.[122] Those who could not pay were subjected to severe beatings, were bound and forced to carry heavy loads or do forest work.

As *majumbe* became instruments of colonial policy, women and other householders began to reject their authority. Left behind in a deteriorating environment, women shifted production to manageable levels by opening up fields in less accessible bush where they could avoid intense colonial control.[123] Reports of people moving away from centers of control to open up new *mashamba* and descriptions of "remnants of villages and devastated fields" preceding the rebellion attest to this movement.[124] One observer described these migrations as a cause of deep dissatisfaction among *majumbe* as German policies eroded their "patriarchal discipline" and they began to lose "the strong hand over the women."[125] Reference to the "loosened morals" of women on the eve of the rebellion, to *jumbe* prosecutions of women for adultery and witchcraft, and memories of women as betrayers of rebel *majumbe* during the uprising suggest that women were at loggerheads with them.[126] Other gendered disputes were becoming rife at this time. As men joined the wage labor nexus, often through compulsion, they neglected their roles in rural society—hunting, clearing new fields, and paying taxes. Households began to break up as men left for extended periods. Reports of women guarding the fields from pigs, and even guarding settlements from lions, suggest that gender roles were in flux, and women were assuming the established roles of men in rural society.[127]

Because peasants rejected colonial demands in increasingly overt ways, *majumbe* were themselves whipped or jailed. Under these circumstances—losing influence among their people, unable to maintain patriarchal authority, beaten and jailed by colonial authorities—many *majumbe* of Rufiji region sought to reclaim their past prestige by confronting the colonial state. Some began to ignore colonial regulations and neglect communal cotton fields.[128] Others sponsored *ngoma* rituals, such as the *jumbe* of Mfullu village north of the Rufiji in early 1905, at a time when drought threatened that year's crop.[129] The *jumbe* of Mtondo village, noted above, sponsored an *ngoma* to distribute *dawa* to protect fields.[130] Most dramatically, when fighting broke out in the Matumbi hills in July 1905, many *majumbe* throughout southern Tanzania took up arms against the German administration and their representatives. Some, such as Kibassira of southern Uzaramo, went almost directly from jail to rebellion.[131] Although most *majumbe* stayed out of the war, many joined in order to reverse the erosion of their control over rural society. Germans who investigated the cause of the uprising recognized this when they pronounced the war in Rufiji region to be a "*jumbenkrieg*," a war of *majumbe*.[132]

The uprising was sparked in mid-July 1905 near the town of Kibata, about thirty miles south of the Rufiji, when the *akida* Sefu bin Amri demanded that a local *jumbe* supply porters for a caravan to Mahenge.[133] When none were forthcoming, the son of the *jumbe* was whipped, and the *jumbe* organized an attack on the *akida*, who then called for German assistance. In the next few weeks rebellious *majumbe* organized attacks on several German cotton plantations scattered in the Matumbi foothills and at Samanga on the coast. The conflict quickly spread to regions where German control was weak, such as the Matumbi hills, the upper Rufiji river, and Donde, where the Liwale military post was attacked and destroyed. Because not all *majumbe* joined the rebels, a "loyalty oath" was required of participants, often forcibly extracted, which took the form of buying *maji* for 2 pesas.[134] In some cases emissaries fanned out to bring *maji* to localities, and in other cases *majumbe* heard rumors of the uprising and sent representatives to collect *maji*.[135] In this way the rebellion became a widely dispersed movement, a grassfire spreading piecemeal throughout the greater Rufiji basin and in the south and southwest of the colony, with a few reports of battles in the north of the colony.[136] Pasi Kitoweo of Uzaramo related how the rebellion came to his village. After Matumbi emissaries brought rumors of war, one villager, Machinga, joined the movement, and demanded that other villagers pay 2 pesas to receive "medicine against the Europeans."[137] Although Pasi Kitoweo said he did not participate in the war because he had syphilis, he also refused to pay 2 pesas for the water, as did many of his people. Said Bai Magimbara of Kihamba village told a similar story. One of his people, Paasi, brought *maji* from Jumbe Kibassira, demanding 2 pesas per person. Magimbara himself was afraid and hid to avoid fighting. It is clear from African testimony and European observations that the rebellion was not a general uprising of rural dwellers, nor could it be, since rural society had been so disrupted by 1905 that men were often far away as wage laborers, and women were preoccupied with maintaining food production under difficult circumstances.[138]

Along the Rufiji river the rebellion was strongest outside the district center at Mohoro, where after the first few weeks of August life went on as normal. Germans reported more than four thousand rebels between Kilwa and Mohoro in early August 1905, and on August 7 German forces engaged four hundred fighters two hours southwest of Mohoro.[139] Germans believed that some five thousand rebels in the Matumbi and Kichi hills were armed with firearms, mostly muskets.[140] On August 25 Germans attacked a troop of some one thousand African opponents about seventy-five km inland on the north bank of the Rufiji.[141] Half of the rebels were armed with firearms, and some seventy-three were killed, many drowning while crossing the Rufiji to escape German forces. At about the same time German forces confronted one thousand "organized rebels" three hours west of Kilwa.[142] Rebels repeatedly cut the telegraph line between Kilwa and Dar es Salaam, and sometimes managed to capture modern rifles.[143] Zaramo and Dengereko rebels flying a black flag attacked the coastal town of Kissiju in October.[144] By November German forces brought most rebel districts around the Rufiji under control even as the war spread south to Lindi district, west to Kilosa on the central caravan route, and to the southwestern highlands, preoccupying German forces for the next year.

Germans desperately sought to uncover a leadership structure for the uprising, at various times believing it to be the brainchild of African "Ethiopian" Christians, Indian traders, Muslim *walimu* or brotherhoods, former *maakida*, or even former *askari*, since some rebel forces exhibited a military-style organization.[145] The Kilwa district office took eleven Indian traders into custody and imprisoned them for several years for selling gunpowder to Africans at the onset of the rebellion.[146] Within weeks of the outbreak of rebellion the official consensus, as propagated by Governor Götzen, was that the uprising stemmed from a conspiracy of "witch doctors" in conjunction with disaffected *majumbe*. Götzen telegraphed the Colonial Office as early as August 10 that the cause of the uprising was "apparently sorcery and copious beer drinking following a good harvest."[147] Even before this conclusion was reached, in early August 1905 several Rufiji spirit mediums were rounded up, charged with inciting the rebellion, and summarily hanged.[148] While *waganga* mediums doubtless supplied *maji* for war protection, Germans viewed even those providing *dawa* to protect fields as complicit in the rebellion. More level-headed observers, including members of the commission sent to investigate the causes of the uprising, dismissed the centrality of spirit mediums, and focused on forced labor, pig plagues, and forest and hunting laws as the main factors feeding rural discontent and *majumbe* rebellion.[149]

REFUGEES AND RURAL BREAKDOWN

In the greater Rufiji region Germans ended the war by late 1905 using scorched earth tactics, summary executions of participants, and labor indemnities from rebellious villages.[150] In so doing, they exacerbated the environmental calamities that had set the rebellion in motion by depriving rural society of manpower to grow crops and protect fields, setting in motion patterns of refugee movement that lasted for years. Germans forcibly conscripted villagers as porters during the war, and burned the huts of people who didn't aid the war effort. This was the case near Kisserawe in Uzaramo, for example, where villagers failed to turn up to carry provisions for a German captain because they were preparing fields for the rainy season.[151] In December 1905 German forces conscripted 1,000 Rufiji people to harvest grain in the rebellious Kichi hills to provide rations for German soldiers and porters.[152] In this way Kichi people were starved into submission, and villages in regions of fighting were often completely destroyed by German troops (See FIGURE 4.4). Even people who did not actively support the rebellion were terrorized into fleeing into the bush.[153] Although Germans recognized that not all people within districts of rebellion participated in the uprising, they nevertheless considered it important to exact punishment on villagers so as to preserve "a permanent memory of their subjugation."[154] In whole regions of the uprising all weapons—firearms, bows, arrows, and spears—were requisitioned, making hunting virtually impossible for the foreseeable future.[155] Iron smiths, who often were spirit mediums, were imprisoned and their forges dismantled, affecting people's ability to farm.[156] Along footpaths and roads, *askari* burned fields to prevent potential rebel

Figure 4.4 Captured Maji Maji chiefs from Songea district. From *Missions-Blaetter* 10, 9 [June, 1906] 130.)

attacks.[157] Meanwhile, German forces conscripted prisoners from the jails of Dar es Salaam, Kilwa, and Lindi as porters alongside some 1,500 local Rufiji people.[158]

In reasserting control over localities of the uprising, German officials demanded a war indemnity of 3 Rp each from all men in areas of rebellion "as a symbol of submission."[159] In 1906 Paasche and his party collected a war indemnity of twelve boxes of copper and silver coins from Rufiji villagers worth several thousand rupees.[160] Those who could not pay the indemnity were put to work on district and private plantations. Colonial officials required areas of rebellion to give up large contingents of men to work as penal laborers for three to six months as a war indemnity. The result was a great household labor shortage in regions of the south and the continued breakdown of rural society. Already strained relations between men and women were exacerbated, and marriages broke up as some men left their homes to find work elsewhere or deserted their families for the duration of wartime famines.[161] Women and children abandoned cultivated fields and resorted to foraging, since German forces confiscated harvests to reward loyalists and to punish suspected participants.[162]

During the war German policy was to use famine as a means to get people to work for a wage. On one occasion Rufiji villagers emerged from the bush and approached German forces.[163] Showing certificates proving that they had paid their war indemnity, they asked if they could have seed corn to begin cultivating their fields again. In response, the German commander told them to go to the *boma* for work if they wanted seed. A great inflation in food prices marked the aftermath of the war so that, even in localities where crops could be grown, the price was so high that people had to work for a wage to buy food.[164] Many Rufiji people journeyed north to Uzaramo to purchase cassava, since, by 1906, the people there were allowed to cultivate their fields and the rains were good.[165]

Even as the war spread to other regions, as early as 1906 in the Rufiji-Kilwa region Germans sought a return to normalcy. When in 1906 the rebellious *jumbe* Said bin Pembe of Donde appeared in Kilwa requesting peace, the district officer agreed to pay him a gratuity of 20 Rp and put him in charge of Liwale with Governor Götzen's reluctant approval.[166] Worried that the loss of people fleeing north to Uzaramo as refugees threatened to destroy the emergent forest and cotton industries of the region, the Rufiji district officer allocated 5,000 Rp for food reserves and seed corn, and another 7,000 Rp to purchase grain to sell to peasants at cost.[167] By the end of the year German authority had once again been reasserted, as suggested by African children playing war games in which some played the role of rebels and others the role of German *askari*.[168] However, a return to normalcy would not take place for the foreseeable future.

The rebellion was a time of great transition in southern Tanzania. Government officials estimated the total number of dead through warfare or war-induced famine in the colony at 75,000, while their critics put the figure at 200,000.[169] Children and old women in particular died in great numbers as a result of the famines that accompanied the uprising. The Rufiji district officer abandoned the demand to conscript one man for every four huts for penal labor because "the inhabitants are almost completely undernourished and are not suited for effective work."[170] At any rate, few men were around, most having scattered in search of food until their wives were able to bring in a crop.

With men absent from regions of rebellion owing to death, penal labor, or migration, insufficient labor was available for regular planting, and environmental control broke down completely. Unable to cultivate fields while guarding against crop predators, women abandoned established agricultural patterns. The trend was for women to de-intensify agriculture by keeping fields small, by depending on simpler crop mixes that required less labor, and by resorting to labor-saving crops, especially cassava. Women increasingly sought to avoid control by German officials and African elites by opening up new fields in inaccessible bush and forest. The District Officer Grass, touring Rufiji region the year after the uprising, complained that the people "don't lay their houses out so that they can be seen when one walks past, rather as much as possible isolate them unseen in the dense bush, each at a respectful distance apart."[171] Such concealment enabled villagers to avoid forced provisioning of government caravans that passed through. Hundreds of refugees remained in the "cassava regions" of Dar es Salaam and Morogoro districts for years after the war. Some villages shrank to a fraction of their former size, and others, especially those along caravan routes, were abandoned completely.

As bush encroached on formerly cultivated acreage, wild pig plagues continued unabated, and, in light of massive depopulation, probably increased.[172] Some Rufiji people continued to live in southwest Uzaramo in 1907 "because Rufiji district is feared because of famine and pigs, which people of the southern border regions speak of in one breath."[173] In 1908 around Kisserawe in Dar es Salaam district, in a region that generally did not participate in the uprising, missionaries described a state of agricultural collapse in the years following the uprising:

> The reason for the continuous calamity lies for the most part in the wild pig plagues. People plant cassava . . . and once it begins growing the wild pigs arrive and root up the field. People must guard the fields every night in order to drive them away, but it is to no avail, since the pigs run all around. . . . People tire of the constant guarding and abandon the fields.[174]

Two years after the rebellion, this was a description much like those that preceded the uprising.

In the war's aftermath, with men away working for a wage, women recognized a palpable and seemingly permanent shift in rural relations. Men had apparently abandoned rural production, and, with the defeat of the rebellion, the colonial state sought to coopt remaining *majumbe* fully by cracking down on any sign of recalcitrance. Any vestige of environmental control was left to women under circumstances in which controlling the environment by established gender divisions was impossible. Like women elsewhere in Africa undergoing a period of uncertainty and cataclysmic transition, women of southern Tanzania resorted to spirit possession and *ngoma* ritual to redress rural imbalances.[175] One description from 1907 is especially telling of the changes taking place. Near Kisserawe in Uzaramo, women dressed as men, brandishing muskets, performed an *ngoma* in which they danced around a well and appealed to "their god" to bring rain to ameliorate the droughts that had beset the region.[176] The adoption of male dress and weaponry suggests women's conscious appropriation of established male roles in rural society, especially those related to protecting fields through hunting. Increasingly hunting and field protection was a task for women due to ruptures created by the colonial economy. As women assumed male roles in rural society, and as men left for labor, divorce became more frequent, marriages were delayed, births declined, and generally women were viewed by colonial officials, *majumbe*, and other men as becoming unruly. The scapegoating and even criminalization of women would become an ongoing feature of colonial society in the last decade of German rule. For their part, women increasingly viewed men as abandoning their roles as husbands, fathers, and protectors of rural society. As the wage labor nexus came to full fruition following the rebellion, such household tensions would become more pronounced.

NOTES

1. "Lokales," *UP*, 24 December 1904, 2.
2. Gilbert Gwassa and John Iliffe, eds., *Records of the Maji Maji Rising* (Dar es Salaam, 1967), 4.
3. Berliner Missionswerk, Kisserawe Tagebuch, III Quartal 1905.
4. BAB/R1001/726, Booth report, 16 January 1906, 132a.
5. TNA G35/1, Forst-Angelegenheiten, Akida Kirumbi bin Kirumbi to Reich, 11 May 1905.
6. Otto Stollowsky, "On the Background to the Rebellion in German East Africa in 1905–1906," *IJAHS* 21, 4 (1988), 683; GStA, Nachlass Schnee, File #62, "An alle Akiden," German and Swahili texts, no date.
7. BAB/R1001/726, Schultz and Booth report, 11 December 1905, 105b.
8. BAB/R1001/726, Haber report, 9 September 1906, 85b.
9. John Iliffe, *A Modern History of Tanganyika* (Cambridge, 1979), 130.
10. James Giblin, *The Politics of Environmental Control in Northeastern Tanzania, 1840–1940* (Philadelphia, 1992); "The Precolonial Politics of Disease Control in the Lowlands of Northeastern Tanzania," in *Custodians of the Land: Ecology and Culture in the History of Tanzania,* ed. Gregory Maddox, James Giblin, and Isaria N. Kimambo (London, 1996), 127–51. See also Helge Kjekshus, *Ecology Control*

and Economic Development in East African History: The Case of Tanganyika 1850–1950 (London, 1996).

11. On the role of tribute labor in rural society see Steven Feierman, *Peasant Intellectuals: Anthropology and History in Tanzania* (Madison, 1990), Chapter 2.

12. Feierman, *Peasant Intellectuals*, Chapter 4.

13. J.K. Robertson, "Mixed or Multiple Cropping in Native Agriculture Practice," *East African Agricultural Journal* (April, 1941), 228–31; H.F.v. Behr, "Die Völker zwischen Rufiyi und Rovuma," *MaddS* 6 (1893), 78.

14. A.R.W. Crosse-Upcott, "Ngindo Famine Subsistence," *TNR* 50 (1950), 1–20.

15. Tanganyika District Books (TDB), Morogoro Province, Rufiji District Book, "Warufiji Tribal History and Legends."

16. William Beardall, "Exploration of the Rufiji River under the orders of the Sultan of Zanzibar," *Proceedings of the Royal Geographical Society* 11 (November 1881), 647.

17. Beardall, "Exploration," 642, 647; Gilbert Gwassa "The Outbreak and Development of the Maji Maji War, 1905–1907," (Ph.D. diss., University of Dar es Salaam, 1973), 43–46.

18. "Nachweisung über die in Deutsch-Ostafrika vorhandenen Privat-Pflanzungen," *BLF* 3, 2 (1907), 41–42; "Selbständige Ansiedler," *Kolonial-Handels-Adressbuch* (1911), 72.

19. Germans designated Rufiji region early on as a cotton zone. BAB/R1001/8179, von Katte report, 18 August 1901, 27–29.

20. F. Elton, "On the Coast Country of East Africa, South of Zanzibar," *Journal of the Royal Geographical Society* 44 (1874), 243; Beardall, "Exploration," 642, 646.

21. The following description of the Rufiji draws on A.H. Savile, "A Study of Recent Alterations in the Flood Regimes of Three Important Rivers in Tanganyika," *EAAJ* (October, 1945), 69–74; L.A. Lewis and L. Berry, *African Environments and Resources* (Boston, 1988), 136–38; R. de la B. Barker, "The Rufiji River," *TNR* (1936), 14; "Der Rufiji," *DOAZ*, 26 April 1911, 1.

22. TDB MF-977 "Land Tenure in the Matumbi Tribal Area," Kilwa District Books; H. Gillman, "Bush Fallowing on the Makonde Plateau," *TNR* 19 (1945), 34–44.

23. TDB, Eastern Province, Rufiji and Mafia District Books, "Land Tenure in the Matumbi Tribal Area."

24. Binti Mohamedi in Marja-Liisa Swantz, *Women in Development: A Creative Role Denied?* (London, 1985), 33; TDB, Eastern Province, Morogoro District, "Rufiji River Floods."

25. *Mlau* agriculture has been discussed in the following: Kjell J. Havnevik, *Tanzania: The Limits to Development from Above* (Motala, 1993), 83, 95; TDB, Eastern Province, Vol. IV, Rufiji and Mafia District Books, "Rufiji River Floods"; B. Muhema, "The Impact of Flooding in Rufiji," *Journal of the Geographical Association of Tanzania* 7 (September 1972), 49–64; H. Marsland, "Mlau Cultivation in the Rufiji Valley," *TNR* 5 (April, 1938), 56–59. Marsland wrote "Mlau has been practiced at least as long as the present elders can remember. . . ."

26. Rufiji land has been held communally in modern times. Havnevik, *Tanzania*, 119.

27. Havnevik, *Tanzania*, 85–86.

28. Ziegenhorn, "Das Rufiyi-Delta," *MaddS* 9 (1886), 78–85; Hermann Paasche, *Deutsch-Ostafrika—Wirtschaftliche Studien* (Hamburg, 1913), 115–21.

29. K. Braun, "Der Reis in Deutsch-Ostafrika," *BLF* 3, 4 (1908), 190–94; BAB/R1001/7908, Reis in Deutsch-Ostafrika; Ziegenhorn, "Rufiyi-Delta," 78–85.

30. Ziegenhorn, "Rufiyi-Delta," 82–83.

31. Elton, "On the Coast," 232; Havnevik, *Tanzania*, 68.

32. Beardall, "Exploration," 656.

33. TDB, Morogoro Province, "Rufiji River Floods"; Havnevik, *Tanzania*, 79.

34. More frequent floods were not caused by increased rainfall, but by increased run-off from regions upriver. Savile, "Recent Alterations," 70–71.

35. TDB "Rufiji River Floods," Rufiji and Mafia District Books.

36. R. de la B. Barker, "The Rufiji River," *TNR* (1936), 14.

37. Barker, "The Rufiji," 15; Prüssing, "Ueber das Rufiji-Delta," *MaddS* 14 (1901), 110.

38. Elton, "On the Coast," 249; Beardall, "Exploration," 649.

39. Elton, "On the Coast," 249; Beardall, "Exploration," 649, 653. Beardall's observations from 1881 could have been affected by the widespread famine that hit the regions that year, exacerbated by Mahenge raids from the west.

40. K. Grass, "Forststatistik für die Waldungen des Rufiyideltas," *BLF* 2 (1904–06), 193; Ziegenhorn, "Rufiyi-Delta," 79–80; Paasche, *Deutsch-Ostafrika*, 129–30.

41. Cattle were scarce in Rufiji region owing to the presence of tsetse. Kjekshus, *Ecology Control*, 164.

42. "Auszüge aus den Berichten der Bezirksämter," *BLF*, 1 (1903), 246; "Zur Abwehr der Wanderheuschrecken," *DKB* 17 (1906), 678.

43. Beardall, "Exploration," 649; Swantz, *Women in Development*, 26–27, 37; Gwassa, "The Outbreak," 451–58, 535–38; "Bezirksamt Rufiji," *BLF* 1 (1903), 244–48; E. Werth, *Das Deutsch-Ostafrikanische Küstenland*, 2 Vols. (Berlin, 1915), 59–60; Ziegenhorn, "Das Rufiyi-Delta," 80–83.

44. Beardall, "Exploration," 646.

45. A description of such towers in Kilwa region are found in Otto Peiper, "Ethnographische Beobachtungen aus dem Bezirke Kilwa, Deutsch-Ostafrika," *Baessler-Archiv* 10 (1926), 24–27. For depictions of other traps and snares used in southern Tanzania see Karl Weule, *Native Life in East Africa* (Chicago, 1969), 91–100.

46. Franz Stuhlmann, "Forschungsreisen in Usaramo," *MaddS* 8 (1894), 230–31.

47. Beardall, "Exploration," 642, 648.

48. Beardall, "Exploration," 644.

49. Ziegenhorn, "Rufiyi-Delta," 78–81.

50. Agents of the Sultan of Zanzibar had a monopoly on the export trade of copal from the coast. Abdul Sheriff, *Slaves, Spices and Ivory in Zanzibar* (Athens, OH, 1987), 119–27.

51. Elton noted that a few men armed with muskets guarded copal diggers. However it was likely that guards were also protecting people from slave traders, who

frequented the coast after trade in slave by sea was curtailed by the 1873 treaty. Elton, "On the Coast," 228, 244, 249; Sheriff, *Slaves, Spices and Ivory*, 223–38; Beardall, "Exploration," 645, 656.

52. Ziegenhorn, "Rufiyi-Delta," 85. See also Erik O. Gilbert, "The Zanzibar Dhow Trade: An Informal Economy on the East African Coast, 1860–1964," (Ph.D. diss., Boston University, 1997).

53. Grass, "Forststatistik," 195.

54. Ziegenhorn, "Rufiyi-Delta," 80. Two *korija* (40 lengths) could pay a year's hut tax, while one *korija* of *boriti* for roof construction brought in 6–8 Rp, double to triple a year's hut tax. Grass, "Forststatistik," 187–92.

55. Prüssing, "Ueber das Rufiyi-Delta," 106–13.

56. Beardall, "Exploration," 644.

57. TNA G8/19, Abgabe Baumwollsaat; F.v. Eberstein, "Ueber die Rechtsanschauungen der Küstenbewohner des Bezirkes Kilwa," *MaddS* 9 (1896), 170–83.

58. In 1888 the *DOAG* concession company assumed rights to the Rufiji forests, but transferred those right to the Colonial Government in 1894. The Sultan of Zanzibar, who maintained rights to Rufiji forest woods during German rule, was allowed to export 100 *korija* of wood per month for a nominal fee. Grass, "Forststatistik," 167–73. See also Hans Schabel, "Tanganyika Forestry under German Colonial Administration, 1891–1919," *Forest and Conservation History* (July, 1990), 130–41.

59. Paasche, *Deutsch-Ostafrika*, 164.

60. The argument was that Africans opened use of forests, fields, and pastures to outsiders, ruling out a sense of communal proprietorship. *Allmende* derives from *Allgemein*, "was alle gemein ist." T. Siebenlist, *Forstwirtschaft in Deutsch-Ostafrika* (Berlin, 1914), 56–57. On German forest polices in Usambara see also Christopher Conte, "Nature Reorganized: Ecological History in the Plateau Forests of the West Usambara Mountains, 1850–1935," in *Custodians of the Land*, ed. Maddox et al., 108–10.

61. L. Sander, *Die geographische Verbreitung einiger tierischer Schädlinge unserer kolonialen Landwirtschaft und die Bedingungen ihres Vorkommens* (Frankfurt a.M., 1903), 41–42.

62. The following is based on TNA G8/19, Abgabe Baumwollsaat, document in Swahili, 1581/94, 60–61. Forest protection laws are found in: TNA G8/508, Forstverordnungen, 12 December 1893, 12–14; *Landesgesetzgebung*, "Forstwirtschaft," 587–92; Siebenlist, *Forstwirtschaft*; BAB/R1001/726, Foreign Office to Götzen, 17 February 1906, 72a; Vincenti and Haber report, 17 January 1906, 111b; Paasche, *Deutsch-Ostafrika*, 384; Werth, *Küstenland*, 191–92.

63. Reports on the southern locust plagues are found in TNA G8/19, Schroeder report, 28 February 1894, 32–33; 17 March 1894, 34–35; 16 May 1894, 71.

64. TNA G8/508, Forstverordnungen, Götzen memo, 20 May 1903, 8.

65. TNA G8/508, Runderlass an alle Bezirksämter, 13 January 1900, 44.

66. TNA G8/19, Swahili document 1581/94 (1894), 60–61.

67. TNA G1/17, Mohoro Verwaltungs-Angelegenheiten, Spieth report, 1 June 1899.

68. Siebenlist, *Forstwirtschaft*, 2–3.

69. BAB/R1001/726, Report by Vincenti and Haber, 17 January 1906, 111; report by Roeder, Booth, Vincenti, Haber, 21 September 1905, 120–21; GStA, Nachlass Schnee, File #62, "Tangazo."

70. Grass, "Forststatistik," 192.

71. BAB/R1001/5075, Strafverzeichnisse Bagamoyo, 118, 122.

72. BAB/R1001/726, Report by Michels, Booth, Vincenti, Haber, 21 December 1905, 120a–b; Grass, "Forststatistik," 193.

73. In 1902 thirty *mapao* poles used for roof supports brought in 3 Rp, but the permit cost 1 Rp (100 heller). Grass, "Forststatistik"; BAB/R1001/726, Report by Schultz, Booth, Vincenti, Haber, 23 December 1905, 121–22.

74. TNA G8/884, Rufiji Forstverwaltung, 17 January 1909.

75. By 1905 people claimed 250 Rp of bounty for 125 pig heads brought to DSM district authorities. BAB/R1001/726, Report by Westhaus, Booth, Vincenti, Haber, 21 December 1905, 122b.

76. BAB/R1001/724, "Denkschrift," 33b; Juhani Koponen, *Development for Exploitation* (Hamburg, 1995), 536–37; Ulrike Wanitzek and Harald Sippel, "Land Rights in Conservation Areas in Tanzania," *GeoJournal* 46 (1998), 114–15. Though Wanitzek and Sippel are skeptical that early hunting proscriptions were enforced, reports from the German era are clear that they were. BAB/R1001/726, Michels et al., 120; Sadi wadi Chande Mkweju received two months in chains for violating the hunting ordinance. BAB/R1001/5075, Strafverzeichnis Kilwa, 28 December 1896, 87.

77. Grass, "Forststatistik," 193; BAB/R1001/726, Booth report, 132.

78. "Auszüge," *BLF* 2 (1904–06), 57.

79. Elton noticed very few wild pigs in his journey down the coast in 1874. "On the Coast," 245.

80. Iliffe, *Modern History*, 165; Giblin, *Politics of Environmental Control*, 130.

81. Schwarze, *Deutsch-Ost-Afrika*, 35, 44; Hans Paasche, *Im Morgenlicht: Kriegs- Jagd- und Reise-Erlebnisse in Ostafrika* (Berlin, 1907), 48.

82. Ziegenhorn, "Rufiyi-Delta," 80.

83. TNA G3/70, District Office Kilwa to Imperial Government, 12 September 1905.

84. "Siku hizi kila kitu kwa amri." BAB/R1001/726, Booth report, 16 January 1906, 28–32.

85. BAB/R1001/726, Booth report, 22 December 1905, 124a.

86. BAB/R1001/726, Winterfeld report, 4 December 1905, 98.

87. Ziegenhorn, "Rufiyi-Delta," 81, 84. Ziegenhorn specified that pigs were a problem for rice fields. Msalla, a village of 50 huts and 100 residents in the Delta, specialized in cassava, as did many villages of the coast north of the Rufiji.

88. Wilhelm Methner, *Unter drei Gouverneuren: 16 Jahre Dienst in deutschen Tropen* (Breslau, 1938), 11–12.

89. Early descriptions of the village agricultural scheme in Dar es Salaam district are found in the report by the district officer Winterfeld in "Auszüge aus den Berichten der Bezirksämter," *BLF* 2 (1904–06), 51–56; "Kommunalschamben und ihre Nachteile," *DOAZ*, 28 November 1903, 1; TNA G4/40, Spieth to Imperial Government, 12 February 1906, 162.

90. BAB/R1001/726, Winterfeld report, 4 December 1905, 9–97.
91. "Zum Thema 'Kommunalschamben'," *DOAZ,* 12 December 1903, 1–2; "Auszüge," *BLF* (1904–06), 52; BAB/R1001/726, Supf to Colonial Office, 23 January 1906, 30b.
92. "Kommunalschamben," *DOAZ,* 12 December 1903, 1.
93. BAB/R1001/726, Booth report, 22 December 1905, 24–25.
94. BAB/R1001/726, Haber report, 9 September 1906, 86a; Geibler et al., 20 December 1905, 116b.
95. BAB/R1001/726, Report by Geibler et al., 20 December 1905, 117.
96. BAB/R1001/726, Supf to Foreign Office, 23 January 1906, 30.
97. TNA G4/82, Wirtschaftsberichte, 6 September 1902; BAB/R1001/233, Götzen to Colonial Office, 31 August 1902. Götzen wrote, "In particular Rufiji is the land where it is likely in the next few years to realize the KWK's cotton plans."
98. "Auszüge," *BLF* (1903), 244–45.
99. TNA G4/82 Wirtschaftsberichte Rufiji, Kommunal-Verband Rufiji, 21 December 1904, 234; *Amtlicher Anzeiger,* "Wirtschaftsplan des Kommunalverbandes Rufiyi auf das Rechnungsjahr 1905."
100. Werth, *Küstenland,* 189–92. For discussions of the German model of scientific forest management that influenced colonial forest conservation models see Christoph Ernst, "An Ecological Revolution? The 'Schlagwaldwirtschaft' in Western Germany in the Eighteenth and Nineteenth Centuries," in *European Woods and Forests: Studies in Cultural History,* ed. Charles Watkins (Cambridge, 1998), 83–92; James Scott, *Seeing Like a State* (New Haven, 1998), 11–22.
101. BAB/R1001/8647, Versuchspflanzung Mohoro, 31 March 1897, Schroeder report, 74.
102. Europeans overseeing delta forestry as well as Arab estate owners complained about the "indolence and actual insubordination among their workers and slaves" and the "increasing insolence of native laborers." Stollowsky, "Background to Rebellion," 683–84; Paasche, *Deutsch-Ostafrika,* 117–21.
103. BerM-Maneromango, Bericht über das I. Quartal 1905, 11 April 1905. The Maneromango worker Stefanos spent his savings of 7.32 Rp to ransom his mother and sister from the *jumbe* of Vihumburu village.
104. Giblin, *Politics of Environmental Control*; Elton, "On the Coast," 244–46; Stuhlmann, "Forschungsreisen in Usaramo," 229–30.
105. BAB/R1001/726, Booth report, 22 December 1905, 124–25.
106. "Auszüge," *BLF* (1904–06), 56–60.
107. BAB/R1001/726, Report by Schultz and Booth, 11 December 1905, 106a.
108. BAB/R1001/726, Winterfeld report, 4 December 1905, 97b.
109. There is an extensive literature on the Maji Maji uprising, but see: Gilbert Gwassa, "The Outbreak" and "Kinjikitile and the Ideology of Maji Maji" in *The Historical Study of African Religion,* ed. T.O. Ranger and I.N. Kimambo (London, 1972); John Iliffe, "The Organization of the Maji Maji Rebellion," *JAH* 8, 3 (1967), 495–512 and *Modern History,* Chapter 6. Both draw on some elements of the *Maji Maji Research Project.* More recently see Marcia Wright, "Maji Maji: Prophecy and Historiography" in *Revealing Prophets: Prophecy in Eastern African History,* ed. David Anderson and Douglas Johnson (London, 1995), 124–42; Jamie Monson, "Relocat-

ing Maji Maji: The Politics of Alliance and Authority in the Southern Highlands of Tanzania, 1870–1918," *JAH* 39 (1998), 95–120; Thaddeus Sunseri, "Famine and Wild Pigs: Gender Struggles and the Outbreak of the Maji Maji War in Uzaramo (Tanzania)," *JAH* 38 (1997), 235–57.

110. *MMRP* 1/68/2/1, I.A.S. Mananga, "The Maji Maji Rising at Msongozi," 1; *MMRP* 9/68/1/3/3, Mzee Hamisi Matanga, 1; 9/68/1/3/6, Mzee Petro Moto, 2.

111. Though mentioned in Götzen's and other German-era accounts of the rebellion, the term "maji maji" was not widely used until British colonial rule. Graf von Götzen, *Deutsch-Ostafrika im Aufstand 1905–6* (Berlin, 1909). On connections between German accounts of the Maji Maji rebellion and other colonial uprisings see Thaddeus Sunseri, "Maji Maji and the Millennium: Abrahamic Sources and the Creation of a Tanzanian Resistance Tradition," *History in Africa* 26 (1999), 365–78. On German involvement in the Boxer rebellion see Joseph Esherick, *The Origins of the Boxer Uprising* (Berkeley, 1987). See also Tilman Dedering, "The Prophet's 'War Against the Whites': Shepherd Stuurman in Namibia and South Africa, 1905–7," *JAH* 40 (1999), 1–19.

112. TDB MF-977, Reel 15, Kilwa District Books, "Land Tenure in Matumbi Tribal Area"; Moritz Merker, "Über die Aufstandsbewegung in Deutsch-Ostafrika während der Monate August bis November 1905," *Militär-Wochenblatt* 45 (1906), 1025; Joseph Safari, "Grundlagen und Auswirkungen des Maji-Maji-Aufstandes von 1905," (Ph.D. diss., University of Cologne, 1972), 64–65.

113. Stollowsky, "On the Background," 684–85.

114. Most notably Gwassa, "Kinjikitile"; Iliffe, *Modern History*, 168–202. For a critique see Sunseri, "Famine and Wild Pigs," 238–42.

115. Stollowsky, "On the Background," 685.

116. Stollowsky, "On the Background," 686–87.

117. BerM-Kisserawe, II. Quartal 1905, 30b.

118. Martin Klamroth, "Beiträge zum Verständnis der religiösen Vorstellungen der Saramo im Bezirk Daressalam," *Zeitschrift für Kolonialsprachen* 1–3 (1910–13), 139–53.

119. Around Morogoro, where the Koleo cult was based, modern Tanzanian informants denied any association between Koleo and the uprising despite persistent attempts by interviewers to elicit a connection. *MMRP* 1/68/2/3/1/2, Deu Chigwa, 2. Also 1/68/2/3/7 Sheikh Salum Mbilu, 2; Iliffe, "The Organization"; BAB/R1001/724, Denkschrift über die Ursachen des Aufstandes in Deutsch-Ostafrika 1905, 5–6; *DOAZ*, 3 March 1906, 6.

120. BAB/R1001/726, Booth report, 22 December 1905, 125.

121. *MMRP* 3/68/1/3/1, Stephen Chang'a, 1.

122. "Mwamini Mungu si mtovu," *Mambo Leo*, August 1937, 122.

123. "Aus der Kolonie," *DOAZ*, 30 Dec 1905, 2; Paasche, *Deutsch-Ostafrika*, 149.

124. BAB/R1001/726, Booth report, 16 January 1906, 133a; BerM-Kisserawe, Bericht der Station für 1904, 8a; Kisserawe, II. Quartal 1905, 30b.

125. BAB/R1001/726, Vincenti and Haber report, 17 January 1906, 112b.

126. BAB/R1001/726, Vincenti and Haber report, 17 January 1906, 112; R.M. Bell, "The Maji Maji Rebellion in Liwale District," *TNR* 28 (1950), 42–43, 47.

127. BAB/R1001/726, Vincenti and Haber report, 17 January 1906, 112b; Bell, "Maji Maji in Liwale," 42, 43, 47; BerM-Maneromango, 1. January bis 31 December 1905.
128. BAB/R1001/726, Report by Vincenti and Haber, 17 January 1906, 113b–114a.
129. BerM-Maneromango, Bericht über das II. Quartal 1905, 30 June 1905, 25.
130. Stollowsky, "On the Background," 684–86.
131. Iliffe, *Modern History*, 173.
132. BAB/R1001/726, Report by Siegel, Booth, Vincenti, Haber, 23 December 1905, 116.
133. BAB/R1001/726, Haber report, 9 September 1906, 88b. This contrasts with Gwassa's interpretation, which sees the rebellion as the product of long-term planning to do battle with the German empire stemming from at least 1903. Gwassa, "The Outbreak," 189–90, 220–21.
134. Application of *maji* water took many forms. Some people applied it by beating their legs with wet leaves, some sprinkled it on crowds, others drank the water or wore it in vials around their necks. *MMRP* 3/68/1/1 Pascal Mhongole, "The Hehe and the Maji Maji Rebellion," 14; *MMRP* 7/68/2/1 P.M. Libaba, "The Maji Maji Rising in Lindi District," 8; *MMRP* 2/68/1/1, D.L. Chipindulla, "The Maji Maji Rising in Kilossa Town," 5.
135. Acceptance or rejection of *maji dawa* followed local patterns of politics and relations with German rulers. Many *majumbe* consciously refused to take the water, understanding it to be a commitment to rebellion. For Tanzania as a whole outside of the outbreak region see the interviews in *MMRP*.
136. On the rebellion in the southwest see Patrick Redmond, "Maji Maji in Ungoni: A Reappraisal of Existing Historiography," *IJAHS* 8 (1975), 407–23; O.B. Mapunda and G.P. Mangara, *The Maji Maji War in Ungoni* (Dar es Salaam, 1969); Monson, "Relocating Maji Maji"; Iliffe, *Modern History*, Chapter 6. Historians commonly confine the rebellion south of the central caravan route, but see the following on the war in Iraqw: BAB/R1001/724, Haber to Foreign Office, 11 June 1906, 84; Haber to Foreign Office, 4 July 1906, 102; "Aufstand in der Landschaft Iraku," *DOAZ*, 16 June 1906, 2; "Aus den Aufstandsgebieten," *DOAZ*, 7 July 1906, 2.
137. BAB/R1001/726, Booth report, 22 December 1905, 124.
138. BerM-Kisserawe, II. Quartal 1905, 30–35; BAB/R1001/726, Report by Vincenti and Haber, 17 January 1906, 110b.
139. BAB/R1001/721, Back to Berlin Admiralty, 6 August 1905, 11; Back to Berlin, 10 August 1905, 29; Gwassa, "The Outbreak," Chapter 4.
140. Bundesarchiv-Militärarchiv Freiburg, AF/RM121/v.441, Amtliche Nachrichten des Gouvernements aus den unruhigen Gebieten, 14 October 1905, 92.
141. BAB/R1001/722, Back to Berlin Admiralty, 25 August 1905, 21.
142. BAB/R1001/722, Götzen to Foreign Office, 27 August 1905, 34.
143. BAB/R1001/722, Götzen to Foreign Office, 26 August 1905, 108; BAB/R1001/721, Götzen to Foreign Office, 17 August 1905, 59.
144. BA-Militärarchiv Freiburg, "Amtliche Nachrichten," 92; BAB/R1001/723, Foreign Office to Götzen, 14 October 1905, 27–28.

145. BAB/R1001/726, Haber report, 9 September 1905, 82b; Stollowsky, "On the Background," 695–96; "Noch Einiges von den Unruhen im Süden," *DOAZ*, 30 September 1905; "Die maji-maji-Lehre arabischen Ursprungs!" *DOAZ*, 13 January 1906, 2–3; John Iliffe, *Tanganyika under German Rule* (Cambridge, 1969), 194. For an overview of Ethiopianism in southern Africa see John L. and Jean Comaroff, *Of Revelation and Revolution: The Dialectics of Modernity on a South African Frontier* Vol. II (Chicago, 1997), 100–06.

146. BAB/R1001/4826, Strafsache der Inder, 1906–1911; *DOAZ*, 13 January 1906, 1–2.

147. BAB/R1001/721, Götzen to Foreign Office, 10 August 1905, 21.

148. BAB/R1001/721, Götzen to Foreign Office, 7 August 1905, 16.

149. Ultimately the commission split on its view of the uprising between those who viewed it as stemming from economic grievances and those, such as Governor Götzen, who adhered to the idea of a witch doctor conspiracy. BAB/R1001/726, Götzen to Colonial Office, 15 March 1906; Schultz and Booth report, 11 December 1905, 103–08.

150. Gwassa and Iliffe, *Records*, 27.

151. TNA G3/72, District Office Dar es Salaam to Imperial Government, 13 December 1905, 241–42.

152. BAB/R1001/723, Glatzel to Berlin, 4 December 1905, 147; Bell, "Maji Maji in Liwale," 51.

153. BAB/R1001/723, Foreign Office to Götzen, 14 October 1905, 27–28.

154. BAB/R1001/724, Haber to Colonial Office, 16 July 1906, 116b.

155. BA-Freiburg, RM 121v/438, "Befehl an die Truppenführer im Aufstandsgebiet," 11 November 1905; Gwassa and Iliffe, *Records*, 22. The reality was that most weapons and firearms were not turned in, and Germans gradually let the provision drop. BAB/R001/724, Haber to Foreign Office, 16 July 1906, 115–17, 120.

156. "Die Reise des hochwürdigen Herrn Bischof Thomas Spreiter nach Matumbi und Kwiro," *Missions-Blaetter* 13, 4 (1909), 123; Weule, *Native Life*, 55; "Landwirtschaftliches aus Ungoni," *Missions-Blaetter* 14 (1910), 52.

157. Paasche, *Deutsch-Ostafrika*, 146.

158. Bell, "Maji Maji in Liwale," 51.

159. BAB/R1001/723, Götzen to Foreign Office, 7 December 1905, 188.

160. Paasche, *Deutsch-Ostafrika*, 153.

161. Gwassa and Iliffe, *Records*, 28.

162. Paasche, *Deutsch-Ostafrika*, 149–50. For Lindi district see TNA G4/74 Kommune Lindi, 5 August 1906.

163. Paasche, *Deutsch-Ostafrika*, 150.

164. BerM-Maneromango, Quartelsberichte vom 1. Januar bis zum 13. März 1906, 23 April 1906; Paasche, *Deutsch-Ostafrika*, 150.

165. BerM-Maneromango, Quartalbericht vom 1 Januar bis zum 31 März 1906.

166. TNA G3/70, District Office Kilwa to Governor, 2 February 1906.

167. TNA G4/81, Kommunalangelegenheiten Mohoro-Rufiji 1906.

168. BerM-Kisserawe, III. Quartal 1906.

169. BAB/R1001/725, Reichstagsangelegenheiten 1912, 62–63.

170. TNA G1/97, Grass to Imperial Government, 23 July 1906.
171. TNA G1/97, Arbeiterverhältnisse Rufiji, Grass to Imperial Government, 23 July 1906.
172. Ambrosius Maier, "Aus den Matumbibergen," *Missions-Blaetter von St. Ottilien* 14 (1910), 116.
173. TNA G8/581, von Wächter report, 29 March 1907, 58.
174. BerM-Kisserawe, Bericht über das I. Quartal 1909.
175. BerM-Kisserawe, III. Quartal 1906, 19 November 1906; "Die Reise des hochwürdigen Herrn Bischof Thomas Spreiter nach Matumbi und Kwiro," *Missions-Blaetter* 13, 4 (January 1909), 49; Landeg White, *Magomero: Portrait of an African Village* (Cambridge, 1989), 176–90.
176. BerM-Kisserawe, IV. Quartal 1907, 24 January 1908, 25. In some African societies women's assumption of male dress was a means of ridiculing men who were not fulfilling their social roles. For another example see John Parker, *Making the Town: Ga State and Society in Early Colonial Accra* (Portsmouth, 2000), 52.

5

AN ANTIDOTE TO THE PLANTATION LABOR SHORTAGE? THE PEASANT COTTON CAMPAIGN IN SOUTHEASTERN TANZANIA

The Maji Maji rebellion ended as the state began a new cotton campaign aimed at peasant householders. Whereas the previous communal campaign had required rural men and women to journey to central villages or private plantations to plant cotton and other cash crops, the new program brought cotton seed to householders and required peasants to plant it on their own *mashamba*. By 1906 colonial officials came to view peasant households as *krisenfest*, secure from crises, because they offered flexibility in planting and use of household labor, and were able to withstand disasters, including floods, crop pests, diseases, and fluctuating market prices better than either plantations or communal fields, which could not even master the labor shortage.[1] The head of the KWK wrote, "in my view the oldest negro woman is able to exceed [the communal *shamba*] yield on her small personal shamba."[2] German policy makers had long viewed the Kilwa-Rufiji region as a promising locus of peasant cotton production, and now targeted it as the foundation of the new program.

Historians have viewed the cotton campaign as symptomatic of an era of improvement that followed the Maji Maji war, when the state created a program of incentives and a marketing and railway infrastructure to facilitate peasant cash crop production.[3] The incentives included free distribution of cotton seed to peasants, the establishment of ginning facilities, market centers, minimum purchase prices, and instruction in scientific methods of growing cotton based on the Mpanganya cotton school on the Rufiji river. In the prevailing view, African "men of initiative" responded positively to these incentives and demonstrated that they could be progressive cotton farmers.[4] Indeed, in this view growing cotton on household *mashamba* offered the advantage of being able to bring in a cash income to pay taxes without mandating that peasants work as wage laborers on any of the ten cotton plantations that Germans founded in Rufiji-Kilwa region following the Maji Maji war.[5] German policy makers believed this course offered the only hope of mastering the cotton question at a time when the German textile industry entered into yet another period of crisis.

These positive views of the "new course" have not taken the realities of peasant-level production and its ecological and gendered dimensions into sufficient consideration. The peasant cotton campaign was inaugurated in an atmosphere of crisis in southeastern Tanzania. In Kilwa-Rufiji region thousands of men and women died in the Maji Maji war, hundreds of men were conscripted as penal laborers to work in northern plantation zones or on the Central Railway, and thousands of people emigrated to Uzaramo to the north or to inland districts where colonial control was weak in order to survive famines that accompanied the war. Many men had long since left the region as wage laborers on the railway, on plantations, or as porters. There was a palpable decline in the rural population that made normal food production difficult enough without adopting a new, non-food cash crop like cotton. Evidence furthermore points to the increase in divorce, household breakdowns, and birth decline following the war, all of which impaired production and posed limits on rural production. On top of the rural labor shortage, district officials intensified colonial conservation policies that attacked hunting, bush burning, and forest use. Colonial officials created forest reserves throughout Rufiji region that severely circumscribed peasant use of the commons or ability to guard fields from crop predators. State officials enlisted *majumbe* village headmen both to carry out the cotton program and to maintain conservation policies, and any hesitation was viewed as opposition to the state, perhaps even a return to rebellion. Under these circumstances environmental control was not possible, and peasant householders, far from being *krisenfest*, were continuously exposed to crisis. In this atmosphere of state intervention in production and resource use, women, who were often single household heads, sought to avoid colonial oversight by moving into forests and bush to open up new fields aimed at subsistence food production.

FAMINE AND AGRICULTURAL INVOLUTION IN THE MAJI MAJI AFTERMATH

Famine and household disruptions were direct consequences of the Maji Maji war. The German policy of ending the war through attrition included burning grain fields in the vicinity of rebel villages or harvesting grain using conscripted and penal labor to supply German troops, thus depriving local people of food. Villagers in rebel districts further lost grain stores through a war indemnity of 3 Rp per household.[6] Finally, the end of the war was marked by refugee movements, the end of environmental controls, plagues of wild pigs, and the destructive flooding of the Rufiji river, all of which contributed to famine.[7] According to Camelius Kiango,

> It was extremely fierce famine and people denied their children and wives. It was only those who really loved each other who remained together. . . . On the other hand, if they did not love each other everyone went his separate way struggling to survive. That is why some men had to marry the same woman twice, for they had deserted them during the famine. When he searched for his former wife her parents asked him "Where did you leave her?" So he had to pay dowry again. This famine was called Fugufugu.[8]

Similar famines accompanied by household breakup and marriage dissolution occurred in other regions of rebellion.[9] Several years after the uprising, missionaries traveling through the war's outbreak regions of Rufiji, the Matumbi hills, and Liwale recorded ample evidence of rural breakdown. Sex ratios were skewed due to men having died in the war, having left the region for wage labor, or having fled to escape colonial controls. The absence of men was obvious in the rise in polygamy and divorce.[10] There were six to twelve women per hut to every man in some parts of the region, increased polygamy being a survival strategy of women widowed or abandoned by husbands or parents.[11] Many cases of divorce resulted from the prolonged absence of husbands as women came to view men as failing to fulfill household obligations. Tanzanian elders confirmed these accounts to an anthropologist who toured the region in British colonial times. Describing famine survival strategies that followed the uprising, Crosse-Upcott concluded, "tacit divorce occurs, the husband merely fending for himself if not actually driving out his wife."[12] Accounts of the increase in women's spirit possession, by which husbands were accused of not fulfilling household and marital obligations, offer further evidence of the social disruption that followed the uprising.[13]

A direct result of household breakup was birth decline. The missionary Maier noted few children in Umatumbi, less than one child per woman in regions that he visited, and other reports claim that for every five women there were only two children.[14] Crosse-Upcott reported that in times of famine, "husband and wife avoid intimacy . . . for fear of conception—a child born in such conditions would be doomed."[15] Another explanation for few children in the region lies in the practice of pawning children in times of crisis so that both children and remaining families had a better chance of survival.[16] An elder in modern Tanzania recalled this practice in Kilwa region following Maji Maji, as many people were sold into slavery onto Mafia Island where conditions were much better in the rebellion's aftermath.[17] However, there can be no doubt that many children and elders succumbed to famines that followed the war, as the Mohoro District Officer reported.[18] Similarly, the anthropologist Weule, traveling through Lindi district in 1906, pronounced the Mwera people to be in deplorable condition, forced to live in the bush without shelter since their villages were "leveled with the ground by our troops."[19] Survivors of the war, especially women and children, were "emaciated to skeletons," many people surviving on famine foods, including beans, roots, pumpkins, gourds, and insects.[20]

Colonial officials were struck by the noticeable population decline in the southeast in the years after the uprising. As a result of the war and its prosecution, "a great many Matumbi perished" and those who survived were dependent on the Kilwa Kommune for food aid.[21] Food and field theft were recurrent crimes. In 1908 sixty-three people of Kilwa district were fined 1 Rp each for breaking into a rice storehouse.[22] Bishop Spreiter, who traveled through the region in 1908, noted that "formerly [the Matumbi] were as numerous as termites, then the war came, followed by smallpox, then famine and typhus, and, finally, worm disease."[23] As towns such as Kibata became military garrisons to control the Matumbi and exact indemnity taxes, many men fled to escape penal labor. Villagers abandoned fertile lands and banana groves near established villages in favor of bush or forest that appeared to offer refuge. The 10,000 people who had lived around Kibata town before the war shrank to 2,000 by 1908.[24] The *jumbe* of Chumo reported that there were 163 huts in his village in 1908 compared to

588 before the war, probably because an *askari* station was established there, motivating people to leave. Many Rufiji people left for the "richer cassava regions of Dar es Salaam and Morogoro" leaving some villages completely evacuated.[25] Women were left to tend fields in once-prosperous villages, where now wild pigs and rats proliferated, attacking the cassava crop that people relied on.[26] In Lindi district plagues of wild pigs were so bad that the district office took bids on effective ways to master the problem, and the Kilwa district office used arsenic against pigs, with little effect.[27] Rufiji villagers fled to Uzaramo to escape pig devastations just north of the river. In the war's aftermath colonial officials confiscated guns, prohibited the sale of gunpowder to Africans, and continued to enforce hunting bans, severely constraining the ability to protect fields and people.[28] Even iron production by local smiths was inhibited by bans on forest use, especially cutting the hardwood needed for charcoal. One result was that in a fifteen-month period from 1908 to 1909 lions and leopards reportedly killed 276 people in Kilwa district.[29] These were conditions of environmental collapse that mirrored the years preceding the rebellion.

Throughout southeastern Tanzania householders left regions of colonial control to hide in forests and bush so as to escape the exactions of the colonial state. People left the main caravan route between Kilwa and Liwale to avoid the plundering of porters and *askari* stationed in the region, some moving into the high escarpments of the Matumbi hills for security, areas that they had formerly considered taboo.[30] Some people of Kilwa district reportedly moved their fields into the forests because crop-destroying baboons avoided leopards that lived there. Bishop Spreiter referred to this forest movement as *pembeni*, living "in the corners," of the land where people could hide and farm in peace, admitting, "if I were a negro I wouldn't want to live along the roadways."[31] In Lindi district as well people opened up new fields, isolated in the bush, so as to avoid forced conscription or food plundering.[32] While the Kilwa district office claimed that post-Maji Maji refugees began to return by 1909, many clearly did not. At the end of German rule, Matumbi migrants resided in significant numbers in Iringa district and as far away as Langenburg-Masoko north of Lake Nyasa, while others made their way to Dar es Salaam and Wilhelmstal, undoubtedly as urban dwellers or labor migrants.[33]

For some southeastern people, forest migrations were an attempt to survive famine conditions by collecting wax, honey, rubber, copra, and mangrove bark to sell to coastal merchants.[34] One pound of wax or one bottle of honey could bring in $^1/_2$ Rp, enough to pay a year's hut tax and the war indemnity with a few weeks of work. Ngindo people near Liwale earned as much as ½ Rp per day tapping wild rubber trees.[35] However, a direct result of these forest pursuits was that agriculture in the region declined as men concentrated on rubber gathering. Overtapping reportedly killed many trees.

While some men moved into forests to extract products for sale, some Matumbi women followed similar patterns by farming land parcels called *matimbe* located along forest riverbanks.[36] Traditionally considered to be subsidiary lands used for famine crops in conjunction with annually cleared *shamba* land, *matimbe* (or *ngwenda*) flooded during the rainy seasons, retaining moisture well into the dry season that facilitated crops such as cassava and *maji ya konoa*, a rice variety that ripened three months after sowing.[37] Hillside soil that washed down onto *matimbe* offered further fertility. *Matimbe* strips were so important to the household that they were not given up as fallow, rather householders maintained possession as long as they resided in the region.[38] *Matimbe* also required a dispersed-field economy, because such river lands were widely scattered throughout the Matumbi hills and lowlands, in contrast to *shamba* lands, the customary basis of bush fallowing and export crops, which were located in the vicinity of villages. Women's use of *matimbe* reflected a major restructuring of land use in southeast Tanzania since women "invaded" land that in times past had been male domains, had represented patrilineal succession, and instilled citizenship on a clan. Men absent for too long lost clan rights to *matimbe* use. Women in effect colonized men's lands in the aftermath of Maji Maji, both preserving clan citizenship and retaining vital famine lands necessary for household survival. However, this shift entailed significant tensions between men and women and across generations (see Chapter 7).

While demographics of the southeast are impossible to gauge with any certainty, it seems clear that many men and women took to the forests during and after the war so as to evade depredations of colonial forces, caravan porters, labor recruiters, and *askari*. Perhaps most importantly, following the war the state began an intensive cotton campaign that targeted householders as the prime growers of the crop. Under these circumstances, living *pembeni*, dispersed in the corners of the landscape, made sense. The colonial state's post-Maji Maji declaration of forest and game reserves throughout the Rufiji-Kilwa region, precisely where the rebellion originated, was a direct response to these "native incursions" into the forests.[39] Twenty-one forest reserves were declared in Rufiji district alone between 1907 and 1911, encompassing some 40,000 hectares.[40] Once district officials declared a forest reserve they informed *majumbe* and local villagers that, henceforth, it was prohibited to lay out new fields, use bush burning as a method of clearing fields, or use products from the forest reserve. In keeping villagers out of the forests, colonial officials also sought to draw them back onto cultivated *shamba* land under the control of *majumbe* to participate in the cotton campaign. Nevertheless, knowing the social landscape following the uprising better than colonial officials, the missionary Maier pronounced, "cotton will never become a *Volkskultur* (peasant crop) in Umatumbi."[41]

PAMBA: THE PEASANT COTTON CAMPAIGN

Even during the Maji Maji uprising, the colonial government introduced cotton on a household basis as soon as regions were secured from rebellion. The Rufiji delta was an early site of these projects, bringing in a cotton crop already in 1906.[42] In June of that year the Rufiji District Officer Grass called an assembly of local people at Mohoro town. After castigating the people for participating in the rebellion, he took out some watches and said "these are gifts for industrious people who plant cotton. They come from Europe from a cotton industrialist (*bwana mkubwa wa pamba*); everyone should work hard to grow cotton!"[43] Grass thereupon presented the watches to three Muslim elites of Mohoro town. In the next few years the administration and the Colonial Economic Committee worked hard to enlist people of the southeast for cotton growing. The KWK pronounced cotton to be a successful peasant crop in Rufiji district by 1910 and in Lindi district by 1912. In 1911 the newspaper *Deutsch-Ostafrikanische Rundschau* pronounced Rufiji to be a peasant district "that offers little room for large-scale European cultivation."[44] The last governor of German East Africa, Heinrich Schnee, defended peasants as the "backbone of cotton growing in the colony" against German planters who believed the colonial state's peasant emphasis deprived them of labor.[45]

Despite these optimistic claims, cotton was only adopted as a peasant crop in these regions of recent famine, population loss, and labor migration owing to the vigorous, ongoing intervention of the state and the KWK. The heart of the cotton campaign was the Mpanganya cotton school located on the Rufiji river.[46] The KWK, which founded Mpanganya in 1904, hoped to replicate a Tuskegee-style education in scientific farming that would teach regional peasants how to grow cotton.[47] Toward this end, the school's director, a German-Texan, recruited "intelligent natives" literate in Swahili from Rufiji, Kilwa, and Lindi districts to act as the nucleus of the region's cotton program.[48] Hoping these students would serve as model farmers for peasants, the

KWK and the state settled the school's first graduates in Rufiji district in 1910.[49] The school also concentrated on breeding cotton seed suitable to the region's climate and soil conditions; sought solutions to problems of drought, flooding, cotton pests and diseases; and experimented with the best rotations for cotton and other crops. As one of a dozen regional cotton plantations, Mpanganya employed several hundred local peasants, and used its gins and presses to process cotton grown on peasant *mashamba*.[50] After 1910 the KWK founded other cotton schools in Kilosa, Tabora, Lindi, and Kilimanjaro districts, although only Mpanganya emerged as more than an experimental cotton plantation.

Mpanganya failed to radiate modern farming to regional peasants and instead became a medium for social control, sending out itinerant teachers annually in conjunction with the Mohoro district office to oversee cotton growing (See FIGURE 5.1). The unsuitability of the southeast for cattle obviated ox-plowing, and regional peasants resisted growing cotton according to government dictates. Instructors exerted great effort teaching proper cotton picking so as to obtain a clean lint. The school's Swahili-language cotton manual emphasized that "Europeans who buy cotton to make cloth don't use traditional cotton (*pamba semani*)" that was interplanted with other crops, a practice that peasants used to save labor time, but which stunted cotton plants.[51] Ali Mwinyinvua Maiti of Morogoro, who grew cotton ten to fifteen times in his lifetime, recalled how intercropping was done:

> The way I remember it you take a certain width, such as our feet, and do like so: there are four or five feet in width. You measure one, two, three and four—a row of cotton. Because in between there are rows of corn. . . . You weren't only able to plant cotton because the children would die. . . .

Maiti emphasized the necessity of weeding and harvesting a row of cotton then a row of corn in succession. "If you plant the cotton well along with corn, you are able to feed the children so that they have enough. That is the way we farmed in those days."[52]

Maiti's recollections underscore the famine consciousness that peasants brought to the cotton campaign that made them resist the restructuring of local production according to Tuskegee principles.

After the first few years KWK officials abandoned "scientific" methods of farming in deference to more expedient peasant methods based on bush fallowing. Mpanganya officials instructed peasants to open up new cotton fields in the bush for greater soil fertility, encroaching on parcels

An Antidote to the Plantation Labor Shortage? 121

Figure 5.1 Children harvesting cotton in southeast German East Africa c. 1910. In the absence of men, children were enlisted to work during the *pamba* campaign that followed the Maji Maji war. (© Bildarchiv Preussischer Kulturbesitz Berlin, 1401 g. Reprinted with permission.)

that would otherwise serve as *kilala* fallow. Peasants must have wondered why the state had banned bush burning for food crops, but encouraged it in the new cotton program:

> If you want to make a cotton field in the bush, you first should obtain a *panga* and cut the bush and all small trees. And then it is necessary for you to cut all the trees in the field with an axe, then burn them because cotton seedlings like to receive sun.[53]

The cotton program relied on colonial agriculture officials and itinerant teachers to oversee field selection, planting and harvest, and to simply make sure that people grew cotton by enlisting *majumbe* support and punishing noncompliance.[54] For example, traveling through the village of Kitundu in 1911, the Rufiji agricultural officer came across "completely neglected cotton fields" intercropped with rice and maize, with no proper attention to ground preparation. Calling the *jumbe* and villagers, the official asked why the cotton teacher hadn't taught them to grow cotton properly. Learning that they had been instructed repeatedly, he ordered the villagers to work on the construction of the Mohoro-Kilindi road for fifteen days as punishment. The official reported "it spread like wildfire that whoever didn't hoe properly would be employed at road construction and in that way most of the cotton fields have been tended to."[55] Although there was no legal obligation to grow cotton, it seems likely that district officials used the threat of penal labor or work on plantations to motivate peasants to grow their own cotton. The criminal statistics for this period are rife with cases of people charged with disobedience or recalcitrance against *majumbe* or state authority. For example, twelve people were charged at Kibata late in 1908 for "resisting state authority" and sentenced to one month in chains, perhaps on the nearby Kilwa Cotton Plantation. Eight people were sentenced to fourteen days in chains for disobedience to their *jumbe* in July 1909.[56] Another thirty-eight men and women received five days in jail with forced labor for "insubordination" against their *jumbe*."[57] Though these reports do not detail the exact nature of the crimes, they do make clear that *majumbe* continued to be an essential layer of colonial social control during the period of the cotton campaign.

As in times past, *maakida*, *majumbe*, and other rural elites were at the forefront of cotton growing. Controlling more land and labor than ordinary peasants, including multiple wives and slaves, the state gave them privileges to grow cotton, including monetary advances, iron hoes, and gifts for well-tended fields, or punished them for infractions such as negligence in service, recalcitrance, or disobedience.[58] "People who controlled slaves" grew most of Lindi district's cotton in 1910, and this was also the case around Mohoro town in the Rufiji delta.[59] In that year agricultural inspectors also gave premiums to 149 cotton growers of Rufiji region, mostly to people living in the delta, where *mlau* cultivation using slave labor was possible.[60] In the Rufiji *akidat* of Kooni 12 farmers received premiums of 12 Rp each and 15 others received 6 Rp each.[61] These recipients were leading members of their villages, descended from prominent clans.[62] On modest estates of 1–4 ha, farmers such as these earned profits ranging from 90 Rp to as much as 500 Rp.[63]

Not content that cotton be confined to regional elites, and wary of recreating a "communal" program like the one that contributed to Maji Maji, colonial officials targeted householders for the cotton campaign. Toward this end the KWK's single biggest expense was the free distribution of seed to peasants.[64] District officials throughout the south ordered *majumbe* and *maakida* to fetch and distribute free seed to villagers in their domains.[65] The KWK also guaranteed a minimum purchase price for any cotton that peasants produced, especially after monopoly manipulations of the German East Africa Corporation and its Indian cotton agents depressed prices to levels that led "bitterly disappointed" peasants to abandon the crop completely.[66] After 1909 peasants received a minimum price of 8–10 *hellers* per lb of unginned cotton, although sometimes market prices rose to much higher levels.[67]

Rashidi Mohamed Mtambo's parents grew cotton in the environs of Kilwa during this time. Born during the Maji Maji war, Rashidi was old enough to participate in cotton growing near the Kikanda plantation of the Kilwa Cotton Corporation. However, he and his parents usually avoided work on the plantation by growing their own plot. "I worked planting the seed. My father made the holes, and I put the seed in."[68] Both parents weeded the *shamba*, and his father brought the crop to market. Rashidi did not remember the Mpanganya school, but recalled that "people were around to teach cotton planting." Rashidi, a Muslim, considered his family to be *waungwana*, and disassociated them from the events of Maji Maji, which he referred to as a fierce war, but "stupidity," adding "it wasn't very important." Because his father did not participate in the war, his family was intact following the uprising, and better able to farm in peace.

Kitenge Muhamed told a similar story. Born at Kilwa-Masoko on the coast, his parents fished and farmed, growing millet, sesame, cassava, and rice before the arrival of the Germans. Kitenge was old enough to remember the German cotton planters Meyer and Jung, who opened up estates near Kilwa-Kivinje before the Maji Maji uprising. Kitenge recalled that cotton fields were supposed to be kept separate from grain fields, the cotton *mashamba* being "isolated, far away." This posed a hardship for peasants who first had to cultivate cotton plots before they could tend to their millet, especially near the coast, where oversight was more pronounced. Kitenge recalled that during German times cotton was the only crop that peasants could sell to get money to pay taxes and buy things they needed, like cloth. When asked whether people could sell food crops to earn such money, Kitenge responded, "It's like today. It's like today. One can make more money working or growing cotton, it's the only way to get things one needs, like *miziki* (cotton garments worn by men) or cloth if one wants a wife. . . . Food is only food."[69] Other elders of modern Tanzania were

Figure 5.2 Women transporting cotton. (Courtesy of Bundesarchiv, Koblenz, 146/78/23/17A. Reprinted with permission.)

more adamant that, from the Rufiji river to Kilwa, villagers preferred to grow and market oil crops (*mafuta*), such as sesame or coconuts, and only grew cotton because of German orders.[70]

Colonial officials and the KWK claimed that cotton had become a successful peasant crop by 1912, when perhaps 2,000 Rufiji-Kilwa peasants grew cotton.[71] Despite the state's optimism, peasants never internalized the crop. In 1907–08, the first concerted year of cotton growing south of the Rufiji, peasants produced some 458 bales of ginned cotton in Rufiji and Kilwa districts together (See FIGURE 5.2).[72] That amount had perhaps doubled by 1913–14 to about 900 bales.[73] By any account these were meager returns. Reports describe peasant cotton *mashamba* as small plots, some no larger than ⅓ to ½ area (about 23 x 23 ft).[74] At the minimum price of 8 *hellers* per lb, a peasant would need about 40 lbs. of unginned cotton, or about 65 x 65 ft., just to earn enough for the 3 Rp tax.[75] Even on larger *mashamba* with family labor available this was a huge burden. If cotton were adopted, peasants invariably intercropped it with grain crops both to save on clearing land and labor time. However, the depletion of soil nutrients that this double-cropping entailed led to involution in the long run, as peasants well knew.

Looking at Matumbi land use and agrarian patterns it is obvious why rural dwellers resisted cotton. In times past Matumbi and other greater-Rufiji agrarian patterns were based on a complex gender division of labor and sensitivity to land and crop types (see Chapter 4).[76] Outside of Rufiji river floodlands, where labor-saving *mlau* cultivation was practiced, agriculture was time-consuming and dependent on household and village labor. For this reason, Matumbi men had refrained from porterage in precolonial times. The population dispersals and other disruptions that followed the Maji Maji rebellion upset these patterns completely. With many men absent it was difficult for women to sustain the three-field Matumbi agricultural system that had once produced grain surpluses for regional markets. Colonial directives to plant cotton preceding the heavy rains that fell in March and April conflicted with the Matumbi seasons of *Mwano, Ntandatu,* and *Nchimbi,* when they planted rice and maize, and when continuous vigilance against wild pigs and birds consumed available family labor. Under these circumstances, peasants could not add cotton to cropping patterns and sustain food production. For this reason, after one or two years many Kilwa-area peasants abandoned both cotton and even *shamba* land near centers of colonial control.[77] Without pressure from African elites and district officials, coupled with the threat of corvée labor or penal labor on European plantations, peasants would very likely never have taken up the crop at all.

PLANTATIONS, COTTON, AND FOOD DECLINE

Following Maji Maji, thirteen German plantations appeared in Rufiji and Kilwa districts. Some, such as the Kilwa Cotton Plantation, were founded by German textile industrialists expressly to produce cotton.[78] Before 1905 these plantations would have been assured of strong state support in procuring a workforce. However, in the atmosphere that prevailed after 1907, state policy was to facilitate a free labor market and uphold labor contracts, but refrain from using force to get peasants to work for a wage. Planters were expected to attract a workforce by offering competitive wages, food rations, and adequate living conditions. For their part, German planters resented the peasant cotton campaign, particularly the free dispensation of seed to peasants, because it made it difficult for them to compete with peasants as cotton growers, and it empowered peasants to avoid wage labor.[79]

Frustrated at their inability to obtain sufficient local labor, some Rufiji district planters initially tried to subvert local peasant cotton growers by prohibiting them from growing cotton.[80] After district officials intervened to prevent such practices, a new planter tactic was to provide local peasants with cotton seed in the hope of buying peasant cotton and then reselling it at higher prices.[81] Planter competition to buy peasant cotton was so intense in Rufiji region that it drove prices as high as 25 *hellers* per lb. in 1913, leading district officials to worry that, at such high prices, peasants would decrease the amount of cotton in their fields.[82] In Kilwa and Lindi districts planters resorted to sharecropping methods to obtain peasant cotton, drawing on a north German practice called *Instwirtschaft* that resembled the squatter economies of Kenya or Rhodesia.[83] The squatter model was for householders to settle with their families on plantation lands in exchange for free housing and land for their own food plots. The household head signed a contract to work for 120 days per year on the plantation for "customary" wages. At planting and harvest times, planters expected other family members to work for them as well. Lindi planters often plowed fields for peasant use, provided high monetary advances for sharecroppers to grow cotton, and bought any cotton that sharecroppers harvested. Most Lindi cotton—perhaps most plantation cotton—was produced by peasant sharecroppers or other local peasants, although planters included such cotton in their overall figures to argue for more government support.

Despite peasant success at avoiding wage labor by growing their own cotton, the proliferation of plantations in conjunction with the intensification of the cotton program contributed to a palpable decline in food production in southern Tanzania and elsewhere in the colony. Tanzanian coastal societies before the German arrival had been growers of surplus rice and millet, much of which they traded on the coast for export into Indian Ocean trade networks. In the 1890s these markets were still vibrant. In 1891 Tanzania exported 2.75 million kg of rice, according to German figures, which are probably underestimates.[84] After 1894, coinciding with locust plagues and the first state attacks on peasant bush fallowing, grain imports far outdistanced exports. In 1909 more than 13 million kg of rice worth 2.7 million marks were imported into German East Africa, a level that remained unchanged to the end of German rule.[85] Due to periodic food shortages following Maji Maji, some Rufiji planters grew grain to attract peasants to settle near their estates.[86] In 1914 some Rufiji peasants went to a planter to buy seed corn at high prices because "there was no maize in the entire region."[87] When the planter had none to sell, they were forced to journey 200 km to the Kilwa market. In Lindi district observers attributed the decline in food directly to cotton growing. The KWK representative reported in 1914 that "just a few years ago Lindi was considered to be the breadbasket of the colony, [as] great loads of millet went from Lindi to Arabia and Aden; now the millet harvest is barely sufficient to feed the district."[88] Often compelled to give a portion of their land and labor over to cotton rather than food, and frequently crippled by the absence of men, peasant subsistence suffered. The conflict between growing cotton and food never abated during German rule, leading peasants to resist the crop overtly or covertly or seek other means of surviving the cotton campaign.

RESISTING COTTON COLONIALISM IN SOUTHEAST TANZANIA

Histories of the post-Maji Maji period in Tanzania typically assert that the ability or willingness of peasants to resist German colonialism came to an end with the war.[89] However, as a wide body of literature on "hidden resistance" makes clear, peasants did not accept cash crop regimes passively, nor could they in light of the damage to the rural physical and social environment that came with colonialism.[90] Resistance was a crucial arena of the colonial economy that took the form of peasant movements and actions that had important consequences for survival. These actions shaped the direction of the colonial economy, despite the best efforts of the state to establish an economic blueprint that meshed with the needs of the German industrial economy.

Peasant resistance was widespread in southeastern Tanzania in the decade of the cotton campaign. In 1912, following a spate of destructive Rufiji floods, peasants refused cotton planting outright in order to put a food crop in the ground.[91] Peasants who did grow cotton in this period typically brought in a deficient, dirty product, neglecting completely the directives of itinerant instructors. The KWK reported, "most peasant cotton comes to market completely unsorted and even blatant waste is often not removed."[92] In Lindi district, peasants who lived *pembeni*, secluded in the bush "distant from Lindi and plantations," didn't even bother to sow the cotton seed that *majumbe* distributed to them.[93] In southern Kilwa district, where state control was weak, peasants simply ignored orders to plant cotton in favor of cassava, well-known as a famine crop.[94] Traveling south of Kilwa in 1909 on an inspection tour, a KWK representative observed extensive fields of cassava in this region where cotton had been promoted intensely. Coming across a village headman, the official asked why no cotton was to be seen. The *jumbe* responded, "If your cotton were cotton on top and cassava on the bottom, then you'd see how much we'd grow."[95] While the KWK agent concluded from his encounter that, "after all, people want to eat," he also understood that local villagers saw more profit to be gained growing cassava in an isolated region between Kilwa and Lindi, where people traveling for two or three days at a time needed to buy food.

In the years of the cotton campaign, some peasants used the presence of regional plantations to their advantage, working as day laborers during low cycles in the agricultural calendar, and returning home daily with wages they could use to buy food or pay taxes.[96] Rufiji planters accused peasants living near their lands of stealing cotton from their fields then marketing it as their own. Yet another grievance for planters was their loss of expensive contract labor to local women. In the absence of husbands, some single or abandoned women formed new relationships with workers on regional plantations, often Ngoni or Mozambican labor migrants on half-year contracts, with whom they reconstituted their households.[97] Planters complained that some of these men broke contract and never returned to work as they blended into local villages (some perhaps abandoning wives in their homelands).

During the cotton campaign a growing rebelliousness permeated peoples from the Rufiji to the Rovuma. Some Rufiji people left the region for Kisaki and Morogoro districts, where local control was less onerous and sometimes nonexistent.[98] Other accounts in the settler press and from planters' associations depict southern Kilwa district around the Mbwemkuru river as a region beyond state control, where "unsavory elements" from Lindi, Kilwa, and Rufiji congregated to escape state controls.[99] There people refused corvée labor, hunted without permits, avoided working for planters, didn't pay taxes, damaged the forests, and "caroused" with beer parties. In 1908 the Lindi district office apprehended two *waganga* spirit mediums from the region who, it claimed, were inciting the people against the German regime.[100] People of the borderland *Grenzwildnis* reportedly carried on the extractive economy of gathering wild rubber, copal, wax, and mangrove bark, and even elephant hunting, spiting the state's efforts to get peasants to produce cotton. The editor of the *Deutsch-Ostafrikanische Zeitung* worried that the passive resistance of these borderland renegades might easily turn into active resistance once again. Claiming that some Lindi villages disintegrated because of the exodus of people to the borderland, the Lindi Planters' Association requested that southern Kilwa be brought under firmer state control because it acted as a haven for southern peasants who refused to grow cotton or work on plantations.[101]

Although fears of rebellion could be attributed to planter paranoia and frustration at not being able to muster sufficient local labor, KWK and state authorities worried about the general state of things in the south on the eve of World War I. So many peasants of Lindi district had become indebted to planters through advances on the next cotton crop that a standing debt peonage was in the making, which, one KWK observer warned, could lead to a repeat of the 1889 or 1905 rebellions.[102] In 1913 the settler press claimed that between the borders of Rufiji and Kilwa districts, in the outbreak region of Maji Maji, an "inciter" using a *dawa* was planning a rebellion directed against local planters.[103] The alleged instigator was apprehended by authorities and brought to the district office in Utete, and there reports of the incident end. However, fears of another rebellion weighed heavily on the minds of colonial officials to the end of colonial rule, leading them to tread carefully in implementing cotton projects.

THE LIMITS OF THE CRISIS-SECURE PEASANT HOUSEHOLD

To the end of colonial rule officials believed that the peasant cotton course was the correct one, and resisted recriminations from settlers, planters, and their industrial backers in Germany who demanded a return to the plantation imperative. Peasant *mashamba*, despite meager returns, still far outdistanced plantations in producing cotton, which policy makers believed was absolutely essential for the stability of the German economy and polity.[104] For this reason, officials proceeded with plans to open up inland regions of the colony along the Central Railway for peasant cotton, ultimately targeting Tabora district as a major arena for future peasant cotton production. Meanwhile, a few dozen large-scale plantations emerged in the colony that succeeded in drawing in thousands of long-distance labor migrants to grow cotton and, increasingly, sisal. Forced to compete with the state's preference for peasant-scale cotton production, planters and their allies in the settler community made the *Arbeiterfrage*, the labor question, the single biggest point of conflict in colonial policy.

While peasants of the southeast demonstrated a resilience in restructuring agriculture to deal with the crisis of the cotton campaign, as seen in Matumbi women's farming of *matimbe* strips, there was no way to insulate rural society from the accumulation of grievances that accompanied colonial rule. Contrary to colonial planners' perceptions that peasants were *krisenfest,* crises were an almost continuous feature of rural households forced to endure the multiple burdens of growing cotton and maintaining subsistence food production, while still paying taxes and providing corvée labor, often absent male labor. In peasant perceptions, the cotton campaign was associated with sharply circumscribed access to the forest commons, and increased vulnerability to wildlife predators. Small wonder, then, that when German colonialism ended with World War I, southeastern peasants quickly abandoned *pamba,* having internalized a distaste for the crop that continued into the era of British rule.[105] As a British agrarian planner stated after a decade spent trying to get Rufiji peasants to grow cotton, "Cotton is a most unpopular crop, and its extension has defied all efforts of the department of agriculture over a long period of years."[106] The cotton campaign created a "prejudice, deep-rooted" toward the crop that outlasted German and British colonial rule.

NOTES

1. Reichskolonialamt, *Der Baumwollbau in den deutschen Schutzgebieten* (Jena, 1914), 38. On *Krisenfestigkeit* see Elizabeth Bright Jones, "Gender and Agricultural Change in Saxony, 1900–1930," (Ph.D. diss., University of Minnesota, 2000); Fritz Klare, *Untersuchung über Einsatz und Ausnutzung der menschlichen Arbeitskräfte in bäuerlichen Betrieben* (Dessau, 1932).

2. BAB/R1001/726, Booth report, 16 January 1906, 130a; Supf to Colonial Office, 23 January 1906.

3. Richard V. Pierard, "The Dernburg Reform Policy in German East Africa," *TNR* 67 (June 1967), 31–38; Harald Sippel, "Aspects of Colonial Land Law in German East Africa," in *Land Law and Land Ownership in Africa*, ed. Robert Debusman and Stefan Arnold (Bayreuth, 1996), 34; Lewis H. Gann, "Marginal Colonialism: The German Case," in *Germans in the Tropics: Essays in German Colonial History*, ed. Arthur Knoll and Lewis H. Gann (Westport, 1987).

4. Most importantly John Iliffe, "The Organization of the Maji Maji Rebellion," *JAH* 8, 3 (1967), 500 and *Agricultural Change in Modern Tanganyika: An Outline History* (Nairobi, 1971), 18–23; Walter Rodney, "The Political Economy of Colonial Tanganyika 1890–1930," in *Tanzania under Colonial Rule*, ed. M.H.Y. Kaniki (Singapore, 1980), 135–36; Juhani Koponen, *Development for Exploitation* (Hamburg, 1995), 427–28; Taasisi ya Elimu, *Historia. Schule za Msingi* (Dar es Salaam, 1985), 27–28.

5. Thaddeus Sunseri, "Peasants and the Struggle for Labor in Cotton Regimes of the Rufiji Basin (Tanzania), 1890–1918," in *Cotton, Colonialism, and Social History in Sub-Saharan Africa*, ed. Allen Isaacman and Richard Roberts (Portsmouth, 1995), 180–99.

6. Gilbert Gwassa and John Iliffe, *Records of the Maji Maji Rising* (Dar es Salaam, 1967), 22.

7. "Habari za njaa," *Kiongozi* (August 1908).

8. Quoted in Gwassa and Iliffe, *Records*, 27–28.

An Antidote to the Plantation Labor Shortage?   *131*

9. *MMRP* 2/68/2/3/7, Mzee Chidege Mwegoha, interviewed by J.R. Mlahagwa, 7 April 1968.

10. Ambrosius Maier, "Aus den Matumbibergen," *Missions-Blaetter* 14 (1910): 115–18; Gwassa and Iliffe, *Records*, 28. Divorce appears to have been especially rife in the Maji Maji outbreak region near Kibata. TNA G11/1 Kibata Strafbücher, 99, 138, 165–66, 237–42, 247–48.

11. "Die Reise des hochwürdigen Herrn Bischof Thomas Spreiter nach Matumbi und Kwiro," *Missions-Blaetter*, 13, 4 (January 1909), 66.

12. Marital breakdown during times of famine has been noted in other cases. Megan Vaughan, *The Story of an African Famine: Gender and Famine in Twentieth-Century Malawi* (Oxford, 1987); Gregory Maddox, "Gender and Famine in Central Tanzania: 1916–1961," *African Studies Review* 39 (1996), 83–101; Thaddeus Sunseri, "Famine and Wild Pigs: Gender Struggles and the Outbreak of the Maji Maji War in Uzaramo (Tanzania)," *JAH* 38 (1997), 235–59.

13. "Die Reise," *Missions-Blaetter*, 13, 4 (1909), 45; Landeg White, *Magomero* (Cambridge, 1987), 178–90.

14. "Die Entwicklung Kilwas im Jahre 1908," *DOAR*, 6 November 1909, 1.

15. A.R.W. Crosse-Upcott, "Ngindo Famine Subsistence," *TNR* 50 (1950), 2.

16. Toyin Falola and Paul Lovejoy, eds., *Pawnship in Africa: Debt Bondage in Historical Perspective* (Boulder, 1994).

17. Interview with Kassam Makao and Hamadi Duma, Mafia-Kilindoni, 26 May 1990.

18. TNA G1/97, Grass to Imperial Government, 23 July 1906.

19. Karl Weule, *Native Life in East Africa* (Chicago, 1969), 53, 58.

20. TNA G4/75, Bezirksrat Lindi, 20b–21a; Gwassa and Iliffe, *Records*, 28.

21. TNA G4/69, Rechnungslegung Kilwa, 28 June 1906, 27–28.

22. TNA G11/1, Kilwa Strafbuch, 31–34.

23. "Die Reise," *Missions-Blaetter*, 53.

24. "Die Reise," *Missions-Blaetter*, 65; Ambrosius Maier, "Aus den Matumbi–bergen," *Missions-Blaetter von St. Ottilien* 14 (1910), 115–18. The district office claimed that population levels had recovered at Kibata that same year. "Entwicklung Kilwas," *DOAR*, 6 November 1909, 1.

25. TNA G1/97, Grass to Imperial Government, 23 July 1906.

26. Maier, "Aus den Matumbibergen," 115–18; "Entwicklung Kilwas," *DOAR*, 6 November 1909, 1.

27. TNA G4/75 Bezirksrat Lindi, 14 March 1906, 3; "Entwicklung Kilwas," *DOAR*, 6 November 1909, 1; "Kilwa im Jahre 1909," *DOAR*, 17 December 1910, 1.

28. TNA G11/1, Kilwa Strafbuch, 83, 206.

29. "Entwicklung Kilwas," *DOAR*, 6 November 1909, 1.

30. The Matumbi belief that forested hill tops were inhabited by *shetani* ill spirits was probably a means to prevent erosion of mountain slopes where people lived and cultivated. Tanganyika Regional and District Books, MF-977, Reel 15, "Land Tenure in Matumbi Tribal Area"; "Die Reise," *Missions-Blaetter*, 49, 66.

31. "Die Reise," *Missions-Blaetter*, 131.

32. Weule, *Native Life*, 58.

33. "Familien-Nachwuchsstatistik über die Eingeborenen von Deutsch-Ostafrika," *DKB* 25 (1914), 448.

34. "Die Reise," *Missions-Blaetter*, 83; "Entwicklung Kilwas," *DOAR*, 10 November 1909, 1; TNA G1/97, Grass to Imperial Government, 23 July 1906.
35. "Die Reise," *Missions-Blaetter*, 129.
36. "Entwicklung Kilwas," *DOAR*, 6 November 1909, 1.
37. K. Braun, "Der Reis in Deutsch-Ostafrika," *BLF* 3, 4 (1908), 195.
38. *Matimbe* land was coterminous with men's *ngwenda* land. Tanzania Regional and District Books, MF-977, Reel 15, "Land Tenure in the Matumbi Tribal Area."
39. TNA G58/98, Jahresbericht der Forstverwaltung Rufiji 1910/11, 30 April 1911, 2–16.
40. The declaration of these forest reserves, including locations and provisions regulating access, are found in TNA G8/672–G8/692.
41. Maier, "Aus den Matumbibergen," 115–18.
42. TNA G4/80, Grass to Imperial Government, 15 September 1906, 126–28.
43. "Mohoro," *Kiongozi* 2, 16 (1906).
44. "Baumwollbau am Rufiji," *DOAR*, 11 March 1911, 1.
45. BAB/R1001/8186, Schnee to RKA, 14 January 1914, 45.
46. RKA, *Der Baumwollbau,* 52–101; TNA G8/901, Baumwollstation Mpanganya 1914, 24.
47. The KWK recruited African American cotton experts from Tuskegee Institute for its cotton projects in Togo. A similar effort for German East Africa was abandoned shortly before Maji Maji. BAB/R1001/8147, Supf to Foreign Office, 13 April 1904, 133–34; Louis R. Harlan, "Booker T. Washington and the White Man's Burden," *American Historical Review* 71 (1966), 442–47.
48. In 1911 nineteen of the school's twenty-nine students came from Rufiji, six from Lindi, three from Kilwa and one from Mafia Island. "Von der Baumwoll-Schule Rufiji," *DOAZ*, 23 June 1906, 2; TNA G8/901, Baumwollstation Mpanganya 1914, 22; RKA, *Der Baumwollbau*, 58–59, 76. The English Universities Mission in Massassi (Lindi district) sent some of its students to Mpanganya. Kolonial-Wirtschaftliches Komitee, *Deutsch-Koloniale Baumwollunternehmungen* 12 (Spring 1910), 162. On environmental effects of the German cotton program see Kapepwa Tambila, "Botanical Imperialism in Action: Germany and Cotton in East Africa, 1886–1914," *Tanzania Zamani* 1, 4 (1996), 27–57.
49. KWK, "Baumwollbericht XII," (1910), 35.
50. *Verhandlungen des KWKs* 2, 9 October 1906, 14; *DKBU* 12 (Spring 1910), 162.
51. GStA, Nachlass Schnee, Schriftstücke in Suaheli, File #69, "Nipande pamba ya namna gani?"
52. Interview with Ali Mwinyinvua Maiti, Morogoro, 5 June 1990.
53. GStA, Nachlass Schnee, Schriftstücke in Suaheli, File #69, "Nipande pamba ya namna gani?"
54. RKA, *Der Baumwollbau*, 66, 98–101; TNA G8/16, Dienstanweisung für Bezirkslandwirte; TNA G8/137, KWK to District Office Mohoro, 6 December 1910; BAB/R1001/541, Kränzlin report, 30 July 1910, 15. Generally one itinerant teacher was assigned to each *akidat*.
55. TNA G8/177, Mohoro District Office to Dar es Salaam, 1 October 1911, 30–31.

56. TNA G11/1, Kibata Strafbuch, 72.
57. TNA G11/1, Kilwa Strafbuch, 106, 210.
58. TNA G11/1, Kilwa Strafbuch, 60, 83, 102, 145; Kibata Strafbuch, 237.
59. KWK, *Verhandlungen der Baumwollbau-Kommission des KWKs*, 2. Sitzung, 27 November 1911, 36.
60. TNA G8/137, KWK to District Office Mohoro, 6 December 1910.
61. KWK, *DKBU* 14 (1911), 8–9.
62. Several recipients claimed descent from the Mlanzi clan, which tradition asserted came to Rufiji region 400 years previously. Tanganyika District Books, Morogoro Province, Rufiji District Book, "Warufiji History and Legends."
63. "Die Baumwolle am Rufiyi," *Koloniale Zeitschrift*, 25 September 1911, 616–19; "Baumwollbau am Rufiji," *DOAR*, 11 March 1911, 1.
64. Of the KWK's 1913 budget of 330,000 RM, 150,000 was used for free cotton seed to peasants. Archiv des Handelskammers Hamburg, KWK to Reichstag, 11 January 1913, Bestand 132-1, 3; RKA, *Der Baumwollbau*, 39.
65. *DKBU* 11 (Spring 1909), 157, 162; GStA, Nachlass Schnee, File #72, Lindi, 18 October 1910.
66. BAB/R1001/8181, Grass to Imperial Government, 18 January 1909, 218–19.
67. RKA, *Der Baumwollbau*, 110; BAB/R1001/8181, Supf to Colonial Office, 1 March 1909, 232–35.
68. Interview with Mzee Rashidi Mohamed Mtambo, Mafia-Kilindoni, 26 May 1990.
69. Interview with Kitenge Muhamed, Kilwa-Masoko, 20 June 1990.
70. Interview with Kassam Makao, Hamadi Duma, Mzee Nganda, Mafia-Kilindoni, 26 May 1990; Abdalla Umati, Kilwa-Masoko, 20 June 1990.
71. This was perhaps 2–5 percent of the region's population. BAB/R1001/8181, Grass to Government, 18 January 1909, 215.
72. KWK, *DKBU* 11 (Spring 1909), 143.
73. BAB/R1001/8186, Ernteschätzung für das Baumwolljahr 1913/14, 86–87. While Rufiji estimates distinguish between peasants and planters, about 500 bales produced by each, the 500 Kilwa bales do not distinguish peasants from planters. The biggest Kilwa cotton plantation averaged about 85 bales per year after 1910. Apparently 71 bales were marketed by the plantation in 1914. TNA G8/197, Leuze to Baumwollpflanzungsgesellschaft Kilwa, 15 August 1912, 102; Museum für Arbeit und Technik, Mannheim, 871.1 Otto-197, 370, 10 February 1914.
74. "Baumwollkultur in Deutsch-Ostafrika," *DOAZ*, 17 April 1909, 13; "Baumwolle am Rufiyi," *Koloniale Zeitschrift*, 12, 39–40, 25 September 1911, 616–19.
75. Quantities of cotton per acre varied widely. In 1911 the average was about 387 unginned lbs per acre. Quantities on peasant *mashamba* were likely far less owing to intercropping with food crops and peasant opposition to the crop. "Deutschkolonialer Baumwollbau," *Ostafrikanischer Pflanzer* 3 (1911), 159.
76. Tanganyika Regional and District Books, MF-977, Reel 15, Kilwa District Books, "Land Tenure in the Matumbi Tribal Area"; David L. Horne, "Mode of Production in the Social and Economic History of Kilwa to 1884," (Ph.D. diss., UCLA, 1984), 140–49; Gilbert Gwassa, "The Outbreak and Development of the Maji Maji War, 1905–1907," (Ph.D. diss., University of Dar es Salaam, 1973), 55–62, 535–38.
77. "Baumwollkultur in Deutsch-Ostafrika," *DOAZ*, 17 April 1909, 13.

78. A list of these plantations is found in KWK, *Kolonial-Handels-Adressbuch* (Berlin, 1911), 63–77.

79. BAB/R1001/8186, DOAG to KWK, 22 January 1914, 20–21; KWK to Imperial Government, 8 January 1914, 11–12.

80. TNA G8/179, Engel to Imperial Government, 22 September 1910, 61.

81. TNA G8/179, Kränzlin report, 1911; KWK to Imperial Government, 27 July 1910.

82. RKA, *Der Baumwollbau*, 111.

83. Rudolf Görnandt, *Die Landarbeiter mit eigener Wirtschaft in Nordwest- und Ostdeutschland* (Berlin, 1910); KWK, *DKBU* 10 (1908), 163; TNA G8/199, Pflanzervereinigung Lindi, 1912; BAB/R1001/8185, Supf to RKA, 11 September 1913, 233.

84. Braun, "Der Reis," *BLF*, 3, 4 (1908), 169.

85. "Die Frage des Reisbaues in den Kolonien," *Verhandlungen des Kolonial-Wirtschaflichen Komitees*, 22, 5 December 1912, 50; "Wirtschaftliche Erkundung im Interessengebiete der Bahnlinie Tabora-Kigoma (Tanganjikasee)," *Verhandlungen des KWKs*, 28 November 1911, 31.

86. "Lehrreiches aus der Bilanz einer kleinen Pflanzung," *DOAZ*, 24 February 1912, 1; BAB/R1001/8185, Supf to RKA, 11 September 1913, 233.

87. "Das Kolonial-Wirtschaftliche Komitee und die Baumwollkultur," *DOAZ*, 11 July 1914, 1.

88. BAB/R1001/8186, Schlosser to KWK, 12 February 1914, 77–78.

89. Rodney, "Political Economy," 135; Iliffe, *Modern History*, 201.

90. Representative of this literature is Allen Isaacman, "Peasants and Rural Social Protest in Africa," in *Confronting Historical Paradigms: Peasants, Labor, and the Capitalist World System in Africa and Latin America*, ed. Frederick Cooper, Florencia Mallon, Steve Stern, Allen Isaacman, and William Roseberry (Madison, 1993), 205–317; Allen Isaacman, *Cotton Is the Mother of Poverty: Peasants, Work, and Rural Struggle in Colonial Mozambique, 1938–1961* (Portsmouth, 1996); James Scott, *Weapons of the Weak: Everyday Forms of Peasant Resistance* (New Haven, 1985); Osumaka Likaka, *Rural Society and Cotton in Colonial Zaire* (Madison, 1997); William Beinart and Colin Bundy, *Hidden Struggles in Rural South Africa* (Berkeley, 1987).

91. "Die wirtschaftliche Lage am Rufiji," *DOAZ*, 25 May 1912, 2; "Eingeborenen- oder Plantagenkultur am Rufiji?" *DOAZ*, 23 April 1913, 2.

92. KWK, *DKBU* 12 (Spring 1910), 41.

93. BAB/R1001/8186, Ernteschätzung und Ernteertrag im Bezirk Lindi, 10 February 1914, 83–85.

94. Louise O. Fresco, *Cassava in Shifting Cultivation* (Amsterdam, 1986), 143–46; J.D. Acland, *East African Crops* (Longman, 1987), 33–38.

95. "Koloniale Volkswirtschaft," *DOAZ*, 17 April 1909, 14.

96. Sunseri, "Peasants and the Struggle for Labor."

97. TNA G8/199, Pflanzervereinigung Lindi 1912, 2.

98. TNA G8/177, Protokoll der Versammlung des 'Wirtschaftlichen Verbandes von Rufiji,' 12 February 1911, 10.

99. TNA G8/199, Pflanzervereinigung Lindi 1912, 2; "Videant consules," *DOAZ*, 8 January 1913, 1–2.

100. "Lindi," *DOAZ*, 16 May 1908, 2.

101. TNA G8/199, Pflanzervereinigung Lindi 1912, 2.
102. BAB/R1001/8186, Schlosser to KWK, 12 February 1914, 77.
103. "Zu den Unruhen im Rufiji-Bezirk," *DOAZ*, 17 September 1913, 22.
104. *DOAR*, 10 April 1912, 2; Rainer Tetzlaff, *Koloniale Entwicklung und Ausbeutung: Wirtschafts- und Sozialgeschichte Deutsch-Ostafrikas, 1885–1914* (Berlin, 1970), 147.
105. "Rufiji River Floods," Tanganyika District Books, Eastern Province, Rufiji and Mafia District Books.
106. BAB/R1001/8185, Schnee to Colonial Secretary, 28 November 1912, 18; D.M.P. McCarthy, *Colonial Bureaucracy and Creating Underdevelopment: Tanganyika 1919–1940* (Ames, 1982), 129.

6

MIGRANT LABOR AND THE SHAPING OF PLANTATION WORK CULTURE

The period after 1906 in German East Africa marked the decisive end of the plantation imperative. The state would no longer privilege plantations in the formulation of colonial policy, particularly in matters of labor procurement. Instead a laissez-faire labor policy emerged in the colony that was to be embedded in the 1909 labor ordinances. *Freizügigkeit*—freedom of movement—was the order of the day, which meant that there was no notion of "influx control" as existed in, for example, German Southwest Africa. Nor were Africans confined to reserves under the control of chiefs and monopsonistic labor recruiters, or deprived of land on which to survive as independent peasants. This liberal labor policy was one geared to the needs of German East Africa in a period of rapid colonial development. The construction of two competing railway lines in addition to the burgeoning demand for porters necessitated a free flow of labor for the foreseeable future. The seasonal needs of peasant agriculture also required that long distance migrants be able to return to their homelands to participate in agricultural pursuits alongside their wives, hopefully growing cash crops of value to the German metropole.

The end of the plantation imperative was demonstrated by a shift in the colonial administration. Bernhard Dernburg, appointed as the first Colonial Minister, did not believe that settlers or plantations were necessary for colonial development. In German East Africa Albrecht von Rechenberg replaced Graf von Götzen as governor and immediately vetoed a quadrupling of the hut tax that planters had long lobbied for to compel more people to work for a wage.[1] Dernburg and Rechenberg were not mavericks. They and their successors represented the will and interests of the German state in the decade before World War I. This meant as much as possible avoiding colonial abuses such as forced labor that many opponents of the regime in Germany believed had been the causes of the 1905 rebellion. The state was furthermore still committed to emancipating itself from the American cotton monopoly. As discussed in Chapter 1, the period after 1907 witnessed escalating crises in the German textile industry accompanied by increased strike activity and other labor struggles at a time when Social Democrats were emerging as the biggest political threat in Germany. Many policy makers believed that the key to industrial stability was to curb the fluctuations in world cotton prices by obtaining secure, German-controlled sources of cotton. Even before the Maji Maji rebellion, the influential Colonial Economic Committee had begun to conclude that cotton was grown most efficiently on small-scale peasant *mashamba*. After the war the colonial administration endorsed this view, and concentrated state policy, including labor matters, in this direction. In so doing, Rechenberg quickly incurred a reputation as the enemy of settler and plantation interests in the colony.[2]

The shift in state policy did not mean an end to plantations in the colony. Indeed, the period after 1906 can be considered to be the high tide of plantation development as the number of small-scale settlers and large corporate plantations tripled in number by 1910. While settlers continued to gravitate to the northeastern Usambara highlands and their foothills, large-scale plantations increasingly took root around Morogoro and Kilosa towns 200 km or so inland along the Central Railway that was making its way into the interior. In 1907, when Dernburg made a study visit to German East Africa to assess the colony's economic potential, he was accompanied by a handful of textile industrialists who went on to found their own cotton plantations in the colony, hoping to supply their own factories completely with colonial-grown cotton.[3] Twelve large plantations alone controlled some 85,000 ha by 1910.[4] Policy makers publicly welcomed new plantation development, particularly because many new undertakings committed themselves to grow some cotton.

Despite public encouragement, privately colonial officials, especially Governor Rechenberg, came to see settlers and plantations as burdens on the colony. Even before the period of rapid plantation development there was an almost insurmountable labor shortage. While many thousands of new wage laborers could still be drawn into the colonial economy from the newly reconquered southwest and the densely populated regions of Ruanda-Urundi, most policy makers understood that the colony simply did not have enough people to sustain both peasant and plantation production regimes. The fear of another rebellion being ignited by forced labor or plantation abuses, even missed wage payments, weighed heavily on the minds of colonial officials.[5] The state therefore focused on peasant food production in plantation districts and peasant cotton growing elsewhere. The free-labor policy meant that planters were dependent on incentives to obtain a seasonal migrant labor force, including high wages, recruitment bonuses, food rations, and amenable plantation living conditions. Under these circumstances, labor migrants held great volition in negotiating the terms of their contracts and shaping plantation work culture. However, the steady rise in numbers of plantations and settlers after the Maji Maji war meant that the labor question would continue to be at the center of colonial policy disputes.

LABOR MIGRATION AND "WILD" RECRUITMENT

The state's laissez-faire attitude toward labor opened the door to a frenzied era of labor procurement known as "wild" recruitment. Before the 1905 rebellion intense settler competition for labor drove wages up, creating an environment of discretionary wage labor and high wages for the thousands of Nyamwezi porters and others who came to work in northern plantation districts. After the rebellion, hundreds of new German settlers arrived, alongside immigrants from South Africa, Russia, Greece, and India. Some had relatively modest labor needs, such as the approximately eighty farmers and ranchers of Arusha district, most of whom were Boers recently arrived from South Africa.[6] However, hundreds of settlers growing coffee, rubber, and sisal had ongoing demands for workers that peaked at important moments of the agricultural season. These middling planters were usually in a poor position to compete with the seventy-five or so large-scale plantations that were founded by joint-stock corporations or private capitalists in Germany, and therefore were often unable to muster financial resources for expensive capital inputs and labor procurement.[7] Besides the European plantation sector, hundreds of Arab and Swahili estates still employed thousands of workers and slaves, and a few hundred thousand men worked annually as porters.[8] By 1907 the construction of two railway lines, the Usambara in the north and the Central Railway on the main caravan route, demanded as many as 25,000 workers annually, intensifying overall competition for labor. Several thousand workers were also employed in the tiny mining and industrial sectors by 1912.[9] Meanwhile, thousands of Nyamwezi and Sukuma who had once migrated to the coast for labor found better opportunities marketing hides and wax, or working as porters for the Mwanza market opened up by the completion of the Uganda railway in Kenya.[10] All of these undertakings created opportunities for peasants to grow and market food crops to feed workers, empowering them to pay taxes and avoid wage labor. The result was a frenzied struggle in the colony for a limited labor supply.

Even before the 1905 uprising planters sent agents into the interior to recruit workers, realizing that the old porterage networks around Bagamoyo would not bring them adequate numbers of workers.[11] Following the Maji Maji uprising, scores of failed planters and recent immigrants found a new occupation as labor brokers, making their living by obtaining workers by any means possible and channeling them to the highest bidders in plantation zones. This "wild" recruitment was fraught with abuse and chicanery. In 1908 the Tanga district office charged Fritz Moritz, a failed coffee farmer, with recruitment under false pretenses for promising several men in Dar es Salaam that they would receive wages and a food ration amounting to 17 Rp per month, far above the going rate of about 10–12 Rp.[12] Other workers came forward with similar stories. Moritz promised three recruits that they would be sent to work on a coconut palm plantation near Bagamoyo. Instead they were sent to sisal plantations near Pangani and Tanga, which many workers avoided because of injuries caused by working around sisal blades. Discovering also that they would receive no *posho* food ration, the recruits "did not consider ourselves to be obligated to work," and promptly deserted. The Tanga District Court exonerated them of charges of contract breaking.

Moritz's "recruitment exaggerations" (*Werbekniffe*) were mild compared to other threats directed at African workers and labor recruits. Cases of mistreatment, negligence, physical abuse leading to death, and forced recruitment surfaced in the first few years afer 1908.[13] Recruiters seeking quick profits, accompanied by armed henchmen, scoured the countryside in search of workers, finding fertile ground in regions recently devastated by the 1905 rebellion, where they bribed loyalist chiefs to compel men to migrate for wages. In Njombe region in 1906, for example, the sultan Merere bin Merere supplied workers to the Greek recruiter Zavaella in exchange for a *bakshish* of 300 Rp.[14] In mid 1908 the recruiter Markos arrived in the district and paid Merere the requisite 300 Rp for a free hand to impress workers with threats and force, chaining some at his recruitment camp. Reports also emerged from coastal plantations that Bena workers from Njombe arrived in an unhealthy state, many having died from the march to the coast.

The government responded to these cases by directing the Iringa military station to suspend labor recruitment immediately, sending an *askari* to free Markos' impressed workers.

Labor recruiters in the era of wild recruitment sometimes provisioned their caravans by pillaging villages. On a march from Songea to Lindi in 1909, the recruiter Wisliceny directed his 200 recruits and porters, including a former *askari*, to raid villages they passed for food.[15] They emptied all the grain storage bins in half a dozen villages, dug potatoes and cassava out of the fields, and plundered stores of rice, beans, and blankets. The villager Kalindo testified that Wisliceny's men stole four *pishi* (about 24 lbs) of salt. When another villager fought a porter who was pillaging his millet field, Wisliceny had him beaten twenty-five times and confiscated all his possessions.

Known cases of recruitment abuse, and the potential for more in an intense atmosphere of labor competition, led the government to enact the first comprehensive labor ordinance in the colony in 1909 to address labor recruiting and wage labor on plantations.[16] To rein in "unscrupulous labor recruiters" the new ordinance required a recruitment permit to be issued by local authorities. District officials could deny permits to persons with records of crime or abuse, as they did in 1910–11 with thirty-four recruiters who were convicted of labor violations.[17] The overseer Frantzis, for example, received three days in jail for recruiting men to work outside Tanga district. Officials revoked the permit of the Swahili Hassani bin Abdrachman because he did not provide the surety that was required for recruited workers. The German Bohl lost his permit after officials charged him with forced recruitment, and many other recruiters received fines and jail terms for violations of the 1909 ordinance.

The 1909 ordinance empowered district officers to restrict recruiting in their regions if they deemed the loss of workers to be unhealthy. It furthermore prohibited recruitment from the densely populated regions of the northwest, especially Ruanda, Urundi, and Ujiji out of fear that "mountain peoples" could not withstand the malarial coast.[18] In so doing, more than 40 percent of the colony's population was off-limits to labor recruitment, a severe loss for plantation development. To ward off the periodic threat of South African labor recruiters, the 1909 ordinance proscribed recruitment for work outside the colony. The dangers and deceptions of working in South Africa were periodically publicized in the Swahili newspaper *Kiongozi*.[19]

Despite limitations on labor recruitment, the colonial state sometimes urged district officers to pressure people to migrate for work if they were not otherwise employed in cash crop growing or did not pay their taxes. In 1911 the Iringa station chief took pains to assure the governor that, despite deep reservations, he was not opposed to labor migration.[20]

Before labor migrants left their homeland the district office verified terms of their contracts, including wage levels, type of work, intended work site, and the duration of their contracts so as to prevent misrepresentation. The office required a surety of a few rupees for every worker recruited to guarantee adequate food provisioning during the journey to plantation regions, which might take several months. Intended to uncover cases of impressment or involuntary labor migration, contract verification was not always rigorous. In 1913 a group of Pogoro recruits testified that they agreed to a labor contract at the Mahenge district office because of pressure from their *jumbe* and intimidation from a local German planter acting as a labor recruiter.[21] District officers often hesitated to delve too deeply into motives for recruitment as long as force was not obvious.

Once contracts were verified, recruits began the trek to the work site. They were rarely accompanied by the recruiter, instead choosing one of their number, perhaps someone who had migrated before, as a leader. Recruits received wage advances of about 4 Rp and an additional 2–3 Rp to buy food from villagers along the way. It was not unusual for recruits to then desert, negotiating new work arrangements with different planters or employers.[22] Such was the case with eleven workers from Iringa district who signed contracts in May 1910, passed through Kilosa by June, but by September had still not arrived at their destination near Tanga.[23] Suspecting that they were working on another plantation, the Tanga district office offered a reward of 10 Rp for their capture. The Tanga *boma* posted a reward of 25 Rp for a contingent of seventeen Sukuma contracted in Mwanza to help construct the Tanga harbor. When the recruits did not arrive after several months, officials assumed that they had been enticed to work for a planter along the way.[24] Employer competition, and the limits of the state's police authority, provided recruits with ample opportunity to desert or to negotiate better working conditions with rival employers.

We can piece together a portrait of *waajiriwa* contracted laborers from a 1913 list of fifty recruits from Mahenge.[25] Recruited in groups of about thirteen, each worker agreed to a 180-day contract at 12 Rp per month, receiving a wage advance of 3–4 Rp, and 1$^1\!/_2$ Rp for provisioning during the two-week journey to a rubber plantation near Morogoro. Thirty-four of the men were Pogoro, the remaining included several Bena and Hehe. Migrants tended to journey with a few cohorts from their village, perhaps for mutual protection during the long march to the work site. Only one of the fifty was accompanied by his wife, who was not a contracted worker, although women and children could legally sign long-term contracts before 1913.[26] The ages of the Mahenge recruits ranged from sixteen to forty, with most men in their mid-twenties, suggesting that labor migration was still a young man's duty. While Mahenge patterns don't necessarily replicate long-established migration networks, such as those from Unyamwezi, they are probably a good picture of the "new" post-Maji Maji migration zones of the south and southwest.

Governor Rechenberg's concern for peasant agriculture and seasonal crop needs was imbedded in the 1909 labor ordinance, which limited contract duration to 180 days. Whether or not contract days were worked off, they were void after nine months, thereby preventing permanent proletarianization. Yet workers could renegotiate labor contracts immediately without returning to their homelands, and could reside permanently at the work site if they wanted, as many did. A South African-style oscillating labor migration, which maintained cheap "single-man's" wages, did not become the pattern in German East Africa. Indeed, many planters tried to settle whole families on their estates, hoping to ensure themselves of labor throughout the year.

Tax policy provided migrants with an incentive to work and reside on plantations for extended periods.[27] The 1905 revisions to the tax ordinance allowed men who worked on plantations for six months continuously to pay only $1^1/_2$ Rp annual tax instead of the usual 3 Rp. Men who resided on plantations longer than six months paid no tax, and many might have used plantations literally as tax havens (See FIGURE 6.1). It is unlikely, however, that the provision brought many new workers to plantations for a sum that could be worked off in a few days, and planters, for their part, considered tax policy to be meaningless, lobbying fruitlessly for a "labor creating" tax and pass controls as existed in South Africa.[28] State officials feared that extreme tax levels would contribute to the exodus of workers out of the colony to Kenya and Northern Rhodesia.[29]

Once migrants agreed to labor contracts, district officials could punish them for breaking contract with whipping, fines, or jail in chains. At the urging of planters, Rechenberg raised the jail term for desertion from fourteen days to three months. However, penal reports from Tabora district in 1913 suggest that fourteen days was the typical punishment for contract breaking at that late date, invariably aimed at railway workers in this plantation-scarce region.[30] The Kibata penal records in Kilwa district probably reflect patterns more typical for the colony as a whole since ten plantations were located nearby. There in 1908–10

Migrant Labor and Plantation Work Culture 143

Figure 6.1 Workers and their overseers on a plantation in German East Africa. (Courtesy of Bundesarchiv, Koblenz, 146/84/67/24. Reprinted with permission.)

contract breakers were punished on average seven to ten days in chains, unless desertion was accompanied by theft or violence.[31] Porters who deserted, in contrast, might receive as much as one month in chains. Despite these penalties, planters' complaints and fugitive reports demonstrate that desertion was widespread, and workers left estates almost at will. In 1908 planters requested, and received, a secret plantation police (*Geheimpolizei*) to root out contract breakers in some districts.[32] Yet contract breaking did not abate, because the fierce labor market gave workers incentive to find new employment almost with impunity. In 1912, for example, the Mombo Rubber Plantation charged the worker Afrika with repeatedly breaking contract, and the Wilhelmstal District Office sentenced him to two months in chains.[33] When he was eventually returned to Mombo to complete his contract, Afrika immediately fled, this time successfully. In 1912 the Wilhelmstal planter Gutsch reported eight Nyamwezi workers who had been recruited together as contract breakers.[34] Gutsch believed that they were working at another plantation in the Luengera Valley.

The problem with finding contract breakers was that it was almost impossible to confirm their identities. Almost immediately upon signing labor contracts or agreeing to work, recruits adopted plantation names. These names often poked fun at plantation work. There were perhaps hundreds of workers named "Mpenda Kula" (likes to eat), "Kazi Bure" (worthless work), "Kazi Mbaya" (bad work), and "Kazi Ulaya" (European work) roaming the plantations of German East Africa.[35] Workers often took the name of towns (Daressalaam, Kilimatinde, Bagamoyo, Stambuli—Istanbul), or objects like "Pesa Mbili" (two pesas) or "Sigara" (cigarette). Near the coast many workers took on Islamic names, immersed as they were in Swahili culture. Plantation names could be changed almost at will, allowing for a floating identity that made it extremely difficult to regulate workers' movement or to capture deserters. One planter complained:

> These Sukuma and Nyamwezi! They abandon their real name as soon as they leave their homelands and take on a travel name: "Pesa Mbili," "Kofia Mbaya," "Kazi Moto," or something like that. Then they are enticed to break contract by a wily *ndugu* [countryman] and they take on a new name as soon as they are introduced to a new employer.[36]

The state refused to create an identification pass system, believing their resources to be too limited for effective policing, so contract breaking plagued employers to the end of German rule. However, planters themselves might have opposed such a system. Desertion was so common and so successful because of planter collusion with deserters. A writer in the *Usambara Post* chastised planters as the root cause of desertion, since they so readily accepted anyone willing to work, no questions asked, and even sent out their overseers to entice workers from neighboring estates.[37] The Baumwolle A.G. Plantation Corporation in Morogoro district charged neighboring planters with harboring some of its deserted workers.[38] Indeed, some recruiters looked at plantations as fertile ground for recruitment. The recruiter Koyakos sent his agent Malim Abdallah to the Kimamba cotton plantation near Kilosa to persuade workers to break contract and sign on with another employer. Abdallah admitted that this was a standard recruiting practice.[39]

Desperate for workers, planters often resorted to impressment to get sufficient laborers onto their estates, especially at peak periods of the year. In one instance an armed contingent apprehended seven Bena labor migrants marching home from Tanga and forced them to carry loads back to Korogwe in the heart of the northeast plantation district.[40] The workers then proceeded with their trek back home to Iringa, passing by the Wami River, where they were again apprehended and taken to pick cotton on the Rudewa plantation near Kilosa. They protested in vain to the plantation director, who confiscated their work cards. The policeman Pacifique, in search of a deserter from a nearby plantation, discovered the forced impressment of the Bena and reported the case to the Kilosa district station, which ordered their release with pay for the work they had done. The Rudewa plantation's overseer, Mluga, admitted that impressment was a common method of obtaining workers.

So dire was the labor problem, even in a "new" plantation district like Morogoro, that tension between planters and surrounding villagers developed when local people refused to work for a wage. An example is the case of two men, one a Manyema and one a Vidundu, who trekked northward from Kidodi to Morogoro to purchase cloth. They met the planter Hürstal, who asked them if they would do a week's work on his estate for $1^1/_2$ Rp, about half of the going wage rate. They explained that they were going to market, and didn't want to work, especially for such a low wage. Hürstal alleged that the two laughed at him when he made the offer "and gave me extremely cheeky answers."[41] Hürstal then beat the travelers with a walking stick and forced them to his estate to clear fields to plant rubber. Eventually the two escaped to Morogoro, filed a complaint of impressment, and also charged that Hürstal kept some 10 Rp they had intended for shopping. Because of Hürstal's reputation for past impressment, the district court sided with the plaintiffs. Hürstal's bitterness toward the district authorities was palpable. "If you provided us with just a little support," he wrote, "these things wouldn't happen."

The truth was that district officials frequently intervened to get people to work on plantations, particularly outside of peasant cotton zones. In the old plantation region of West Usambara the district officer introduced a *kipande* "work card" system in 1907 that required all men in the region to work for thirty days every four months.[42] The Morogoro district officer Lambrecht also introduced a work card that required men to work for a wage for thirty days each year.[43] He also timed tax collection to pressure *majumbe* to get people to work on nearby plantations. Lambrecht assured the director of the Morogoro Cotton Plantation Corporation, for example, that he would support him "in every way" in matters of labor recruitment.[44] The Cotton Corporation came to think of surrounding villages as a private labor reserve, even agreeing to pay the taxes of anyone who would come to work on the plantation. Expressing satisfaction at workers rounded up by the tax collector Isidor, the plantation director vented his frustration with others.[45] The tax collector Muhamadi produced no workers for him, and out of forty *vipande* work cards issued to Jumbe Bambarawe in 1911, only one worker showed up. Five *majumbe* ignored the requests for workers altogether. Those *majumbe* who put too much pressure on their people to do wage work risked losing them to emigration. In 1914, for example, Jumbe Kisere appeared at the Morogoro district office demanding the return of three of his people who he believed had moved to Bagamoyo, undoubtedly to earn higher wages elsewhere.[46] So, too, did Jumbe Mtitu of Ngerengere arrive at the Morogoro *boma* requesting that two of his people who had moved to Dar es Salaam be made to return. However, the principle of *Freizügigkeit* (freedom of movement) that formed the basis of labor policy in German East Africa meant that any villager could migrate wherever he or she wanted, and many used this option.

Even the *kipande* systems used in Usambara and Morogoro did not guarantee that plantations would get workers. In 1913 the Morogoro district officer ordered Akida Jarmias "to look for people hiding so as to avoid working for Europeans" in order to procure workers for the Mikesse rubber plantation.[47] In this case, as in others, many men simply left work card regions for other parts of the colony, as Rechenberg predicted would happen when the system was introduced.[48] Men could work off their cards anywhere they wanted. Morogoro workers usually preferred railway work, which offered better wages and more choice in tasks. In Usambara, Shambaa workers were known to travel twelve hours distant to work for better wages and conditions rather than work for nearby planters that had reputations for violence and low wages.[49]

While district officers generally tried to facilitate labor recruitment, planters' incessant demands for workers, and frequent abusive treatment, soured relations with district authorities. A case from Songea is illustrative. The district officer Keudel initially urged local people to work for the rubber planter Blohm, who settled in the region in 1912.[50] However Blohm quickly established a reputation for poor treatment, low wages, and no provisioning of *posho*. Most workers of the district preferred to migrate several hundred miles to the north or to the coast rather than work for him. In 1912 seventeen Matengo who had worked for Blohm appeared at the Mahenge *boma* complaining that they had not been paid or provided with *posho*. When Blohm refused to meet the workers' demands, Keudel turned decidedly against the planter. Blaming Blohm for his problems in procuring workers, Keudel pronounced that he would henceforth no longer obtain workers for him because "labor recruitment is solely a private matter." A relationship of deep antagonism developed between the two, a pattern that became common between local officials and planters elsewhere in the colony. So, too, did the initial amicable relationship between the Baumwolle A.G. Plantation and the Morogoro district officer sour after Lambrecht refused to ban northern labor recruiters from the district.[51]

Short of outright compulsion to work, planters were never satisfied with the role of local authorities. Indeed, many officials reminded villagers and their *majumbe* that, so long as they paid their taxes, they didn't have to work for a wage. As a result, many people resisted demands to work that did not come directly from district officials. This was the case with Dozi bin Mgido, a Luguru from Morogoro district, who worked off his *kipande* for the East Africa Plantation Corporation at Madamu. After leaving employment and returning home, Dozi was seized by Akida Sol Kopi, who, claiming to be acting on the plantation's behalf, accused Dozi of breaking contract, saying he would be brought to the Morogoro *boma* for punishment. Instead Kopi brought Dozi to his own *shamba* and put him to work protecting his fields from wild pigs. After working for some time, Dozi questioned whether his punishment was really by order of the government. Kopi responded, "Here it is the same as the *boma*. Don't you see a gun barrel? You will work here until your punishment is over."[52] Instead Dozi got word of his impressment to the Morogoro district office, which ordered his immediate release and payment for the work he had done.

In spite of the 1909 labor ordinance, many recruiters continued their abuses until caught. It was common for a recruiter to simply arrive in a locality and pay an *akida* or chief a *bakshish* of 5 Rp per worker, who would then pass the word down to *majumbe* to muster workers. According to one source critical of the method,

> [The sultan] gets the word from his authorities to supply the recruiter with people, and he must do no more than sit on his throne and give the order to his jumbes and village elders "amri ya serkal kupeleka watu mia moja"—[the district office orders you to supply one hundred people]. And the people, whether they want to or not, are brought to the district office by misuse of the name "serkal" [district office].[53]

Despite such cases, local *majumbe* increasingly did not simply obey the dictates of recruiters, chiefs, or *maakida*, often turning to district authorities for support.[54] In 1910 the recruiter Samaras appeared in the village of Jumbe Gawaya near Lake Nyasa and demanded workers for railway construction by order of the New Langenburg *boma*.[55]

Gawaya replied that some of his people had just returned from railway work and needed to plant their fields, while others were still working on the railway. Gawaya also pointed out that he had a letter from the *boma* that stated that people didn't have to work on the railway if they didn't want to. Similarly, in 1911 the recruiter Georgiades sent a messenger to *majumbe* around Singidda, north of the railway line, with a piece of paper that he alleged was an order from the *boma* to supply workers for railway construction. Several *majumbe*, having been previously warned by district authorities, knew this to be untrue, and simply refused to comply.[56]

The open labor market in German East Africa gave workers substantial leverage. Even when extra pressure was placed on them to work, they could choose their employers, decide the length of their contract or work with no contract at all, negotiate wage levels, and desert if conditions were bad or wages low. When the Baumwolle A.G. Plantation ran out of money to provide *posho*, a group of workers and two overseers deserted, finding work immediately on neighboring plantations.[57] Recruits did not hesitate to travel hours distant to avoid planters with bad reputations, whom they branded as "Bwana Mkali" (a cruel employer). Once in receipt of such a nickname, it was extraordinarily difficult for a planter to obtain workers. Many labor migrants simply refused to sign contracts with recruiters, migrating on their own to the railway or plantations to negotiate their own agreements with employers desperate for labor.[58] Non-contractual migrants such as these gave up free provisioning along the march and recruitment bonuses in favor of greater autonomy. Many entered into work agreements of two or three months, rather than 180 days, so that they could return to their homelands in time to help their wives with field work. Migrants understood the leverage that they held over planters, and used it to create the most favorable working conditions possible within the constraints of a colonial economy.

THE PEASANTIZATION OF PLANTATION WORK

In 1911 a planter wrote, "about once or twice every week I sponsor an *ngoma* and provide a few pots of beer, which the wife of one of my overseers brews almost continuously. The *ngoma* seldom last past 11:00, and only on Saturdays, except when it is necessary to extend them in order to drive out devils."[59] If this planter's description of his operation is to be believed, he went far to cater to the tastes of his workers. He encouraged men to settle with their families. He built houses with beds for his workers, provisioned the plantation *duka* weekly with fresh meat, and provided workers who agreed to sign contract extensions with wool blankets and *kanzu* garments as an incentive to stay longer. Though the planter probably exaggerated his generosity, his awareness of worker desires demonstrates how some planters came to understand that, in order to retain workers, they had to accommodate themselves to a work culture shaped by the demands and tastes of labor migrants.

This work culture was embedded in the 1909 labor ordinances, the colonial state's most far-reaching attempt to regulate working and living conditions on plantations, which required planters to provide long-distance migrants with housing, medical clinics, food rations, a ten-hour daily work limit, and a Sunday day of rest.[60] The administration appointed labor commissars to monitor work conditions and enforce labor contracts on plantations. The labor ordinance was in part a response to past abuses and poor working conditions that had threatened to create a climate of rebellion among thousands of annual labor migrants. Most planters viewed the labor ordinance with deep hostility. Following its enactment, the *Usambara Post* pronounced the Colonial Minister Dernburg to be "an enemy of German colonists in East Africa" for frustrating their "honorable struggle against the Rechenberg system" that outlawed forced labor and encouraged peasant farming.[61] Planters saw the labor ordinance as giving far too much volition to workers in negotiating wage levels, length of contract, and work and living conditions. Lamenting that their fates were dependent on the good will of district officials who acted as a "threatening sword over their heads," planters came to view the state as their implacable enemy.[62]

Planters attempted to master the labor environment by forming regional pressure groups and employers' associations that tried to control workers by colluding over maximum wage levels and by agreeing not to hire suspected contract breakers.[63] Such measures failed. Large plantations and small estates were often at odds over labor issues, the former in a much better position to pay high wages. Planter associations were extremely territorial, and hostile to labor recruiters who tried to draw people out of their districts. Most employers were willing to accept workers under any circumstances, whether or not they were contract breakers, and tried actively to entice their neighbors' workers onto their estates. With little expectation of aid from the state, or cooperation from their neighbors, planters did what they could to attract and retain workers on their estates. Wild recruitment moved from inland networks to plantation zones themselves. The result was a commodification of the workplace as planters learned to cater to worker likes and dislikes. In so doing, workers and local villagers shaped plantation culture and even the plantation work regime.

While long-distance labor migrants received most attention in colonial discourses on the labor shortage, most wage workers were men and women who lived in close proximity to plantations, towns, market centers, and mission stations. Local people usually worked on a short-term basis, for thirty days or less, perhaps only a few days at a time. These workers were uncounted in colonial statistics, but undoubtedly outnumbered the 57,525 long-distance migrants on plantations in 1912.[64] "New" plantation regions, such as Lindi, Rufiji, and Morogoro, obtained the bulk of their workers from local people. The advantage to planters was that local workers, living close to their homes, received no *posho* or housing, and received lower wages than long-distance migrants. They furthermore could be called upon at peak periods in planting schedules, and thus offered a more flexible labor supply. Planters situated their estates close to peasant villages, hoping to tap into the local labor market. In 1907, for example, the Kilwa Cotton Corporation established a plantation at Mtingi near the outbreak site of the 1905 rebellion.[65] Located adjacent to nine villages, and displacing some thirty-two households when it was founded, the Kilwa Corporation expected to draw local people onto its several plantations.[66] Likewise, along the Rufiji river ten German plantations competed intensely for local African labor, erroneously believing that they would not suffer the labor shortages of the northeastern plantation districts, where hundreds of settlers competed for local labor.[67]

For villagers, local wage labor was part of the household economy. Between planting and harvest times women and men might make a daily sojourn to a local employer, returning home before nightfall in time to cook or weed their fields. At planting or harvest times these workers abandoned plantation work altogether, frustrating employers who were powerless to prevent the exodus. While Iliffe and Koponen have argued that local labor was overwhelmingly forced, a careful reading of the evidence points to a different conclusion.[68] Peasants, especially women, used local labor as a supplement to household production, only working when necessary. A thirty-day work contract might be worked off gradually over half a year or longer, making it clear that local labor was discretionary. So successful were peasants at controlling local labor patterns that the state agreed to regulations in 1913 that required a thirty-day contract to be worked off within four months.[69] Even then, peasants still decided whether or not to sign a contract that might take seven days of their labor per month, typically during the dry season when their household crops were already in the fields awaiting maturation and harvest. Local workers were not to be had during planting and harvest times, as planters frequently complained.

In some cases whole villages of men and women traveled on a daily basis to plantations, returning home before nightfall to tend their own fields. Local workers refused to extend their contracts if plantation conditions were bad, if wage payments were irregular, or if a better deal could be obtained on a neighboring plantation. Workers often disappeared at planting and harvest times, whether or not they signed a contract. Planters complained frequently about local people's refusal to come to work, often resorting to compulsion in their desperation. One German planter in Rufiji district kidnapped and sexually abused the wives of an "eminent Swahili *jumbe*" for failing to muster workers, earning the wrath of district authorities in this region of the Maji Maji outbreak.[70] Northern planters were equally notorious for their bad relations with local people who refused work on their estates. One Wilhelmstal planter encouraged his workers to steal crops from local people to drive them away, hoping to expand his estate onto their lands.[71] Local labor was the arena of plantation work most open to negotiation, contestation, and conflict between planters and villagers.

A case study of the Otto Cotton Plantation near Kilosa illustrates how plantation work regimes and social life were forged through the ongoing interaction between long-distance and local laborers, who gradually came to "peasantize" plantation work regimes and culture.[72] Founded in 1907 by a German textile manufacturer who hoped to become self-sufficient in cotton, the Otto plantation was an example of the industrial predilection for intensive agricultural operations on a grand scale.[73] The symbol of Otto's self-emancipation was his purchase of two steam-powered tractors that he hoped would free the plantation from dependence on African labor. Through capital and technology, Otto expected to lead the way in colonial development. Otto planned a massive irrigation system, and diversified his operation by planting maize to provision his workers in addition to cotton, sisal, and rubber for export. Otto hired a half-dozen European overseers, including a manager with experience growing cotton in India. With seemingly unlimited capital resources, Otto spared no expense in his aim of emancipating himself from American cotton, even if German industry as a whole would remain dependent for the foreseeable future.

German planters like Otto attempted to create a disciplined factory-style work environment, "education for work" being a mantra of colonial development. However, there is very little evidence that these

Figure 6.2 A row of plantation workers doing field work in German East Africa, c. 1905. Planters attempted to regulate worker movement through call-and-response singing. Often a thin string or chain connected workers to maintain straight lines. (© Bildarchiv Preussischer Kulturbesitz Berlin, 1401 g. Reprinted with permission.)

efforts succeeded. On large plantations like Otto's, overseers called people to work every morning with a drum, and workers showed up with a work card that was marked once in the morning and once in the evening. Workers received their wages when their cards were marked thirty times. Using African overseers for every cadre of twenty-five workers, rows of workers were bound together with rope or chain to poke seed holes in regular, straight rows to facilitate the use of the steam tractors (See FIGURE 6.2).[74] Behind a lead row of men, a row of women deposited cotton or grain seed. Overseers attempted to regulate worker motions through call-and-response singing. However, these methods failed because work rhythms were under the control of African singers.

Widespread absenteeism also subverted the "time discipline" of calling workers together each morning with a drum.[75] Typically on large plantations, a great percentage of the work force simply refused to come to work daily. One planter claimed that one-quarter of resident laborers might actually be working at any given moment despite continuous efforts to get people to work.[76] Workers might spend a few days at plantation work, then a few cultivating their own parcels set aside by planters to attract workers. It was typical for a worker to take several months to complete a thirty-day card. Contracts of 180 days might be extended far longer than the nine-month limit stipulated by the 1909 ordinance. Though some historians have viewed the long time needed to work off contracts as a sign of planter manipulations of workers, the opposite seems more realistic.[77] Planters were unhappy about the lack of discipline and pressured the state to intervene. Toward this end, the amended 1913 labor ordinance provided that migrants who worked for less than twenty days per month could be punished, since "often on a plantation of 1,200 workers only about 300 actually work at any time, while the rest loaf around."[78] Yet attempts like this to rein in absenteeism generally failed, since workers could always find other planters desperate for their labor.

Capitalist planters like Otto hoped technology would solve the labor problem. Far from emancipating his plantation from labor, Otto's two steam tractors created their own labor demand. The two tractors operated in tandem, not pulling a plow, but rather dragging the plow along a cable connected to winches mounted on the two machines (see Figure 1.1). Requiring continuous supplies of fuel wood and water, the tractors employed whole cadres of workers to cut and transport wood, procure water, and to dig wells. Tractor agriculture required that fields be cleared painstakingly, since plowshares were easily broken by stones, stumps, and roots. Five to six times more labor was needed for clearing fields for a tractor than for hoe agriculture. Since fertilizer was too expensive an option for the soil-depleting cotton crop, new land had to be cleared every few years as with extensive "peasant" agriculture. The tractors were useless during the rainy season, becoming deeply mired and requiring days to be dug out (See FIGURE 6.3). For all their expense, steam tractors could plow no more than about one hectare per day. With a four-month window of opportunity at best before the rainy season set in, a modest extent of 120 ha or so could be expected from tractors per year, a fraction of the 5,000 ha that Otto leased, and far below the 10 percent of acreage Otto needed to bring under cultivation each year as part of his lease agreement with the state. Indeed, the limitations of labor meant that all planters invariably reached a bottleneck that limited productive land to a fraction of overall land leased from the government, perhaps no more than 10 percent.[79] Within a few years Otto realized that his was just as dependent on African labor as any other plantation in the colony.

Figure 6.3 One of the steam tractors of the Otto Cotton Plantation near Kilossa, mired in mud. Intended to emancipate the plantation from the labor shortage, steam tractors instead created a huge labor demand. (From R. Kaundinya, *Erinnerungen aus meinen Pflanzerjahren in Deutsch-Ostafrika* [Leipzig, 1916], opposite 89.)

By 1912 most production on the Otto plantation was done by "a living machine" of men and women using hoes and other peasant technologies.[80] As the steam tractors gave way to hoes, the regimen of gang labor also collapsed, as workers broke ranks and "hoed back and forth in all directions."[81]

Just as the work regime was peasantized, plantation culture was shaped largely by the interaction between local villagers and long distance migrants. Planters relied on this interaction, since most of the food used to provision workers came from local people. Furthermore, workers were attracted to estates largely because of the social life made possible by proximity to local villages. Planters who facilitated such a social milieu could better compete with neighbors for scarce labor. As a result, plantations were scenes of intense social activity. The Otto plantation was not unusual in setting aside parcels of land for workers to reside on with their families as labor tenants, hoping to retain workers in this way for as long as possible.[82] Claiming three villages of some 2,000 people altogether, worker villages like Otto's attracted local people who had grain, meat, or beer to sell, or who wanted to purchase wares from the plantation markets.[83] Most planters learned that, to attract workers and maintain a semi-permanent work force that could meet seasonal needs, a symbiotic relationship with local villagers like this was necessary.

The presence of women was a necessary facet of plantation social life. Long-distance migrants were sometimes accompanied by their wives, who cooked, farmed their own land parcels, and otherwise replicated domestic life. Based on the few recruitment lists available, about 2 percent of migrants from southwest districts were accompanied by women compared to 10 percent of workers from the more established Nyamwezi labor networks.[84] It was far more common for local women to work for short stints on plantations, or earn money by selling food, water, fuel wood, *tembo* palm wine, *pombe* beer, or sex. Some male migrants settled permanently near plantations and married local women, never to return home. Rufiji and Lindi planters complained that their expensive Ngoni recruits married local women, sometimes abandoning plantation work completely.[85] However, most employers understood the importance of having women on plantations to attract men, and founded bordellos or otherwise "procured women" for workers.[86] According to a missionary, "if one wants to retain workers continuously, one must build a bordello in the worker camp."[87] While missionaries believed plantation prostitution to be a major problem, they also believed that it was a necessary evil.[88] Practical plantation owners also allowed, and even sponsored, *ngoma* dances, provided extra *posho* to brew beer, and sometimes distributed meat to encourage workers to stay longer. By facilitating a social life, one plantation might attract workers from its neighbors without significantly raising its operating costs or violating recruitment ordinances.

The ongoing interaction between workers and local villages was a double-edged sword for planters. While plantation social life attracted workers, many planters complained that *ngomas* and *pombe* drinking subverted labor discipline.[89] After an *ngoma* with heavy drinking, workers might not show up for work for several days, whiling away the time in neighboring villages. Villages furthermore offered refuge to contract breakers, since planters did not have a good sense of their workers' identities. An underground economy between plantation workers and local villagers also facilitated work avoidance. Some workers on the Otto plantation showed up in the morning to have their work cards marked off, then spent days unsupervised, cutting wood in the adjacent forest to sell locally.[90] At night some of Otto's workers tapped rubber trees and stole maize that they then sold on the underground market.[91] Guarding fields at night from workers and local villagers was a regular activity for plantation overseers and watchdogs.

As thousands of migrants came to work annually on plantations and the railways, men and women from different regions, representing different cultures and languages, crossed paths. Even though men tended to migrate together from the same village and region, it was inevitable that a cultural mixing took place at the point of production, in plantation or village markets, at *ngoma* dances, beer huts, and bordellos. While dance competitions could be arenas of cultural competition, there is little evidence of the faction fighting and violence at the work site that existed in the compounds and worker camps of South Africa.[92] Nor is there much evidence that employers used ethnicity to divide their workers. More apparent were mediums for building worker solidarity. Swahili was the common language of plantations, and dissemination of the language increased with labor migration.[93] Perhaps the most important medium for cultural blending was Islam. Missionaries and district officials reported with great alarm the return of labor migrants from "the coast" with at least some trappings of Islam, often circumcised, with Muslim plantation names and coastal dress.[94] Muslim *walimu* started Koranic schools on plantations and in railway camps. South of the Rufiji, Islam made great inroads among plantation workers in the aftermath of Maji Maji.[95] A Swahili and Muslim hegemony induced labor migrants to a nominal conversion. The coastal disdain for *washenzi* or *kafiri*—heathens—was expressed in the plantation division of labor, where Swahili and other Muslims monopolized privileged positions as artisans, messengers, overseers, or domestic servants.[96] Near the coast, Muslim prostitutes were characterized as "apostles of Islam" because they disdained association with uncircumcised men.[97] If labor migrants agreed to circumcision and the trappings of Islam, they could enter mosques, socialize more freely with Muslim women, and assert a seniority on plantations that came with frequent sojourns to the coast. While planters had no sympathy for Islam, it did not interfere with plantation work. In contrast, Christian mission stations and schools ushered in "sharp attacks" on the labor availability of plantations as "a great number of half-grown boys are lost as workers on the plantations."[98] While worker solidarity on plantations might have resulted from the adoption of Islam, tension between male migrants and their wives also ensued as men returned home circumcised with Muslim names and dress, often disdaining local religious traditions that women preserved as the basis of their identity. Furthermore, some liaisons between newly converted plantation workers and Muslim women became permanent unions, and some men deserted their homelands and wives altogether as a result.

Plantations generally created poor health environments, and the 1909 legislation tried to address conditions by requiring clinics on large estates, blankets in cold weather, and latrines away from water sources. Epidemics of hook worm disease, caused by unsanitary water and congested living conditions, hit many estates.[99] Worm sickness outbreaks were so rife that failure to build proper outhouses was perhaps the single most widespread criminal infraction directed against Africans in some regions.[100] Clinics appear to have been miserable places that workers avoided, some believing that they were sent there to die. On the Tungi plantation in Morogoro district conditions were so bad that several groups of workers deserted the plantation clinic outright, showing up at district offices in Morogoro and Mahenge to complain of abuse, overwork, and lack of *posho*.[101] Such poor health conditions point to the reason for plantation social life. Workers who lived in their own huts with their wives or local women, who procured their own food from gardens, who frequented local villages, poached in forests, and who enjoyed *pombe*, were healthier than others. By avoiding plantation barracks, by controlling the time spent working off their contracts, by resisting "time discipline," workers carved out realms of autonomy that shaped the labor regime and social life away from home. While planters complained about these freedoms, most also came to realize that in the intense atmosphere of labor competition that existed in the era of wild recruitment it was prudent to succumb to the migrant's vision of plantation culture.

CONCLUSION: WORKERS AND THE SHAPING OF THE COLONIAL STATE

This analysis of labor migration and plantation work life has suggested an alternative picture of labor relations in German East Africa than those which view labor migrants simply as forced workers. Labor was costly for German planters, and myriad factors in the development of the colony, including the actions of labor migrants themselves, increased its costs every year of colonial rule. Planters' efforts to solve the labor shortage with industrial techniques and technologies—steam tractors, European managers, irrigation, and time discipline—failed to master the work environment during this period. No plantation in German East Africa was intensive in the strict sense of the word, and the vision of transforming the

Tanzanian landscape into a *Kulturland* of European-style production was never realized. Instead, a steady peasantization of plantations took place that was largely the creation of labor migrants and local villagers. Bush fallowing, green manuring, hand labor using axes and hoes, even the reliance on locally grown maize to feed plantation workers all became features of German plantations. Finally, peasant work rhythms and social life, necessary to attract and retain a work force, emerged as the basis of plantation culture.

Illustrative of the failure of planters to control their own environments was the Kilwa Cotton Plantation, which a consortium of cotton industrialists founded in 1907 on a parcel of over 1,000 ha in the region of the Maji Maji outbreak.[102] The only plantation of note in a radius of fifty miles, the plantation nevertheless struggled to obtain workers. Local people assiduously avoided the plantation, and even harbored plantation deserters and truants. Long-distance labor migrants from the south generally refused contracts for longer than three months so that they could return to their homelands to help their wives with field work. The plantation therefore freely accepted tax defaulters and ransomed slaves sent by the district office for seasonal work.[103] While on the plantation, the workers lived in self-sufficient villages, and, complained one observer, after a few days on the job, each worker "takes not only a blue Monday, but sometimes also a blue week."[104] By World War I the Kilwa plantation had invested close to a million Marks for an average of about eighty bales of cotton per year, much of which was likely purchased from local peasants.[105] Such grand expenditures for meager returns were typical of large-scale plantations, many of which could not even afford to pay their workers. Held hostage to high wages, the fear of worker desertion, or even another uprising, neither planters nor the colonial state were in control of the laboring environment in the last few years of German rule.

The disappointing returns and danger to social stability from plantations led German colonial officials to abandon the plantation vision that inaugurated German rule. Some historians have asserted that, on the eve of World War I, the colonial state was moving back in the direction of a plantation imperative.[106] Indeed, in 1913, under the administration of Governor Schnee, the labor ordinances were revised to allow male labor migrants to sign contracts for up to 240 days per year, an extension of two months from 1909 levels.[107] However, this provision did not rescue the plantation sector in any meaningful way. Contract labor was still discretionary, wages continued to rise, and the inability to retain or pay workers led to frequent plantation failures.[108] No planter succeeded in farming as much as half of his estate. Settlers, for their part, remained embittered over labor policy to the end of colonial rule, believing that the state had abandoned them as the anchor of the colonial economy.[109] The last governor, Heinrich Schnee, rejected planter calls for forced labor, and vetoed pass controls as too great a burden on limited government personnel.[110] Colonial officials believed that forced labor would "nourish discontent in the land, breed insurrection, and endanger all the cultural work undertaken to date."[111] The last Colonial Minister concluded after a study visit to the colony in 1912 that German East Africa would never become "White Man's Country."[112]

NOTES

1. BAB/R1001/6985, Verhandlungen des Kolonialrats 1906, 209–18; "Antwort des Gouverneurs," *DOAZ*, 24 March 1906, 5; "Aus der letzten Gouvernementsratssitzung," *DOAZ*, 31 March 1906, 2–3.

2. "Noch ein Warnruf vor unserer neuen Eingeborenen-Politik," *UP*, 14 December 1907, 1; "Rechenberg in Berlin über die Arbeiterfrage," *DOAZ*, 5 February 1908, 1; "Der beste Ostafrikakenner hat gesprochen!" *DOAZ*, 14 March 1908, 1; "Über die Besiedelungsfähigkeit der deutsch-ostafrikanischen Hochländer," *DOAZ*, 8 April 1908, 2.

3. BAB/R1001/300, Schubert to Dernburg, 18 February 1907, 2–3; BA-Koblenz, Nachlass Dernburg, File #47, R101 I/48.

4. Franz Stuhlmann, "Die Pflanzungsunternehmungen der Europäer in den deutschen Schutzgebieten," *Jahrbuch über die deutschen Kolonien* 3 (1910), 121–47.

5. BAB/R1001/237, Rechenberg to RKA, 21 December 1910, 76.

6. Selbständige Ansiedler, *Kolonial-Handels-Adressbuch*, 73–74.

7. "Kontraktbruch," *UP*, 10 August 1907, 1; "Die Monopolisierung der Arbeiterbörse," *DOAZ*, 6 October 1906, 1; "Vom Pflanzertag in Tanga," *DOAZ*, 9 September 1908, 1. Northern settlers proposed in vain that railway wages be set at one-third below plantation wages.

8. Eighty-four thousand porters left Tabora annually, most drawn toward the caravan trade of Lake Victoria that was stimulated after 1902 by the completion of the Uganda Railway in Kenya. *DOAR*, 17 October 1908, 2.

9. "Volkswirtschaft und Wirtschaftspolitik in D.O.A." *DOAR*, 3 April 1912, 1–2.

10. Laird Jones, "Merchants of Slaughter: The Expansion of the Hide Trade in the Mwanza Region of Tanzania, 1903–1916," paper presented to the African Studies Association Annual Conference, Toronto, 1994.

11. "Arbeiterfrage," *UP*, 9 September 1911, 3.

12. TNA G8/194, District Office Dar es Salaam to Imperial Government, 5 February 1908; testimony in Tanga, 24 December 1907.

13. TNA G21/157, Ermittlungssache gegen den Pflanzer Max Richard Grabow, 1907–1908; TNA G21/165, Strafsache gegen den Brauer Kuhnigk, 1907; TNA G21/

180, Ermittlungsache gegen den Angestellten Ernst Pfeiffer, 1908. See also Siegfried Krebs, "Zwangsarbeit in der ehemaligen deutschen Kolonie Ostafrikas," *Wissenschaftliche Zeitschrift der Karl-Marx-Universität Leipzig* 9 (1959–60), 395–400.

14. TNA G21/211, Georg Markos, 13 April 1908.

15. TNA G1/65, Streitsache des Jumben Kiondomari zu Ssongea, 8–14 September 1909. Wisliceny recruited for the Kikwetu plantation of the Ostafrika-Kompanie.

16. *Landesgesetzgebung*, Verordnung, betreffend die Anwerbung von Eingeborenen in Deutsch-Ostafrika, 27 February 1909, 311–17.

17. TNA G1/95, Verzeichnis der Personen die wegen Vergehens gegen die Arbeiteranwerbeordnung bestraft werden, 1913.

18. TNA G8/171, Rechenberg to Colonial Office, 21 July 1910, 41.

19. "Tangazo," *Kiongozi*, 4, 63, 1910. The article warned of the danger of working underground: ". . . kazi yake ni ya hatari mno, sababu ni ya kuchimba chini sana ndani ya arzi." However German authorities didn't express the same concern about working in the Morogoro mica mines, which sometimes took the lives of African workers. TNA G21/291, Ermittlungssache gegen den Angestellten der Morogoro-Glimmerwerke, 1910–11.

20. TNA G1/7, Jahresbericht Iringa 1911, 42–43.

21. TNA G21/562, Strafsache Morogoro, Staff Doctor to District Commissioner, 18 March 1914.

22. A Wilhelmstal planter complained that "20–50 percent of recruited people run away on the march to the work site or shortly after arrival." TNA G8/127, Wilkins to Lindequist, 19 July 1909, 95b.

23. "Wanatafutwa," *Kiongozi* 4, 66 (1910).

24. "Wamepotea," *Kiongozi*, 4, 67 (1910).

25. TNA G21/562, Strafsache Morogoro, Verzeichnisse Nr. 1–4, 24–27.

26. Photographic evidence and discussions in the Government Council verify the widespread use of child labor on plantations. BAK, Photo Archive, DOA 6143 Land- und Forstwirtschaft, DOA 6143 Baumwollernte; DOA 6482/453 Baumwollfeld; DOA 6424/387 Baumwollernte. It is most likely that child workers came from local villages. After 1913 it was prohibited to recruit women and children as long-distance migrants, though they could accompany husbands, brothers, and fathers. R. Kaundinya, *Erinnerungen aus meinen Pflanzerjahren in Deutsch-Ostafrika* (Leipzig, 1918), 105; *Verhandlungen des Gouvernementsrats*, 21 January 1913, 17; *Amtlicher Anzeiger*, Verordnung betreffend die Anwerbung von Eingeborenen, 1 March 1913, 1.

27. Alexander Bursian, *Die Häuser- und Hüttensteuer in Deutsch- Ostafrika* (Jena, 1910), 15–16.

28. "Beiträge zur Lösung der Arbeiterfrage," *UP*, 12 August 1911, 1; J. Lambert, "From Independence to Rebellion: African Society in Crisis, c. 1880–1910," in *Natal and Zululand*, ed. Duminy and Guest, 389.

29. In 1911 the German Consul in Johannesburg took up the issue of Africans leaving German East Africa "in great numbers" for Rhodesia. Fearing that labor recruitment to German Southwest Africa from South Africa would be "permanently forbidden" if they retaliated against the British colony, he did not pursue the matter. Zimbabwe National Archives, BSAP CID HQ/S 1231, Kaiserlich Deutsches Konsulat Johannesburg, 4 January 1911.

30. TNA G50/10, Tabora Strafbuch, 8 January 1913–10 August 1914.
31. TNA G11/1, Kibata Strafbuch, 1 April 1908–29 March 1910.
32. TNA G8/171, Daebeler to Imperial Government, 25 June 1908; TNA G23/39, Straf gegen den Goanese Joachim Cotta, 1912–13; TNA G9/48, District Office Morogoro, 29 December 1912, 101.
33. TNA G54/22, Kaiserliches Bezirksamt Wilhelmstal, 13 December 1912.
34. TNA G54/22, Gutsch to Wilhelmstal, 30 December 1912; Wilhelmstal to Akida Abdallah, Bumbuli, 31 December 1912.
35. Some representative lists of plantation workers and porters are found in TNA G55/1, Baumwollpflanzungsgesellschaft Kilwa; TNA G8/150, "Südküste" Gesellschaft; TNA G21/562, Strafsache Morogoro; BAB/R1001/301, Dernburgs Reise.
36. "Kontraktbruch," *UP*, 10 August 1907, 3.
37. "Kontraktbruch," *UP*, 10 August 1907, 1–2.
38. TNA G21/348, Strafanzeige Baumwolle A.G., 21 March 1911.
39. TNA G21/645, Kilossa Ermittlungssache, 13 March 1915.
40. TNA G21/666, Ermittlungssache gegen den Pflanzer Haugg, 1914–15.
41. TNA G21/219, Ermittlungssache gegen Eugen Hürstel, Morogoro, 20 January 1909.
42. This was the infamous "Wilhelmstal system." John Iliffe, *Tanganyika under German Rule* (Cambridge, 1969), 135–36.
43. TNA G8/177, Protokoll der Versammlung des Wirtschaflichen Verbandes von Rufiji, 12 February 1911, 9b; Koponen, *Development*, 402.
44. TNA G43/21, Lambrecht to BAG, 22 December 1910.
45. TNA G43/21, Becker to Lambrecht, 31 January 1911.
46. GStA, Nachlass Schnee, Schriftstück #63, 29 January 1914.
47. GStA, Nachlass Schnee, File #63, District Office Morogoro to Akida Jarmias, 8 July 1913.
48. TNA G8/171, Rechenberg to Colonial Office, 21 July 1910, 49–50.
49. TNA G8/142, Bethel Mission to District Office Wilhelmstal, 8 October 1913; "Gegenüber falschen Ansichten," *UP*, 17 July 1909, 1.
50. TNA G21/432, Strafanzeige R. Blohm, Songea, 8–9 January 1912, 5–9.
51. TNA G43/21, Korsch to District Office Morogoro, 18 December 1910, 24.
52. GStA, Nachlass Schnee, Schriftstück #63, Dozi bin Mgido, 9 March 1914; TNA G68/28 Verhandlung der Landkommission für den Bezirk Morogoro, 17 June 1913.
53. "Hongo," *DOAR*, 10 June 1911, 1.
54. For an analysis of an episode of labor recruitment and abuse see Norbert Aas and Harald Sippel, *Konflikte im Kolonialen Alltag: Eine rechtshistorische Untersuchung der Auseinandersetzung des Siedlers Heinrich Karl Langkopp mit der Kolonialverwaltung in Deutsch-Ostafrika (1910–1915)* (Bayreuth, 1992).
55. TNA G21/296, Hager report, Muaja, 17 May 1910, 10–11.
56. TNA G21/412, Singidda testimony, 1–3 August 1911, 2–5.
57. TNA G21/348, Stafanzeige Baumwolle A.G., 21 March 1911, 7–8.
58. "Volkswirtschaft und Wirtschaftspolitik in D.O.A.," *DOAR*, 3 April 1912, 1.
59. "Pflanzerbrief," *DOAR*, 24 May 1911, 1.
60. Verordnung, betreffend die Rechtsverhältnisse eingeborener Arbeiter, *Landesgesetzgebung*, 27 February 1909, 319–27.

61. "Der Kolonialstaatssekretär als Feind deutschen Kolonistentums," *UP*, 10 April 1909, 1–2.

62. "Bericht über die letzte Hauptversammlung des Wirtschaftlichen Verbandes der Nordbezirke," *UP*, 5 March 1910, 2.

63. Settler pressure groups are most thoroughly discussed in Detlef Bald, *Deutsch-Ostafrika 1900–1914* (Munich, 1970), 106–22.

64. "Volkswirtschaft und Wirtschaftspolitik in D.O.A.," *DOAR*, 3 April 1912, 1.

65. TNA G8/197, Kilwa Cotton Corporation, 1907–1913; TNA G55/61, Matters Concerning the Kilwa Cotton Corporation, 1908–1911.

66. The plantation bought a total of 32 ha. belonging to some 42 villagers for 874 Rp, ranging from about 100 Rp going to Binti Ali, who owned land with coconut and mango trees, to the far more typical 3 or 4 Rp paid for small-scale *mashamba* of perhaps two acres. Most of the villagers didn't show up for the 1910 phase of this transaction, and some were dead by that time. TNA G8/197, Kronlandverhandlung Nr. 25, 22 November 1907.

67. Thaddeus Sunseri, "Peasants and the Struggle for Labor in Cotton Regimes of the Rufiji Basin (Tanzania), 1890–1918," in *Cotton, Colonialism, and Social History in Sub-Saharan Africa,* ed. Allen Isaacman and Richard Roberts (Portsmouth, 1995), 180–99.

68. Iliffe, *Tanganyika under German Rule*, 138–39; Koponen, *Development*, 383.

69. Verordnung betreffend die Rechtsverhältnisse des eingeborenen Arbeiter, *Amtlicher Anzeiger*, 1 March 1913, 32. Work arrangements for less than thirty days were void after a month.

70. TNA G8/177, Bericht über die Bereisung der Plantagen des Bezirks Mohoro, December 1910 to April 1911, 13b.

71. TNA G8/142, Kinyassi testimony, Wilhelmstal, 6 January 1913, 74.

72. Sources for the Otto Plantation derive primarily from Kaundinya, *Erinnerungen;* TNA G8/894, Angelegenheiten der Pflanzung Otto, 1908–1916; BAB/R1001/8189–8190 Landwirtschaft; Archiv des Museums für Arbeit und Technik, Mannheim, 871.1 Otto; Gerhard Bleifuss and Gerhard Hergenröder, "Die 'Otto-Pflanzung Kilossa': Eine Unternehmung württembergischer Textilindustrieller in Deutsch-Ostafrika, 1907–1914," in *Kolonisation und Dekolonisation,* ed. Helmut Christmann (Schwäbisch Gmünd, 1989).

73. I have discussed another case study, that of the Leipzig Cotton Spinnery's plantation near Sadani in Thaddeus Sunseri, "The *Baumwollfrage*: Cotton Colonialism in German East Africa," *Central European History* 34, 1 (2001), 31–51.

74. Kaundinya, *Erinnerungen*, 105.

75. E.P. Thompson, "Time, Work-Discipline and Industrial Capitalism," *Past and Present*, 38 (1967), 56–97; Frederick Cooper, "Colonizing Time: Work Rhythms and Labor Conflict in Colonial Mombasa," in *Colonialism and Culture,* ed. Nicholas Dirks (Ann Arbor, 1992), 209–46.

76. Meinhardt in *Verhandlungen des Gouvernementsrats,* 21 January 1913, 19.

77. Rodney considered the long periods needed to work off even a thirty-day contract as proof that planters tied the work force unjustly to the plantation. Rodney, "The Political Economy," 37–39. See also Shivji, *Law, State and the Working Class*, 21.

78. *Verhandlungen des Gouvernementsrats*, 21 January 1913, 19.

79. H. Waltz, "Die Pflanzungen der Europäer in unseren Kolonien im Jahre 1913," *Jahrbuch über die deutschen Kolonien* 6 (1913), 131–33. Though pessimistic about plantation production, Waltz's assertion that about 50 percent of plantation lands were productive are undoubtedly exaggerated.

80. Kaundinya, *Erinnerungen*, 106.

81. Kaundinya, *Erinnerungen*, 107.

82. "Kommunen und Pflanzungen," *DOAZ*, 3 June 1911, 2; Kaundinya, *Erinnerungen*, 141.

83. "Die Verpflegung der Arbeiter," *DOAR*, 5 September 1908, 1; Kaundinya, *Erinnerungen*, 76, 134.

84. Thirty men and three women were included on a list of Nyamwezi recruits to Wilhelmstal. TNA G8/142, Tabora district office to Imperial Government, 8 May 1914, 118.

85. TNA G8/177, "Der Rufiji," Wirtschaftlicher Verband Rufiji; TNA G8/199, Pflanzervereinigung Lindi 1912, 2.

86. Paul Fuchs, *Die Wirtschaftliche Erkundung einer ostafrikanischen Südbahn* (Berlin, 1905), 232–33; "Kommunen und Pflanzungen," *DOAZ*, 6 March 1911, 2; BAB/R1001/6040, Verfügung betr. Geschlechtskrankheiten, 1 December 1910.

87. Martin Klamroth, *Der Islam in Deutsch-Ostafrika* (Berlin, 1912), 13.

88. Missionsarchiv St. Ottilien, Abbot Norbert to Jalwigh, 22 December 1912; Governor Schnee to Bishop Spreiter, 9 October 1912; *Verhandlungen des Gouvernementsrats*, 21 January 1913, 14; Klamroth, *Der Islam*, 12–13.

89. Kaundinya, *Erinnerungen*, 134–35.

90. BAB/R1001/8190, Rechenberg to Colonial Office, 1 November 1910.

91. Kaundinya, *Erinnerungen*, 126.

92. Terence Ranger, *Dance and Society in Eastern Africa* (Berkeley and Los Angeles, 1975), 34–44; Patrick Harries, *Work, Culture, and Identity: Migrant Laborers in Mozambique and South Africa, c. 1860–1910* (Portsmouth, 1994), Chapter 5.

93. Charles Pike, "History and Imagination: Swahili Literature and Resistance to German Language Imperialism in Tanzania, 1885–1910," *IJAHS* 19 (1986), 211–33.

94. TNA G9/48, District Office Tabora to Schnee, 24 January 1913, 125–26; Bericht über die beobachteten Fortschritte der islamitischen Propaganda, Korogwe, 29 December 1912, 134; District Office Morogoro to Schnee, 29 December 1912, 101–03; Klamroth, *Der Islam*, 10–13.

95. Klamroth, *Der Islam*, 11.

96. Kaundinya, *Erinnerungen*, 89.

97. Klamroth, *Der Islam*, 12–13.

98. TNA G9/48, District Office Morogoro to Governor, 29 December 1912, 102.

99. "Die Gesundheitsverhältnisse in unseren Kolonien," *Jahrbuch über die deutschen Kolonien* 1 (1908), 51; Koponen, *Development*, 489–91.

100. TNA G11/1, Kilwa Strafbuch 1908–1910.

101. TNA G21/562, Statement of Pogoro workers, Morogoro, 16–18 March 1914, 2–3.

102. TNA G8/197, Baumwollpflanzungsgesellschaft Kilwa, 1907–1913; TNA G55/7, Kilwa Pflanzungsangelegenheiten 1912–1916; TNA G55/61, Angelegenheiten der Baumwollpflanzungsgesellschaft Kilwa 1909–1911; Landesmuseum für Technik und Arbeit in Mannheim, 871.1 Otto.

103. TNA G55/7, Baumwollpflanzungsgesellschaft Kilwa, Haberland to Bezirksnebenstelle Kibata, 2 August 1913; Streubel to Bezirksnebenstelle Kibata, 1 December 1913.

104. BAB/R1001/157, Bickel to Baumwollpflanzungsgesellschaft Kilwa, 7 January 1911.

105. TNA G8/197, Bericht über die Bestellzeit 1912, 102; Museum für Arbeit und Technik, Mannheim, 10 February 1914, 871.1 Otto-197, 370. In 1914 the Kilwa plantation marketed 71 bales of cotton in Germany.

106. Iliffe, *Modern History*, 150–51; Koponen, *Development*, 669.

107. *Amtlicher Anzeiger* 14, 12, 1 March 1913, 29–35. An abbreviated Swahili version of the legislation is found in *Kiongozi* 11, 9 (November 1913).

108. Waltz, "Pflanzungen," 20; "Die Nordbezirke gesperrt!" *UP*, 1 June 1912, 1; TNA G8/127, Wilkins to Lindequist, 19 July 1909, 95.

109. BAK, NL-53, Nachlass Solf, Reisetagebuch, 60. At a delegation of settlers Colonial Minister Solf and Governor Schnee were so shocked at settler attacks on the administration that Solf wrote, "I considered for a moment whether I should leave the hall."

110. *Verhandlungen des Gouvernementsrats*, 21 January 1913, 14, 27.

111. "Die Verhandlungen des Gouvernementsrats," *DOAR*, 22 June 1912, 2.

112. BAK, NL-53, Nachlass Solf, Reisetagebuch, 54–55, 79.

7

"WAMEKWENDA VILIMANI!": TRANSFORMATIONS IN RURAL SOCIETY

In the first two decades of German rule in East Africa the state and planters aspired to draw men and women from the interior as coastal workers, believing that the future of the colony lay in the northeast plantation sector. At that time they were prepared to resettle whole villages from distant inland regions. As the colonial priority shifted to peasant production of cotton for German industry, the geographical focus of development shifted to the south and the inland, where climate favored cotton. Representative of this peasant development vision was the construction of the Central Railway, begun at Dar es Salaam early in 1905, which made its way inland toward the caravan town of Tabora until 1912. Thereafter the railway was extended to Lake Tanganyika. Hoping to replicate the apparent success of peasant cotton growing in the British colony of Uganda and near Mwanza, German policy makers aimed to extend cotton production to Unyamwezi in western Tanzania, homeland of tens of thousands of men who had migrated for years as porters, plantation workers, and, increasingly, railway workers.[1] Long the major labor reservoir for colonial development, Unyamwezi's reputation for agricultural prosperity was also well known. A colonial myth developed that Unyamwezi could provide unlimited numbers of men for seasonal wage work while sustaining an agricultural economy capable of becoming an oasis of cotton production. This goal of developing the interior intensified as plantations, constrained by labor scarcity and inefficiency, proved incapable of liberating Germany from its dependence on American cotton.

As plans for an inland peasant economy materialized, first missionaries, then colonial officials, became uneasy about what appeared to be the depopulation and decay of the interior. Observers feared that the migration of laborers to the railways and plantations was upsetting the future development of an already sparsely populated colony. Patterns of seasonal labor migration, whereby migrants returned home in order to participate alongside families in agricultural production, appeared to be breaking down, leaving women and the elderly to maintain rural production. The social consequences of continuous migration, including divorce and household dissolution, threatened German plans for a peasant cash crop economy. Furthermore, childbirth was apparently in decline, many missionaries complaining that a typical woman bore only one child. Others believed that abortion and infanticide were becoming widespread practices. As these fears surfaced, policy makers directed their attention at the role of African women in the labor migration nexus, increasingly castigating them as the cause of divorce, birth decline, the spread of disease, and agricultural deterioration.

Rural women were keenly aware of the effects of labor migration, as their husbands in many cases ceased to appear home regularly. African elites, especially in regions of chiefly control such as Unyamwezi, turned to women to perform local work, such as porterage, wood procurement, farming chiefs' lands, or provisioning state caravans. As the local demand for female labor increased in the absence of men, so too did the burden of agriculture on household *mashamba*. Many men were not around for the harvest or even planting stages that were so crucial for food production. The solution that many Nyamwezi women found, as did women in other parts of the colony, was to evacuate areas of elite control and open up new fields in less accessible regions where they could concentrate on growing food. By dispersing their fields into the corners of the land in this way, they could hopefully survive the era of labor migration. In so doing, the landscape of peasant production was altered from a surplus-generating semi-intensive farming to a subsistence-oriented extensive pattern. Women in effect demonstrated their resilience by opting out of cash crop production in order to sustain a food economy. These actions pitted women against chiefs and husbands, and against the colonial blueprint that was based on peasant cotton production.

This chapter examines household disruption and population decline within the context of intensified labor migration, especially looking at railway labor and its effects on Unyamwezi and other regions of western Tanzania, areas most affected by the loss of labor. In general, better working conditions, higher wages, and more autonomy attracted men and some women to the railway, enabling many to avoid plantations altogether, or at least negotiate better working arrangements. As the railway advanced inland, it drew in thousands of workers who had previously avoided wage labor. The irony was that the "peasant" railway appeared to be the main cause of inland depopulation. By the time it reached Tabora in 1912, it appeared that there were not enough intact households to sustain a cash crop economy, especially as women householders themselves began to abandon once-prosperous villages. Colonial officials believed that depopulation allowed forests, bush, and tsetse zones to spread, threatening all plans to develop an inland cash crop economy.[2] This concern led them to reassess labor migration, the role of women as labor migrants, wives, and farmers, and the effects of migration on household production and the landscape. The reconstitution and repeasantization of the inland became a state obsession in the last years of German colonial rule.

RAILWAY WORK AND TRANSFORMATIONS IN LABOR MIGRATION

In order to understand how migration to the Central Railway altered the structure of rural society in Unyamwezi it is necessary to analyze the changing patterns that brought men and women to the railway for work. Begun at Dar es Salaam in 1905, early railway workers included tax defaulters, corvée labor, hired slaves, penal laborers from Maji Maji districts, as well as many free wage laborers.[3] Yet even at this early stage, when many workers were involuntary, railway work for many young men was an alternative to working for virtually no pay on state cotton projects, in forest reserves, or even for competitive wages on settler plantations in the northeast.[4] As famine developed throughout the southeast before and after Maji Maji, men, women, and children fled famine districts for the secure remuneration and guaranteed *posho* food ration that came with railway work.[5] In the year after the rebellion some 800–1,000 Rufiji people left their homes for the railway to escape famine, and, in so doing, made it more difficult for those left behind to master their own agrarian environments.[6] The railway contributed to famine in Uzaramo as railway managers paid such high prices for food to feed workers that peasants sold their reserves of cassava and grain at inflated prices, leaving inadequate local supplies.[7] As the rail line proceeded past Morogoro after 1907, district officials and labor recruiters channeled inland people who had until then avoided paying taxes, such as Gogo and Kaguru, directly to railway work.[8] By 1910 railway workers were drawn from almost all regions of the interior west of Morogoro.[9] Although planters and settlers initially welcomed the railway, believing it would expedite labor recruitment from the interior, the railway's most immediate (and, as it turned out, permanent) effect was to entice workers away from plantations.[10]

Nyamwezi labor migrants and porters enlisted for railway work almost from the beginning. Many already had experience working on the Usambara railway since the 1890s, and some 15,000 worked on the British Uganda line after 1895.[11] By 1912 55 percent of railway workers were Nyamwezi, a number that reached 70 percent in the last year of railway construction after it by-passed their homeland around Tabora.[12] Railway work enabled Nyamwezi men to preserve their strong traditions of porterage that had served as a rite of passage for young men in the nineteenth century.[13] It furthermore led many men to withdraw from plantation districts in favor of jobs that, although often more dangerous, gave them greater autonomy and control over their work. To be sure, the kind of duplicity that existed in plantation recruitment existed on the railway.[14] Yet, in general, workers learned to avoid abusive recruiters and track overseers, and colonial officials were attentive about mitigating abuses for fear of losing workers if conditions were bad. Railway workers received regular *posho*, wages two or three rupees higher than on plantations, and often controlled their work days with little oversight.

Railway recruitment in Unyamwezi was more organized than the "wild" recruitment that existed for plantations. After 1908 the railway construction firm Holzmann & Co. sent three recruitment commissars to Unyamwezi, who in turn hired local agents to fan out into the countryside seeking workers.[15] Recruitment stations were bedecked with flags and slogans, and recruiters dressed conspicuously as they traveled into the countryside to muster workers. Setting up camps near villages, recruiters brought cash, cloth, and commodities such as clocks, gaiters, khaki suits, shoes, perfume, and rubber boots, which they gave as advances to get potential recruits to sign contracts. Once a sufficient number of workers was assembled, they marched to the Tabora district office to have their contracts verified.[16] Undoubtedly recruits selected aliases at the *boma*, then made the long march to the work site under a chosen leader, usually someone who had prior experience migrating to the coast or railway. Many men came to work on the railway without signing a contract (one-third of all workers by some accounts), a strategy that allowed them to negotiate duration and type of work and wage levels, or to leave whenever they wanted.[17] Workers resisted bad conditions, as in the case of some 250 Nyamwezi who deserted the railway near Dodoma because of inadequate food and water.[18] In this case the railway firm improved conditions in time to prevent them from signing onto a nearby plantation. Although railway desertion was always common, it became a plague as the railhead neared Unyamwezi in 1911. Contract breaking accounted for 85 percent of crime in Tabora in 1911 and 90 percent in 1912 compared to 20 percent in 1910, when the railhead was more distant.[19] Nyamwezi workers made up over 70 percent of contract breakers in 1911–12, with neighboring peoples such as Ha and Manyema strongly represented among the remainder. Such desertion took the form of temporary sojourns to visit homes and villages. Missionary complaints made clear that far more men fled to the railway than away from the work site.

Just as women worked as day laborers on plantations in proximity to their homes, women also came to the railway to work as it passed through their lands, some migrating considerable distances.[20] Women performed tasks such as clearing ground for the railway bed, hauling baskets of earth and gravel, and procuring water. Many of these tasks were paid as piece work, bringing in as little as 8 Rp per month (including *posho*) for 15 baskets of gravel per day, or as much as 18 Rp for a worker who could haul 50 baskets per day.[21] Women received anywhere from 50 percent to 80 percent of the wages of men, though some worked for *posho* alone. Women came to the railway in even greater numbers as wives, marketers of food, cooks, beer brewers, and prostitutes. In these capacities women created the kind of social life that existed on plantations. Women and girls who accompanied their husbands or brothers built and maintained temporary huts, pounded grain, cooked, brewed beer, and procured water and firewood (See FIGURE 7.1). A Sandawe girl named Adaa, for example, cooked for her brother Ndegera while he worked on the railway near Kilimatinde.[22] Local or migrant women provided similar services for single men for a fee.[23] Since men often received *posho* in kind, usually a daily *kibaba* (about a pint) of rice, corn, or millet, women sometimes pounded and cooked grain as a paid service.[24] Men who received *posho* in cash sought out local markets, and nearby villagers responded by bringing their food and wares for sale.

Perhaps the most lucrative activity on the railway was beer brewing and marketing. The equivalent amount of grain brewed into beer could bring much greater profits to entrepreneurial women than if sold as meal.[25] The missionary Gaarde, who visited the work camps, noted:

Figure 7.1 Workers and overseers on the construction of the Central Railway between Morogoro and Tabora, c. 1910. Many labor migrants brought wives and sisters to the railhead to provide domestic services. Note the presence of the child. (© Bildarchiv Preussischer Kulturbesitz Berlin, 1401 g. Reprinted with permission.)

> After the day's work is over many workers go to the market for the pots of beer. The beer women are sanctioned [by the construction firm]. Most employers know the weak side of the negro. They know that they win them over by giving them opportunity for beer drinking and once in a while they treat them to beer themselves.[26]

Just as on plantations, *ngoma* dances accompanied by copious drinking often led to an unruly atmosphere that might end in fighting between workers.[27] Also, as on plantations, a night of drinking might be followed by a "blue Monday," absenteeism being a regular feature of railway work.

Alongside beer markets, prostitution was rife on the railway. The engineer Fuchs observed that a railway construction firm could not think of attracting sufficient workers unless women were present because "if women are present, men stay longer and make long contracts."[28] Entrepreneurs established bordellos in major caravan towns like Tabora, and women catered as much to railway workers as to the 300–400 European recruiters and overseers on the railway.[29] When the missionary Gaarde approached a camp to preach, workers assumed he was looking for a prostitute.[30]

Railway social life was vibrant. Camps scattered up and down the railway were inhabited by anywhere from a few dozen workers to several thousand at the railhead. Besides some 13,000 railway workers, local villagers came to sell grain, vegetables, beer, and meat. Indian merchants set up shops to sell cloth and other wares. Muslim *walimu* and Christian missionaries frequented the work camps. The social life of the railway was as much an attraction for workers as were the relatively high wages, secure food rations, and autonomy at work. Combined with continued plantation labor and porterage, by 1910 migration to the railway had a palpable effect on the structure of rural societies, particularly in western and southwestern districts. As the railway approached Tabora, missionaries and colonial officials cited it as the chief cause of regional depopulation and an array of social ills that beset the region.

DISPERSING THE FIELDS:
WOMEN'S RESPONSE TO LABOR MIGRATION

As the colonial economy created exponential demands for wage labor, more men and some women began to work for a wage and ceased to return home annually, to the detriment of their homeland economies. In precolonial days caravan porters had timed their sojourns to and from the coast so as to be home for planting and harvesting.[31] One such porter was Ingereza Ng'wana Sweya, a Nyamwezi who came of age on the eve of German colonialism. Ingereza made five trips to the coast as an ivory porter as a young man, earning enough money to buy cloth, then returning home to help his mother cultivate her fields.[32] After the German arrival Ingereza worked as a carrier on government military expeditions, helped build the *boma* at Iringa, and earned enough to return home and marry. One last time in about 1900 Ingereza carried ivory to the coast, then remained as a worker on a Tanga plantation for two years, missing at least two agricultural seasons before returning home. Nevertheless, Ingereza then settled permanently, in contrast to a slightly younger cohort, who worked for much longer stints away from home, neglecting season after season of agricultural activity. Some men departed indefinitely for colonial work, forming new marriages near the coast, along the railway line, or in towns like Tanga, Dar es Salaam, or Tabora. As one source reported for the regions of Ugalla and Ukonogo 200–300 km southwest of Tabora, which were recent arenas of labor migration in 1910, "village elders and women complain bitterly that the men have been away for years."[33] The result was that women made up 75 percent of the inhabitants of many villages, while other villages were in ruins or had simply been abandoned "precisely as in Unyamwezi."[34] In light of colonial labor migration, it was difficult for rural women to maintain household agriculture according to established practices.

A look at the nineteenth-century Nyamwezi agricultural system illustrates rural reliance on the labor of all household members for part of the year. By the end of November each year porters returned home to clear fields for planting as the big rains set in.[35] Men cleared fields by burning the bush and working it into the ground as fertilizer. Some householders obtained old cattle enclosures that were exceptionally fertile for their new fields. If sufficient labor were available, household members spread soil from ant hills over their gardens for added fertility.[36] Meanwhile, villagers still used old fields in their rotations, designating different crops for different lands depending on soil and rain conditions. Men and women used iron hoes to cut furrows "as deep as a plow would," and built up ridges to retain water and choke off weeds, an extremely labor-intensive practice. Once the ground was prepared in this manner, women planted seeds, weeded frequently, and cared for several fields of millet, sorghum, rice, sweet potatoes, and peanuts planted at intervals in the season. Women also brewed beer to assemble work parties for time-consuming tasks, such as building fences at the ends of fields to keep out crop predators.[37] So important was beer brewing in southern Unyamwezi that the chief's first wife was called the *umwaampombwe*, the "brewer of beer."[38] Some single men worked on the fields of others in exchange for a share of the harvest before leaving as porters around May.[39] Surpluses created by this semi-intensive cropping system allowed men to undertake porterage for as long as six months each year.

A second arena of nineteenth-century Nyamwezi agriculture was the semi-intensive cultivation of grain crops on the estates of *watemi* chiefs and other Nyamwezi officials. Before the onset of German rule these elites established defensive settlements that drew in hundreds of men and women, including slaves, creating an artificially dense concentration of people able to produce a surplus capable of supplying the caravan traffic.[40] In the Ushirombo chiefdom of Unyamwezi alone there were some 120 villages, many with populations exceeding 1,000.[41] Village officials managed the construction of palisades surrounding these settlements, some four or five miles around, to protect fields from baboons, antelopes, and wild pigs.[42] Chiefs' councillors organized communal parties to farm, hunt, build nets and traps, and otherwise maintain environmental control.[43] Concentrated villages had the further advantage of pushing bush away from settlements, destroying the habitat of tsetse flies, thus controlling the spread of trypanosomiasis. A cattle industry was thereby possible as a major feature of the Nyamwezi economy, attracting Tutsi migrants from the northwest, who tended cattle as clients of Nyamwezi villagers. The household agricultural system, combined with concentrated production on chiefs' estates, made Unyamwezi into a regional granary, producing enough millet in 1900 to feed "all the famine districts" in the rest of the colony.[44] Chiefs also used surplus grain to build up patronage relations with villagers, provide famine relief, attract dependents, and thereby increase the ability to control the environment.

The breakdown of Unyamwezi as a breadbasket began as men and women sought to escape the predations of local elites and colonial officials after the turn of the century, when Germans were especially demanding of taxes and corvée labor.[45] Many chiefs and *majumbe* were eager to prove their loyalty to the regime by enforcing colonial ordinances, collecting taxes, and mustering people for public work. Chiefs furthermore sought to carve out new arenas of power and wealth because colonial authorities curtailed slave trading and elephant and game hunting, and took over the taxation of caravans that had once been an important source of their revenue.[46] During the period of "wild" recruitment before 1909 many chiefs coerced men into labor migration for the capitation fees they received from labor recruiters. Others required those people who remained behind, increasingly women, to work on their estates or perform other types of labor owing to the decline in numbers of slaves. Around Tabora the approach of the railway created a demand for lumber for railway and town construction that chiefs sought to monopolize. Already in 1905 they required "large trains of women and men accompanied by their children" to discharge their tax or corvée obligations by transporting tree trunks to Tabora.[47] The chief of Ngulu paid conscripted workers about 20 *heller* per day to fell two trees, a wage about half that of railway work. Chief Ngurukisi of Ugunda and "Queen" Kalunde of Usoke illegally conscripted people to transport lumber to Tabora, claiming that it was the order of the *boma*.[48] Some chiefs coerced villagers to transport lumber or undertake local porterage with great violence, sometimes taking people away in the night.[49] Owing to such activity, there was a palpable breakdown in the moral economy of Unyamwezi as people turned against the authority of chiefs.[50] The Tabora crime statistics record many instances of repeated disobedience, resistance, and even rebellion against regional chiefs. Two men, for example, were charged with plotting the murder of Queen Kalunde, another six men received fifteen days in chains for repeated "grievous insubordination" against her.[51] Five other Nyamwezi men were charged with "repeated rebelliousness" against their chief in 1910. As state officials propped up local despotic rule and punished such rebelliousness, many men fled the region as porters and labor migrants.

In addition to escaping the abuses of chiefs, men began to leave rural Unyamwezi because colonial laws prohibited or sharply curtailed their agrarian activities. As in other parts of the colony, colonial officials regulated hunting by setting aside game reserves, requiring hunting licenses, prohibiting collective net hunting, and by limiting the availability of guns and gunpowder in the Maji Maji aftermath.[52] The typical punishment for poaching after the turn of the century was three months in chains, and often an older generation of men in their forties and fifties were cited for this crime.[53] Colonial conservation measures proscribed field burning around Tabora forest enclaves.[54] Finally, young men not obviously employed were sometimes charged with vagrancy and put to work on chain gangs with minimal compensation for as long as a month.[55] With less ability to participate in the agrarian economy according to the old division of labor, and subject to labor conscription locally for poor pay, men extended their sojourns as labor migrants to the coast and railways indefinitely. The age of labor migrants expanded to include both younger and older men, and some men migrated with their sons.[56]

As men migrated, women and elders sought to escape the predatory behavior of elites by gravitating to mission stations, to more lenient chiefs, or, increasingly, by leaving chiefs' villages and opening up new fields in less accessible regions off major caravan routes and away from centers of control.[57] Ingereza Ng'wana Sweya and his wife moved their *shamba* away from the local *mtemi* chief and caravan road because "we had no opportunity to do any work after harvest as we were called up to do communal work for him."[58] Missionaries claimed that villages emptied because people fled into "the fields and woods" out of fear of Europeans.[59] As a result of these population movements, a new, less intensive agrarian economy was in the making. Palisades deteriorated, ridging declined, wild pigs and baboons returned, and *pori* replaced cultivated land in many abandoned villages.[60] Women opened up new fields that could be maintained with available household labor and work parties. Distant from centralized villages and colonial control, it was easier to thwart prohibitions on bush burning and net hunting. Newly fired fields were fertile enough to maintain subsistence production if rotated frequently.[61] A more genuine swidden agriculture was the result, allowing for a subsistence economy that was not geared for surplus production. As women and elders "dispersed the fields," they in effect retrenched the peasant economy in light of the serious absence of men. By de-intensifying agriculture, women were able to produce more food given the labor scarcity than if they had attempted to maintain nineteenth-century semi-intensive Nyamwezi agrarian patterns with inadequate labor.

The dispersed-field economy was fraught with tension. Already by 1907 chiefs complained that they were losing control over their people in light of labor migration.[62] In 1910 the chief of Sikonge lamented that the villages in his land were dying out because the people were leaving.[63] The Moravian missionary Löbner believed that the population of the region had declined by half from 1906 to 1914, writing "where previously there were blossoming villages, one now only encounters miserable remnants, and the occupants are mostly old people, women and children, and only a very few of the latter."[64] In Sikonge another missionary noted "often for two hours march only old people and children are to be seen. Many of the villages are empty of people."[65] A Catholic missionary lamented that "everywhere one comes across evacuated or half-empty villages, everywhere one encounters traces of previously planted fields."[66] Almost with one voice these observers believed the cause of evacuated villages to be labor migration, especially men's migration to the railway and the coast. One observer described labor migration from Unyamwezi to be a cancer on the region, ushering in a general neglect of agriculture.[67] Peasants who remained in Unyamwezi believed that the railway caused drought.[68] The settler press reported that it was rare for Nyamwezi men to return to their homelands to participate in agriculture as they once did regularly: "many remain permanently hanging around the coast; others remain distant from their homelands for years on end, preferring to work first on one plantation, then on another, then on the railway."[69] The result was that the "one time granary of the interior and model of agriculture has completely deteriorated owing to the migration of the men." The judge Karstedt reported:

> Four years ago I traveled through north and northwest Unyamwezi for weeks at a time, not only along the great caravan roads . . . many a

day I went through three or four villages that were completely evacuated and ruined. In others only a few old people were left behind, and when asked where the villagers were, the typical answer was: *wamekwenda vilimani!*, that is, they have gone to the coast to work.[70]

Many attributed the depopulation of Unyamwezi and other western districts specifically to the arrival of the railway, and the attraction of the high wages that it brought.[71] While the 1909 labor ordinance and its 1913 revisions capped the duration of contracts so that men could return home for seasonal agriculture, nothing prevented men from extending contracts immediately or moving on to other employers. As the Tabora district officer pointed out to a missionary who complained about the effects of labor migration, "freedom of movement exists in the colony, and nobody can be prevented from voluntarily going to work on coastal plantations."[72] Most Nyamwezi labor migrants developed a pattern of continuous work outside their homeland. A missionary reported, "Not even one third return home. . . . Many mothers and women wait for seven, eight, or ten years in vain for their son or husband, not knowing if he is alive or dead."[73]

While male migration was considered to be the root cause of depopulation and agricultural decline, the movement of women was perhaps more important in reshaping the agrarian environment. Although it was exceptional for women and children to agree to long-term labor contracts, the fear of inland depopulation led the state to prohibit women from signing contracts for long-distance labor after 1913. More consequential for rural change was the local migration of women away from chiefly control.[74] Some women moved into Tabora town or to the railway camps as hawkers of *pombe* beer, especially as the railway arrived in 1912 and proceeded to Kigoma on Lake Tanganyika (See FIGURE 7.2).[75] Even more frequent was the movement of women into the woodlands "hidden and protected from obligations to the king," where they could farm more effectively on newly opened fields.[76] Because they thwarted established conventions, women's actions elicited great concern from colonial officials, patriarchal elites, and even husbands and fathers. For example, in Ukimbu there was a gendered forest-field opposition, with the forests as a male domain, the location of hunting, initiation rituals, and ancillary economic activities like bee keeping and wax collection.[77] In contrast, women as the principle farmers dominated the fields and cleared spaces. A Kimbu folktale reinforced this opposition with the story of a young girl who upset convention by breaking the rules and entering into the forest, resulting in the scattering of the Kimbu people. However, it was

Figure 7.2 The market at Tabora. The arrival of the Central Railway in 1912 increased market activity and provided women and men alternatives to farming under the constraints of colonial policies. (Courtesy of Laird Jones.)

just this entry into the forests to open up new fields that took place as a result of men's absence "at the coast." Men described this recalcitrant behavior in unflattering terms. A Kimbu men's song included the line "She is mad; she wants to disperse the homestead."[78] Women's dispersal of fields, both an act of survival and an expression of resilience in light of labor migration, reshaped established social conventions and gender norms.

The Nyamwezi landscape changed as a result of women's migration into the forests, where it was possible to practice bush fallowing less inhibited by state control. In the dry savanna of Unyamwezi, *miombo* woodlands rapidly expanded on fired bush.[79] Because *miombo* harbored tsetse, the cattle economy of Unyamwezi was affected adversely. Reports noted that, in place of cultivated land, the "endless *miombo*" dominated the landscape, and cattle keeping was becoming rare or isolated to small pockets.[80] Women's field dispersals thus thwarted one of the rationales for the construction of the Central Railway, i.e., the rewinning of the trade in hides to Lake Victoria and Kenya for the economy of German East Africa.

Even more worrisome for colonial officials were the declining prospects for cotton growing in Unyamwezi. Since the Maji Maji uprising new governors and colonial ministers, accompanied by textile industrialists, made regular pilgrimages to Unyamwezi to gauge the region's potential for peasant cotton.[81] In 1911 the KWK founded a cotton trial station at Mabama, west of Tabora, hoping to foster the crop on a wide scale.[82] However, very quickly the station officer became deeply pessimistic, noting that many people had moved away from the main caravan route, where the railway would soon arrive, in order to escape the burden of provisioning the caravan traffic.[83] Overturning a decade of optimism on the agricultural prospects of Unyamwezi, the Mabama officer pronounced the land to be deficient and the population far too sparse to support large-scale cotton production.[84] Owing to population dispersals, he believed, Unyamwezi's days as an agricultural oasis were over. Although the blame for agrarian decline might have been placed on local chiefs who drove people away, on men who stayed away too long as labor migrants, or on colonial officials who burdened rural society with unrealistic demands, colonial officials instead singled out women as the subverters of colonial development, a reaction that appears to have been colony-wide.

As women dispersed fields or migrated to towns like Tabora or to the railway to reassert control over their productive lives in the absence of men, men came to lose control over women. Representative is the complaint of Noha, a Moravian mission adherent at Sikonge in Unyamwezi, whose wife Tabea took up with other men before ultimately sundering her marriage to Noha, "leaving him to harvest his fields on his own."[85] So too did the woman Safi binti Mayaruka leave her husband to take up with another man in Kisaki, refusing her husband's pleas to return home despite his having paid a 50 Rp brideprice. Safi's husband appealed to the Morogoro district officer, "I want the government to return my wife, I don't want money."[86] The colonial record provides many examples of women who refused to accept the patriarchal controls of elites and husbands, leading officials to attempt to reassert control over women in the last decade of colonial rule.

BIRTH DECLINE AND THE CRIMINALIZATION OF WOMEN'S BEHAVIOR

While official anxieties about the increasing unruliness of women were colony-wide, the best surviving evidence comes from southern districts. In 1910 the Lindi district officer wrote a directive to local *maakida*:

Transformations in Rural Society

> I have heard that these days many women don't want to have children. If they get pregnant they often abort their fetuses. . . . Women who end their pregnancies this way will never give birth the rest of their lives. I don't approve of this behavior. I want women to bear many children with their husbands like in days past. I want all akidas and liwalis to investigate cases like this. In particular, I want all women who are seen with such medicines, as well as the *waganga* who make them, to be apprehended and brought to the *boma* for questioning as quickly as possible.[87]

This extraordinary concern about birth and the behavior of women was not isolated to Lindi district, but was on the agenda of officials throughout the colony. Almost with one voice colonial officials and missionaries decried what appeared to be a drop in birth rates, fearing the stunting of colonial development for lack of sufficient people to work or grow cash crops.[88] Because the labor question was one of "biology and health," the government's goal in the last years of colonial rule was to reverse population decline and infant mortality. Although many suspected that the cause of birth decline was labor migration and its ensuing rural disruption, most considered African women to be responsible for the problem and therefore sought to alter their behavior.

In the era of labor migration colonial officials cultivated an image of African women as responsible for household instability. Typical was the complaint of the Iringa station chief, who asserted that labor migrants often returned home to find their wives in the arms of other men.[89] Missionaries in Unyamwezi believed that family life suffered greatly from men's prolonged absence, leading women to adultery, extramarital pregnancies, infanticide, and abortion.[90] Dissolution of marriage indeed appears to have been widespread at this time, so much so that some regions made adultery (*Ehebruch*) a crime punishable by up to one month in chains (See FIGURE 7.3).[91] In some cases women sought divorce due to the prolonged absence of husbands. For example, in January 1914 Mama Msafiri binti Chuma appeared at the Morogoro District Office complaining that her husband, Selemani bin Pazi, was working on the railway in Tabora with no intention of returning home. She requested the *boma*'s aid in securing a divorce because "it's been two and a half years since I've known my husband or his food."[92] Some wives and mothers went for years hearing no news from husbands or sons, not knowing whether they were dead or alive.[93] Children furthermore ceased to know their fathers owing to prolonged absence. This was the complaint of Panya Manyema, who arrived at the Morogoro *boma* hoping to contact his father who had abandoned him and his mother. Hearing that his father was

Figure 7.3 Women prisoners at the Tabora *boma*. Colonial cooption of chiefs after the turn of the century increased demands on local people, leading many to oppose chiefly authority. (© Bildarchiv Preussischer Kulturbesitz Berlin, 1401 f. Reprinted with permission.)

working in Dodoma region, Panya requested that his father be notified "that I am his child and I am here in Morogoro, and he should come and look for me at once."[94]

As cases of marriage and family dissolution reached the ears of missionaries and colonial officials, women, not men, were portrayed as the root of the problem. Illustrative are colonial discourses on syphilis, which many believed was rife throughout the labor markets.[95] A planter opined that "while men work, a great many of the women undertake the business of prostitution. They go from plantation to plantation and take the last heller from the workers. Most women are syphilitic."[96] According to that writer, owing to plantation prostitution, "most workers return from the coast to their homelands afflicted with syphilis." The result of the spread of syphilis, to colonial thinkers, was widespread sterility, spontaneous abortions, and a dramatic decline in the birth rate. One planter claimed that "for every 20 women . . . there is barely one child."[97] Some also pointed to polygamy as the cause of women's moral degeneration since many women entered into polygamous households with much older men at a time when missionaries were promoting monogamy. The medical chief of Ujiji claimed:

> Common people have as many as six wives, some sultans as many as twenty. The consequence is a type of prostitution. The dissatisfied women go from one man to another, and the result is that many men remain unmarried. By this means venereal disease becomes widespread.[98]

Missionaries and health officials viewed polygamy as a symptom of unstable households, veiled prostitution, a medium for the spread of syphilis and thus a cause of low birth rates.[99]

Policy makers also suspected that women intentionally limited the number of births through practices such as postpartum sexual abstinence and prolonged nursing. Indeed, among some peoples it was taboo to have sex while breast feeding, a period that might last several years.[100] Koponen believes that such practices were breaking down under colonial rule, and thus cannot account for birth decline.[101] However, limited anecdotal evidence shows postpartum abstinence as a point of conflict during the German period. In 1914 Mlamuingu binti Salim, a woman from Mafissa, appeared at the Morogoro *boma* complaining that her husband, who worked as a domestic servant, wanted to have sex with her (*anataka ngono kwangu*) every time she visited him at work. Binti Salim implored, "A woman who has a small child is not allowed to sleep with her husband, and if she does, the child will be injured."[102] Because Binti Salim refused her husband's advances, he beat her, and wouldn't allow her to give porridge to the baby. In fact, prolonged nursing allowed a woman to devote all her efforts to the health of one child in infancy, and was perhaps most important during times of social and economic stress, such as during colonial rule, when food and men's labor were not always available.[103] Colonial officials viewed the practice as stymieing the reproduction of the labor force.

Sober medical thinkers pointed to other factors in birth decline and child mortality. Poor nutrition for mothers and children, malaria, intestinal diseases, or just plain starvation were all features of the colonial economy.[104] Intestinal sickness such as hook worms, spread by poor health conditions on plantations and worker camps, was the single biggest cause of child mortality, with malaria second. Rarely did colonial officials consider how their policies contributed to child mortality by decreasing food production at the expense of cash crops and by promoting long absences of men from their homelands. Most of the attention instead went into trying to control the behavior of women as the cause of the death of children.

While officials and missionaries deemed prolonged nursing, polygamy, and sexual abstinence to be regressive cultural problems, a more serious suspicion was that abortion and infanticide were widespread practices.[105] Many colonial observers believed that abortion was a direct consequence of women's adulterous behavior in the absence of their husbands. Although knowledge of abortion medicines was reported to be a specialty of the "wives of askari and Swahili," officials related abortion directly to *waganga* spirit mediums who were still associated with the Maji Maji rebellion and general rural disorder.[106] Toward this end, officials and missionaries actively combated the influence of spirit mediums and their supposed role in promoting abortion and infanticide.[107]

Perhaps the most dramatic case of the colonial state criminalizing women's behavior was a case from Iringa district that emerged in 1908 and preoccupied the German court system to the end of colonial rule. In that case the military chief charged twelve Bena people, mostly women, with murder and cannibalism.[108] According to testimony, the group of alleged cannibals were controlled by a Bena man purported to be a sorcerer, who provided knowledge of poisons and magic that could be used against one's enemies. This *mganga* demanded the sacrifice and collective eating of children for his knowledge. German officials were most appalled that local women who were among the accused admitted to poisoning and eating their own children. Several of the accused at first strongly denied having anything to do with cannibalism. The woman Sihiligire, for example, replied to the accusations against her, "I deny everything completely. I know nothing about any sorcery, I've never eaten human flesh."[109] Gradually, however, often after vehement denials, each of the accused admitted her guilt, and all were sentenced to death by hanging.

Two months later, in another village, six other Bena were tried and sentenced to death for murder and cannibalism.[110] Of the six, only one was a man, who was convicted of complicity in murder. The convictions in this case rested on the testimony of a twelve-year-old boy who local officials regarded as mentally incompetent. Of the five women defendants, four were hanged for contemplated murder and cannibalism, and one for abetting murder. The second case, coming so closely after the first, caught the attention of local missionaries, who wrote letters to the military commander at Iringa, the governor in Dar es Salaam, and the Colonial Office in Germany strongly protesting the verdicts, asserting unequivocally that cannibalism did not exist among the Bena.[111] Several missionaries went to the villages of the accused to investigate, going so far as to unearth the graves of the alleged victims, where they found bodies intact, although, according to the court testimony, their skulls had been removed to be used for sorcery. Despite such strong evidence ruling out cannibalism, the governor in Dar es Salaam upheld the verdict, and the second group of Bena were hanged.

These cases perhaps led directly to a third in Kibata, in the Maji Maji outbreak region, where four elderly and infirm women were accused of murdering and consuming a twelve-year-old boy. One of the accused was hanged, the other three were sentenced to life imprisonment in chains for abetting cannibalism. The details of this case are sketchy, and court officials admitted that they could uncover no motive, and that the guilt of three of the accused was probable but "not sufficiently proven."[112] The accused claimed that they were made to admit their guilt through force and threats. As in the Bena cases, the use of *madawa* medicines and the implication of sorcery were pronounced elements of the Kibata case.

The timing of these cases is important. They came at the end of several years of upheaval, war, and famine associated with the Maji Maji rebellion, which came late to southwest Tanzania, but lingered well after other regions had been quelled. Maji Maji was fought with scorched earth tactics, burning fields and confiscating livestock, to the extent that malnutrition created low population densities for a generation.[113] Labor migration following Maji Maji also contributed to social and economic decline in Ubena. Immediately following the war, planters and recruiters tapped Iringa district for labor, and men responded in order to escape deteriorating circumstances that included famine. A few years later the Iringa military chief reported disruptions in family life, marriage dissolution, adulterous relationships, and fierce competition for land and livestock to recoup Maji Maji losses.[114] Indeed, as the Bena cannibalism case unraveled, there were hints that local enemies seeking to dispossess them of their land targeted the accused. The use of ordeal, by which a needle poked through the earlobes of the accused, if obstructed, substantiated guilt, was a subjective method that allowed the accusers to pronounce guilt on almost anyone. Those who admitted their guilt did so because they believed that local methods of uncovering guilt were correct. Trial transcripts also suggest that witnesses who initially denied their guilt were intimidated by *askari* into admitting their complicity.

Similar circumstances reigned in Kibata region in the years after Maji Maji, the major exception being a pronounced colonial presence in the form of state campaigns to grow cotton. Yet, in this region so central to colonial development plans, disorder seemed to reign.[115] The crime of adultery, i.e., the colonial fear of household break-up, was especially rife in the region, as were many instances of resistance to state authority and to *maakida* and *majumbe*. Child mortality was an ongoing colonial concern in Kilwa-Rufiji region as in other parts of the colony.[116] Finally, famine was recurrent in the region owing to Rufiji river flooding and crop losses.

The prominent role of *madawa* medicine and sorcery in both cannibal cases, so close after Maji Maji, encouraged German officials to intervene, always fearing another colonial rebellion.[117] Most importantly, German officials held a preconceived belief that women were intentionally responsible for birth decline. Thus, in the colonial imagination, the cannibalism cases were extreme examples of a phenomenon that was widespread throughout the colony. As the Lindi district officer wrote, and Iringa officials concurred, "Some women who have husbands at home commit adultery with men from the outside, and then they have illegitimate pregnancies that they are afraid to tell their husbands about, so they seek strong medicines in order to abort their pregnancies."[118] In this atmosphere of declining births, sundered marriages, labor shortage, and the inability to control women's actions, officials were quick to criminalize women's behavior. One German judge who upheld the Bena cannibalism case concluded his report with the following words:

> The truth is that the dwellers of [Iringa] district are pleased that the government took firm action. Presently, in Ubena, poison is continuously being made for the purpose of *mothers* killing their children in large numbers. The reason for this is mainly because, according to custom, women must refrain from sex while nursing, and therefore they instead remove the obstacle [that is, the infants].[119]

While clearheaded opinion recognized that falling birth rates and failed marriages were consequences of colonial economic policies and poor nutrition, German colonial rulers became fixated on the cannibalism cases because they resonated with their growing fears that they were losing control of women in rural society.

CONCLUSION:
COLONIAL VILLAGIZATION AND PEASANT RESILIENCE

Colonial designs to develop southern and western Tanzania through peasant production of cotton and other cash crops were thwarted by depopulation and the breakdown of the prosperous agricultural systems that Germans had noticed when they arrived in East Africa. Households were breaking apart, births were down, child mortality apparently up, all considered to be women's reactions to labor migration. At the end of colonial rule, state authorities sought to reverse these problems by reversing inland depopulation and agricultural decline. In so doing, they resisted pressure from planters to effect the permanent settlement of inland societies to coastal districts as a labor force, warning that labor policy must not prevent future colonial development.

Revisions to the labor ordinances in 1913 demonstrate the state's concern for inland stability. The 1909 prohibitions on recruiting workers from the densely-populated regions of Rwanda, Urundi, and Ujiji were upheld, even intensified for fear that migrants from those regions were carriers of sleeping sickness.[120] District officers were empowered to prohibit recruitment from their regions if they deemed migration to be locally detrimental, and many acted accordingly.[121] By 1913 written permission from the governor was required to recruit men for work outside their home districts.[122] District officers were directed to make sure that labor recruitment "does not collide with the field preparations of the natives."[123] In order to guarantee the return of men to their wives in the inland, missionaries lobbied for the setting of a maximum bride price at 15 Rp, believing that men who paid a bride price in full were more apt to return home to their wives rather than form new relationships elsewhere.[124] Yet, toward maintaining family stability and combating prostitution and syphilis, colonial officials allowed wives to continue to migrate with their husbands so that "family life will be preserved." Finally, after 1911 planters were required to use the railway to transport their workers to and from their homelands, and to pay for workers' journeys home "to prevent the depopulation of inland districts."[125] Though significantly raising the cost of labor recruitment and incurring the ire of planters, it helped ensure a healthier workforce and faster repatriation of workers so that they could participate in household agrarian activities.

In light of ongoing population loss, the state tried to repeasantize Unyamwezi and other western districts, believing that, "The negro farmer without doubt provides more for the preservation and increase in the people than all of the fluctuating plantation workers."[126] This was done with a policy of "villagization," by which colonial officials established concentrated villages along the railway line and major caravan routes to recreate the semi-intensive economy of the past. Officials pronounced such a settlement of Ngoni at Runzewe in Unyamwezi a success, and a model for other such schemes.[127] Denser populations would furthermore help combat sleeping sickness by allowing the bush to once again be mastered, allowing for the revival of the cattle economy that had once been so important to the region.[128] As the railway reached Tabora in 1912, officials induced Nyamwezi workers to settle in base camps that, hopefully, would attract other people, just as railway camps had spawned marketing centers.[129]

Colonial villagization schemes were generally fitful, going against the grain of peasant aspirations at the time. Women and men still acted to avoid elite and state control over their labor and agricultural practices. Settlement schemes did the opposite by bringing production under stricter state control. For most rural dwellers, colonial measures that prohibited environmental control, including proscriptions on field burning, net hunting, hunting without a license, prohibitions on the sale of gunpowder, and the establishment of forest reserves, were unacceptable encumbrances on the rural economy. In one settlement in the environs of Tabora, under the shadow of the *boma*, peasants were prevented from constructing pitfalls and using nets to hunt crop predators that were devastating their fields.[130] The result was that people evacuated these villages, some moving into Tabora town, while others moved into the forests where, far from state control, they were able to ignore constraints on environmental control. In so doing, rural householders demonstrated their resilience in spite of the pressures of colonial rule.

NOTES

1. "Baumwolle in Deutsch-Ostafrika und Uganda," *DOAR*, 30 November 1912, 1; Reichskolonialamt, *Der Baumwollbau in den deutschen Schutzgebieten* (Jena, 1914), 116–17; "Die Entwicklung einer ostafrikanischen Kolonie," *KR* 6 (1911), 337–41.

2. BAB/R1001/227, Charisius to Imperial Government, 16 January 1907, 6.

3. "Thätigkeit des Arbeiter-Komissariats," *DOAZ*, 18 August 1906, 2; "Strafarbeiter für den Bahnbau," *DOAZ*, 10 June 1906, 3. Amendments to the corvée labor ordinance were made in March 1905 stipulating that labor conscripts could be used in other ways besides road clearing and maintenance. *Landesgesetzgebung*, Arbeiterrecht, 22 March 1905, 308–09.

4. For example, near Kisserawe on the railway line from Dar es Salaam, the Zaramo men Munipembe and Seliman were at work on the railway as the Maji Maji war engulfed the region. In their absence German forces burned down their houses. TNA G3/72, Entschädigungsansprüchen aus dem Aufstand, 30 September 1905, 236–37.

5. BerM-Kisserawe, Report from September 1905 to November 1906, 73; Bericht über das erste Quartal 1909, 2.

6. TNA G4/81, Grass to Government, 10 December 1906.
7. BerM-Kisserawe, II. Quartal 1905, 31b; Tagebuch vom II. Quartal 1906, 58a.
8. TNA G1/5, Jahresbericht Mpapua 1908/09, 16. Koponen uses this source to assert that railway workers generally were forced laborers. Juhani Koponen, *Development for Exploitation*, (Hamburg, 1995), 344–45, 410.
9. "Die Arbeiterverhältnisse beim Bau der Ostafrikanischen Mittellandbahn," *DKB* 22 (1911), 708.
10. Settlers proposed that railway wages be set at one-third less than plantation wages to prevent the exodus of workers. "Beiträge zur Lösung der Arbeiterfrage," *UP*, 12 August 1911, 1.
11. BAB/R1001/6466, Jahresberichte aus Ostafrika 1894–96 and RKA 6479 Jahresbericht aus Ostafrika Januar 1905 bis September 1906 in Achim Gottberg, ed., *Unyamwesi: Quellensammlung und Geschichte* (Berlin, 1971), 388, 392; "Über die Arbeiterfrage in Zukunft für die Nordbezirke und D.O.A," *UP*, 21 September 1907, 5.
12. BAB/R1001/6569, Manuskripte zu den Denkschriften über die Entwicklung der Schutzgebiete D.O.A. 1912–13 in Gottberg, *Unyamwesi*, 393; TNA G12/6, Eisenbahn-Tabora, 1913–1914.
13. Stephen Rockel, "Wage Labor and the Culture of Porterage in Nineteenth Century Tanzania: the Central Caravan Routes," *Comparative Studies of South Asia, Africa and the Middle East* 15, 2 (1995), 14–24.
14. TNA G21/299, Ermittlungssache gegen die Aufseher Tschortsch und Georges Ihliades, 1910; TNA G21/395, Strafanzeige des Griechen Spiro Petritsopoulos, 1911; TNA G27/29, Strafsache gegen den Unternehmer Jean Zimopulos, 1912–1914.
15. "Zur Arbeiterfrage," *DOAR*, 3 October 1908, 1; "Arbeiteranwerbung in Deutsch-Ostafrika," *DOAZ*, 17 March 1909, 1–2; "Eingeborenen-Kontrolle und Arbeitspflicht," *UP*, 13 March 1909, 1–2.
16. ABU-Herrnhut, Jahresbericht von Sikonge-Ngulu, 1912; Jahresbericht der Missionsstation Ipole, 1906.
17. TNA G12/6, Eisenbahn-Tabora, 1913–1914.
18. TNA G21/341, Ermittlungssache Garbe, Morogoro, 1911.
19. TNA G50/10, Strafbuch Tabora, 1909–1912.
20. "Zentralbahn und Plantagenarbeiter," *DOAZ*, 18 December 1907, 1; F. Baltzer, *Die Kolonialbahnen mit besonderer Berücksichtigung Afrikas* (Berlin, 1916), 337.
21. "Die Arbeiterverhältnisse," *DKB* 22 (1911), 709.
22. TNA G27/53, Strafsache gegen den Unternehmer Emanuel Jeronimakis, 1911–1912.
23. ABU-Herrnhut, Bericht über den Anfang der Bahnmission, October–December 1910.
24. "Die Arbeiterverhältnisse," *DKB* 22 (1911), 708.
25. Elizabeth Schmidt, *Peasants, Traders and Wives: Shona Women in the History of Zimbabwe 1870–1939* (Portsmouth, 1992), 59–60.
26. ABU-Herrnhut, Bericht über den Anfang der Bahnmission.
27. B.S. Hoyle, *Gillman of Tanganyika: The Life and Work of a Pioneer Geographer* (Aldershot, 1987), 77–79.
28. Paul Fuchs, *Die Wirtschaftliche Erkundung einer ostafrikanischen Südbahn* (Berlin 1905), 234. Social Democrats in the Reichstag accused labor recruiters of

tricking women into prostitution. "Der Kolonialetat im Reichstagsplenum," *DOAR*, 1 June 1912, 6.

29. Wilhelm Methner, *Unter drei Gouverneuren: 16 Jahre Dienst in deutschen Tropen* (Breslau, 1938), 265–66.

30. ABU-Herrnhut, Bericht über den Anfang; Bericht über die Bahnmission, 1 January to 31 December 1911; F. Baltzer, *Die Kolonialbahnen mit besonderer Berücksichtigung Afrikas* (Berlin, 1916), 333.

31. Stephen J. Rockel, "Caravan Porters of the *Nyika*: Labour, Culture, and Society in Nineteenth Century Tanzania," (Ph.D. diss., University of Toronto, 1997), Chapter 4.

32. "Ingereza Ng'wana Sweya: His Own Story and His Agricultural Practices," *East African Agricultural Journal* (1939), 211–15.

33. TNA G12/165, District Station Bismarckburg (Kasanga) to Imperial Government, 30 September 1910, 99.

34. TNA G12/165, District Station Bismarckburg to Imperial Government, 99.

35. Report of Pater Müller in Gottberg, *Unyamwesi*, 103–04; Juhani Koponen, "Agricultural Systems in Late Pre-colonial Tanzania," in *The Transformation of Rural Society in the Third World*, ed. Magnus Mörner and Thommy Svensson (London, 1991), 193, 202; Wilhelm Blohm, *Die Nyamwezi: Land und Wirtschaft* (Hamburg, 1931), 117–24; Rockel, "Caravan Porters," 107.

36. "Ingereza Ng'wana Sweya," *EAAJ* (1939), 211–12.

37. "Fragebogen-Beantwortung für ganz Wanyamwezi durch Missionar M.H. Löbner," in Gottberg, *Unyamwesi*, 128, 160.

38. Aylward Shorter, *Chiefship in Western Tanzania: A Political History of the Kimbu* (Oxford, 1972), 24, 112.

39. Blohm, *Land und Wirtschaft*, 121.

40. Wilhelm Blohm, *Die Nyamwezi: Gesellschaft und Weltbild* (Hamburg, 1933), 68–71.

41. J.M.M. van der Burgt, "Zur Entvölkerungsfrage Unjamwesis und Ussumbwas," *KR* 12 (1913), 706.

42. Shorter, *Chiefship*, 42; Blohm, *Gesellschaft und Weltbild*, 36–38.

43. Blohm, *Land und Wirtschaft*, 105–06. On the concept of environmental control see Chapter 4 above and James Giblin, *The Politics of Environmental Control in Northeastern Tanzania* (Philadelphia, 1992).

44. Heinrich Dauber, *'Nicht als Abentheurer bin ich hierhergekommen . . . ': 100 Jahre Entwicklungs- 'Hilfe'* (Frankfurt am Main, 1991), 173.

45. For example see ABU-Herrnhut, Jahresbericht der Station Ipole 1907, 11–12.

46. TNA G50/9, Strafbuch der Militär-Station Tabora, 1902–1904.

47. The lumber industry emerging in Unyamwezi at this time is described in ABU-Herrnhut, Bericht der Bahnmission, 1 April to 30 June 1911; Jahresbericht der Station Sikonge 1905; Löbner to Tabora District Office, 22 June 1910; BAB/R1001/227, Löbner to Tabora District Office, 20 June 1910; Antwort des Bezirksamtes, 22 June 1910.

48. In this case the district administration punished the chief for forced labor, sentencing him to 15 canings, five weeks of chains, and he was required to carry lumber from Ugunda to Tabora. ABU-Herrnhut, Zweiter Vierteljahresbericht der Missionsstation Ipole, 1913.

49. BAB/R1001/831, Trägerverkehr, 5 December 1913, 28.
50. BAB/R1001/831 *Missions-Blatt der Brüdergemeine* 10 (1913), 228–29.
51. TNA G50/10, Tabora Strafbuch, 1910.
52. ABU-Herrnhut, Jahresbericht der Missions-Station Ipole 1906, 2. The boundaries of the Tabora game reserve (Ngulu chiefdom) were delineated in BAB/R1001/7776, Jagdschutzverordnung für das deutsch-ostafrikanische Schutzgebiet, 1 June 1903, 356.
53. TNA G50/10, Tabora Strafbuch, 1904. Men were often punished collectively in cases of poaching, suggesting a communal activity.
54. Koponen, *Development*, 534–35; T. Siebenlist, *Forstwirtschaft in Deutsch-Ostafrika* (Berlin, 1914), 7, 13–17; F.O. Karstedt, "Betrachtungen zur Sozialpolitik in Ostafrika," *KR* 13 (1914) 138.
55. TNA G50/10, Tabora Strafbuch 1913, 20.
56. BAB/R1001/846, Jahresbericht über das Missionswerk der Brüdergemeine für das Jahr 1912, 51.
57. For another example of protective forest adaptation in Guinea see James Fairhead and Melissa Leach, "Rethinking the Forest-Savanna Mosaic: Colonial Science and Its Relics in West Africa," in *The Lie of the Land: Challenging Received Wisdom on the African Environment*, ed. Melissa Leach and Robin Mearns (London, 1996), 105–21.
58. "Ingereza Ng'wana Sweya," *EAAJ* (1939), 212. For a similar example of dispersing fields in light of labor migration in Northern Rhodesia see Henrietta L. Moore and Megan Vaughan, *Cutting Down Trees: Gender, Nutrition, and Agricultural Change in the Northern Province of Zambia, 1890–1990* (Portsmouth, 1994).
59. ABU-Herrnhut, Jahresbericht der Station Sikonge 1910.
60. Karstedt, "Betrachtungen," 133.
61. On the advantages of extensive agriculture over intensive in light of low population levels see Robert McC. Netting, *Smallholders, Householders: Farm Families and the Ecology of Intensive, Sustainable Agriculture* (Stanford, 1993), 105–08; Sara Berry, *No Condition Is Permanent: The Social Dynamics of Agrarian Change in Sub-Saharan Africa* (Madison, 1993), 188–89.
62. BAB/R1001/227, Tabora, 16 January 1907, 4b; BAB/R1001/580, Bericht Oberleutnant Glaunings, 7 December 1899 in Gottberg, *Unyamwesi*, 384–85.
63. ABU-Herrnhut, Jahresbericht der Station Sikonge 1910.
64. M.H. Löbner, "Zur Entvölkerungsfrage Unyamwezis," *KR* 13 (1914), 267–70; idem, *Unyamwezi und Tabora: Land, Volk und Missionsarbeit* (Herrnhut, 1914), 5.
65. ABU-Herrnhut, Jahresbericht der Station Sikonge 1910.
66. Van der Burgt, "Zur Entvölkerungsfrage," 706–07.
67. "Hans Meyer über die Arbeiterfrage in Deutsch-Ostafrika," *DOAZ*, 20 January 1912, 1; "Reiseberichte von Professor Dr. Hans Meyer aus Deutsch-Ostafrika," *MaddS* 24 (1911), 219–21, 342–59.
68. ABU-Herrnhut, Jahresbericht der Station Sikonge 1910.
69. "Der gegenwärtige Stand der Arbeiterverhältnisse in Deutsch-Ostafrika," *DOAZ*, 10 December 1910, 1.
70. Karstedt, "Betrachtungen," 133.
71. "Eisenbahnen und Menschen," *KR* 13 (1914), 388; TNA G12/165, Gräff to Imperial Government, 30 September 1910, 99.

72. BAB/R1001/227, Hermann to Löbner, 9 July 1908, 1.
73. Siegfried Krebs, "Zwangsarbeit in der ehemaligen deutschen Kolonie Ostafrikas," *Wissenschaftliche Zeitschrift der Karl-Marx-Universität Leipzig* 9 (1959–60), 398.
74. J.M.M. van der Burgt, "Zur Bevölkerungsfrage Unjamwesis und Ussumbwas," *KR* 13 (1914), 26.
75. TNA G50/10, Tabora Strafbuch 1913, 22–26.
76. ABU-Herrnhut, Jahresbericht der Station Sikonge 1910; Krebs, "Zwangsarbeit," 396.
77. This discussion of Kimbu conventions is drawn from Shorter, *Chiefship*, 58–61.
78. Shorter, *Chiefship*, 60.
79. L.A. Lewis and L. Berry, *African Environments and Resources* (Boston, 1988), 224–31. For an analysis of *miombo* regeneration in Zambia see Shuichi Oyama, "Regeneration Process of the Miombo Woodland at Abandoned Citimene Fields of Northern Zambia," *African Study Monographs* 17, 3 (1996), 101–16.
80. BAB/R1001/227, Charisius report, 16 January 1907, 5–6; BAB/R1001/8186, Bericht der Baumwollstation Mabama, 30b.
81. BAB/R1001/300, Bericht ueber eine vom 13. Juli bis 30. Oktober 1907 nach Ostafrika ausgefuehrte Dienstreise; Schubert to Dernburg, 18 February 1907, 2–3; BAK, Nachlass Solf, Reisetagebuch, 18 August 1912, 65.
82. BAB/R1001/8186, Bericht der Baumwollstation Mabama, 24 November 1911 bis 31 March 1913.
83. "Wirtschaftliche Erkundung im Interessengebiete der Bahnlinie Tabora-Kigoma," *Verhandlungen des KWKs*, 28 November 1911, 32–33.
84. BAB/R1001/8186, Schnee to Colonial Office, 24 June 1914, 150b.
85. ABU-Herrnhut, Jahresbericht von Sikonge-Ngulu 1912.
86. GStA, Nachlass Schnee, File #63, Morogoro, 28 November 1913.
87. GStA, Nachlass Schnee, File #72, Lindi, 24 July 1910.
88. Methner, *Unter drei Gouverneuren*, 331; "Zur Arbeiterfrage," *DOAZ*, 10 August 1907, 2.
89. TNA G1/7, Iringa Jahresbericht 1911, 5, 42.
90. Löbner, *Unyamwezi*, 6, 11.
91. TNA G9/13, Schumann to Imperial Government, 24 March 1909, 31–34; TNA G11/1 Kibata Strafbuch, 99, 138, 165–66, 247–48; Chole Strafbuch, 227; Liwale Strafbuch, 250.
92. GStA, Nachlass Schnee, Schriftstück No. 71, 20 January 1914.
93. Krebs, "Zwangsarbeit," 398.
94. "amenitupa tangu zamani." GStA, Nachlass Schnee, Schriftstück No. 63, 31 October 1912.
95. Löbner, *Unyamwezi*, 11–12; TNA G1/7, Iringa Jahresbericht 1911, 5; "Die Gesundheitsverhältnisse in unseren Kolonien," *Jahrbuch über die deutschen Kolonien* 1 (1908), 51. Colonial attitudes about syphilis and its treatment in Uganda are explored in Michael Tuck, "Syphilis, Sexuality, and Social Control: A History of Venereal Disease in Colonial Uganda," (Ph.D. diss., Northwestern University, 1997) and "Venereal Disease, Sexuality and Society in Uganda," in *Sex, Sin and Suffering:*

Venereal Disease and European Society since 1870, ed. Roger Davidson and Lesley A. Hall (London, 2001), 191–204.

96. Benediktiner Mission Archives, St. Ottilien, #406, "Der Geburtenrückgang und die Kindersterblichkeit," 22 December 1912.

97. Benediktiner Mission Archives, St. Ottilien, "Der Geburtenrückgang und die Kindersterblichkeit," 22 December 1912, 1.

98. "Familien-Nachwuchsstatistik über die Eingeborenen von Deutsch-Ostafrika," *DKB* 25 (1914), 441.

99. Ambrosius Maier, "Aus den Matumbibergen," *Missions-Blaetter* 14 (1910), 117; "Familien-Nachwuchsstatistik," *DKB* 25 (1914), 441; Josef Froberger, "Die Polygamie und deren kulturelle Schäden," *Verhandlungen des Deutschen Kolonialkongresses 1910* (Berlin, 1910), 717–32.

100. "Familien-Nachwuchsstatistik," *DKB* (1914), 441; "Säuglings- und Kinder-Ernährung," *DKB* (1914) 354–65.

101. Juhani Koponen, "Population: A Dependent Variable," in Maddox et al., *Custodians of the Land*, 34. Koponen's evidence is based on later periods of Tanzanian history.

102. GStA, Nachlass Schnee, File #63, Morogoro, 20 February 1914.

103. For a discussion of colonial perceptions of postpartum abstinence see Nancy Hunt, "Le Bebe en Brousse: European Women, African Birth Spacing and Colonial Intervention in Breast Feeding in the Belgian Congo," *IJAHS* 21, 3 (1988), 401–32.

104. "Säuglings- und Kinder-Ernährung in Deutsch-Ostafrika," *DKB* 25 (1914), 354–65; Familien-Nachwuchsstatistik," *DKB,* 25 (1914), 440–57; Ann Beck, *Medicine and Society in Tanganyika 1890–1930. A Historical Inquiry* (Philadelphia, 1977).

105. "Familien-Nachwuchsstatistik," 440–41.

106. "Familien-Nachwuchsstatistik," 441; "Lindi," *DOAZ,* 16 May 1908, 2.

107. For another example of German fears of infanticide associated with spirit mediums see Giblin, *Politics of Environmental Control,* 105–11.

108. BAB/R1001/827, Kannibalismus in Deutsch-Ostafrika, "Oeffentliches Shauri," 29 December 1908, 5–15; "Ein Mordprozess gegen Menschenfresser," *DKB* 20 (1909), 261; TNA G9/13, Schuman to Imperial Government, 24 March 1909, 31–34.

109. BAB/R1001/827, "Oeffentliches Shauri," 10.

110. BAB/R1001/827, Berner to RKA, 16 March 1910, 40–46.

111. BAB/R1001/827, "Aus einem Brief von Missionar Nauhaus-Kidugala an Missionsinspektor Lic. Axenfeld," 2 July 1909, 20–26.

112. TNA G11/1, Kilwa Strafbuch, 13 October 1909–2 November 1909, 177–82.

113. A.T. Culwick and G.M. Culwick, "A Study of Population in Ulanga, Tanganyika Territory," *Sociological Review* 30 (1938), 375; Koponen, "Population," 31–32; Jamie Monson, "Relocating Maji Maji: The Politics of Alliance and Authority in the Southern Highlands of Tanzania, 1870–1918," *JAH* 39 (1998), 113–19.

114. TNA G1/7, Iringa Jahresbericht 1911, 42–43. Patterns of marriage disruption and wife abandonment owing to labor migration in Njombe district continued well beyond the German period. James Giblin, "Family Life, Indigenous Culture, and Christianity in Colonial Njombe," in *East African Expressions of Christianity,* ed. Thomas Spear and Isaria N. Kimambo (Oxford, 1999), 313.

115. TNA G11/1, Kilwa Strafbuch, 1908–1910.
116. "Familien-Nachwuchsstatistik," *DKB* 25 (1914), 440–43.
117. For a similar example see "Lindi," *DOAZ*, 16 May 1908, 2.
118. GStA, Nachlass Schnee, Lindi, 24 July 1910. The Iringa station chief shared these fears about low population in light of birth decline. TNA G1/7, Iringa Jahresbericht 1911, 5, 42–43. For background to colonial relations at the Iringa station see Marcia Wright, *Strategies of Slaves and Women: Life-Stories from East/ Central Africa* (New York, 1993), 206.
119. BAB/R1001/827, Oberrichter Vortisch, 22 May 1910, 64.
120. *Landesgesetzgebung*, 27 February 1909, 314; TNA G12/165, Medizinalreferat to Bezirksämter Mwanza, Tabora, und Residentur Urundi, 21 August 1909, 60.
121. "Beiträge zur Lösung der Arbeiterfrage," *UP*, 15 July 1911, 2.
122. Verordnung, *Amtlicher Anzeiger*, 1 March 1913, 1; Karstedt, "Betrachtungen," 140–41.
123. TNA G12/165, Sperling to Imperial Government, 13 April 1912, 145.
124. Van der Burgt, "Zur Entvölkerungsfrage," 723–24. The tensions between bride wealth payments and labor migration continued into the British period of rule in Tanganyika. See Margot Lovett, "On Power and Powerlessness: Marriage and Political Metaphor in Colonial Western Tanzania," *IJAHS* 27, 2 (1994), 291–96.
125. "Arbeitertransport," *DOAR*, 14 October 1911, 1; H. Waltz, "Die Pflanzungen der Europäer in unseren tropischen Kolonien im Jahre 1912," *Jahrbuch über die deutschen Kolonien* 6 (1913), 206–07.
126. BAB/R1001/813, Verhandlungen des Gouvernementsrats, 20 June 1912, 196.
127. BAB/R1001/227, Charisius report, 16 January 1907, 6–7.
128. The association between dense settlements and the control of *miombo* forests is seen in "Aus dem Bezirke Tabora," *DKB* 18 (1907), 459–62.
129. Löbner, *Unyamwezi*, 5.
130. Karstedt, "Betrachtungen," 138.

EPILOGUE

Virtually all colonized societies underwent profound changes as a result of labor migration. Some, such as the extreme cases of southern Africa, where adult men, forced to migrate for much of their lives, left behind rural environments dramatically altered by state intervention, stand out in African history. While the scale of labor migration in German East Africa is not exceptional, it is important for understanding Tanzanian and colonial history.

Colonial rule in Tanzania was built on previously established labor patterns, especially porterage and slavery. As much as colonial rulers sought to shape the economy in the direction of capitalist-scale production by drawing on German precedents, porters, slaves, and other workers, many with preexisting traditions of paid labor, subverted this plantation imperative. Workers were not simply a pliable labor force that could be shaped by colonial fiat, coercion, or tax pressure. Worker leverage was to a large degree a factor of a labor scarcity that never abated during German rule. Scarce labor was made costlier by the determination of migrants to resist colonial labor demands or only work under relatively favorable conditions. Those who agreed to work on plantations shaped work regimes and social life at the work site. Plantations furthermore depended on neighboring peasant householders for food to feed their workers, taking local people out of the wage labor nexus for most of each year. Even before the Maji Maji rebellion of 1905–07, many colonial thinkers had concluded that the economy of German East Africa could not rely on a plantation sector based on labor coercion.

The weight that German policy makers gave to East Africa to solve problems of metropolitan cotton supply and social stability ultimately led them to conclude that the peasant sector must be preserved in order to compensate for disappointing plantation returns. For this to work, Africans could not be deprived of adequate land and labor for small-scale cash crop production, as they were in the migrant labor economies of southern Africa. However, when German rulers shifted their priorities from plantation to household production, they did so with misconceptions about peasant economies. They began with a conviction that peasant households offered a flexibility in terms of scale of production and access to family labor that made them "crisis free," and thus able to bear the addition of cash crops like cotton. Yet they also believed that peasant farming was a comparatively primitive *Urproduktion* that could be improved through colonial intervention. Before 1905 colonialists believed that peasant cash crop production must take the form of smallholder farms using family labor, draft animals, plows, irrigation, and scientific agriculture. Colonial rulers therefore attacked peasant farming techniques, especially bush burning to clear new fields and the widespread use of fallows. Colonialists also denied the use of commons as an important feature of African farming. This was seen in the establishment of forest and wildlife reserves that sharply curtailed the peasant use of forests and the ability to protect fields from crop predators. Hunting prohibitions furthermore inhibited villagers from guarding their crops. Even though Germans began to rely on peasant agriculture in their colonial planning, they seriously hemmed in the ability of householders to produce surpluses by ignoring the ecological realities of the rural sector.

Labor policy further impaired peasant agriculture. For most of German rule, colonial officials believed that labor migration could operate hand-in-hand with rural household production. Patterns of labor migration that predated colonial rule saw men leave on coastal sojourns for part of the year, then return to participate in household agrarian activities at planting and harvesting times. Several aspects of labor migration, however, were unanticipated in colonial planning. Given a colonial economy based on freedom of movement, labor migrants ceased to return to their homelands annually to help out in agricultural production, particularly in light of local corvée labor demands and conservation controls. The movement of female householders from centers of colonial control such as the villages of *maakida*, chiefs, and *majumbe*, also ran counter to the colonial blueprint. Indeed, rather than juggle the constraints of household subsistence and the pressure to grow cash crops like cotton, women moved *pembeni,* into the corners of the landscape, where they carved out new fields away from colonial controls. In dispersing the fields in this manner, women altered the landscape and preserved subsistence production in order to avoid colonial control. Scholars of the post-colonial period have long noted the "traditional" village structure of dispersed settlements that characterized much of rural Tanzania in the twentieth century.[1] Yet they have not sufficiently considered how patterns of labor migration that were ushered in by colonial rule led directly to the scattering of villages and fields as a defensive mechanism.[2] In light of these movements, this study has suggested that one of the most tangible consequences of colonialism was the abandonment of households by men, leading to the disruption of rural society, the increase in marital conflict and divorce, and birth decline. Far from being crisis-free, peasant households were prone to ongoing crisis as a direct result of colonial rule.

The role of labor migration in shaping the economy of German East Africa has been obscured by studies that have taken British Tanganyika as their starting point, when political and economic circumstances were vastly different. Following World War I the colony went from being the core of the German overseas empire to a periphery of the British empire. Though the plantation cotton sector was never seriously revived under British rule, a Tanganyikan specialization in sisal production became the basis of the continued recruitment of labor migrants for plantation work.[3] The greater autonomy that tens of thousands of migrants preserved working as porters or on railway construction was sharply curtailed with the completion of the railway line from Tabora to Mwanza in 1928. Under the British and post-colonial governments the trend was toward periodic labor gluts that impaired the ability of migrants to negotiate terms of hire. For this reason, historical studies have taken the British-era term for Tanganyikan labor migrants, *manamba* "numbers," somewhat too literally as signifying that migrants in all periods of Tanzanian history, including German East Africa, had no agency, but were mere pawns of colonial and capitalist forces.[4] While this surely goes too far, it does reflect the reality of a diminishing bargaining power over time. The social effects of British-era recruitment mirrored that of German rule, and included instances of migrant workers abandoning wives and higher incidences of adultery and divorce.[5] In some regions women responded to the prolonged absence of husbands by relying on less labor-intensive crops, in effect preserving the subsistence-oriented household as a survival strategy.

Conservation policies inaugurated by German rule, including the establishment of forest and wildlife reserves that were off-limits to African agrarian (and pastoral) activity, were expanded in subsequent periods of Tanzanian history.[6] The 30,000 sq km of German East Africa reserved for wildlife protection tripled to about 90,000 sq km at the end of the twentieth century. Forest and conservation reserves multiplied eight-fold, from about 8,000 sq km to about 50,000 sq km. Meanwhile, the country's population (excluding Ruanda and Burundi) has multiplied by about five times since German times. British and post-colonial conservation intervention was also much more rigorously enforced than under German times, when the state was weaker.[7] The establishment of forest and wildlife reserves has included the forced removal of rural dwellers, the creation of protected zones for wildlife that often act as crop predators, and the elimination of the commons for thousands of people. Ecological constraints introduced by German colonialism have continued to hem in rural production and foster labor migration.

Patterns of labor migration and rural change that originated under German rule continue to have relevance for modern Tanzania. The contemporary impermanence of migrating for work resembles colonial patterns, when full proletarianization was exceptional. Indeed, since the 1980s, when economic liberalization has been unleashed in full force, urban unemployment has led to a decline, even reversal of rural-to-urban migration that is probably temporary.[8] Nevertheless, Tanzanian rural society continues to be characterized by an insufficient availability of male labor resulting in the overburdening of rural women. The direct consequence for women has been to turn to coping mechanisms that include supplementing household income through petty marketing, resisting cash crop production and state labor demands, and avoiding agricultural intensification.[9] Modern resistance to forced settlement in concentrated *ujamaa* villages under rigorous state control also has its colonial-era precedents.[10] These are all survival strategies that women learned under colonial rule in response to the loss of male labor "at the coast."

NOTES

1. R.G. Abrahams, *The Political Organization of Unyamwezi* (Cambridge, 1967), 13; Aylward Shorter, *Chiefship in Western Tanzania: A Political History of the Kimbu* (Oxford, 1972), 61–65, 117–20; Idris S. Kikula, *Policy Implications on Environment: The Case of Villagisation in Tanzania* (Uppsala, 1997), 18–19.

2. Kikula, *Policy Implications*, 18.

3. R. Cecil Wood, "Cotton in Tanganyika Territory," *Empire Cotton Growing Review* 1, 1 (1924), 31–41; A.J. Kirby, "The Progress of Cotton Growing in the Tanganyika Territory," *Empire Cotton Growing Review* 7, 3 (1930), 169–80; Deborah Fahy Bryceson, *Food Insecurity and the Social Division of Labour in Tanzania, 1919–85* (New York, 1990), 93–98; Nicholas Westcott, "The East African Sisal Industry, 1929–1949: The Marketing of a Colonial Commodity during Depression and War," *JAH* 25 (1984), 445–61.

4. John Iliffe, *A Modern History of Tanganyika* (Cambridge, 1979), 306; Issa Shivji, *Law, State, and the Working Class in Tanzania* (London, 1986), 21.

5. James Giblin, "Family Life, Indigenous Culture, and Christianity in Colonial Njombe," in *East African Expressions of Christianity*, ed. Thomas Spear and Isaria Kimambo (Athens, OH, 1999), 310–14; Gregory Maddox, "Environment and Population Growth in Ugogo, Central Tanzania," in Maddox et al., *Custodians of the Land*, 56–59.

6. Juhani Koponen, *Development for Exploitation* (Hamburg, 1995), 529–42. Figures for modern Tanzania are derived from C. George Kahama, T.L. Maliyamkono, and Stuart Wells, *The Challenge for Tanzania's Economy* (London, 1986), 102; Byarugaba Kamara, "The Impact of Structural Adjustment Programmes on Natural Resources with Particular Reference to Wildlife Conservation in Tanzania," in *Policy Reform and the Environment in Tanzania*, ed. M.S.D. Bagachwa and Festus Limbu (Dar es Salaam, 1995), 173–75.

7. Helge Kjekshus, *Ecology Control and Economic Development in East Africa: The Case of Tanganyika 1850–1950* (London, 1996); Roderick Neumann, *Imposing Wilderness: Struggles over Livelihood and Nature Preservation in Africa* (Berkeley, 1998); Rodger Yeager and Norman Miller, *Wildlife, Wild Death: Land Use and Survival in Eastern Africa* (Albany, 1986).

8. T.L. Maliyamkono and M.S.D. Bagachwa, *The Second Economy in Tanzania* (London, 1990), 35–36; Aili Mari Tripp, *Changing the Rules: The Politics of Liberalisation and the Urban Informal Economy in Tanzania* (Berkeley, 1997), 52–53.

9. Ulla Vuorela, "The Crisis, Women, and Social Reproduction," in *The IMF and Tanzania: The Dynamics of Liberalisation*, ed. Horace Campbell and Howard Stein (Harare, 1991), 153–74; Japheth M.M. Ndaro, "Local Coping Strategies in Dodoma District, Tanzania," in *Development from Within: Survival in Rural Africa*, ed. D.R.F. Taylor and Fiona MacKenzie (London, 1992), 178–80.

10. Dean McHenry, Jr., *Tanzania's Ujamaa Villages: The Implementation of a Rural Development Strategy* (Berkeley, 1979); James Scott, *Seeing Like a State* (New Haven, 1998).

BIBLIOGRAPHY

Aas, Norbert, and Harald Sippel. *Konflikte im Kolonialen Alltag: Eine rechthistorische Untersuchung der Auseinandersetzung des Siedlers Heinrich Karl Langkopp mit der Kolonialverwaltung in Deutsch-Ostafrika (1910–1915)*. Bayreuth, 1992.
Abrahams, R.G. *The Political Organization of Unyamwezi*. Cambridge, 1967.
———. *The Nyamwezi Today*. Cambridge, 1981.
Acland, J.D. *East African Crops*. Longman, 1987.
Akinola, G.A. "Slavery and Slave Revolts in the Sultanate of Zanzibar in the Nineteenth Century," *Journal of the Historical Society of Nigeria* 6, 2 (1972), 215–28.
Anderson, David M. "Master and Servant in Colonial Kenya, 1895–1939," *JAH* 41 (2000), 459–85.
Atkins, Keletso. *The Moon Is Dead! Give Us Our Money! The Cultural Origins of a Zulu Work Ethic*. Portsmouth, 1993.
Bade, Klaus. "Antisklavereibewegung in Deutschland und Kolonialkrieg in Deutsch-Ostafrika 1888–1890: Bismarck und Friedrich Fabri," *Geschichte und Gesellschaft* 3, 1 (1977), 31–58.
———. "Labour, Migration, and the State: Germany from the Late 19th Century to the Onset of the Great Depression," in *Population, Labour and Migration in 19th- and 20th-Century Germany*, ed. Klaus Bade. Leamington Spa, 1987, 59–85.
Bakari, Mtoro bin Mwinyi. *The Customs of the Swahili People*, ed. and trans. J.W.T. Allen. Berkeley, 1981.
Bald, Detlef. *Deutsch-Ostafrika 1900–1914. Eine Studie über Verwaltung, Interessengruppen und wirtschaftliche Erschliessung*. Munich, 1970.
Baltzer, F. *Die Kolonialbahnen mit besonderer Berücksichtigung Afrikas*. Berlin, 1916.
Barker, R. de la B. "The Rufiji River," *TNR* (1936), 10–16.
Barkin, Ken. *The Controversy over German Industrialization*. Chicago, 1970.

Basset, Thomas J. "Introduction: The Land Question and Agricultural Transformation in Sub-Saharan Africa," in *Land in African Agrarian Systems*, ed. Thomas J. Basset and Donald E. Crummey. Madison, 1993, 3–31.

Bauer, Adalbert. *Der Arbeitszwang in Deutsch-Ostafrika*. Würzburg, 1919.

Baumann, Oskar. *Usambara und seine Nachgbargebiete*. Berlin, 1891.

Beardall, William. "Exploration of the Rufiji River under the Orders of the Sultan of Zanzibar," *Proceedings of the Royal Geographical Society* 11 (November 1881), 641–56.

Beck, Ann. *Medicine and Society in Tanganyika 1890–1930. A Historical Inquiry*. Philadelphia, 1977.

Behr, H.F.v. "Die Völker zwischen Rufiyi und Rovuma," *MaddS* 6 (1893), 69–87.

Beinart, William, and Colin Bundy. *Hidden Struggles in Rural South Africa*. Berkeley, 1987.

Bell, R.M. "The Maji Maji Rebellion in Liwale District," *TNR* 28 (1950), 38–57.

Benl, Georg. *Die handelspolitischen Interessen der deutschen Spinnerei und Weberei von Baumwolle und Wolle seit 1862*. Berlin, 1930.

Berlepsch, Hans-Jörg von. *"Neuer Kurs" im Kaiserreich? Die Arbeiterpolitik des Freiherrn von Berlepsch 1890 bis 1896*. Düsseldorf, 1987.

Berman, Bruce, and John Lonsdale. *Unhappy Valley: Conflict in Kenya and Africa*. London, 1992.

Bernstein, Henry, "African Peasantries: A Theoretical Perspective," *Journal of Peasant Studies* 6, 4 (1979), 421–43.

Berry, Sara. *No Condition Is Permanent: The Social Dynamics of Agrarian Change in Sub-Saharan Africa*. Madison, 1993.

Bielefeldt, Karl. *Das Eindringen des Kapitalismus in die Landwirtschaft*. Berlin, 1910.

Biermann, Werner. *Tanganyika Railways—Carriers of Colonialism: An Account of Economic Indicators and Social Fragments*. Münster, 1995.

Bleifuss, Gerhard, and Gerhard Hergenröder. "Die 'Otto-Pflanzung Kilossa': Eine Unternehmung württembergischer Textilindustrieller in Deutsch-Ostafrika, 1907–1914," in *Kolonisation und Dekolonisation*, ed. Helmut Christmann. Schwäbisch Gmünd, 1989, 244–60.

Blohm, Wilhelm. *Die Nyamwezi: Land und Wirtschaft*. Hamburg, 1931.

———. *Die Nyamwezi: Gesellschaft und Weltbild*. Hamburg, 1933.

Böhme, Helmut. *Deutschlands Weg zur Grossmacht: Studien zum Verhältnis von Wirtschaft und Staat während der Reichsgründungszeit 1848–1881*. Köln, 1966.

Born, Karl Erich. *Wirtschafts- und Sozialgeschichte des Deutschen Kaiserreichs (1867/71–1914)*. Stuttgart, 1985.

Brain, Joy. "Natal's Indians, 1860–1910," in *Natal and Zululand from Earliest Times to 1910*, ed. Andrew Duminy and Bill Guest. Pietermaritzburg, 1989, 249–74.

Braun, K. "Der Reis in Deutsch-Ostafrika," *BLF* 3, 4 (1908), 167–217.

Bryceson, Deborah Fahy. *Food Insecurity and the Social Division of Labour in Tanzania, 1919–85*. New York, 1990.

Burgt, J.M.M. van der. "Zur Entvölkerungsfrage Unjamwesis und Ussumbwas," *KR* 12 (1913), 705–28.

———. "Zur Bevölkerungsfrage Unjamwesis und Ussumbwas," *KR* 13 (1914), 24–27.

Bursian, Alexander. *Die Häuser- und Hüttensteuer in Deutsch-Ostafrika.* Jena, 1910.

Büsgen, M. "Forstwirtschaft in den Kolonien," *Verhandlungen des Deutschen Kolonialkongresses.* Berlin, 1910, 801–17.

Canning, Kathleen. *Languages of Labor and Gender: Female Factory Work in Germany, 1850–1914.* Ithaca, 1996.

Caplan, Pat. "Gender, Ideology and Modes of Production on the Coast of East Africa," *Paideuma* 28 (1982), 29–43.

Clark, W.A. Graham. *Cotton Fabrics in Middle Europe: Germany, Austria-Hungary, Switzerland.* Washington, 1908.

Comaroff, John L., and Jean Comaroff. *Of Revelation and Revolution: The Dialectics of Modernity on a South African Frontier* Vol. II. Chicago, 1997.

Conte, Christopher. "Nature Reorganized: Ecological History in the Plateau Forests of the West Usambara Mountains, 1850–1935," in *Custodians of the Land,* ed. Gregory Maddox et al., 96–121.

Cooper, Frederick. *Plantation Slavery on the East Coast of Africa.* New Haven, 1977.

———. *From Slaves to Squatters: Plantation Labour and Agriculture in Zanzibar and Coastal Kenya 1890–1925.* New Haven, 1980.

———. *On the African Waterfront: Urban Disorder and the Transformation of Work in Colonial Mombasa.* New Haven, 1987.

———. "Colonizing Time: Work Rhythms and Labor Conflict in Colonial Mombasa," in *Colonialism and Culture,* ed. Nicholas Dirks. Ann Arbor, 1992, 209–46.

Crosse-Upcott, A.R.W. "Ngindo Famine Subsistence," *TNR* 50 (1950), 1–20.

Culwick, A.T., and G.M. Culwick. "A Study of Population in Ulanga, Tanganyika Territory," *Sociological Review* 30 (1938), 365–79.

Dahl, Edmund. *Nyamwezi-Wörterbuch.* Hamburg, 1915.

Dauber, Heinrich. *"Nicht als Abentheurer bin ich hierhergekommen . . . ": 100 Jahre Entwicklungs- "Hilfe." Tagebücher und Briefe aus Deutsch-Ostafrika, 1896–1902.* Frankfurt am Main, 1991.

Dedering, Tilman. "The Prophet's 'War Against the Whites': Shepherd Stuurman in Namibia and South Africa, 1905–7," *JAH* 40 (1999), 1–19.

Delius, Peter. *A Lion amongst the Cattle: Reconstruction and Resistance in the Northern Transvaal.* Portsmouth, 1996.

Deutsch, Georg. "The 'Freeing' of Slaves in German East Africa: The Statistical Record, 1890–1914," *Slavery and Abolition* 2 (1998), 109–32.

Deutscher Landwirtschaftsrat. *Sesshaftigkeit und Abwanderung der weiblichen Jugend vom Lande.* Berlin, 1905.

Eastman, Carol M. "Women, Slaves, and Foreigners: African Cultural Influences and Group Processes in the Formation of Northern Swahili Coastal Society," *IJAHS* 21, 1 (1988), 1–20.

Eberstein, F.v. "Ueber die Rechtsanschauungen der Küstenbewohner des Bezirkes Kilwa," *MaddS* 9 (1896), 170–83.

Eismann, Gustav. "Über Baumwolle in Deutsch-Ostafrika," *Der Pflanzer* (1905), 56–57.
Elton, F. "On the Coast Country of East Africa, South of Zanzibar," *Journal of the Royal Geographical Society* 44 (1874), 227–51.
Ernst, Christoph. "An Ecological Revolution? The 'Schlagwaldwirtschaft' in Western Germany in the Eighteenth and Nineteenth Centuries," in *European Woods and Forests: Studies in Cultural History,* ed. Charles Watkins. Cambridge, 1998, 83–92.
Esherick, Joseph. *The Origins of the Boxer Uprising.* Berkeley, 1987.
Fairhead, James, and Melissa Leach. "Rethinking the Forest-Savanna Mosaic: Colonial Science and Its Relics in West Africa," in *The Lie of the Land: Challenging the Received Wisdom on the African Environment,* ed. Melissa Leach and Robin Mearns. London, 1996, 105–21.
Falola, Toyin, and Paul Lovejoy, eds. *Pawnship in Africa: Debt Bondage in Historical Perspective.* Boulder, 1994.
Feierman, Steven. *Peasant Intellectuals: Anthropology and History in Tanzania.* Madison, 1990.
Fischer, Ferdinand. *Die Industrie Deutschlands und seiner Kolonien.* Leipzig, 1908.
FitzGerald, W.W.A. *Travels in British East Africa, Zanzibar and Pemba.* London, 1898.
Frankenstein, Kuno. "Königreich Sachsen," *Schriften des Vereins für Sozialpolitik* 54 (Leipzig, 1892).
Franz, Eckhart, and Peter Geissler, eds. *Guide to the German Records* 2 Vols. Dar es Salaam/Marburg, 1984.
Fresco, Louise O. *Cassava in Shifting Cultivation.* Amsterdam, 1986.
Freund, Bill. *Insiders and Outsiders: The Indian Working Class in Natal.* Portsmouth, 1994.
Froberger, Josef. "Die Polygamie und deren kulturelle Schäden," *Verhandlungen des Deutschen Kolonialkongresses 1910* (Berlin, 1910), 717–32.
Fuchs, Paul. Die Wirtschaftliche Erkundung einer ostafrikanischen Südbahn. Berlin, 1905.
Gann, Lewis H. "Marginal Colonialism: The German Case," in *Germans in the Tropics: Essays in German Colonial History,* ed. Arthur Knoll and Lewis H. Gann. Westport, 1987.
Gewald, Jan-Bart. *Herero Heroes: A Socio-Political History of the Herero of Namibia, 1890–1923.* Oxford, 1999.
———. "The Issue of Forced Labour in the Onjembo: German South West Africa 1904–1908," *Itinerario* 19, 1 (1995), 97–104.
Giblin, James. *The Politics of Environmental Control in Northeastern Tanzania, 1840–1940.* Philadelphia, 1992.
———. "The Precolonial Politics of Disease Control in the Lowlands of Northeastern Tanzania," in *Custodians of the Land,* ed. Maddox et al., 127–51.
———. "Family Life, Indigenous Culture, and Christianity in Colonial Njombe," in *East African Expressions of Christianity,* ed. Thomas Spear and Isaria N. Kimambo. Athens, OH, 1999, 309–23.
Gilbert, Erik O. "The Zanzibar Dhow Trade: An Informal Economy on the East African Coast, 1860–1964," (Ph.D. diss, Boston University, 1997).

Gillman, C. "A Short History of the Tanganyika Railways," *TNR* 13 (1942), 14–56.
Gillman, H. "Bush Fallowing on the Makonde Plateau," *TNR* 19 (1945), 34–44.
Glassman, Jonathon. "The Bondsman's New Clothes: The Contradictory Consciousness of Slave Resistance on the Swahili Coast," *JAH* 32 (1991), 277–312.
———. *Feasts and Riot: Revelry, Rebellion, and Popular Consciousness on the Swahili Coast, 1856–1888.* Portsmouth, 1995.
Goebes, Gisela. "Die sozialpolitische Bedeutung des Crimmitschauer Textilarbeiterstreiks 1903–04," (M.A. thesis, University of Konstanz, 1975).
Görnandt, Rudolf. *Die Landarbeiter mit eigener Wirtschaft in Nordwest- und Ostdeutschland.* Berlin, 1910.
Götzen, G.A. von. *Deutsch-Ostafrika im Aufstand 1905–6.* Berlin, 1909.
Gottberg, Achim, ed. *Unyamwesi. Quellensammlung und Geschichte.* Berlin, 1971.
Grass, Karl. "Forststatistik für die Waldungen des Rufiyideltas," *BLF* 2 (1904–06), 165–96.
Gregory, Robert G. *India and East Africa.* London, 1971.
Groh, Dieter. "Intensification of Work and Industrial Conflict in Germany, 1896–1914," *Politics and Society* 8 (1978), 349–97.
Gunzert, Theodor. "Service in German East Africa," mimeographed extract, n.d.
Gwassa, Gilbert C.K. "Kinjikitile and the Ideology of Maji Maji," in *The Historical Study of African Religion,* ed. T.O. Ranger and I.N. Kimambo. London, 1972, 202–17.
———. "The Outbreak and Development of the Maji Maji War, 1905–1907," (Ph.D. diss., University of Dar es Salaam, 1973).
Gwassa, G.C.K., and John Iliffe, eds. *Records of the Maji Maji Rising.* Dar es Salaam, 1967.
Hacker, Paul. *Die Beiräte für besondere Gebiete der Staatstätigkeit.* Tübingen, 1903.
Harlan, Louis R. "Booker T. Washington and the White Man's Burden," *American Historical Review* 71 (1966), 442–47.
Harries, Patrick. *Work, Culture, and Identity: Migrant Laborers in Mozambique and South Africa, c. 1860–1910.* Portsmouth, 1994.
Hartnoll, A.V., and N.R. Fuggles Couchman. "The 'Mashokora' Cultivations of the Coast," *TNR* 3 (1937), 34–39.
Havnevik, Kjell J. *Tanzania: The Limits to Development from Above.* Motala, 1993.
Henderson, W.O. *The Rise of German Industrial Power 1834–1914.* London, 1975.
Henning, Hans-Joachim, ed. *Die Sozialpolitik in den letzten Friedensjahren des Kaiserreichs.* Wiesbaden, 1982.
Hennings, R. "Der Baumwollkulturkampf," *Beiträge zur Kolonialpolitik* 7 (1905), 906–14.
Hesse, H. "Strafgewalt über die Eingeborenen in den deutschen Schutzgebieten," *Beiträge zur Kolonialpolitik* 6 (1904), 122–25.
Hindorf, Richard. *Der Sisalbau in Deutsch-Ostafrika.* Berlin, 1925.
Horne, David L. "Mode of Production in the Social and Economic History of Kilwa to 1884," (Ph.D. diss., UCLA, 1984).
Hoyle, B.S. *Gillman of Tanganyika: The Life and Work of a Pioneer Geographer.* Aldershot, 1987.

Hunt, Nancy. "Le Bebe en Brousse: European Women, African Birth Spacing and Colonial Intervention in Breast Feeding in the Belgian Congo," *IJAHS* 21, 3 (1988), 401–32.
Iliffe, John. "The Organization of the Maji Maji Rebellion," *JAH* 8, 3 (1967), 495–512.
———. "The Effects of the Maji Maji Rebellion of 1905–1906 on German Occupation Policy in East Africa," in *Britain and Germany in Africa: Imperial Rivalry and Colonial Rule,* ed. Prosser Gifford and William Roger Louis. New Haven, 1967, 557–75.
———. *Tanganyika under German Rule 1905–1912.* Cambridge, 1969.
———. *Agricultural Change in Modern Tanganyika: An Outline History.* Nairobi, 1971.
———. *A Modern History of Tanganyika.* Cambridge, 1979.
Isaacman, Allen. "Peasants and Rural Social Protest in Africa," in *Confronting Historical Paradigms: Peasants, Labor, and the Capitalist World System in Africa and Latin America,* ed. Frederick Cooper, Florencia E. Mallon, Steve J. Stern, Allen Isaacman, and William Roseberry. Madison, 1993, 205–317.
———. *Cotton Is the Mother of Poverty: Peasants, Work, and Rural Struggle in Colonial Mozambique, 1938–1961.* Portsmouth, 1996.
Jones, Elizabeth Bright. "Gender and Agricultural Change in Saxony, 1900–1930," (Ph.D. diss., University of Minnesota, 2000).
Jones, Laird. "Merchants of Slaughter: The Expansion of the Hide Trade in the Mwanza Region of Tanzania, 1903–1916," paper presented to the African Studies Association Annual Conference, Toronto, 1994.
———. "Target Wage Workers or Targeted Consumers?: Caravan Porters, Migrant Laborers and Imported Goods, 1880–1914," paper presented to the African Studies Association Annual Conference, Philadelphia, November 1999.
Jungblut, Carl. *Vierzig Jahre Afrika 1900–1940.* Berlin-Friedenau, 1941.
Kähler, Wilhelm. *Gesindewesen und Gesinderecht in Deutschland.* Jena, 1896.
Kahama, C. George, T.L. Maliyamkono, and Stuart Wells. *The Challenge for Tanzania's Economy.* London, 1986.
Kamara, Byarugaba. "The Impact of Structural Adjustment Programmes on Natural Resources with Particular Reference to Wildlife Conservation in Tanzania," in *Policy Reform and the Environment in Tanzania,* ed. M.S.D. Bagachwa and Festus Limbu. Dar es Salaam, 1995, 173–95.
Karstedt, F.O. "Betrachtungen zur Sozialpolitik in Ostafrika," *KR* 13 (1914), 133–41.
———. "Zur Sklavenfrage in Deutsch-Ostafrika," *KR* 12 (1913), 616–21.
Kaundinya, R. *Erinnerungen aus meinen Pflanzerjahren in Deutsch-Ostafrika.* Leipzig, 1918.
Kempf, Rosa. *Die deutsche Frau nach der Volks-, Berufs-, und Betriebszählung von 1925.* Mannheim, 1931.
Kerner, Donna O. "Land Scarcity and Rights of Control in the Development of Commercial Farming in Northeast Tanzania," in *Land and Society in Contemporary Africa,* ed. R.E. Downs and S.P. Reyna. Hanover, 1988, 159–91.

Kieran, J.A. "Abushiri and the Germans," in *Hadith 2,* ed. Bethwell Ogot. Nairobi, 1970, 157–201.
Kikula, Idris S. *Policy Implications on Environment: The Case of Villagisation in Tanzania.* Uppsala, 1997.
Kimambo, Isaria N. *Penetration and Protest in Tanzania: The Impact of the World Economy on the Pare 1860–1960.* London, 1991.
Kirby, A.J. "The Progress of Cotton Growing in the Tanganyika Territory," *Empire Cotton Growing Review* 7, 3 (1930), 169–80.
Kirchhain, Günter. "Das Wachstum der deutschen Baumwollindustrie im 19. Jahrhundert," (Ph.D. diss., University of Münster, 1973).
Kjekshus, Helge. *Ecology Control and Economic Development in East African History: The Case of Tanganyika 1850–1950.* London, 1996.
Klamroth, Martin. *Der Islam in Deutschostafrika.* Berlin, 1912.
———. "Beiträge zum Verständnis der religiösen Vorstellungen der Saramo im Bezirk Daressalam," *Zeitschrift für Kolonialsprachen* 1–3 (1910–13), 37–70, 118–53, 189–223.
Klare, Fritz. *Untersuchung über Einsatz und Ausnutzung der menschlichen Arbeitskräfte in bäuerlichen Betrieben.* Dessau, 1932.
Kolonialpraxis. Handbuch für Kaufleute, Industrielle, Banken, Behörden und Kapitalisten. Berlin, 1911.
Kolonial-Wirtschaftliches Komitee. *Unsere Kolonialwirtschaft in ihrer Bedeutung für Industrie und Arbeiterschaft.* Berlin, 1909.
———. *Kolonial-Handels-Adressbuch.* Berlin, 1911.
Koponen, Juhani. *People and Production in Late Precolonial Tanzania.* Jyväskylä, 1988.
———. *Development for Exploitation: German Colonial Policies in Mainland Tanzania, 1884–1914.* Hamburg, 1995.
———. "Agricultural Systems in Late Pre-colonial Tanzania," in *The Transformation of Rural Society in the Third World,* ed. Magnus Mörner and Thommy Svensson. London, 1991, 189–216.
———. "Population: A Dependent Variable," in *Custodians of the Land,* ed. Gregory Maddox et al., 19–42.
Krebs, Siegfried. "Zwangsarbeit in der ehemaligen deutschen Kolonie Ostafrikas," *Wissenschaftliche Zeitschrift der Karl-Marx-Universität Leipzig* 9 (1959–60), 395–400.
Kuntze, F. "Der Sklaven-Freikauf in Deutsch-Ostafrika," *Kolonie und Heimat* 2, 7 (1908–09), 8.
Lambert, John. "From Independence to Rebellion: African Society in Crisis, c. 1880–1910," in *Natal and Zululand from Earliest Times to 1910,* ed. Andrew Duminy and Bill Guest. Pietermaritzburg, 1989, 373–401.
Lamden, S.C. "Some Aspects of Porterage in East Africa," *TNR* 61 (1963), 155–64.
Leue, A. "Die Sklaverei in Deutsch-Ostafrika," *Beiträge zur Kolonialpolitik* 2 (1900–01), 606–08, 617–25.
Levy, Benas. "Baumwolle," *KR* 9 (1910), 746–65.
———. "Die Baumwollfrage und die deutschen Kolonien," *KR* 12 (1913), 391–414.

Lewis, L.A., and L. Berry. *African Environments and Resources.* Boston, 1988.
Likaka, Osumaka. *Rural Society and Cotton in Colonial Zaire.* Madison, 1997.
Linton, Derek. "Between School and Marriage, Workshop and Household: Young Working Women as a Social Problem in Late Imperial Germany," *European History Quarterly* 18 (1988), 387–408.
Löbner, M.H. *Unyamwezi und Tabora: Land, Volk und Missionsarbeit.* Herrnhut, 1914.
———. "Zur Entvölkerungsfrage Unyamwezis," *KR* 13 (1914), 267–70.
Lochmüller, W. *Zur Entwicklung der Baumwollindustrie in Deutschland.* Jena, 1906.
Lovett, Margot. "On Power and Powerlessness: Marriage and Metaphor in Colonial Western Tanzania," *IJAHS* 27, 2 (1994), 273–301.
Lwoga, C.M.F. "From Long-Term to Seasonal Labour Migration in Iringa Region, Tanzania: A Legacy of the Colonial Forced Labour System," in *Forced Labour and Migration: Patterns of Movement within Africa,* ed. Abebe Zegeye and Shubi Ishemo. London, 1989, 180–210.
Maddox, Gregory. "Gender and Famine in Central Tanzania: 1916–1961," *African Studies Review* 39 (1996), 83–101.
———. "Environment and Population Growth in Ugogo, Central Tanzania," in Maddox et al., *Custodians of the Land,* 43–65.
Maddox, Gregory, James Giblin, and Isaria N. Kimambo, eds. *Custodians of the Land: Ecology and Culture in the History of Tanzania.* London, 1996.
Maier, Ambrosius. "Aus den Matumbibergen," *Missions-Blaetter von St. Ottilien* 14 (1910), 115–18.
Maji Maji Research Project: Collected Papers. University College Dar es Salaam, Department of History, 1968.
Maliyamkono, T.L., and M.S.D. Bagachwa. *The Second Economy in Tanzania.* London, 1990.
Mandala, Elias. "Peasant Cotton Agriculture, Gender, and Inter-Generational Relationships: The Lower Tchiri (Shire) Valley of Malawi, 1906–1940," *African Studies* 25, 2–3 (1982), 27–44.
Mapunda, O.B., and G.P. Mangara. *The Maji Maji War in Ungoni.* Dar es Salaam, 1969.
Marks, Shula, and Richard Rathbone, eds. *Industrialization and Social Change in South Africa: African Class-formation, Culture and Consciousness, 1870–1930.* Hong Kong, 1985.
Marsland, H. "Mlau Cultivation in the Rufiji Valley," *TNR* 5 (April 1938), 56–59.
Martin, Rudolf. *Die Ausschliessung der Verheirateten Frauen aus der Fabrik: Eine Studie an der Textil-Industrie.* Tübingen, 1896.
McCarthy, D.M.P. *Colonial Bureaucracy and Creating Underdevelopment: Tanganyika 1919–1940.* Ames, IA, 1982.
McHenry, Dean. *Tanzania's Ujamaa Villages: The Implementation of a Rural Development Strategy.* Berkeley, 1979.
Merker, Moritz. "Über die Aufstandsbewegung in Deutsch-Ostafrika während der Monate August bis November 1905," *Militär-Wochenblatt* 45 (1906), 1021–30.

Methner, Wilhelm. *Unter drei Gouverneuren: 16 Jahre Dienst in deutschen Tropen.* Breslau, 1938.
Meyknecht, Ernst. *Die Krisen in der deutschen Woll- und Baumwollindustrie von 1900 bis 1914.* Gütersloh, 1928.
Mihanjo, E.P., and N.N. Luanda. "The South-East Economic Backwater and the Urban Floating Wamachinga," in *The Making of a Periphery: Economic Development and Cultural Encounters in Southern Tanzania,* ed. Pekka Seppälä and Bertha Koda. Uppsala, 1998, 222–32.
Mintz, Sidney. *Caribbean Transformations.* New York, 1989.
———. "Slavery and the Rise of Peasantries," *Historical Reflections* 6, 1 (1979), 213–42.
Monson, Jamie. "Relocating Maji Maji: The Politics of Alliance and Authority in the Southern Highlands of Tanzania, 1870–1918," *JAH* 39 (1998), 95–120.
Moore, Henrietta L., and Megan Vaughan. *Cutting Down Trees: Gender, Nutrition, and Agricultural Change in the Northern Province of Zambia, 1890–1990.* Portsmouth, 1994.
Moore, Sally Falk. *Social Facts and Fabrications: "Customary" Law on Kilimanjaro, 1880–1980.* Cambridge, 1986.
Muhema, B. "The Impact of Flooding in Rufiji," *Journal of the Geographical Association of Tanzania* 7 (September 1972), 49–64.
Müller, F.F. *Deutschland-Zanzibar-Ostafrika. Geschichte einer deutschen Kolonialeroberung 1884–1890.* Berlin, 1959.
Murray, Colin. *Families Divided: The Impact of Migrant Labour in Lesotho.* Cambridge, 1981.
Ndaro, Japheth M.M. "Local Coping Strategies in Dodoma District, Tanzania," in *Development from Within: Survival in Rural Africa,* ed. D.R.F. Taylor and Fiona MacKenzie. London, 1992, 170–213.
Netting, Robert McC. *Smallholders, Householders: Farm Families and the Ecology of Intensive, Sustainable Agriculture.* Stanford, 1993.
Neumann, Roderick. *Imposing Wilderness: Struggles over Livelihood and Nature Preservation in Africa.* Berkeley, 1998.
Nussbaum, Helga. *Unternehmer gegen Monopole: Über Struktur und Aktionen antimonopolitischer bürgerlichen Gruppen zu Beginn des 20. Jahrhunderts.* Berlin, 1966.
Oppel, A. *Die deutsche Textilindustrie.* Leipzig, 1912.
Otto, Rose. *Über Fabrikarbeit verheirateter Frauen.* Stuttgart, 1910.
Oyama, Shuichi. "Regeneration Process of the Miombo Woodland at Abandoned Citimene Fields of Northern Zambia," *African Study Monographs* 17, 3 (1996), 101–16.
Paasche, Hans. *Im Morgenlicht: Kriegs-, Jagd- und Reise-Erlebnisse in Ostafrika.* Berlin, 1907.
Paasche, Hermann. *Deutsch-Ostafrika: Wirtschaftliche Studien.* Hamburg, 1913.
Parker, John. *Making the Town: Ga State and Society in Early Colonial Accra.* Portsmouth, 2000.
Peiper, Otto. "Ethnographische Beobachtungen aus dem Bezirke Kilwa, Deutsch-Ostafrika," *Baessler-Archiv* 10 (1926), 24–27.

Pentzel, Otto. *Heimat Ostafrika.* Leipzig, 1936.
Pfüller, A. "Über Baumwollkultur," *Der Pflanzer* (1905), 97–100.
Pierard, Richard V. "The Dernburg Reform Policy in German East Africa," *TNR* 67 (June 1967), 31–38.
———. "A Case Study in German Economic Imperialism: The Colonial Economic Committee, 1896–1914," *Scandinavian Economic History Review* 26, 2 (1968), 155–67.
Pike, Charles. "History and Imagination: Swahili Literature and Resistance to German Language Imperialism in Tanzania, 1885–1910," *IJAHS* 19 (1986), 211–33.
Prüsse, Albert. *Zwanzig Jahre Ansiedler in Deutsch-Ostafrika.* Stuttgart, 1929.
Prüssing, K. "Ueber das Rufiji-Delta," *MaddS* 14 (1901), 106–13.
Quante, Peter. *Die Flucht aus der Landwirtschaft.* Berlin, 1933.
Ranger, Terence. *Dance and Society in Eastern Africa.* Berkeley and Los Angeles, 1975.
Redmond, Patrick. "Maji Maji in Ungoni: A Reappraisal of Existing Historiography," *IJAHS* 8 (1975), 407–23.
Reichsamt des Innern. *Die Beschäftigung verheiratheter Frauen in Fabriken.* Berlin, 1901.
Reichskolonialamt. *Die Baumwollfrage: Denkschrift über Produktion und Verbrauch von Baumwolle. Massnahmen gegen die Baumwollnot.* Jena, 1911.
———. *Der Baumwollbau in den deutschen Schutzgebieten.* Jena, 1914.
Roberts, Richard. "Representation, Structure and Agency: Divorce in the French Soudan during the Early Twentieth Century," *JAH* 40 (1999), 389–410.
Roberts, Richard, and Suzanne Miers, eds. *The End of Slavery in Africa.* Madison, 1989.
Robertson, J.K. "Mixed or Multiple Cropping in Native Agriculture Practice," *East African Agricultural Journal* (April 1941), 228–31.
Rockel, Stephen J. "Wage Labor and the Culture of Porterage in Nineteenth Century Tanzania: the Central Caravan Routes," *Comparative Studies of South Asia, Africa and the Middle East* 15, 2 (1995), 14–24.
———. "Caravan Porters of the *Nyika*: Labour, Culture, and Society in Nineteenth Century Tanzania," (Ph.D. diss., University of Toronto, 1997).
Rodney, Walter. "The Political Economy of Colonial Tanganyika 1890–1930," in *Tanzania under Colonial Rule,* ed. M.H.Y. Kaniki. Singapore, 1980, 128–63.
Rodney, Walter, Kapepwa Tambila, and Laurent Sago. *Migrant Labour in Tanzania during the Colonial Period: Case Studies of Recruitment and Conditions of Labour in the Sisal Industry.* Hamburg, 1983.
Rounce, N.V. "Ingereza Ng'wana Sweya: His Own Story and His Agricultural Practices," *East African Agricultural Journal* (1939), 211–15.
Safari, Joseph. "Grundlagen und Auswirkungen des Maji-Maji- Aufstandes von 1905," (Ph.D. diss., University of Cologne, 1972).
Sander, L. *Die geographische Verbreitung einiger tierischer Schädlinge unserer kolonialen Landwirtschaft und die Bedingungen ihres Vorkommens.* Frankfurt am Main, 1903.

Savile, A.H. "A Study of Recent Alterations in the Flood Regimes of Three Important Rivers in Tanganyika," *East African Agricultural Journal* (October 1945), 69–74.
Schabel, Hans. "Tanganyika Forestry under German Colonial Administration, 1891–1919," *Forest and Conservation History* (July 1990), 130–41.
Schanz, Moritz. *Baumwollbau in den deutschen Kolonien.* Manchester, 1910.
———. "Der koloniale Baumwollenbau," *Verhandlungen des Deutschen Kolonialkongresses* (Berlin, 1910), 817–41.
Schmidt, Elizabeth. *Peasants, Traders and Wives: Shona Women in the History of Zimbabwe 1870–1939.* Portsmouth, 1992.
Schmidt, George. *Das Kolonial-Wirtschaftliche Komitee.* Berlin, 1934.
Schnee, Heinrich, ed. *Deutsches Kolonial-Lexicon* Vol. I. Leipzig, 1920.
Schrader, Rudolf. *Die Zwangsarbeit in Ostafrika nach deutschem und britischem Kolonialrecht.* Hamburg, 1919.
Schroeder, Friedrich, "Einiges über Arbeiterverhältnisse in Usambara," *DKZ* 5, 28 (1988), 220–22.
Schwarze, W. *Deutsch-Ost-Afrika.* Berlin, 1907.
Scott, James. *Weapons of the Weak: Everyday Forms of Peasant Resistance.* New Haven, 1985.
———. *Seeing Like a State: How Certain Schemes to Improve the Human Condition Have Failed.* New Haven, 1998.
Sheriff, Abdul. *Slaves, Spices and Ivory in Zanzibar.* London, 1987.
Shivji, Issa. *Law, State and the Working Class in Tanzania.* London, 1986.
———. "The Roots of an Agrarian Crisis in Tanzania: A Theoretical Perspective," in *The Tanzanian Peasantry: Economy in Crisis*, ed. Peter G. Forster and Sam Maghimbi. Avebury, 1992, 124–50.
Shorter, Aylward. *Chiefship in Western Tanzania: A Political History of the Kimbu.* Oxford, 1972.
Siebenlist, T. *Forstwirtschaft in Deutsch-Ostafrika.* Berlin, 1914.
Simon, Helen. *Der Anteil der Frau an der deutschen Industrie.* Jena, 1910.
Sippel, Harald. "Aspects of Colonial Land Law in German East Africa," in *Land Law and Land Ownership in Africa,* ed. Robert Debusman and Stefan Arnold. Bayreuth, 1996, 3–38.
Spear, Thomas. *Mountain Farmers.* Berkeley, 1997.
Stegmann, Dirk. *Die Erben Bismarcks: Parteien und Verbände in der Spätphase des Wilhelminischen Deutschlands.* Cologne, 1970.
Stichter, Sharon. *Migrant Labour in Kenya: Capitalism and the African Response 1895–1975.* London, 1982.
Stoecker, Helmuth, ed. *German Imperialism in Africa.* London, 1986.
Stollowsky, Otto. "On the Background to the Rebellion in German East Africa in 1905–1906," trans. John East, *IJAHS* 21, 4 (1988), 677–97.
———. "Die Aufhebung der Sklaverei in Deutsch-Ostafrika," *Koloniale Zeitschrift* (31 April 1912), 348–49.
Stuhlmann, Franz. "Forschungsreisen in Usaramo," *MaddS*, 8 (1894), 223–32.
———. "Vierter Jahresbericht des Kaiserlichen Biologisch-Landwirtschaftlichen Instituts Amani," *BLF* (1904–06).

———. "Die Pflanzungsunternehmungen der Europäer in den deutschen Schutzgebieten," *Jahrbuch über die deutschen Kolonien* 3 (1910), 121–47.
Sunseri, Thaddeus. "Slave Ransoming in German East Africa, 1885–1922," *IJAHS* 26, 3 (1993), 481–511.
———. "Peasants and the Struggle for Labor in Cotton Regimes of the Rufiji Basin (Tanzania), 1890–1918," in *Cotton, Colonialism, and Social History in Sub-Saharan Africa*, ed. Allen Isaacman and Richard Roberts. Portsmouth, 1995, 180–99.
———. "Labor Migration in Colonial Tanzania and the Hegemony of South African Historiography," *African Affairs* 95, 381 (1996), 581–98.
———. "Famine and Wild Pigs: Gender Struggles and the Outbreak of the Maji Maji War in Uzaramo (Tanzania)," *JAH* 38 (1997), 235–59.
———. "Dispersing the Fields: Railway Labor and Rural Change in Early Colonial Tanzania," *Canadian Journal of African Studies* 32, 3 (1998), 558–83.
———. "Maji Maji and the Millennium: Abrahamic Sources and the Creation of a Tanzanian Resistance Tradition," *History in Africa* 26 (1999), 365–78.
———. "The *Baumwollfrage*: Cotton Colonialism in German East Africa," *Central European History* 34, 1 (2001), 31–51.
Supf, Karl. "Zur Baumwollfrage," *Der Tropenpflanzer* 4, 6 (1900), 263–73.
———. "Die Arbeit des Kolonial-Wirtschaftlichen Komitees, 1896–1906," *Der Tropenpflanzer* 10, 12 (1906), 769–77.
Supf, Wilhelm. *Das Ende deutscher Kolonialwirtschaft?* Berlin, 1921.
Swantz, Marja-Liisa. *Women in Development: A Creative Role Denied?* London, 1985.
Sybel, Heinrich. "Die Baumwollindustrie," *Schriften des Vereins für Socialpolitik* 105 (Leipzig, 1903), 127–55.
Taasisi ya Elimu. *Historia. Shule ya Msingi*. Dar es Salaam, 1985.
Tambila, Kapepwa. "Botanical Imperialism in Action: Germany and Cotton in East Africa, 1886–1914," *Tanzania Zamani* 1, 4 (1996), 27–57.
Tanzanian Institute of Curriculum Development. *East Africa from 1850 to the Present*. Dar es Salaam, 1988.
Tetzlaff, Rainer. *Koloniale Entwicklung und Ausbeutung: Wirtschafts- und Sozialgeschichte Deutsch-Ostafrikas, 1885–1914*. Berlin, 1970.
Thompson, E.P. "Time, Work-Discipline and Industrial Capitalism," *Past and Present* 38 (1967), 56–97.
Tripp, Aili Mari. *Changing the Rules: The Politics of Liberalization and the Urban Informal Economy in Tanzania*. Berkeley, 1997.
Tuck, Michael. "Syphilis, Sexuality, and Social Control: A History of Venereal Disease in Colonial Uganda," (Ph.D. diss., Northwestern University, 1997).
———. "Venereal Disease, Sexuality and Society in Uganda," in *Sex, Sin and Suffering: Venereal Disease and European Society since 1870*, ed. Roger Davidson and Lesley A. Hall. London, 2001, 191–204.
Ullmann, Hans-Peter. "Unternehmerschaft, Arbeitgeberverbände und Streikbewegung 1890–1914," in *Streik: Zur Geschichte des Arbeitskampfes in Deutschland während der Industrialisierung*, ed. Klaus Tenfelde and H. Volkmann. Munich, 1981.

Vaughan, Megan. *The Story of an African Famine: Gender and Famine in Twentieth-Century Malawi.* Oxford, 1987.
Velten, Carl. *Swahili Prose Texts,* ed. and trans. L. Harries. London, 1965.
Verein für Sozialpolitik. *Bäuerliche Verhältnisse im Königreich Sachsen.* Leipzig, 1892.
Vuorela, Ulla. "The Crisis, Women, and Social Reproduction," in *The IMF and Tanzania: The Dynamics of Liberalisation,* ed. Horace Campbell and Howard Stein. Harare, 1991, 153–74.
Wagner, Woldemar. "Der Crimmitschauer Textilarbeiterstreik in den Jahren 1903–1905," (Ph.D. diss., University of Leipzig, 1960).
Waller, Richard. "Emutai: Crisis and Response in Maasailand, 1883–1902," in *The Ecology of Survival: Case Studies from Northeast African History,* ed. Douglas Johnson and David Anderson. Boulder, 1988, 73–112.
Waltz, H. "Die Pflanzungen der Europäer in unseren Kolonien im Jahre 1913," *Jahrbuch über die deutschen Kolonien* 6 (1913).
Wanitzek, Ulrike, and Harald Sippel. "Land Rights in Conservation Areas in Tanzania," *GeoJournal* 46 (1998), 113–28.
Wege, Arthur. *Die rechtlichen Bestimmungen über die Sklaverei in den deutschen afrikanischen Schutzgebieten.* Berlin, 1915.
Weidner, Fritz. *Die Hausssklaverei in Ostafrika.* Jena, 1915.
Werth, Emil. *Das Deutsch-Ostafrikanische Küstenland und die Vorgelagerten Inseln* Vol. II. Berlin, 1915.
Westcott, Nicholas. "The East African Sisal Industry, 1929–1949: The Marketing of a Colonial Commodity during Depression and War," *JAH* 25 (1984), 445–61.
Weule, Karl. *Native Life in East Africa.* Chicago, 1969.
White, Landeg. *Magomero: Portrait of an African Village.* Cambridge, 1987.
Willms, Angelika. "Modernisierung durch Frauenarbeit? Zum Zusammenhang von wirtschaftlichem Strukturwandel und weiblicher Arbeitsmarktlage in Deutschland, 1882–1939," in *Historische Arbeitsmarktforschung: Entstehung, Entwicklung und Probleme der Vermarktung von Arbeitskraft,* ed. Toni Pierenkemper and Richard Tilly. Göttingen, 1982, 37–77.
Wood, R. Cecil. "Cotton in Tanganyika Territory," *Empire Cotton Growing Review* 1, 1 (1924), 31–41.
Worger, William. *South Africa's City of Diamonds.* New Haven, 1987.
Wright, Marcia. *Strategies of Slaves and Women: Life-Stories from East/Central Africa.* New York, 1993.
———. "Maji Maji: Prophecy and Historiography," in *Revealing Prophets: Prophecy in Eastern African History,* ed. David Anderson and Douglas Johnson. London, 1995, 124–42.
Yeager, Rodger, and Norman Miller. *Wildlife, Wild Death: Land Use and Survival in Eastern Africa.* Albany, 1986.
Ziegenhorn. "Das Rufiyi-Delta," *MaddS* 9 (1886), 78–85.

ARCHIVES AND LIBRARY COLLECTIONS

Berlin-Dahlem, Geheimes Staatsarchiv-Preussischer Kulturbesitz (GStA)
Berlin, Berlin Missionswerk

Berlin, Bundesarchiv (BAB)
Bielefeld, Bethelarchiv
Dar es Salaam, Tanzania National Archives (TNA)
Dresden, Sächsisches Hauptstaatsarchiv
Frankfurt, Stadt- und Universitätsbibliothek, Abteilung Orient und Afrika
Freiburg, Bundesarchiv-Militärarchiv (BAF)
Hamburg, Staatsarchiv
Hamburg, Weltwirtschaftsarchiv (HWWA)
Hamburg, Archiv des Handelskammers
Herrnhut, Archiv der Brüder Unität, Moravian Mission (ABU)
Koblenz, Bundesarchiv (BAK)
Leipzig, Hauptstaatsarchiv
Mannheim, Landesmuseum für Teknik und Arbeit
Munich, Bayerisches Hauptstaatsarchiv
St. Ottilien, Archiv der Benedektiner Mission
Stuttgart-Hohenheim, Wirtschaftsarchiv Baden-Württemberg
Stuttgart, Hauptstaatsarchiv

INTERVIEWS

Interviews were conducted in Swahili. Unrecorded interviews have been marked (UR).
Jalala Hamisi Sumail, Bagamoyo, 6 May 1990. (UR)
Mlisho Kazi, Bagamoyo, 6 May 1990.
Hella Saidi, Bagamoyo, 7 May 1990.
Athumani Kongo, Mafia-Kirongwe, 21 May 1990.
Mwandazi Juma, Mama Mwandazi, Mafia-Kirongwe, 21 May 1990.
Mshangama Mohamed, Mafia-Juani, 26 May 1990.
Rashidi Mohamed Mtambo, Mafia-Kilindoni, 26 May 1990.
Kassam Makao, Mafia-Kilindoni, 26 May 1990.
Hamadi Duma, Mafia-Kilindoni, 26 May 1990.
Mzee Nganda, Mafia-Kilindoni, 26 May 1990.
Mashaka Salehe, Morogoro, 4 June 1990.
Bila Jina, Morogoro, 4 June 1990.
Najabu bin Najabu, Morogoro, 4 June 1990.
Ali Mwinyinvua Maiti, Morogoro, 5 June 1990.
Mzee Magongo, Morogoro, 5 June 1990. (UR)
Saifu Athumani, Kilosa, 10 June 1990.
Abdul Mohamed, Kilosa, 10 June 1990.
Shumali Abedi Tandika, Kilosa, 10 June 1990.
Alfani Nyembe, Kilosa, 10 June 1990.
Kitenge Muhamed, Kilwa-Masoko, 20 June 1990.
Abdalla Umati, Kilwa-Masoko, 20 June 1990.
Ali Abdalla Omari Ndimba, Kilwa-Masoko, 20 June 1990.
Jusuf Muhamed Mshirazi, Kilwa-Kisiwani, 21 June 1990.
Muhamed Timani, Kilwa-Kisiwani, 21 June 1990.

NEWSPAPERS, JOURNALS, AND OFFICIAL PUBLICATIONS

Afrika: Monatschrift für die sittliche und soziale Entwicklung der deutschen Schutzgebieten
Askari: Fahndungsblatt
Beiträge zur Kolonialpolitik
Der Pflanzer
Der Textil-Arbeiter
Deutsch-Ostafrikanische Zeitung
Deutsch-Ostafrikanische Rundschau
Deutsche Kolonialzeitung
Deutsche Kolonialzeitschrift
Deutsche Kolonialpost
East African Agricultural Journal
Empire Cotton Growing Review
Handel und Gewerbe
Jahrbuch über die deutschen Kolonien
Journal of the Royal Geographical Society
Kiongozi
Koloniale Monatsblätter—Zeitschrift für Kolonialpolitik, Kolonialrecht, und Kolonialwirtschaft
Koloniale Rundschau
Koloniale Zeitschrift
Kolonie und Heimat
Leipziger Monatschrift für die Textilindustrie
Mambo Leo
Missionsblaetter von St. Ottilien
Mitteilungen aus den deutschen Schutzgebieten
Ostafrikanischer Pflanzer
Politische Nachrichten
Sächsische Landwirtschaftliche Zeitung
Sächsische Arbeiter-Zeitung
Textilarbeiter-Zeitung
Usambara Post
Verhandlungen der deutschen Kolonialkongresse

Publications of the Government of German East Africa (Kaiserliches Gouvernement von Deutsch-Ostafrika):

Amtlicher Anzeiger für Deutsch-Ostafrika
Amtlicher Anzeiger für Tanga
Berichte über Land- und Forstwirtschaft
Die Landesgesetzgebung des Deutsch-Ostafrikanischen Schutzgebietes (Tanga/Dar es Salaam, 1911)
Verhandlungen des Gouvernementsrats (Dar es Salaam)

Publications of the Colonial Office (Reichskolonialamt):

Deutsches Kolonialblatt
Der Baumwollbau in den deutschen Schutzgebieten: seine Entwicklung seit dem Jahre 1910 (Jena, 1914)
Die Baumwollfrage (Jena, 1911)
Jahresberichte über die Entwicklung der deutschen Schutzgebiete in Afrika und der Südsee.

Publications of the Colonial Economic Committee (KWK)

Beihefte zum Tropenpflanzer.
Der Tropenpflanzer. Zeitschrift für tropische Landwirtschaft.
Deutsch-Koloniale Baumwollunternehmungen.
Kolonial-Handels-Adressbuch.
Verhandlungen der Baumwoll-Kommission des KWKs.
Verhandlungen des Kolonial-wirtschaftlichen Komitees

Other Official Publications:

Stenographische Berichte über die Verhandlungen des Reichstages

INDEX

Abortion, 166, 179–80, 182
Aden, 127
Adultery, 96, 179–84
African-American farmers, 14, 132 n.47. *See also* Tuskegee Institute
Akida (pl. *maakida*), xiii, 27, 66, 70, 78, 82, 88, 89, 91, 92, 94, 97, 98, 122, 123, 147, 178, 179, 184, 194. *See also* Local elites
Akidat, xiii, 122
Algeria, 4
Allmende. See Commons
Amani research station, 17
Arabia, 127
Arab planters and traders, xxi, 17, 26, 41, 81, 108 n.102, 138
Arbeiterfrage (labor question), xiv, 2, 129
Arusha, 138
Askari (police), xiii, xxx, 63, 64, 68, 98–99, 101, 117–18, 140, 182–83
Association of German Cotton Yarn Consumers, 6
Association of South German Cotton Industrialists, 6

Bagamoyo, xxxi, 53, 56, 60, 66, 89, 139, 146
Bakshish, xiii, 89, 139, 147

Baumwollfrage (cotton question), xiv, 2
Baumwolle A.G. Plantation, 144, 145, 147, 148
Beer. *See Pombe* beer
Bena, 139, 141, 144, 145, 182–84
Benedictine Mission, xxix
Berlepsch, Freiherr von, 8
Berlin Mission, xxix
Birth decline, 179–85
Bismarckburg, 65
Boers, 138
Boxer rebellion, 95
Bremen, xxx; Cotton Börse in, 5
Britain, British, 3, 83, 130, 165, 195–96
Brussels Anti-Slavery Conference, 30
Bukoba, xxv
Bülow, Chancellor Bernhard von, 6
Bush (*pori*), xiv, 15, 92, 99, 101, 102, 115–17, 167, 173–75. *See also* Commons
Bush fallowing and burning, xxiv, 14, 15, 16, 76, 78, 79, 82, 84, 87–94, 114, 118–19, 121, 126, 172–73, 175, 177, 186, 194
Bushiri uprising, 4, 129

Call-and-response singing, 152

Cannibalism fears, 182–84
Capitalism, xxii, xiv, xxv, 195; on plantations, xxvii, 193
Caravans, xxi, 43, 56, 57, 59, 65, 76, 77, 79, 83, 98, 101, 117, 140, 165, 166, 171–75, 178; *Caravanserais*, 60–61. See also Slavery; Porters
Cash crops, xxii–xxix, xxxii–xxxiii, 12, 16, 17, 19 n.3, 43, 51, 53, 64, 76, 77, 79, 88, 91, 113–14, 127, 136, 140, 166–67, 179, 181, 184, 194, 196. See also *individual crops*
Cassava, 78, 85, 91, 101–102, 107 n.87, 117–18, 123, 127, 128, 140, 167
Catholic Center Party, 27
Cattle, 32, 60, 65, 67, 79, 105 n.41, 120, 172, 173, 177, 186
Central Africa, xxi
Chain gangs. See Labor, penal
Children, xxxii, 36, 38, 43, 44, 54, 66, 77, 85, 93, 100, 101, 116, 120, 121, 142, 156, 160 n.26, 167, 170, 173, 175–84
China, 55
Chole Island, xxxi, 37, 38
Christianity, 10, 98, 156, 171
Cloth, xiii, 4, 32, 83, 86, 87, 94, 123, 145, 149, 156, 168, 171
Cloves, 32
Coconuts, 31, 32, 37, 53, 68, 124, 139. See also Copra
Coffee, xxii, 2, 16, 53, 54, 55, 68, 138, 139
Colonial Economic Committee. See KWK
Colonial Office, 98, 182
Commons (*Allmende*), xiv, 87–88, 106 n.60, 114, 130, 194, 196
Communal fields and obligations, 91–94, 96, 97, 113, 122
Congo, 67, 80
Conservation, xxiv, xxvi, xxxi, xxxiii, 77, 79, 90, 114, 174, 194–96
Copal, 15, 67, 84, 86, 105 n.51, 128
Copra, xxii, 37, 65, 117. See also Coconuts

Cotton, xxii–xxiii, xxvi–xxx, 1–4, 8, 14, 17, 37, 43, 52, 65, 67, 68, 76, 77, 81, 92, 93, 97, 101, 137, 145, 152, 167, 184, 194; Cotton Famine, 4, 5, 6, 10, 18, 137; German dependence on American, xxv, 1–10, 13, 137, 151, 165, 194; prices, 5, 11, 14, 21 n.21; as a peasant crop, 53, 91, 113–30, 138, 165, 178
Crime and criminality, 40–44, 52, 55, 63, 64, 69, 103, 116, 122, 140, 157, 169, 174, 178–86. See also Labor, penal
Crimmitschau textile strike, 6
Crop pests and predators, xx, 15, 77, 80, 84, 85, 87, 90, 95, 101, 113–14, 117, 125, 130, 173–74, 194, 196. See also Locusts; Wild pigs

Dar es Salaam, xix, 53, 55, 60, 63, 69, 70, 76, 88–92, 98, 100–101, 117, 139, 146, 165, 167, 172, 182–83, 186 n.4
Dawa (medicine), xiii, 94–95, 97–99, 110 n.135, 129, 179, 183–84
Dependency theory, xxii
Dernburg, Colonial Minister Bernhard, xxx, 7, 12, 136–37, 149
Desertion. See Labor; Slavery
Deutsch-Ostafrikanische Rundschau (*DOAR*), xxix, 119
Deutsch-Ostafrikanische Zeitung (*DOAZ*), xxviii, 67, 128
Dienstbote, xiv, 62. See also Domestic servants
Dienstbuch (*kitabu cha kazi*), xiv, 35, 62, 64
Dienstherrschaft (Master-Servant Relationship), xiv, 32, 39, 62
Disease, xiv, xxxi, 116, 157, 166, 181. See also Hook Worms; Malaria; Sleeping sickness; Syphilis
Divorce. See Marriage dissolution
DOAG (*Deutsch-Ostafrikanische Gesellschaft*), 13, 16, 23 n.74, 26, 54, 55, 60, 63, 68, 106 n.58, 123

Index

Dodoma, 169, 180
Domestic servants, 26, 30, 32, 39, 63, 64, 68, 181
Donde, 97
Dresden, xxx, 6

East Africa Plantation Corporation, 147
Economic liberalization, 196
Egypt, 4, 10
Environment and ecology, xxiv, xxxiii, 15, 65, 79-84, 92, 95, 96, 99, 114, 117, 132 n.48, 193-96; environmental control, 15, 79-80, 89, 93, 102-103, 114-15, 173, 186
Ethiopianism, 98

Fallow (*kilala*), xiii, 92, 94, 118, 121, 158, 194. *See also* Bush fallowing and burning
Famine, xiv, xxvii, xxxii, 17, 29, 41, 65, 77, 78, 80-87, 93-96, 99, 101-102, 114-20, 167, 173, 183-84
Field dispersal, 96, 102, 118, 165, 171-78, 194-96
Fire. *See* Bush fallowing and burning
Floods and floodlands, 82-83, 85, 115, 118, 120, 125, 127. *See also Mlau*
Food production and subsistence, xxiii-xxiv, xxvii-xxviii, 11, 14, 16, 52, 54, 78, 82-84, 98, 114-15, 125, 127, 130, 138, 166, 175
Food rations (*posho*), xiv, 52, 93, 139, 145, 148, 150, 155, 157, 167-69, 171
Foreign Office, 5, 6, 91
Forests, xxvi, xxvii-xxx, 13, 15, 16, 76-78, 81, 84-89, 91, 96, 98, 101, 102, 106 nn.58,60, 108 nn.100,102, 114-19, 128, 130, 131 n.30, 156-57, 167, 174-77, 186, 194-96
Frauenindustrie (women's industry), 7
Freedom of movement, xiv, xxvii, xxxiii, 9, 33, 44, 136, 146, 176, 194
Freibrief (*hati ya huru*), xiii, xiv, 33-36, 39
Freikauf. See Slavery, ransoming

Freizügigkeit. See Freedom of movement
Geheimpolizei (plantation police), 143, 145
Gender, xxiii-xxiv, xxxi, 7-9, 40-41, 84, 96, 102, 114, 125, 176-77
Gerengere trial estate, 17, 81
German Colonial Society (DKG), 21 n.28
German East African Corporation. *See DOAG*
Gesinde/Gesindewesen, xiv, xxxiii, 26-27, 32-40, 44, 47 n.51, 52, 62
Giblin, James, 79
Glassman, Jonathon, 40
Gogo, 75 n.88, 167
Götzen, Governor Adolf Graf von, 5, 59, 67, 91, 98, 99, 101, 136
Gramsci, Antonio, 40, 43
Grass, Karl, 102, 119
Great Depression, xxi
Greece, Greeks, 138, 139
Grenzwildnis, xv, 128
Grossbetrieb, xv, 11. *See also* Plantations

Ha, 169
Hamburg, xxx, 5
Hannover, 13
Hati ya huru (certificate of freedom). *See Freibrief*
Hehe, 96, 141
Hemp, 60
Hermann, Freiherr von, 5
Holzmann & Co., 72 n.22, 168-69
Honey, 15, 117
Hook worms, 116, 157, 181
Households, xxii-xxiii, 17, 84-85, 118, 125, 129-30, 150, 167, 181, 194; division of labor, 15-16, 125, 172-73, 175; household conflict, xxxii, 65, 77, 88, 96, 100, 102-103, 114-116, 118, 166, 175, 179-85, 195. *See also Krisenfest*
Hunting, 15, 67-68, 76-80, 84, 90-96, 99, 103, 107 n.76, 114, 117,

128, 157, 173–76, 186, 189 n.53, 194

Iliffe, John, xxii, 150
India, 1, 4, 138, 151; Indian Emigration Act, 55
Indian Ocean, xix, 28, 81, 82, 87, 126
Indians (South Asians), 30, 55; farmers,14, 17; planters, 26, 81; traders, xxi, 83, 86, 94, 98, 123, 171
Industry and industrialization, German, xix, xxv, xxxii, xxxiii, 2, 3, 26, 127, 129, 165. See also Textile industry, German
Infanticide, 166, 179–84
Instwirtschaft (sharecropping, squatting), v, 126
Interior Ministry, 5, 6, 91
Iringa, 117, 140, 141, 145, 171, 179, 182–84
Iron smiths, 87, 99, 117
Irrigation, 12–14, 17, 65, 151, 157, 194
Islam, 40, 123, 144, 156, 157, 171. See also Koranic schools; *Walimu*
Ivory, 15, 65, 171

Johannesburg, 160 n.29
Jumbe (pl. *majumbe*), xiii, xxvi–xxvii, xxxii, 27, 64–66, 70, 76, 77, 82, 88–99, 101, 103, 108 n.103, 110 n.135, 114, 116, 118, 119, 121, 122, 123, 127, 141, 145, 146, 147, 148, 151, 173, 184, 194. See also Local elites

Kaguru, 167
Kalunda, Queen, 173–74
Katanga, 80
Kenya, xxiii, 59, 62, 126, 139, 142, 177
Keudel, Maximilian, 146
Kibassira, Jumbe, 97–98
Kibata, 97, 116, 122, 142, 183
Kichi hills, 80, 82, 94, 97–99
Kigoma, 176
Kikale, 95
Kikanda, 18, 123

Kikogwe cotton plantation, 13
Kilimanjaro, 120
Kilimatinde, 169
Kilindi, 122
Kilindoni, xxxi
Kilosa, 18, 35, 60, 66, 98, 120, 137, 141, 144, 145, 151, 154
Kilwa (Kivinje), xxvii, xxx, xxxi, 16, 17, 27, 29, 37–43, 52, 59, 76, 80–85, 88, 91, 98, 100, 101, 113–30, 142, 184
Kilwa Cotton Plantation, 33, 36, 122, 123, 125, 150, 158, 162 n.66
Kilwa-Masoko, 123
Kimbu, 176–77
Kiongozi, 140
Kipande (work card), 145–47
Kisaki, 128, 178
Kisserawe, 98, 102, 103, 186 n.28
Kissidju, 98
Kitunda, 121
Kjekshus, Helge, xxiv
Koleo cult, 95, 109 n.119
Kolonialrat (Colonial Council), xv, 4, 20 n.20, 54
Kommune, xv, 91, 116. See also Communal fields and obligations
Kooni, 122
Koponen, Juhani, xxii, 150, 181
Koranic schools, 156
Korogwe, 144
Krisenfest, xv, 113–14, 129, 194–95
Kulturland, xv, 12, 15–16, 88, 158
Kwai cotton estate, 17
KWK (Kolonial-Wirtschaftliches Komitee), 5–6, 9, 10, 17–18, 21 n.28, 52, 67, 92, 113, 119–20, 122–23, 127–29, 132 n.47, 137, 178

Labor: absenteeism and "blue Monday," 150–56, 158, 170; agency and autonomy, xxiii, xxvii, 28, 51, 53, 64, 70, 76, 138, 148, 149, 150–51, 157–58, 166, 168, 171, 195; aliases and plantation names, 144, 156; Asian indentured xxi,

Index 219

xxvi, 11, 39, 53, 54, 55, 56, 70, 71 n.15; Bagamoyo brokerage, 56; contracted (*waajiriwa*), xxiv, 39, 64, 125, 128, 141, 142, 153, 158; contract breaking and desertion, xxix, 43, 52, 55, 61–71, 128, 141–48, 157–58, 160 n.22, 169; corvée, xxi, 52, 62, 66, 77, 80, 92, 122, 125, 128, 130, 167, 173, 194; forced, xxviii, xxxii, 17–18, 51, 53, 54, 64, 67, 70, 77, 93–94, 96, 98, 125, 137–51, 157, 159, 167, 173, 188 n.48; free labor market, xxvii, 32, 125, 136, 148; labor gluts and unemployment, 195–96; local and day (*kibarua*), xiii, 26, 39, 54, 68, 126, 128, 150–51, 153, 169; long distance migration, xxii–xxviii, xxxi, xxxiii, 2, 26, 39, 44, 51, 52, 56–62, 69, 76, 77, 82, 117, 119, 128, 129, 136–59, 166, 173–79, 183, 185, 193–96; *manamba*, xxi, xxxi, 195; numbers on contract, 27; ordinances, 136, 140, 142, 147, 149, 153, 157, 158, 176, 185; penal, xxi, xxvi, 39, 42, 53, 55–56, 60–63, 70, 88, 89, 93–94, 100–101, 114–16, 122, 125, 143, 167, 174; plantation, xxiii, xxvi, 54, 100, 125, 165–66, 193; railway, 54, 114, 142, 146, 148, 156, 165–71, 175, 186 n.4, 195; recruitment, xxvii, xxxi, 11, 118, 136, 168; resistance, xxiii, xxvii, xxx, 2, 4, 28, 63, 64, 193; and slavery, 32–40; shortage xxi, xxiii, 17, 27, 31, 52–53, 59–70, 100–101, 113–14, 137, 139, 150, 154, 175, 184, 193; wage levels, 139, 141, 145, 150, 168–69, 173; wage work, xix, xxi, xxv, xxx, 2, 39, 76, 98, 101, 114–15, 125, 139, 149, 159 n.7, 168; as war indemnity, 98, 100; "wild" recruitment 138–49, 168, 173; worker subculture and social life, 69, 154–57, 169–71, 193. *See also* Arbeiterfrage; Porters; Slavery; Women; Workers, German

Lake Nyasa, 65, 117, 147
Lake Tanganyika, 165, 176
Lake Victoria, xxi, 56, 59, 159 n.8, 177
Lambrecht, Arnold, 145, 147
Landflucht, xv, 9, 23 n.61
Langenburg, 117
Leipzig Cotton Plantation and Spinnery, 12, 18
Lessel Plantation, 38
Lewa plantation, 54, 63
Liebert, Governor Eduard von, 5
Lindi, 27, 31, 35, 41, 52, 60, 91, 98, 100, 116, 117, 119, 120, 122, 126, 127, 128, 129, 140, 150, 155, 178, 179, 184
Lindi Planters' Association, 128
Liwale, 97, 101, 114, 117, 118
Liwali (pl. *maliwali*; alt. *wali*), xiii, 27, 42, 179
Local elites, xxviii, xxix, 4, 14, 16, 27, 28, 31, 36, 41, 43, 51, 53, 64, 66, 70, 80, 82, 93, 96, 102, 119, 122, 125, 166, 172–74, 178, 186
Locusts, 15, 16, 29, 41, 65, 78, 80, 83–85, 88, 91, 94, 95, 126
Luguru, 147

Maasai, 29, 46 n.42, 75 n.88
Mabama, 178
Mafia Island, xxxi, 37–39, 43, 86, 116, 132 n.48
Mafia Plantation, 38
Mahenge, 141, 142, 146, 157
Maize, 16, 19 n.3, 65, 82–85, 92–94, 121, 125–26, 151, 156, 158
Maji water, xiv, 94, 97–99, 110 n.134
Maji Maji rebellion, xxvi–xxvii, xxx–xxxiii, 2, 17–18, 29, 36, 43, 51, 53, 70, 77, 78, 84, 90, 91, 93, 94–103, 109 n.111, 113–19, 121–29, 137–39, 142, 150, 151, 156, 158, 167, 174, 178, 182–84, 186 n.4, 193
Maji Maji Research Project, xxxii
Malaria, 140, 181
Mangroves, 81, 84, 86–90, 92, 117, 128

Manyema, 30, 145, 169
Marriage dissolution, xxxii, 100, 102, 115–16, 131 n.12, 166, 178–84, 195
Master-and-servant relationship. See *Dienstherrschaft*; *Gesinde/Gesindewesen*
Matengo, 146
Matimbe, xiv, 118, 129
Matumbi people, 15, 16, 80, 95, 116, 118, 129, 131 n.30; Matumbi region (Umatumbi), 78, 82, 97, 98, 115–17, 119, 125
Mbwemkuru river, 128
Meru- und Kilimanjaro Zeitung, xxviii
Mfullu village, 97
Mganga (pl. *waganga*) spirit medium, xiv, 95, 99, 128, 179, 182–84
Migration. *See* Labor; Population of German East Africa
Mikesse rubber plantation, 146
Mikindani, 41–43
Minaki Plantation, 38, 39, 44
Mining, 138, 160 n.19
Miombo bush, xxi, 177
Missionaries, xxix, xxx, 17, 91, 94, 116, 155, 156, 165–67, 169, 171, 174–76, 179–85
Mlau, xiv, 82–83, 88, 92–93, 122, 125
Mohoro, 16, 55, 80, 83, 88, 93, 95, 98, 116, 118, 120, 122
Mombo rubber plantation, 143
Moravian mission, xxix
Morogoro, xxvii, xxxiii, 64, 66, 91, 102, 117, 120, 128, 137, 141, 144, 145, 146, 150, 157, 167, 168, 170, 178, 179, 180, 181
Mozambique, 128
Mpanganya cotton school, 17, 114, 119–23, 132 n.48
Mpwapwa, 60
Mtingi, 150
Mtondo, 95, 97
Mtoro bin Bakari, 44
Mtumbwi (pl. *mitumbwi*) canoes, xiv, 86–87
Mtumwa (pl. *watumwa*). *See* Slavery

Muskets and firearms, 86, 90, 98, 99, 103, 105 n.51, 111 n.155, 117, 147, 174
Mwanza, 139, 141, 165, 195
Mwera, 116

Ndengereko (Dengereko), 80, 93, 98
Ndugu, xiv, 69, 144
New Langenburg, 147
Ngarambe, 95
Ngindo, 16, 75 n.88, 80, 118
Ngoma, xiv, 44, 94, 97, 102, 148, 155–56, 170
Ngoni, 155, 185
Ngulu, 173
Njombe, 139
North America, 86
Northern Rhodesia, 142
Nyamwezi people, 15, 56, 60–62, 67, 69, 70, 75 n.88, 138, 143, 155, 166–78, 186
Nyamwezi region (Unyamwezi), xix, xxi, xxiv, xxviii, 60–61, 67, 142, 165, 167, 185. *See also* Tabora

Omanis, 28
Otto Cotton Plantation, xxxi, 18, 151–56

Paasche, Wilhelm, 100
Pamba. See Cotton, as a peasant crop
Pangani, 13, 27, 32, 33, 41, 42, 53, 54, 139
Pass controls, xxxiii, 55, 144, 159
Pastoralists, 29, 195
Patrons, patronage, 79–80, 93, 94, 95, 173
Pawning. *See* Slavery
Peasant breach, 29
Pemba, 26, 30, 36
Pembeni, xiv, 117, 118, 127, 194. *See also* Population of German East Africa, dispersals; Refugees
Plantations, xix–xxxiii, 27, 32, 38, 44, 51–56, 63, 70, 77, 81, 88, 93, 113, 125–29, 136–59, 167, 175; American, xx; competition from railways,

Index

168; cotton, 1, 10, 18, 32, 114, 133 n.73, 137, 195; dependence on local villages, 52, 54, 154–55, 193; health conditions, 157, 181; labor bottlenecks on, 153; numbers of, 74 n.84; peasantization of, 148–59; plantation imperative, xxv–xxvi, 2, 11–18, 28, 52, 62, 71, 129, 158, 193; as tax havens, 142; time discipline on, 152–53, 157; work culture, 148–59. See also Labor; Settlers, European
Plows, 14, 15, 17, 120, 194
Pogoro, 80, 95, 141
Polygamy, 16, 115, 122, 181–82
Pombe beer, xiv, 94, 95, 128, 148, 155–57, 169–72, 176
Population of German East Africa, xxiii, 14–15, 196; decline of, 65, 102, 114, 116, 119, 166–67, 171–72, 175–85; dispersals, xix, 101, 114, 125, 127, 174–78, 194; forced removal, 196
Porters, xix, xxi, xxvi, 2, 15, 30, 52, 54, 56–62, 65, 67, 70, 77, 82, 84, 93, 99, 114, 117, 118, 125, 136, 138, 139, 140, 143, 159 n.8, 165–66, 171, 172, 174, 193, 195; desertion, 59, 60; numbers, 56–58. See also Caravans; Slavery
Prisoners, 65. See also Labor, penal
Prostitution, 30, 155–56, 169–71, 180–81, 185
Prussian law, 31, 46 n.37

Railways, xix, 53, 54, 62, 67, 70, 77, 88, 93, 113, 136, 148, 176, 178, 185–86; Central, xxi, xxvii, xxviii, 18, 114, 129, 137, 138, 165–71, 177; Northern (Usambara), xxi, 60, 168. See also Labor, railway
Rebellion, 128–29, 149, 174, 184. See also Bushiri uprising; Maji Maji rebellion
Rechenberg, Governor Albrecht von, 69, 136–37, 142, 146
Refugees, xxvii, 77, 94, 96, 99–103, 115–17. See also *Pembeni*; Population of German East Africa, dispersals
Reichstag, 10, 18, 27, 187 n.28
Rheinische coffee and rubber plantation, 39
Rhodesia (Southern), 126, 160 n.29
Rice, 31, 81–84, 88, 91–94, 107 n.87, 116, 118, 121, 123, 126, 169, 172
Rinderpest, 29, 89
Rovuma river, 128
Ruanda (Rwanda), xxiii, xxv, 27, 137, 140, 185, 196
Rubber, xxii, 1–3, 11, 15, 16, 18, 19 n.2, 65, 67, 86, 92, 117–18, 128, 138, 145, 146, 151, 156
Rudewa rubber plantation, 145
Rufiji Industrial Syndicate, 88
Rufiji people, 15, 80–103, 167
Rufiji region, xxvii, xxx, xxxiii, 16, 31, 37, 77, 78, 80–103, 113–30, 150, 151
Rufiji River, xxiv, xxvi, 77, 80–103, 156

Sachsengänger, xv, 59, 72 n.40
Sadani, 12, 17, 18, 35
Samanga, 16, 83, 95
Sandawe, 169
Saxony, xxx, 6, 7, 9
Schele, Governor Friedrich, 31
Schnee, Heinrich, Governor, xxx, 119, 158, 164 n.109
Schultz beer brewery, 90
Senegambia, 4
Serfdom in Germany, 26
Sesame, 14, 65, 77, 81, 93, 123–24
Settlers, European, xxii–xxix, 2, 16–18, 32, 35, 51, 55, 62, 67–70, 76, 81, 90–94, 129, 136–38, 149–50, 159, 164 n.109, 167–68. See also Plantations
Shambaa, 75 n.88, 146
Sikonge, 175, 178
Singidda, 148
Sisal, xxii, xxxi, 2, 3, 11, 16, 18, 19 n.2, 62, 63, 68, 129, 138, 139, 151, 195

Slavery, xiv, xix–xxvi, xxxii–xxxiii, 2, 14, 26–44, 62, 79, 93, 96, 122, 138, 172, 173, 193; abolition in Tanganyika, 27, 32, 36; abolition in Zanzibar, 27; autonomy of slaves, 30, 37, 39, 44; on caravans, 26, 28, 43, 59; hiring of slaves, 30–33, 167; *huru* freedmen, 33–36, 48 n.59, 39, 44, 68; manumission, 35, 36, 37, 49 n.77; numbers of slaves, 27, 45 n.5; pawning, 27, 29, 31, 116; on plantations, 27, 53; ransoming (*Freikauf*), xxv, 27–29, 32–44, 48 nn.59, 64, 56, 68, 70, 158; slave consciousness, 40; slave desertion and resistance, xiv, 29–33, 39–44, 60; Swahili customs regarding, 27; trade, 28, 30, 35, 46 n.30, 83, 105–106 n.51, 116, 173; types of, 28–30; wages, 30–35. *See also* Women, slaves

Sleeping sickness (trypanosomiasis), 14, 57, 173, 185–86

Social Democrats, xxiii, 1, 10, 27, 137, 187 n.28

Soden, Governor Julius von, 13, 31

Solf, Colonial Minister Wilhelm, xxx, 164 n.109

Songea, 100, 140, 146

South Africa, xxiii, 55, 88, 138, 140, 156; labor matters in, 68, 142, 160 n.29, 193–94

Southwest Africa, 53, 136, 160 n.29

Spirit possession, 116

State, colonial: abandonment of forced labor policy, 18, 70, 125, 136, 138; coercion, use of, xxiii–xxvi, xxviii, 60, 67, 122; and colonial cotton, 10, 113–14, 118–20, 124, 129, 184; conservation controls, 91, 93, 118, 126, 177; control of women, 176, 178–84; and German textile industry, xxii–xxv, 8, 12, 136; historiographical views of, xxii, xxv, 51; as an industrial state, xxxii, 12, 127; intervention in labor control and supply, xxiii–xvi, 2, 13, 52–53, 55, 62–63, 70, 77, 125, 140–41, 149–50, 153, 193; limits of state power, xxvi, xxxii, 2, 18, 53, 60, 67, 70, 127–28, 141, 158, 186, 196; and local elite, 31, 65–66, 93, 97, 102, 114, 122, 174; and plantation imperative,1–2, 18, 51, 136–37, 158; promotion of peasant cash crops, xxvii–xxviii, 16, 53, 67, 76, 92, 119, 136–38, 166–67, 185–86; relation with settlers and planters xxii–xxiii, 2, 69, 149, 158; and slavery, 31–32

Steam tractors, 151–54, 157

Strike activity in Germany, 8, 137. *See also* Crimmitschau textile strike

Stuttgart, xxx, 18

Subaltern culture, xxvi, 28, 39, 44. *See also* Plantations, work culture

Sugar plantations, 28, 31, 32, 41, 77, 81, 82

Sukuma, 56, 138, 141

Supf, Karl, 5, 10, 62

Swahili, 14, 75 n.88, 89, 151, 156, 182; culture and society, xxviii–xxxii, 29, 40, 86, 119, 120, 140, 144; planters, xxi, 26, 81, 87, 138; slavery, 27, 28–30, 40

Syphilis, 98, 180–81, 185

Tabora, xxxiii, 60, 120, 129, 142, 159 n.8, 165–80, 186, 195

Tanga, xxix, 17, 27, 33, 35, 36, 39, 40, 53, 55, 60, 63, 67, 68, 139, 140, 141, 144, 171, 172

Tanga Planters' Association, 56

Tanganyika, xxi, xxviii, 195

Tanzania, geography, 14

Taxes, xxi, xxiii, xxviii, xxxi, xxxii, 51–54, 58, 60, 64–67, 80, 93–94, 96, 114, 117, 123, 128, 130, 136, 139, 141, 142, 145, 146, 173, 193; in the Belgian Congo, 67; in cash, 65–66; defaulting, 93, 167; in kind, 65, 67; in labor, 65; as Maji Maji war indemnity, 100–101, 115–16,

Index

118; in South Africa, 67; on slave selling, 30
Technology, xxix, 12–13, 151, 153, 157
Texas, 5
Textile industry, German, xxii–xxiii, 1–18, 91, 114, 119, 125, 137, 151, 158; African market, 4; American, 3; British, 3, 6. *See also* Workers, German
Tobacco, 1, 2, 53–55, 60, 77, 81, 82
Tsetse, 14, 15, 167, 173, 177. *See also* Sleeping sickness
Tungi plantation, 157
Tuskegee Institute, 119, 120, 132 n.47
Tutsi, 173

Ugalla, 172
Uganda, 165; Uganda railway, 59, 62, 139, 159 n.8, 168
Ugunda, 173
Ujamaa villages, 196
Ujiji, 140, 181, 185
Ukonogo, xxi, 172
United States, 1–6
Urproduktion, xv, 15, 194
Urundi (Burundi), xxiii, xxv, 27, 137, 140, 185, 196; Mrundi, 30
Usambara, 16, 17, 54, 55, 59, 67, 137, 138, 145, 146
Ushirombo, 172–73
Usambara Post, xxviii, 67, 144, 149
Usoke, 173
Utete, 129

Vidundu, 145
Villagization, 185
Vilimani, xiv, xxi, xxxiv, 165, 176–77, 196
Volkskultur, 119

Walimu (mwalimu), xiv, 98, 171
Wami River, 145
Washington, D.C., 5
Waungwana, 123

Wax, 15, 65, 67, 86, 117, 128, 139, 176
West Africa, 1
Weule, Karl, 116
Wildlife and game reserves, xxiv, xxvi, 118, 130, 174, 189 n.52, 194–96
Wild pigs, 67, 78–80, 84–87, 89, 91, 93–96, 99, 102, 107 n.87, 115, 125, 147, 173–74
Wilhelm II, Kaiser, 6
Wilhelmstal, 117, 143, 151
Winterfeld, Deputy Governor Carl von, 91
Witu enclave, 32
Women, xxi, xxiv, xxvii, xxviii, xxxi–xxxii, 15, 65–68, 76–79, 84–88, 93–103, 114, 118, 124–29, 136, 142, 150–52, 155–57, 185–86, 194–96; beer brewing, 169–70, 172; cross-dressing, 103, 112 n.176; and crime, 40–44, 55, 63, 103, 178–84; in Germany, 1, 7–9; marketers, xxiv, 169, 177; porters, 166; on the railway, 167–71; and rural change, 171–84; slaves, xxiv, 26–44, 48 n.66; wage laborers, xxiv, 11, 167; wage levels in Germany, 8. *See also* Gender; Households; Labor; Slavery
Workers, German, xix, xxi, xxiii, 1, 3, 7–11, 19 n.1; unionization, 8, 10. *See also Frauenindustrie*; *Gesinde/Gesindewesar*; *Landflucht*; Strike activity in Germany; Women, in Germany
World War I, xxviii, xxxi, 37, 129, 130, 137, 158, 195

Zanzibar, 26, 28, 32, 81, 82, 86, 92, 106 n.58
Zaramo people, 15, 59, 75 n.88, 80, 90, 95, 98, 186 n.4
Zaramo region (Uzaramo), 78, 94, 97, 99, 101, 103, 114, 167
Zigua, 31

ABOUT THE AUTHOR

THADDEUS SUNSERI is associate professor of history at Colorado State University. His articles on the social and labor history of Tanzania under German rule have appeared in the *Journal of African History*, the *International Journal of African Historical Studies*, *African Affairs*, and the *Canadian Journal of African Studies*.